Out of Adventism

To Donald + Ruth
With blessings!
Jerry

Out of Adventism

A Theologian's Journey

JERRY GLADSON

Foreword by Edwin Zackrison

WIPF & STOCK · Eugene, Oregon

1 Aug 2019 Gift of the author. DEW

OUT OF ADVENTISM
A Theologian's Journey

Wipf & Stock
An Imprint of Wipf and Stock Publishers
199 W. 8th Ave., Suite 3
Eugene, OR 97401

www.wipfandstock.com

PAPERBACK ISBN: 978-1-5326-3124-5
HARDCOVER ISBN: 978-1-5326-3126-9
EBOOK ISBN: 978-1-5326-3125-2

Manufactured in the U.S.A.   SEPTEMBER 14, 2017

To
our daughters, JoAnna Noorbergen and Paula Gladson,
our grandsons, Spencer, Josh, Aidan, and Jasper,
my beloved wife, Laura, who shared this journey with me

Contents

Permissions

Scripture quotations marked (CEV) are taken from the Contemporary English Version, copyright ©1995 by the American Bible Society. Used by permission. All rights reserved.

Scripture quotations from The ESV® Bible (The Holy Bible, English Standard Version®), copyright ©2001 by Crossway, a publishing ministry of Good News Publishers. Used by permission. All rights reserved.

Scripture taken from the NEW AMERICAN STANDARD BIBLE®, Copyright ©1960, 1962, 1963, 1968, 1971, 1972, 1973, 1975, 1977, 1995 by the Lockman Foundation. Used by permission.

The text of THE NEW AMERICAN BIBLE contained in this book is reproduced by license of the Confraternity of Christian Doctrine, Washington, DC, ©1970, the owner of the copyright of said document. All rights reserved. Used by permission.

Scripture quotations marked (NLT) are taken from the *Holy Bible*, New Living Translation, copyright ©1996. Used by permission of Tyndale House Publishers, Inc., Wheaton, Illinois 60189. All rights reserved.

Scripture quotations contained herein, unless otherwise indicated, are from the New Revised Standard Version Bible, copyright ©1989. Division of Christian Education of the National Council of Churches of Christ in the U.S.A. Used by permission. All rights reserved.

Scripture quotations marked (RSV) are from the Revised Standard Version Bible, copyright ©1971 (second edition) by Division of Christian Education of the National Council of Churches of Christ in the U.S.A. Used by permission. All rights reserved.

Foreword

This is a "journey book." It narrates the odyssey of a theological scholar and his attempt to find truth through the trail that other believers have blazed. The author attempts simply to relate the real travels that a faithful and honest scholar faces. This story will present many surprises to those who have known Jerry Gladson throughout his experience in pastoral and academic settings.

Although similar, a journey book is not technically a diary. It uses diary material as a primary source, but it also draws on phone records, minutes from business meetings, correspondence, letters, personal memories and insights. It tells the authentic story of a settled life of both the person on the journey as well as a number of significant other people connected with the storyteller. The ultimate outlook is a conclusion from the evidence.

Neither is a journey book technically an autobiography. It involves a great deal of autobiographical material but it does not attempt to justify or vilify anyone's actions. That is left to the reader as the story unfolds. It simply shares the developing actions of the principal characters. It relates thoughts and interpretations as the subject of the story tries to deal with facts of life.

This story does not attempt to make a victim out of the main character. It reveals the choices individuals make in their ways and determination to accomplish their purpose in life. Hence it unfolds the tactics one must create to shape a meaningful life. The reader will not always be happy with the results of all the characters involved.

This journey book tells the story of my colleague who set out to pursue a religious life in a setting that required certain dogmas and a prescribed intellectual perspective. I came to know Jerry Gladson forty-five years ago. I first read copies of his preliminary manuscript in Denver at a convention of the Christian Church (Disciples of Christ) in 1997. His narrative largely covers the latter part of his Adventist denominational life. I had been working on just such a manuscript of my own life, but we had never compared our narratives, though we were aware that each was writing.

I was immediately amazed at how similar our experiences were. There were expected parallels since we were both going through much of the same experience during that period from 1972–1984.

We lived in Collegedale, Tennessee; we taught in the Southern Missionary College (now Southern Adventist University) Religion Department. We lived on the same street. We were conservative theologians and at times we competed for effective ministry. This is not to suggest that we agreed with each other on everything. No two theologians agree on everything. We are both creative intelligent beings made by God who are given minds that can be directed by the Spirit of God.

This story is a narrative of exciting events and painful woe. It gives insight through the eyes of one of Adventism's most honest scholars. In 1972 both of us began our professional teaching careers at Southern Missionary College. We built houses across the street from each other. We both had two young children approximately the same age that we planned to rear faithfully as Seventh-day Adventists. We were both involved in Adventist religious activities as part of the extracurricular work of our academic life.

As time went on we were encouraged to continue our education to further qualify us for the teaching ministry at the school. The college financed our education. Jerry went to Vanderbilt University in Nashville where he was already enrolled when he received the invitation to teach at Southern. There he earned an MA and later a PhD, each in Hebrew Scripture. I went to Andrews University for a PhD program in theological studies.

Southern Missionary College was founded in 1892 in Graysville, Tennessee. Soon after the founding of the school it was moved to Collegedale, seventeen miles from Chattanooga. There it served a church's geographical segment for evangelistically appealing to the Adventists of the Southern states. Through the years the school gained the reputation of spirituality and loyalty to a denomination that was steadily growing and developing.

Tracing the developments of these realities in the South is revealing. Jerry became an Adventist as a teenager. He poured his life into the church's mission. He pursued his assigned task of deepening his scholarship. But he ran into a series of episodes that seemed to undercut work as a scholar in a tightly controlled ecclesiastical system.

Jerry's story is a microcosm of the common criticism of Adventism: the denomination wants people with advanced degrees and will pay dearly to enable people to earn doctoral degrees, but in the end wants no change in the scholar from before he or she started on that quest. In short, those in denominational leadership often want nothing to happen in the development of scholars except that they can now have the prestige of academic letters behind their names. But what the denomination fails to appreciate is that too often the scholarly pursuit results in an intellectual shift away from Adventist dogma.

This book shows not only this continual process of growth, but also the resistance of certain people against such natural intellectual development. Dr. Gladson was continually astonished at what happened to him as he faithfully attempted to enlarge his qualifications to teach the message of Adventism. The reader will vicariously suffer some of the frustration that he experienced, as well as the changes he had to make when he finally exited out of Adventism.

Get ready for a journey that often accompanies the Christian scholar on an odyssey that brings reaction and response from shocked onlookers as they grapple with what it means to pursue truth and integrity.

Edwin Zackrison, PhD
Department of Humanities (Retired)
University of Phoenix/Chattanooga

Preface

W hen I first started over twenty years ago to set down this story, I was emotionally unable to continue. The pain of the events it chronicled was too fresh, too painful for any coherent telling. It took me the better part of a decade to write the final draft, published under the title, *A Theologian's Journey from Seventh-day Adventism to Mainstream Christianity* (2000). Now I have completed the task of revising, enlarging, and greatly expanding that original edition under a new title.

A few years ago, while in a restaurant in Southern California, I looked up to find sitting at the table next to me a smartly dressed, attractive woman in her late thirties who seemed vaguely familiar. Suddenly, I recognized her. She had once lived in the Seventh-day Adventist college community where I had taught for fifteen years, and where much of what is related in this book took place. "Jane!" I said. "Fancy seeing you! It's been awhile, hasn't it?"

"Professor Gladson, I haven't seen you for years! Where have you been?" she responded in a surprised tone.

Reaching into my pocket, I retrieved a business card. "As you can tell, I have become a pastor once more." She looked at the card, *Senior Minister, First Christian Church (Disciples of Christ), Garden Grove, California*. Her mouth fell open. She grimaced like she'd seen a ghost.

"You aren't? . . . You're now . . . a minister in the Christian Church (Disciples of Christ)?" She fumbled over her words, incredulous. "How could you? . . . What happened? . . . How could you abandon the Adventist church? What about the Sabbath? The Investigative Judgment? Ellen White? The Sunday laws?"

Her astonished response will surprise most readers. After all, people— even clergy—change churches and denominations every day, and think little of it. Her reaction, however, is typical of most Seventh-day Adventists, who find it hard to believe that a person who once served as an ordained minister, pastored several congregations, taught religion in a Seventh-day Adventist college, and served on top-level theological research committees for the Adventist church would leave to become clergy in another Christian denomination.

Seventh-day Adventists believe their movement, a term they prefer to denomination, enjoys a privileged, unique destiny. They are the people called of God to bring reformation to all of Christendom. They are, by virtue of this divine calling, the "remnant," or final authentic expression of the church. They are destined to restore all the truths once held dear in the New Testament or apostolic church, but lost sight of by all other denominations. They are, as many of their evangelists characteristically put it, somewhat more strongly, the *true* church. All other churches, denominations, and sects are to a greater or lesser degree outside the will of God. Adventists lump all these bodies together as "Babylon," a mysterious epithet found in the book of Revelation, whose name evokes the Hebrew word *babel*, "confusion," the "dwelling place of demons, a haunt of every foul bird, a haunt of every foul and hateful beast" (Rev 18:2). The mission of Adventism, they believe, is to urge people to separate from all the other denominations, sects, and churches, and unite with Seventh-day Adventists in keeping the Sabbath and other mandates.

That is why it is highly unusual for an individual who pastored six Adventist congregations, served as the founding pastor of another, who taught religion at an Adventist college, held full professorial rank there, and who for thirty-four years believed, lived, and worked in the Adventist culture and environment, suddenly to change denominations and start all over again.

Why? Why did I do it?

That is the story you are about to read. It is at once a story of intellectual, spiritual, and emotional struggle, a religious coming-of-age, political intrigue, and betrayal set against a backdrop of an entire denomination in crisis. It is a story of a personal and family tragedy caused, in large part, by the ensuing religious chaos. More than this, it is a story of the search for spiritual integrity and honesty. It is also a story of recovery and redemption.

Since it is impossible to go back and reconstruct the events chronicled here, I have made use of contemporary documents, recent Adventist theological studies, articles, books, and detailed journal notes that I made at the time these events transpired. Notes and memory are always faulty, however—mine being no exception—so where possible, I have tried to corroborate my account with the recollections of actual participants in the story. Even the conversations recounted are from notes made, in most cases, only hours from the time the incidents took place, and thus reflect closely the actual words or at least the essential substance of what was said. The resulting narrative is as accurate as I am capable of making it. I make no claim for infallibility. I welcome the stories of others who participated, as did I, in the crisis of American Seventh-day Adventism. In hearing many voices we come closer to recovering the polyphonic nature of truth. As unbelievable as some of the incidents I mention may sound, they actually occurred.

As a memoir, this book tells my personal experience as clergy within Seventh-day Adventist denomination, and the subsequent disillusionment I experienced. My travail within Adventism and ongoing recovery from its religious abuses serves as an example of what many fundamentalist religious movements—at their core—are like, especially when they arrogate to themselves the only pure truth of Christianity. The denomination's stubborn failure to deal honestly with its theological problems resulted in the departure of hundreds of clergy, including me, along with thousands of lay members.

As a cautionary tale, my story is a plea for Seventh-day Adventism and denominations like it to be more open and transparent in their internal political and theological difficulties. It is a plea for denominational openness to change, even when it involves critical, theological matters. No doctrine or belief should be held to be beyond revision, especially when new discoveries in theology or biblical studies plead for it. Even though I have been out of Adventism for more than two decades, I still hold out the hope—albeit slender—that it might eventually change in these respects. If this book plays even a small role in encouraging such change, I will be more than gratified. It means that experiences like mine would not have to be repeated over and over, as they have been during the denomination's more than one-hundred-fifty-year history.

I could not have written this memoir without the help of many persons. For the moral and spiritual support of the congregations in Kentucky, Tennessee, California, and Georgia I have pastored through the years, filled with caring, loving people whose names are too numerous to mention here, I give credit to them all. I gratefully remember all the students who have studied with me in the classrooms of the several universities and seminaries where I have taught. They have taught me much.

Melvin Campbell and Edwin Zackrison, who along with me lived through many of the experiences chronicled here, after having read the manuscript, added to my story recollections long since forgotten by me. Rick Esterline, a friend and former student, has helped me understand more clearly the current mood inside the Adventist Church. My friend, Heather Hunnicutt, seminarian and professional editor, whose sharp editorial eye and astute attention to style, as well as her good theological sensitivity, has more than once kept me from embarrassing errors in literary style and substance. I am grateful to Aage Rendalen, a teacher of foreign languages and former editor, for his astute editorial suggestions after reading the manuscript. My friend and former student, Warren Taylor, now an addictions counselor, has read the manuscript with great interest. He, too, experienced some of the events described.

Finally, I cannot forget my family, who figure so prominently in this story. Laura, my darling wife and best friend, contributed her experiences and recollections to the writing. Our daughters, JoAnna Noorbergen and Paula Gladson, in keeping with the exemplary women they have become, gave me lots of encouragement. They, too, are survivors, and they have become outstanding mothers of our grandsons, Josh, Spencer, Aidan, and Jasper. To all these, I gratefully say, thank you!

Jerry A. Gladson
Kennesaw, Georgia

List of Abbreviations

ABD   *The Anchor Bible Dictionary*. 6 vols. Edited by David N.
      Freedman. New York: Doubleday, 1992.

ANET   *Ancient Near Eastern Text Related to the Old Testament*. 3rd
      ed. Edited by James Pritchard. Princeton: Princeton University
      Press, 1969.

BDB   Brown, Francis, S. R. Driver, and Charles A. Briggs. *A Hebrew
      and English Lexicon of the Old Testament*. Oxford, UK:
      Clarendon Press, 1907.

BRICOM Biblical Research Institute Committee of the Seventh-day
      Adventist Church

BRISCO Biblical Research Institute Committee on Science and
      Religion, a subsidiary of the Seventh-day Adventist Biblical
      Research Institute (BRICOM).

EGWEnc *The Ellen G. White Encyclopedia*. Edited by Dennis Fortin and
      Jerry Moon. Washington, DC: Review & Herald, 2013.

IDBSup *The Interpreter's Dictionary of the Bible: Supplement Volume*.
      Edited by Keith Crim. Nashville: Abingdon, 1976.

KBL   Koehler, Ludwig, and Walter Baumgartner. *Lexicon in Veteris
      Testamenti Libros*. Leiden: E. J. Brill, 1958.

NIB   *The New Interpreter's Bible*. 12 vols. Edited by Leander Keck.
      Nashville: Abingdon, 1994–2002.

NIDB   *The New Interpreter's Dictionary of the Bible.* 5 vols. Edited by
            Katharine Doob Sakenfeld. Nashville: Abingdon, 2006–2009.

NJBC   *The New Jerome Biblical Commentary.* Edited by R. E. Brown,
            J. A. Fitzmyer, and R. E. Murphy. Englewood Cliffs, NJ:
            Prentice Hall, 1990.

SDABC   *The Seventh-day Adventist Bible Commentary.* 7 vols. Edited
            by Francis D. Nichol. Washington, DC: Review & Herald,
            1954–1956.

TDNT   *Theological Dictionary of the New Testament.* 10 vols. Edited
            by Gerhard Kittel and Gerhard Friedrich. Translated by
            Geoffrey W. Bromiley. Grand Rapids, MI: Eerdmans,
            1964–1976.

PART ONE

Beginnings

1

The Lure of Adventism

Nothing happens unless first a dream.

—*CARL SANDBERG*

The baby blue designer phone beside the bed jangled irritatingly, stirring Laura, my wife, and me out of peaceful, early morning dreams. Blinking bleary, unfocused eyes, I glanced out the window. Already the milky dawn seeped in under the darkness, casting the room in an eerie, surreal morning light. I glanced at the digital clock: 6:00 AM. Who could be calling this early? An emergency? A church member in crisis?

Laura, as usual, had already snatched the phone before I had half-awakened. Holding her hand over the receiver, she whispered, "It's Douglas Bennett!"

"Sorry to call so early, but I felt I'd be more likely to reach you at this early hour." The familiar voice I hadn't heard in more than seven years jolted me into full consciousness. Douglas Bennett was the newly appointed chair of the religion department at Southern Adventist University.[1] He had been my favorite professor, as well as mentor and spiritual advisor, when Laura and I were in college nearly a decade before. At that time he'd newly arrived at the University fresh from a highly successful pastorate, brimming with thrilling ideas that fledgling theological students would be anxious to try in

---

1. At the time of this telephone call Southern Adventist University, in Collegedale, Tennessee, near Chattanooga, was known as Southern Missionary College. Despite the anachronism, to avoid confusion I will refer to it throughout this book under its current name: Southern Adventist University, or simply "Southern" or "University" for short.

their pastoral field assignments. As an upper level undergraduate student, I had served as the religion department's supervisor of Southern's student minister field placement under Bennett's direction. On Saturdays (Seventh-day Adventists observe Saturday as the Sabbath) the University sent out its upper-level theological students to fill the pulpits of some local Adventist churches. This program functioned as a kind of internship and was an excellent, hands-on introduction to pastoral work.

"Jerry, we want you and Laura to come for a visit and look over the campus to see if we can entice you to join the religion faculty." Was Bennett for real? This couldn't be happening! I was the senior minister of the third largest congregation in the Seventh-day Adventist Kentucky-Tennessee Conference. The Adventist denomination at its basic level is organized into Conferences, usually made up of a state or sometimes two. At the top hierarchical level, a General Conference heads the worldwide church, followed by Divisions, which embrace entire continents, such as North America; then Unions, which are specific geographical regions. Like all local church pastors, I held ordained ministerial credentials in a local Conference. That meant I was licensed to administer the sacraments, provide pastoral care, preach and teach, and conduct the administrative affairs of Adventist churches anywhere in the world.

My particular congregation was located in Madison, Tennessee, just off Donelson Parkway, twenty miles northeast of Nashville and some ten miles west of the Hermitage, the historic home of President Andrew Jackson. The five-hundred member congregation worshipped in an attractive building, constructed in popular 1960s architectural style. A healthy group of vibrant young families usually filled the light brownstone edifice on Saturday mornings. I was concluding my third year at the church, and thoroughly enjoying pastoral ministry. Never had I given a moment's thought to leaving the parish for academia. Bennett's early morning telephone call sparked memory of a comment by Bruce Johnston, then the chair of the religion department. I was then preparing to graduate. "Jerry, you should go out into the parish, get some good pastoral experience," Johnston said, "then come back and teach, maybe here or at some other college." *Not on your life*, I thought. I wanted to be a pastor—in the pulpit—not spend my life in an "ivory tower" in academia. That was final! I was certain of it.

Bennett's invitation, however, whetted more than my curiosity. Perhaps he touched some deep yearning within, a longing for deeper academic study, a buried but almost forgotten desire actually to become a theological scholar. If I were to join the University faculty, I would literally be following in Bennett's footsteps. That was a heady thought! Bennett had served my present congregation, the Boulevard Seventh-day Adventist Church, just before joining the faculty at the University. He had led the congregation in constructing its present modern facility.

I had no idea then how his early morning telephone call—the events it set in motion—would alter my life and almost completely destroy my ministry. Ironically, it would also free me from a spiritual bondage as yet unrecognized but already stealthily coiling its tentacles around my soul.

Collegedale, home of Southern Adventist University, lies nestled in a bu-colic valley, sheltered by green, low-lying hills, not far from Chattanooga, Tennessee. The University, founded in 1892 by an Adventist teacher, George Colcord, had been originally a one-room school. Colcord already had an-other college founding to his credit in Walla Walla, Washington. Just before World War I, Southern had migrated from Graysville, Tennessee, in a cara-van of slow-moving, horse-drawn wagons and a herd of cattle a distance of forty miles to the newly purchased Thatcher farm. Once in the new loca-tion it was christened Southern Junior College, and the village that grew up around it, Collegedale.

The college would undergo several more name changes, each reflect-ing further maturation of its fledgling, sponsoring denomination. Earlier, in 1897, while still at Graysville, it had been called the Southern Industrial School; in 1901, Southern Training School; in 1955, when it became a senior college, Southern Missionary College, a name it bore at the time I joined the faculty. Later, it was renamed Southern College of Seventh-day Adventists, and then, in 1997, having finally achieved university status, Southern Ad-ventist University. From a one-room school with twenty-three students it had grown by the 1970s into a thriving liberal arts college of two thousand, one of nine Seventh-day Adventist colleges in the United States and Canada.

Now, in the spring of 1972, having discovered I was already at work on my MA in Old Testament at Vanderbilt University, Bennett had invited me to return to my alma mater to teach. Rarely do universities appoint faculty who do not hold at least one graduate degree; I was therefore more than a little surprised. I would have to start out at the lowest faculty rank (Instruc-tor) and work my way up the academic ladder.

"The University wants you to finish your MA, of course," he explained, outlining further the provisions of the offer, "and then seek the PhD, either at Vanderbilt or another university." The implicit caveat was that no Adven-tist university at the time offered a doctorate specifically in the field of Old Testament. For several years I had quietly nurtured a desire to earn a PhD in the field of religious studies while continuing to work as an active pastor.

I had already settled upon the field of study: Old Testament or, as it is now usually called, Hebrew Bible/Scripture. With the University's offer to sponsor me for the PhD, the concern over how I could pay for such an expensive education was resolved.

September rolled around. I faced three rather large classes of excited, yet terrified freshman students signed up to take my hastily constructed course in the history and development of the Seventh-day Adventist denomination. I was as frightened as they! By lecturing on Mondays, Wednesdays, and Fridays, and then driving a hundred fifty miles to Vanderbilt University in Nashville on Tuesdays and Thursdays, I managed to complete my MA that year and then embark on what turned out to be a rigorous six-year path that led to the PhD in Old Testament. As I stood in front of my first class, I couldn't help but be humbled by the journey that had led to my being there.

I had first heard about Southern Adventist University shortly after a short, balding man, dressed in tie, white shirt, and dark blue suit, representing the local Seventh-day Adventist church, called at our home one lazy summer Saturday afternoon. I was twelve years old at the time. His purpose in calling at our doorstep was to offer our family a series of in-home audiovisual Bible presentations. We lived on McFalls Street in Dalton, Georgia, a growing textile manufacturing town, destined eventually to become the carpet and flooring trade center of the nation. It lay about thirty miles south of Chattanooga in a valley at the mountainous tip where the Appalachians exhaust themselves into northern Georgia.

My brother, Raymond, fifteen years older than I, had married five years earlier and moved with his wife, Billie, to Danville, Virginia. Our family—my parents, Howard and Laura, my sister, Deena, brother, Michael, and I—lived in a small white, three-bedroom stuccoed house that my father had personally built. The house perched on a modest swell of red clay soil beside a graveled road. The road trekked from the main highway that ran from Dalton to Cleveland, Tennessee, down to a tiny, sluggish stream almost hidden in a maze of swamp willows, and then up past our house. Dusty roads snaking through the neighborhood provided choice bicycle paths over which my friends and I roamed during the lazy summer days. We had no television—TV stations were remote and reception was poor, anyway—so when the Whitfield County library bookmobile rolled through on its regular route, I checked out ten or twelve sports novels or biographies to read until it returned the next month. This fed my growing, unquenchable passion for reading that has turned me into a lifelong book lover.

Although my father's sister, Maude, had become a Seventh-day Adventist in the 1940s while living in Columbia, South Carolina, I knew very little about the faith, and as a soon-to-be teenager, cared even less. Aunt Maude struck me as emotionally distant, strict, and religiously fanatical, although I scarcely knew what such words meant. This early impression was wholly unfair, because she was always kind and treated me with great respect. She did, however, interminably argue with my dad, trying as an older sister to convince him that Adventists were right about Christianity. Her attire reflected that of many devout Adventists—plain, neat, and homely, devoid of makeup or jewelry. Traditionally, Adventists believe in simple, unadorned dress, and do not approve of the wearing of jewelry, even engagement or wedding bands. Such accouterments are considered ostentatious. I just couldn't comprehend her strange religion. Every Saturday, when she came for a visit, she faithfully attended the local Adventist Church, a red brick building with amber-tinted windows, located on the opposite side of town from where we lived, across the street from the Dalton High School football stadium. Sometimes my mother went with her. But I never did. I wanted nothing to do with such an odd religion.

Each Saturday evening around 6:30, the same man who had come to our door in the dark suit returned. He now brought with him an older, white-haired man I later learned was his father-in-law, who also happened to be the pastor of the Dalton Seventh-day Adventist Church. The duo set up a black metallic filmstrip projector mounted on a large, cumbersome reel-to-reel tape recorder. The tiny screen they placed at the far side of our small living room soon sprang to life with vivid, colorful images of the strange animal-like creatures artistically inspired by the books of Daniel and Revelation, embellished by scriptural quotations, and backgrounded by hauntingly beautiful music. Since our family had no television, I was captivated by this, and really looked forward to these dramatic presentations, although I didn't really understand them. We were being subtly introduced to Seventh-day Adventism. Adventists, like Jehovah's Witnesses and Mormons, commonly use home-based Bible studies as a method of winning converts to the faith. Jehovah's Witnesses may have actually borrowed this method from Adventists. When I later became an Adventist minister, I would also conduct similar Bible studies, both with the aid of a filmstrip slide projector, and often simply with a Bible and a family gathered around the kitchen table.

These home-based Bible studies were intentionally planned to climax at about the same time as an Adventist evangelist arrived in Dalton to begin a series of public evangelistic lectures in an old, abandoned theater that had been scrubbed and cleaned by volunteers from the local Adventist church.

Arnold Kurtz, the evangelist, illustrated his sermons with colorful, backlit images of the same apocalyptic animals I'd seen on the slides presented in our home. Kurtz was a very effective preacher (he later taught preaching at the church's principal seminary, Andrews University). At the close of the evangelistic crusade, my mother, Laura, and sister, Deena, decided to join the Adventist church. I began attending the Adventist church along with them, and a year later, also converted. My dad, Howard, while he frequented the public evangelistic meetings, never converted, nor afterwards showed any discernible interest in Adventism. Much later he confided to me, "I respect your religion, but I have real difficulty with Ellen G. White." Largely self-taught, with only nine grades of education, dad was very perceptive. It was as though he intuitively sensed there were serious, unresolved problems with Ellen White. His intuition later proved uncannily accurate.

The Dalton Adventist church had fewer than one hundred members, but boasted in its numbers at least four or five physicians and several nurses who, along with their medical talents, brought musical ability into the worship and offered much-needed leadership in church life. The church was vital and active. It operated a small, one-room private Christian elementary school in a two-story, pale yellow masonry block building next door, which most of its school age children attended. In order to counteract the secular forces of society on the minds of the young, Adventists operate a parochial education system that spans kindergarten to graduate school. Its parochial educational system is one of the largest within Protestantism. In an upstairs apartment over the classroom lived the teacher, while the lower level doubled as a classroom and fellowship hall. The members seemed thoughtful and genuine, and accepted us graciously into their community. I really came to feel "at home" there.

Yet becoming Seventh-day Adventists posed for our normal family routine a troubling predicament. Before Adventism, Saturday nights at the local drive-in theater watching movies with Charlton Heston or John Wayne led to long Sunday afternoon drives along dusty roads in the country, stopping to swim in the clear waters of Rock Creek, or to visiting relatives, and then ending up at the local Dairy Queen. Family life now drastically changed. No more movies. Bacon and sausage disappeared from the breakfast table. Saturdays (the Adventist Sabbath) were totally dedicated to church and church activities. On weekends my dad now felt isolated and alone. I could feel new, escalating tension between him and my mother over some of these issues, and hear their painful, bitter arguments, usually about religion. I feared divorce. It seemed our family was about to come apart. What was happening? "I have come to set a man against his father," well-intentioned church members both warned and encouraged mother, quoting

Jesus. "One's foes will be members of one's own household" (Matt 10:35–36). Chafing under this new not-so-subtle designation as the so-called enemy of our family, dad emotionally withdrew and never really re-engaged in family life except superficially. Our home, although never physically sundered, was irrevocably split by a deep, religious chasm. Mother was married to an "unbeliever," in an unfortunate marriage that never should have been, according to Adventism. All she could do was to tolerate the situation and pray for dad's conversion.

My dad had grown up in Eastern Tennessee, on the edge of North Carolina, near the town of Murphy, the oldest male in a family of six children. When his father abandoned the family, leaving his wife and six children all but penniless, dad found it necessary to drop out of high school to support his mother and siblings. He did so mostly by working as a farm laborer and later as a carpenter's apprentice.

A quiet, unassuming man, barely over five feet tall, with thinning light brown hair, he always keenly felt his lack of formal education. He compensated for this deficiency by voracious reading, gradually improving himself until his acquaintances considered him well-educated. He especially enjoyed mathematics, spending leisure time working algebraic formulas and adding huge sums of figures on the backs of old envelopes or on scraps of paper. He had dreamed of becoming an engineer, but since family circumstances had extinguished that vision, he focused on the next best thing, carpentry, eventually mastering the craft and becoming proficient at both the designing and building of houses. To these skills he added a knack for working with anything mechanical. After he met and married my mother, he entered the textile industry, then just getting started in Dalton, as a maintenance mechanic. Uncomfortable in crowds, he much preferred to spend his leisure time reading, especially mystery novels, and going to the movies with the family.

My mother, Laura, with attractive brown eyes and a winning smile to match, presented a sharp contrast to my dad's shy, reserved nature. Gregarious, sociable, active in church life, she was the religious one of the family. Like dad, she had grown up in a large family that during the Great Depression had barely eked an existence from the soil of Gilmer and Murray Counties, Georgia, on farms nestled in the rugged mountainous terrain at the southern tip of the Appalachians. Used to a life where people had to make do with what they had, mother knew how to organize and get things done. Through most of my childhood, she also worked in the textile mills alongside my dad. Every week, however, she dutifully made sure we children were in church. In a sense, choosing Adventism reinforced her sense of duty. She literally thrived as an Adventist, even though the faith brought discord into our family.

I was now officially an Adventist. But my real conversion was yet to come.

2

Reluctant Convert

How are they to call on one in whom they have not believed? And how are they to believe in one of whom they have never heard? And how are they to hear without someone to proclaim him? And how are they to proclaim him unless they are sent?

—St. Paul

E very June, in the sweltering summer heat, for ten days Adventist churches all across Georgia and parts of Tennessee, suspend regular weekly services, and lock their doors. Thousands of Adventists pour into Collegedale, site of Southern Adventist University, for the annual, old-style camp meeting. Spirited preaching, revival music, and stirring evangelistic sermons thrill the crowds in meetings that harken back to the southern mass camp meetings in the nineteenth century. There are separate convocations for children, youth, and adults. While attending one of these camp meetings I first felt a desire for the vocation of Christian ministry.

In partnership with his brother, Jim, a retired U.S. army lieutenant colonel, my dad had purchased a one-hundred-sixty acre farm near Chatsworth, Georgia, nestled in the Northwest Georgia Mountains, not far from where my mother had grown up. The two Gladson brothers, with families in tow, took up joint residence in a spacious, two-story, restored white column plantation house on the property, and together operated the farm. The plan was that dad would continue to work at his job in the textile mill in Dalton, and do things around the farm in his spare time, while Jim would devote himself full time to the farm, which had a large commercial apple orchard and acres of cotton and corn, as well as a small herd of beef cattle.

There was no Adventist church in the vicinity. We lived an hour's drive away from our church in Dalton. With an exciting new life on a working farm with its many distractions, getting acquainted at a new school, my attendance at the church waned. It became sporadic, and then gradually ceased altogether. It was just a lot less bother to stay home on Saturday mornings and play baseball with my cousin Jimmy, or explore the nearby forest on the property. The embers of what little spiritual awakening I'd experienced by joining the Adventist church gradually faded.

The co-operative venture of the farm didn't work out due to tensions between the two families, so after almost two years our family decided to return to Dalton. Now in my teens, by this time I had pretty much decided that religion simply wasn't for me. As soon as I was ready for college and could leave home, I reasoned, I would drop out of the Adventist church. Entering my freshman year at North Whitfield High School, and enduring painful social embarrassment because I couldn't go to football and basketball games on Friday nights, the opening hours of the Sabbath,[1] reinforced these troubling feelings.

Upon completing my freshman year, however, something happened that checked this growing indifference. I was a passionate reader, imitating my dad, and so spent many delightful summer leisure hours reading beneath the trees shading our house, a two-storied, white frame structure, nestled modestly among tall pines and oaks, and fronting a dusty, gravel road. Since we didn't have air conditioning, when automobiles or trucks roared by, dust wafted over the lawn and seeped into the open windows, leaving a fine residue on chairs and tables. It must have been in late June or early July that year when I noticed a book lying on the living room coffee table. Mother had purchased it at the Adventist Bible Book store during the annual camp meeting. Had she deliberately left it there for me? I never found out, but it bore the intriguing title, *Lambs among Wolves*. At the time, I didn't care to read anything even remotely religious. To the contrary, I avoided religion, but for some reason this book attracted me. I was curious.

So one afternoon I picked it up, after settling into my usual spot in the front yard under the oak trees. The book was about Christian life. MacGuire, then a well-known Adventist minister, used the metaphor of sheep and wolves, which he drew from Jesus' instruction to the seventy missionaries, "I am sending you out like lambs into the midst of wolves" (Luke 10:3).

---

1. Adventists follow the Jewish custom of reckoning the Sabbath (Saturday) from sundown Friday to sundown Saturday (see Lev 23:32; Luke 23:54—24:1). Sporting events are taboo during the Sabbath hours.

The sheep or lambs, he declared, carefully working out the analogy, represented Christians; the wolves, the unconverted or unbelievers. When a person becomes a Christian, he pointed out, one assumes the characteristics of a sheep. "My sheep hear my voice," Jesus said. "I know them, and they follow me" (John 10:26). Once a Christian, a person develops the character of a sheep, so to speak. One begins to act like a sheep, and ceases behaving like a savage wolf. If that person continues afterward to behave like a wolf, that person has not really been converted, not really changed.

MacGuire's carefully nuanced prose struck a nerve. I suddenly felt like he was describing me. People wouldn't have considered me markedly wicked, at least not outwardly. I complied with most traditional decorum expected of me. Inwardly, however, it was different. Inside, I was a rebel. I was apathetic to religious faith. I didn't want to be around it, or around those who practiced it. Paradoxically, I was also conflicted. The internal spiritual conflict was more acute than I was willing to admit. Now, suddenly I realized I'd started heading in the wrong direction. Unexpectedly, strangely, against all my normal instincts, *I wanted to be a sheep*, to use MacQuire's metaphor. I no longer wanted a "wolf" kind of life. What should I do? Stammering, hesitantly, not fully understanding even what it meant, under those shady green oak trees, I made a commitment to change my life.

Like Augustine, I trace my Christian conversion to this solitary experience. Wayne Oates, a leading pastoral counselor, notes that some conversions are constructive and lead to reconciliation and positive change in a person's life, while others are fruitless, abrasive, and bring misery to the individual and those around them.[2] Mine was constructive, because my life began to change for the better. I surprised my mother by immediately resuming church attendance. (I had dropped out more than a year before.) I cooperated more reliably with my parents. I started treating my sister, Deena, and brother, Michael, with more respect. That I hadn't always done!

The Adventist faith, previously only an embarrassment, now suddenly became an object of renewed religious interest. The idea that the Seventh-day Adventist church was God's select, chosen people with a special mission in the world mesmerized me. That Adventism was the "remnant" community, actually identified in Revelation, tasked with proclaiming the final divine message for the world, deeply thrilled me. All other Christian denominations or communities were in error, or worse, compromised and in horrible apostasy. They, in fact, were identified as Babylon, that mysterious abomination in the book of Revelation (18:1–4). Adventists were intent upon calling other Christians to abandon corrupt denominations and join Adventists in

2. Oates, *Christian Pastor*, 15.

preparing for the second coming of Christ. The Adventist church was, in effect, the *true* church, as all its evangelists commonly proclaimed. All this bolstered my innate need to feel important.

Laying aside sports novels, voraciously I now devoured all the Adventist literature I could get my hands on and thrilled—somewhat exultantly—in brandishing my newfound biblical familiarity to challenge my Baptist and Methodist high school friends about the teachings of Adventism. Some wisely ignored me, because I was going about zealously like new converts often do, bubbling over with enthusiasm. I became a bothersome nuisance. Undoubtedly I embarrassed people. But I did successfully persuade one of my friends, August Pellom, a member of the Church of God of Prophecy, where he planned eventually to become a minister, to leave that denomination and join the Adventist church. He was my first convert! The morning of his baptism into the Adventist church, his mother, desperately clinging to his arm, begged him tearfully not to take this step.

One day I was futilely trying to convince Carolyn, a classmate, of some Adventist idea. She interrupted me in mid-sentence, and abruptly changed the subject. "Jerry," she said, wryly smiling, looking straight into my eyes, "What do you plan to do when you graduate?"

It was a legitimate question, one high school students often ask themselves. I had thought some about it, but never verbalized what I was beginning to feel deep within. I knew that my dad, denied a good education, had his heart set on my pursuing a career in engineering.

"A minister—a member of the clergy," I replied, surprising even myself. When I later told dad, he reacted quietly, as was his way. "That's all right. Are you going to college? I just want to make sure you get a college education." I could tell, however, that deep down he was disappointed, in part, not only because I was choosing a career path in the Adventist church, but because I wouldn't be following his dream of civil engineering. Of course, my mother was more than thrilled. So the Adventist ministry it would be!

3

Parish Parson

I am no prophet, nor a prophet's son; but I am a herdsman, and a dresser of sycamore trees, and the Lord took me from following the flock, and the Lord said to me, "Go, prophesy to my people Israel."

—*THE PROPHET AMOS*

In the mid-1960s, professional requirements for the ministry in the Seventh-day Adventist church meant obtaining a baccalaureate degree in religion or related field of studies, preferably at an Adventist college and, if the employing church administrative unit so indicated, getting an MA in theology, Christian history, or biblical studies at the Seventh-day Adventist Theological Seminary at Andrews University, located in Berrien Springs, Michigan. Naturally, if for no other reason than it was located near where we then lived, I opted to attend Southern Adventist University in Collegedale, Tennessee, for my undergraduate studies. I would major in Theology (a pre-seminary curriculum).

The world I discovered at Southern differed from anything I had known in high school. Moving into the dormitory the summer before I started classes in the fall, I was astonished to find that men and women students were required to enter the cafeteria by separate doors on opposite sides of the building to prevent couples who were dating from sitting together during meals. It was thought that too much intermingling of the sexes at informal gatherings distracted from one's studies—and especially one's faith. The regulation aimed to put the brakes on budding romances. Nor could men and women leave campus together to go shopping without a designated chaperone tagging along. These strange Victorian notions discouraged any deep romantic involvements and, obviously, any premarital sex. Dormitory deans, it seemed, treated residents more like children than young adults. Since I had experienced much more social freedom in high school, I chafed under these bizarre, archaic regulations. The rationale supporting them, to me, seemed tortuous. But I wanted to be a good Adventist, so I complied.

When classes began, I quickly became fascinated by one of the young religion professors. Tall, trim, and athletic, in his late thirties, Robert Francis always wore a black, blue, or gray suit, white shirt and black tie, even on swelteringly hot days (classrooms weren't air conditioned), and knew how to entertain as well as academically interest his students. He had come to college teaching from an Adventist high school, so didn't lecture like most professors. Instead of lecturing, he performed. He acted, sarcastically pantomiming and caricaturing humorously the lifestyle of non-Christians. He and his wife had no children, so the students in his classes must have provided something of an outlet for his parental instincts. His classes so intrigued me I could hardly wait to attend. Over the four years I was there, I think I took almost every class he taught.

One thing bothered me, however. Although his courses appeared in the college bulletin under the biblical studies category, Francis relied almost entirely on the writings of Ellen G. White. We read the Bible, of course, but specifically we were assigned lengthy readings from Ellen White's five-volume retelling of the biblical story, known as the Conflict of the Ages series. Francis openly—without apology—interpreted the biblical text *through* Ellen White. Because he reasoned that she was a prophet essentially on par with biblical prophets, he regarded her writings as the key to understanding the Bible. I found this frustrating because I had come to college to learn more about the Bible. As a dutiful Adventist, I respected Ellen White, but longed for more exposure to the Bible.

Whether it was Francis's influence or merely the Adventist ambiance of the school, I gradually came to accept—albeit somewhat hesitantly—that Ellen White, as a prophet, was a religious authority only slightly less important than the Bible. I embraced some of Ellen White's ideas that sound peculiar to me now. Women were not wear pants or jeans (they were forbidden for women at the University). Women who do so are an "abomination" in the sight of God, declared Ellen White.[1] I left off eating Milky Way bars

---

1. White, *Testimonies for Church*, 1:421, 457–60. These prohibitions come from 1864 and 1867, respectively. This prohibition ultimately goes back to a literal appropriation of the Deuteronomic Code ("A woman shall not wear a man's apparel, nor shall a man put on a woman's garment; for whoever does such things is abhorrent to the Lord

because White claimed that to eat even a single bite between meals was to offend God.[2] Who wanted to offend God? In some of her earliest writings, she claimed that to participate in the worship services of other denominations was to place oneself upon the devil's ground.[3] All the churches other than the Adventist were "Babylon." They were complicit with Roman Catholics in leading humanity astray. "Fallen, fallen is Babylon the great! She has made all nations drink of the wine of the wrath of her fornication" (Rev 14:8). For a time I avoided attending worship services in any other denomination, even when non-Adventist friends invited me.

When I visited home, my dad, a man of uncommon wisdom, noticed these subtle changes. "Jerry, aren't you becoming a little too fanatical in some of this? I'm not certain that University is good for you." I was offended. We argued heatedly about the interpretation of the Bible, and until I had studied ancient Koine Greek (the colloquial Greek language of the New Testament) and could throw in a few Greek words, he managed to hold his own. Such arguments, however, left him further alienated from the rest of the family and, to my dismay, from Adventism.

Despite my dad's warning, I gradually embraced the Francis's austere perfectionism. He taught that, at the beginning of our Christian life, we are totally dependent upon God's grace. At conversion, we are saved by grace. But as we spiritually mature, we should come to depend less and less on the grace of God and more and more on our own sanctified abilities until we reach the place where we could claim Christian perfection. What was this perfection? Perfection, he explained, represented a life free from conscious sin. His views, I couldn't help but notice, sounded much like what I had read in MacGuire's *Lambs among Wolves*. It represented a species of religious perfectionism that had dogged Christianity almost from the beginning. Adventism, I would later discover, had been infected by a particularly virulent strain of perfectionism, stemming from its nineteenth-century roots, and to it would return again and again like a moth to a flame. Through all my thirty years in Adventism, the shrill voices of perfectionism never abated. Sometimes they came from top church leadership. Frequently they were sounded from various pulpits. The denomination was peculiarly vulnerable

---

your God" [Deut 22:5]).

2. "Never should a morsel of food pass the lips between meals" (White, *Counsels on Health*, 118). This statement is dated 1890.

3. "I saw that neither young nor old should attend their meetings . . . God is displeased with us when we go to listen to error, without being obliged to go . . . The angels cease their watchful care over us, and we are left to the buffetings of the enemy . . . and the light around us becomes contaminated with the darkness" (White, *Early Writings*, 124–25).

to perfectionism because it claimed to be preparing people for the second coming of Christ. What did this mean? To many, this indicated that Adventists ought to "clean up their act" and get their character in order to stand blameless before a Holy God when Jesus returned to earth.

Other professors, less extreme in their views, introduced me to *Questions on Doctrine*, a book that had been published by the Adventist General Conference in 1957 as a result of top-level discussions between the Adventist denomination and evangelical scholars Donald Grey Barnhouse, then pastor of Tenth Presbyterian Church, Philadelphia, and Walter Martin, a Southern Baptist polemicist and cult specialist. At the time of the discussions, Martin was researching a book about Adventists he later published under the title, *The Truth about Seventh-day Adventists*. These discussions persuaded Martin that Adventists were genuine Christians, not a cult, as he had previously thought.[4]

Questions on Doctrine went further than any previous denominational work in emphasizing the common ground between Adventists and other conservative Christian denominations, identifying almost a score of doctrines that were virtually identical to those held by others. Included among these was the belief that the "vicarious, atoning death of Jesus Christ, once for all, is all-sufficient for the redemption of a lost race." As I read these words in *Questions on Doctrine*, I noticed that the expression, all-sufficiency of Christ, was clearly at odds with my favorite professor's views. He foresaw a time when the people of God would have to endure terrible distress without any dependency upon Christ. The book also favorably evaluated other denominations, insisting that Adventists "repudiate any implication that we [Adventists] alone are beloved of God and have a claim upon heaven."[5] *Questions on Doctrine*, introduced to the church under the authority of the General Conference, the highest administrative level of the denomination, would later become highly controversial. Thereupon, after briefly being withdrawn from publication, *Questions on Doctrine* would later be reissued with new editorial annotations.[6]

It was not until my senior year that I hit the first real, personal theological bump. The University allowed a senior religion major to develop a research project on a topic of interest—something like a mini-thesis—in lieu of a conventional classroom course. The student was to work closely with a faculty advisor and eventually submit the resulting thesis for evaluation.

4. An Adventist scholar, Leroy E. Froom, tells the story of this dialogue in his *Movement of Destiny*, 476–92.

5. *Questions on Doctrine* (1957), 21–23, 196.

6. Edited by George Knight this appeared in 2003. Citations herein from *Questions on Doctrine* are from the original anonymous edition (1957).

I chose to examine why Adventists hold that the kosher laws pertaining to clean and unclean foods, which forbid foods like pork and shellfish, are mandatory. These restrictions are part of the Pentateuch (Torah), but most Christians think that such kosher laws are no longer obligatory, like many other restrictions in the Torah that Christians don't observe. Taking the whole New Testament into my purview, I wanted to know why Adventists still observed these kosher restrictions. You couldn't eat bacon or sausage and be considered a good Adventist. Although unlikely, a person could theoretically be excommunicated for such taboo violations.[7] My conclusion regarding these kosher laws closely followed *Questions on Doctrine*: Adventists do not observe these laws because the Torah (Lev 11; Deut 14) is binding upon Christians, but because these foods are inherently detrimental. Foods designated as unclean in the Torah are such because they are basically unhealthy. It is thus a matter of the best health practice, not obedience to an ancient purity law.

Despite this conclusion, there was one passage in the New Testament that simply wouldn't fit the Adventist interpretation. My faculty advisor, in a note on the margin of my paper, called attention to the fact I hadn't considered this significant passage. I don't know whether singling out this passage indicated he shared some uncertainty about this Adventist tenet, or whether he was just making certain I had been thorough in my research. The passage occurs as a parenthetical or editorial comment on Jesus' words in Mark 7:19. With that parenthetical expression indicated in italics, here I translate the passage literally: "Since it [that which defiles] does not enter his heart but into the stomach, and exits into the latrine, *cleansing all foods*." What is meant by "cleansing all foods"? I wondered. The context relates a dispute between Jesus and the religious leaders over whether one is defiled by partaking of a meal without ritually washing the hands (Mark 7:1–5). This cleansing ritual had to do with purity laws. Both Pharisees and Essenes insisted their followers take their meals in a state of ritual purity, hence the requirement to wash the hands, food, and food containers (Mark 7:2–4). In answer, Jesus emphasized that only what defiles the heart—the inner core of a person—truly contaminates. "It is from within, from the human heart, that evil intentions come: fornication, theft, murder, adultery, avarice, wickedness, deceit, licentiousness, envy, slander, pride, folly. All these evil things come from within, and they defile a person" (7:21–23).

7. Although breaking of these kosher laws is not as serious as other offenses, it is sometimes considered along with the taboos on alcohol, tobacco, and drugs, as a basis for church discipline ([General Conference of Seventh-day Adventists], *Adventist Church Manual*, 162).

Of the Synoptic Gospels, only Mark, includes the parenthetical note, "cleansing all foods." Matthew omits it (see Matt 15:17); neither Luke nor John relates the story. This confirms the suspicion that an editor, or perhaps even the original gospel writer, placed the note here. Written for a Roman audience, it was apparently intended as an explanation for readers unfamiliar with Jewish purity laws. Did it imply a suspension of the kosher laws of clean and unclean? Were Christians—at least Mark's readers—no longer under obligation to follow the purity distinctions between clean and unclean foods? Many commentators think so.[8] I found no apparent answer to my question in either *Questions on Doctrine* or in the seven-volume *Seventh-day Adventist Commentary.*[9] I had inadvertently stumbled across an unresolved problem in Adventist doctrine.

Nonetheless, I didn't let such problems overly trouble me. One reason why I had chosen an Adventist college was my desire to meet someone of the same faith with whom I might come to love and later marry. My freshman year I dated Rita, but that came to a predictable end when I discovered she was not a Seventh-day Adventist, nor really interested in becoming one. We continued to see each other, but my reason for dating her shifted into an effort to convert her to Adventism. I guess she had hopes things might be different and so continued the relationship. She discreetly resisted my attempts at converting her, and did not return to the University the next year. She could easily tell the difference between romance and evangelism!

That summer, I lived with my brother, Raymond, in Danville, Virginia, and worked as a colporteur, or door-to-door salesman of Adventist literature. The denomination awarded student scholarships for this kind of work, which it understood as a form of witnessing or evangelism. My assigned territory was located just over the Virginia state line in North Carolina. Five days a week, I knocked on doors and was moderately successful in the cold-call sale of the brightly printed copies of Bible story books and colorful Adventist reference guides to the Bible. I was successful enough, in fact, to

8. Daniel Harrington, although writing subsequent to my paper, is typical: "Jesus appears to abrogate the OT laws dealing with ritual impurity and food." Harrington demurs slightly, however, when he goes on: "If Jesus had been so explicit about the observance of Jewish food laws, why were there so many debates on this matter in the early church?" ("Book of Mark," 612). On Mark 7:19 Perkins concludes, "Kosher food rules have been abrogated" ("Gospel of Mark," 607).

9. The Adventist commentary explains it as a reference to eating foods without ritually washing the hands, not the unclean foods of the Torah (Nichol, *SDABC*, 5:625). Most scholars see the kashrut laws as a way of distinguishing Israel from other peoples. They thus have a national or ethnic basis, not a health rationale. "The distinctions mirror and reinforce the distinction between Israelites and other peoples, and within Israel between priests and people" (Goldingay, *Israel's Faith*, 204–5).

earn a scholarship that paid my entire tuition, along with room and board, at the University for the coming school year.

During those hot summer months, I pored over the photos in the University yearbook to figure out which students I thought I would like to date. Ten women stood out. Why I settled on ten, I don't recall. It sounded like a nice round number! When I go back to the University in September, I told myself, during the registration process I would ask the first one of these select ten I came across for a date. Surely enough, not long after registration began, I bumped into one of the persons on my list. But she was with a young man who appeared to be her new beau! Drat it! Climbing the stairs of the University's Lynn Wood Hall, which then housed the administrative offices, I joined the long line waiting for the registrar's official signature on the class schedules (this was before computerized, online registration). Looking up from the registration forms I had in my hand, I suddenly realized I was standing behind Laura Hayes, *who was on my list*! Laura, a slender, attractive blond, with startling azure eyes, came from Greenwood, South Carolina, where her father, Wilson, operated a dairy farm. A lifelong Adventist, she had attended Adventist schools throughout her educational life, beginning with home schooling by her mother, Pansy, an elementary school teacher. Laura turned down my initial offer of a date (she was already committed), but accepted for a future one. We thus started dating regularly, and continued our courtship for the last three years of college. It was in front of that same Lynn Wood Hall, under the soft white antique street lamp one Saturday night, I looked into her blue eyes and said for the first time to a woman, "I love you." I proposed at the conclusion of our junior year. Beyond my wildest dreams, she accepted! Two weeks after graduation, on June 20, we were married in the small Kinard Methodist Church (there was no Adventist Church in the Greenwood area at the time). Laura, the love of my life, to my immense delight, confided that she had always dreamed of marrying a minister. From the beginning, we delighted in love.

Upon graduation from the University, I was employed by the Kentucky-Tennessee Conference, one of the seven state-wide judicatories of the Adventist organization in the South. The Conference decided against my attending seminary; rather, I was immediately assigned to work with a local congregation. At the time, the denomination was in transition between requiring an MA and the conventional Master of Divinity (MDiv). The transition to the MDiv had caused confusion. Some conferences were slow to adapt to this new policy. Each conference tended to act independently. E. L. Marley, the president of the Kentucky-Tennessee Conference, eyed the Adventist seminary warily. "It ruins young ministers," he argued. "Better have young pastors get some experience in the local churches, and then perhaps attend the seminary." His philosophy, it usually turned out, meant that few of his fledgling ministers would end up actually going to seminary. Unfortunately, Marley's anti-intellectual prejudice against seminary education was widely shared, particularly in the southern states.

To my own detriment, I happened to agree with Marley. Reading Ellen White had convinced me that spending further time in academic training was unessential, even wasteful, especially in view of the nearness of the Second Advent.[10] Jesus was coming soon; I just knew it. I believed that when the last trumpet blew and the earth rumbled beneath my feet as Jesus descended from heaven, I wouldn't want to be trapped in a stuffy seminary library reading some erudite tome. Instead, I planned to be actively sharing the Adventist message with poor benighted, lost individuals. I wanted to be in the evangelistic arena, saving souls for Jesus and the Adventist message. In only a few years, I would realize how mistaken and shortsighted this notion was. At some level I still ironically nurtured a desire for further education, but I repressed it in compliance with Ellen White's inspired counsel. I was utterly convinced Jesus would return in a year or so. At this early stage in my career, naively I had seriously short-changed myself. As it moved toward requiring a three-year seminary degree in addition to a baccalaureate, the denomination conveniently ignored Ellen White on the length of ministerial training.

My theological disposition at this time could accurately be characterized as conservative. I was what some might consider a "fundamentalist" Adventist; many at the time probably thought of me as fanatical. I was at the zenith of my devotion to the Adventist cause. In my first assignment as associate pastor of the large Fourth Street Seventh-day Adventist Church in Louisville, Kentucky, I encountered a senior pastor and mentor who more or less complemented my fundamentalist principles: Joe Crews. Six days a week—rarely taking a day off—Crews began pastoral visits at 9:00 AM sharp, and continued until at least 9:00 PM. When he caught people preparing for bed, he stopped for the day. "Jesus will soon return," he often repeated. "We can't afford to waste time even by taking a day off each week." When I became physically and emotionally exhausted on such a schedule and pled for time off, he grumbled, "*You* take a day off, but *I'm* going to make visits and give Bible studies." He took Ellen White more literally than anyone I'd ever

10. In 1895 Ellen White warned the administrators at Battle Creek College [Michigan]: "Do not encourage students, who come to you burdened for the work of saving their fellow men, to enter upon course after course of study. Do not lengthen out the time for obtaining an education to many years . . . Precious probationary time will not permit of long protracted years of drill . . . Do you believe that the Lord is coming, and that the last great crisis is about to break upon the world?" (*Fundamentals of Education*, 355–56). At the time, the ministerial training program at Battle Creek College was only 2–3 years in length, a little short of today's baccalaureate degree.

known. He sternly forbad the women in his congregation to wear pants or jeans, in keeping with the Deuteronomic restriction (Deut 22:5). Woe to any female church member whom he caught in public wearing jeans! If a woman dared wear jewelry—even a modest wedding band—Crews banned that person from serving in church leadership. Jewelry to him was nothing but a residue of idolatry. Wedding bands were absolutely forbidden. In order to be baptized into the church, a wedding band simply had to go. Crews fearlessly preached these extreme views from the pulpit. He railed against television, movies, and even labor unions. Crews would later go on to found *Amazing Facts*, a conservative Adventist radio (and later TV) ministry.

I idolized him during the brief three months we worked together at Louisville. I absorbed uncritically massive doses of his fundamentalist ideas. He became a model of what conservative Adventism was all about. In my mind, Joe Crews was a *true* Adventist.

His influence followed me into my first pastorate, where I led a small congregation in Ashland, the only such Adventist congregation in a ten-county region of northeastern Kentucky, bordering the Ohio River. There I modeled my evangelistic sermons after those of Crews, which Crews had duplicated and generously made available. My first evangelistic crusade, held in a downtown hotel in Ashland, saw five individuals, including three teenagers, embrace Adventism. Again imitating Crews, I zealously roamed throughout northeastern Kentucky in my light-green Volkswagen, making hundreds of personal visits. Overcoming local prejudice against Adventism in that part of Kentucky proved difficult, but I did experience a modicum of success. In the two years Laura and I served the Ashland church, more than thirty people joined, and the church grew from seventy to more than one hundred members.

Monday was our day off. Laura and I usually went shopping, often only to browse the merchandise in the stores, seldom buying anything (our budget was tight). We frequented good restaurants and had a nice lunch. Eventually, we made our way to the public library, where we discovered an entire room with floor to ceiling shelves stocked with religious literature, biblical commentaries, works on theology, pastoral life, history of religion, and devotional literature—from a variety of perspectives. I've haven't seen such a rich collection of religious literature in any local public library since. On many Mondays Laura and I went to the library, where we checked out armloads of books. (Laura is every bit the book lover as I). In the evening, we put quiet music on the stereo and dived into our new reads.

Delighted with this library treasure trove, I started to investigate some of the standard religious literature published outside the Adventist church. I'd often wondered why, in my religion classes at Southern, we almost always

used textbooks written by Adventist authors. Our courses neglected reading material—of excellent quality—offered by non-Adventist writers. Now I
had the chance to read some of this neglected material. I felt this would help
me keep up my studies as well as better inform me about the world—particularly the religious world—around me. There was a danger here, I knew.
Such reading might "jeopardize Adventist beliefs," Marley, my Conference
president, warned, when I told him what I was doing. I ignored his warning,
confident I could minimize dangerous ideas by carefully picking out the
good from the bad. After all, if Adventists have the truth, why would alternative viewpoints pose a threat? Truth would surely prevail over any error.

My schedule was extremely busy, leaving almost no time, except Mondays, for such elective reading. While continuing a heavy pastoral visiting
schedule, it was all I could manage to prepare a weekly sermon and a mid-
week Bible study. As I made pastoral visits spread all over the ten Kentucky
Counties assigned to me, I hit upon the idea of taking a lunch break at a convenient restaurant and, while I ate lunch, spending the hour reading some
of this theological literature. The non-Adventist authors, Christians all,
proved fascinating. One favorite was F. F. Bruce, a New Testament scholar at
Manchester University in Great Britain, considered a moderate evangelical
scholar, and then in his prime. I also became acquainted with the writings
of C. S. Lewis, an Anglican, but also professor of literature at Oxford and
Cambridge, whose books on the Christian faith had inspired thousands. A
whole new world suddenly began to open. Over the months during these
solitary lunches, I meandered through works on the Old and New Testament, systematic theology, and pastoral theology. Keen theological insights
leaped out at me, many of them far more profound than anything I had ever
come across in Adventist literature. *Why wasn't I exposed to this rich theological literature at the University?* I mused. Many of these books had stood
on the shelves of the University library, but few professors referred to them,
sending us instead, whenever possible, to pertinent Adventist literature. At
the Adventist theological seminary, I realized, I would have had a different
experience. This was also why some church leaders, such as Marley, opposed the seminary. It exposed students to dangerous, non-Adventist ideas.
It "corrupted" young minds.

Among my reads I came across David Wilkerson's moving account
of his ministry among the heroin and cocaine addicts of New York City in
The Cross and the Switchblade. Wilkerson, an Assemblies of God minister,
introduced his converts to a baptism of the Holy Spirit characterized by
speaking in unknown tongues, a phenomenon known as *glossolalia*. This
practice is best known from Paul's reference to people in the ancient Corin-
thian church who were regularly "speaking mysteries in the Spirit" to God,

but whose verbal expression had no semantical significance to those around them (1 Cor 14:2), or the disciples speaking to the crowd on the day of Pentecost so that the people heard them in their own languages and dialects, despite the fact the disciples were probably speaking in their native Aramaic (Acts 2:1–11). In the 1960s there had been a much-publicized revival of glossolalia that spread across denominational boundaries. Adventism had strongly resisted and contemptuously dismissed the whole movement as "of the devil."

In Wilkerson's account, those who received the Spirit in this manner apparently lost all desire for heroin and cocaine. My professors had taught— based on Ellen White—that speaking in tongues was of the devil, so at first I assumed that Wilkerson's "success" with drug addicts was patently false, a satanic delusion.[11] How could such ministry be of God? Clean-cut, former heroin addicts now witnessing to the power of Christ! A revival seemed to be going on in the ghettoes of Manhattan! How could it be false? When I got the chance to hear one of Wilkerson's converts—a former heroin addict named Nicky Cruz—preach at a local church, I came away more bewildered than ever. How could I seriously deny such an obviously altered life? How could I condemn the genuineness of Cruz's religious experience that had freed him from the clutches of heroin addiction? And if these former drug addicts experienced the renewal of the Holy Spirit—outside Adventism—what difference did all Adventism's special truths really make? If God bestowed grace and the Holy Spirit upon those ignorant of the seventh-day Sabbath, Ellen White, and the special understanding of the prophecies of Daniel and Revelation, why all the fuss over the so-called Adventist "truths" the world simply had urgently to hear? When it came to personal salvation, did these special truths really matter? If God seemingly ignored what Adventists deemed so important, and worked redemptively outside Adventism, how could the Adventist message be so crucial?

I was reminded of Peter's comment at the apostolic council in Acts 15, when the church debated whether the Gentile converts ought to keep the laws of the Torah. "God, who knows the human heart, testified to them [the Gentiles] by giving them the Holy Spirit, just as he did to us; and in

---

11. According to Ellen White, ecstatic tongue-speaking is a false manifestation of the Spirit. Speaking of an outbreak of glossolalia in the mid-1850s, she asserts: "They have an unmeaning gibberish which they call the unknown tongue, which is unknown not only by man but by the Lord and all heaven. Such gifts are manufactured by men and women, aided by the great deceiver" (*Testimonies for Church*, 1:412). Glossolalia has appeared sporadically in the church throughout the centuries, but Adventism, with few exceptions, has consistently opposed such ecstatic speech.

cleansing their hearts by faith he has made no distinction between them and us" (15:8–9).

A tiny doubt about the validity—the efficacy—of the Adventist faith now crept into my thinking. A new crack, a tiny, spidery fissure appeared in Adventism's otherwise seamless theology. For several days I turned this question over in my mind. To an ordinary Christian who isn't closed-minded the matter would seem inconsequential. God's Spirit is at work everywhere in the world, regardless of denominational label. "Where can I go from your spirit? Or where can I flee from your presence?" (Ps 139:7). But for an Adventist brought up on the idea that the Adventist church has a lock on both the intellectual and experiential truth of God, finding that truth manifest elsewhere was extremely unsettling.

Nevertheless, once more I repressed my growing doubts. Soon afterward, the Conference reassigned us to southeastern Kentucky, where we were to co-pastor with Terry and Jean McComb three struggling churches and a newly founded congregation. The year we spent with Terry and Jean would prove to be the happiest of our entire Adventist life. Working in that part of Kentucky, however, brought me into an even closer association with many sincere, dedicated Christians in other denominations—Baptist, Methodist, Church of God, Holiness—whose passion for Christ simply couldn't be denied. This only aggravated the uneasiness Wilkinson's book and hearing Nicky Cruz had generated. How could people attend church on Sunday, the *false* Sabbath, knowing nothing of the seventh-day Sabbath or of the Adventist message, and yet experience such a remarkable sense of the presence of God? Coming upon such devout Christians made my theologically "correct" faith seem stale by comparison. Adventism did not seem to correspond to the reality I was experiencing. My carefully crafted Adventist worldview suddenly seemed hounded by uncomfortable questions. Why do these people have a spiritual experience I don't have? I know the Truth. They don't. They live in miserable spiritual ignorance of the fine points of the true theology. Yet they experience divine grace and assurance in a manner I've never known. What's wrong?

I didn't know why my Adventist faith seemed so devoid of an experience of God's grace, but I now intended to find out. I turned anew to the rich vein of theological reflection I'd discovered while reading non-Adventist literature. It reinforced what I was viscerally experiencing in my daily contact with non-Adventist Christians. Once more surfaced the repressed desire to attend seminary, where I might have a better opportunity than on my own to explore the theology and religious experiences I found so captivating. Now, however, the thought of seminary was joined with a different, more dangerous aspiration. I now wanted to attend a *non-Adventist* seminary. I wanted a more objective environment where I could test Adventist theology against common Christian faith.

When our first daughter, JoAnna, came into our life at this time, it made me begin to wonder about the value of rearing her in the exclusive, narrow world of Adventism. The joy of our life, she spent her first night in our home the same evening Neil Armstrong walked on the moon. The world watched and listened with baited breath. "This is one small step for man and one giant step for mankind," Armstrong said as his foot touched the dusty, scarred surface of the moon, more than two hundred thousand miles away. Tiny JoAnna, oblivious to it all, celebrated by crying for her bottle!

That summer completed my formal internship in ministry. In the Adventist system, a candidate for ministry, upon completing college and/ or seminary, serves an internship of four years or more in a parish. At the successful conclusion of the internship, the candidate is ordained to the ministry. I was ordained on June 14, 1969, in Portland, Tennessee. I had finally achieved my life goal of becoming a full-fledged Adventist minister!

The year in southeastern Kentucky ended all too soon. JoAnna was only two months old when I received an invitation to become the pastor of a suburban congregation of five hundred in Madison, Tennessee, one of the largest Adventist congregations in the Kentucky-Tennessee Conference. This was really an unexpected promotion, since the Boulevard Seventh-day Adventist church was considered one of the elite congregations in the Conference. I was then only twenty-six. That first Sabbath (Saturday) in September, trembling inside because I knew I was following in the footsteps of a much more mature, seasoned pastor, I entered the dais in a new pin-stripe black suit, white Oxford button-down shirt, and red striped tie. If the congregation had any reservations about me, they hid it well. Instead, they warmly welcomed Laura, JoAnna, and me into their hearts and lives.

A few months later, after we'd gotten acquainted with the congregation, and members felt more comfortable about approaching us, a physician in the church requested a private meeting. His demeanor screamed "urgent"! The gathering twilight darkness engulfed the church interior as I switched on the lamp in my study and awaited his arrival. Shortly, he appeared, shirt collar unbuttoned, tie askew. His face, framed by a full head of gray hair, sagged gloomily. Ordinarily quiet and reserved, now he poured out a tale of woe about the denominational politics in nearby Madison Hospital, an Adventist institution. It seemed as though, without warning, he had suddenly lost his position as head of the surgery department at the hospital. "I've been horribly wounded and betrayed," he moaned. "This thing caught me by surprise. I'm embarrassed. My wife is embarrassed, my children humiliated." Then, he grew silent, pausing as if in deep, concentration, not sure of what he wanted to say. He looked me in the eye. "You are, if I won't embarrass you by saying so, a rising 'star' in Adventism. Here you are, in your mid-twenties, pastor of one of largest, most distinguished congregations in the Conference. You have the potential to go far in the denomination."

I stared blankly, not sure where he was going with this. "What do you mean? I don't understand."

"You're an honest person. You stand for truth and fairness. The Adventist leadership, you will eventually discover, isn't really honest. One of these days," he said slowly and deliberately as if to draw out each word, "this denomination is going to hit you and hit you hard."

What did he mean? I puzzled. I'm a committed Seventh-day Adventist. No one is going to "hit me hard." Of course, there was political maneuvering in the church. That was only human, I thought. I could endure the politics in the system, because I still believed Adventism's essential, core message.

When the surgeon walked out the door, leaving me alone with my thoughts, I immediately began to argue with myself about his strange prediction. Was he just saying this because of his own bitterness over losing his position at the hospital? Had he become cynical? When he calms down, won't he look at things in a better light? Yet I've never forgotten what he said. In time his cynical prediction would prove eerily accurate.

Life soon presented us with our second joy, Paula, born at Madison Hospital. With the responsibility of two young daughters, I felt more keenly than ever the aspiration to succeed in my ministry and, by further training and experience, improve my pastoral and theological education. Despite what seemed tiny, inconsequential reservations, my career as a Seventh-day Adventist minister never looked brighter.

Nashville, not far from Madison, is home to Vanderbilt University Divinity School. Upon coming to the Nashville area, I would now be within range of one of the best seminaries in the nation. If I could get into Vanderbilt, I could test Adventist theology against the best Christian thought, reasoning that if it could survive such a rigorous test and come out unscathed, it had to be credible and significant. Gingerly testing the waters, I persuaded a new, but reluctant Conference president, Kimber Johnson, to allow me to enroll—at my own expense and on my own time—in a course in biblical Hebrew. Thus far in parish experience, I'd found my Greek (I had minored in Greek in college) to be so valuable, I wanted to study Hebrew, and thus learn to read the Old Testament in its original language. Johnson's concern about how Vanderbilt might affect my faith, however, was not unwarranted. Enrolling at Vanderbilt was a step that would change my life even more than I had ever imagined.

PART TWO

Crisis

4

Unsettling Questions

Faith keeps many doubts in her pay. If I could not doubt, I should not believe.
—*HENRY DAVID THOREAU*

Aﬅer three years we leﬅ the Boulevard Seventh-day Adventist Church to join the faculty at Southern Adventist University. Shortly after we had settled in Collegedale, my dad, Howard, suffered a massive stroke, from which he never really regained consciousness. As I stood at his bedside in the ICU, I thought back to his refusal to join the Adventist church and naturally wondered about his final destiny. Through my tears I prayed for God's generous mercy and grace. A couple of days later, we laid him to rest in a hillside cemetery in Dalton, the city where he'd spent most of his life. The cemetery spread along the hillside, only about two blocks from the site of the Adventist church where I had been baptized into Adventism and which my dad had obstinately rejected.

I was still an ardent, committed Adventist, but my strict, fundamentalist convictions had begun to erode. I no longer viscerally reacted when I saw an Adventist wearing a wedding band, or drinking a cup of coffee, both forbidden by traditional Adventism. Yet I remained intent on maintaining my Adventist convictions. That was why I found it utterly inconceivable that Vanderbilt professor Daniel Patte would claim that the apostle Paul had not written the Pastoral Epistles—1–2 Timothy, and Titus—or possibly even Ephesians and Colossians! More passionately, since it had to do with the Old Testament, my chosen field of study, I clashed with Professor David Hay's argument against the Mosaic authorship of the Pentateuch. Instead of Moses, as I fervidly believed, Hay claimed the Pentateuch was actually the result of the merging of at least four strands of literary material. The Yahwist, designated by the letter "J" wrote first, then came the Elohist (E), followed by the Deuteronomist (D), and finally P, the Priestly writer. This is known as the Documentary Hypothesis of the origin of the Pentateuch. It is commonly accepted, yet not without reservation, in most of the scholarly world.

When it came to modern methods or approaches to the study of the Bible, which the Vanderbilt faculty simply took for granted, I recoiled completely, rejecting outright the historical-critical method because it threatened cherished traditional opinions about the origin, development, and historical content of the books in the Bible.[1] The Documentary Hypothesis is a signatory achievement of the historical-critical method. My wary, defensive reaction to historical-criticism sent me scrambling through all the available scholarly Adventist literature on which I could get my hands. Unfortunately, there was very little available.[2] That didn't stop me from a self-righteous condemnation of my professors because they really didn't know "the truth"—the Adventist message and its conservative approach to Scripture. Hoping to open their eyes to the Adventist truth, like many Adventists in similar circumstances, I plied them generously with Adventist theological literature.

Vanderbilt's course of study, typical for such an academic discipline, led me through Hebrew, Aramaic, Greek, French, German, Old and New Testament introduction and exegesis, hermeneutical theory, theology, ancient history, philosophy, and philology. Despite beginning the curriculum virtually in a state of theological denial, little by little I started intellectually to become open to other approaches and ways of thinking. I kept coming across inconsistencies in Adventist teachings. To compensate, I imagined a fictional "shelf," much like a shelf in a library, where I could intellectually "shelve" the nagging problems until I had the opportunity to re-examine them carefully. This mental construct helped. But the problems kept

1. The historical-critical method "seeks to understand the ancient text in light of its historical origins, the time and place in which it was written, its sources, if any, the events, dates, persons, places, things, customs, etc., mentioned or implied in the text" (Soulen and Soulen, *Handbook*, 79).

2. The Adventist North American Bible Conferences of 1974 addressed biblical criticism. In one paper, Gerhard Hasel dismissed historical criticism as the application of an alien philosophy to the text. "The practice of employing a particular philosophy . . . as a prerequisite for engaging in the task of interpretation and exegesis is to superimpose an external category on Scripture and to make Scripture subordinate to the thoughts of men" ("General Principles of Interpretation," 10).

accumulating. There are surely answers to these dilemmas somewhere, I kept reassuring myself.

One area, in particular, where the problems with Adventist theology abounded was in the interpretation of the biblical apocalyptic literature. From this literature, Adventism had constructed the entire backbone of its theological system. Adventism is really an *apocalyptic* movement. I read through most of the surviving ancient Jewish and Christian apocalyptic texts, including the biblical books of Daniel, Revelation, and 1 Enoch, a non-canonical apocalypse accepted by the Ethiopian Church but actually quoted in the New Testament (see Jude 14–15), written during the heyday of this style of literature (c. 250 BCE–100 CE). Careful examination convinced me that apocalypses were actually works of creative imagination. More akin to poetry than prose, they could not legitimately be read as literal predictions and blueprints of the future. As symbolic texts, their chief role lay in the inspiration, encouragement, and hopes they provided that God would eventually overcome all evil in the world. They were not road maps of future events predetermined to take place during the course of human history, as I had been taught in Adventism, and on which the denomination staked its very existence.

The books of Daniel and Revelation are prime examples of biblical apocalyptic literature. Daniel contains several narratives about the conflict some Judean exiles endured at the hands of their Babylonian captors (Dan 1–6), but the bulk of the book (Dan 7–12) is in apocalyptic style. Apocalyptic writings typically recount divine, heavenly revelation mediated by an otherworldly, angelic being to a human author. The revelation itself concerns the transcendent or heavenly realm and indicates divine sovereignty over and interaction with the temporal, historical affairs of the world. Apocalyptic visionary writings use bizarre animal images; dragon-like creatures; radiant angelic beings poised between earth and heaven; and symbolic numbers such as sevens, tens, and twelves. Apocalyptic literature generally focuses on the end of human history, which is always understood to be imminent.[3]

Such symbolism has puzzled readers for centuries. How should we in modern times understand apocalyptic literature? How may we read it intelligently? I questioned. This is especially true of the biblical books of Daniel and Revelation. Over the centuries, interpreters have tried at least four approaches. One school of thought—known as *futurism*—finds most of Revelation, especially Rev 4–22, and some parts of Daniel (Dan 2, 7–12), as predictive of the distant future from the perspective of the original writing.

3. This characterization follows Collins, *Apocalypse*, 9. Within the Bible most scholars identify the following passages as proto-apocalyptic or apocalyptic: Isa 24–27; Ezek 38–39; Joel 3; Daniel; Zech 9–14; Matt 24; Mark 13: Luke 21; 2 Thess 2; Revelation.

When Revelation was written—near the end of the first century CE—the author was shown events that would transpire in the distant future. Most of these events are still yet to occur, although they are imminent. The recent success of the *Left Behind Series*,[4] with its vision of a world torn apart by the Antichrist, shows how popular is futurism as an interpretive mode. This way of reading apocalyptic is truly alive and well in the modern world.

Opposed to futurism stands another mode of interpretation: *preterism*. Preterism takes seriously the historical circumstances under which Daniel and Revelation were written. Revelation primarily has to do with the first century CE, not some far off future events in the twentieth or twenty-first centuries, as in futurism. Daniel comes from the second century BCE, although some parts of it may be older.

A third way of reading apocalyptic takes the literary images in the text as symbolic. They are allegorical or metaphorical and thus devoid of most historical significance. They merely speak metaphorically and offer spiritual encouragement and hope against all the evil encountered in life. This represents the *idealist* or symbolic approach.

Adventists follow a method of interpretation that was especially popular during much of the nineteenth century when the Adventist movement was born. This is the fourth or *historicist* approach. Adventists situate the gradual, continuous fulfillment or unfolding of the prophecies of Daniel and Revelation during the course of Western history, not merely clustered at the end of time. Thus they find in these books amazing details about Islam, the Roman Catholic Church, the rise of modern Protestantism, the development of the United States, as well as the rapidly unfolding crisis of the end times. What disturbed me most about the Adventist advocates of historicism was that they always seemed to locate the climactic events of apocalyptic *in their own day*, whether that was the nineteenth, twentieth, or twenty-first centuries. This exposed the fatal weakness of the historicist approach. An interpreter using the historicist approach seems always to find the fulfillment of an apocalyptic vision in the present or near future. A historicist constantly looks to the newspaper or current events to find the fulfillment of some apocalyptic prediction. This is why Adventists claim that we are living in the last days—the Second Advent must occur very, very soon. "Aren't the signs of the end all around us?" they say. "Time can't last much longer!" The sense of urgency has dimmed somewhat since the denomination has repeated the same message for almost two hundred years.

4. The *Left Behind Series* consists of 16 books, written by Jerry Jenkins and Tim LaHaye in the late 1990s and early 2000s, published by Tyndale House. In novelistic form, these set forth the futurist vision of the end of times. The series spawned several Hollywood movies.

Within the Adventist community this has engendered a troubling "crisis of delay" that strongly hints that the church may have misinterpreted the very apocalyptic texts upon which the movement has been built. The church has had an increasingly difficult time explaining why, after so many urgent warnings, the end of the world has not yet arrived.

Examining the apocalyptic texts against their cultural background convinced me that, instead of historicism or futurism, a preterist interpretation was most appropriate for apocalyptic. Preterist interpretation, to repeat, approaches apocalyptic literature as primarily rooted in the contemporary social and historical setting of the original apocalyptic writers. Everything it foretold, noted Desmond Ford, who later would become prominent in Adventism's controversies, "could speedily have been fulfilled to the generation that first read its pages."[5] Revelation, in fact, makes this very point: "The revelation of Jesus Christ, which God gave him to show his servants *what must soon take place*" (1:1). The book of Revelation found application primarily before and during the early Christian era (first and second centuries CE). Apocalyptic does not predict the eighteenth, nineteenth, and twentieth centuries, as Adventists have claimed.[6] Thus, when we read apocalyptic, we overhear what the ancient author was saying to the first readers, who may have readily understood most of the symbols. The apocalyptic author was not speaking about the distant future.

My rethinking of apocalyptic interpretation during my studies at Vanderbilt disturbingly left me squarely at odds with Adventism and its major emphasis upon a *historicist* reading of Daniel and Revelation. Since the whole fundamental conceptual framework of the Adventist movement came out of Daniel and Revelation, I gradually found myself unable any longer to accept my denomination's raison d'etre. This did not bode well for the future, I realized. Here I was, pursuing a doctoral degree on my denomination's ticket, while my studies were subtly undermining that very sponsoring denomination. What was I to do? I'd heard of a few Adventist scholars who'd dropped out of their universities because they couldn't handle what they were learning. If I'd wanted to avoid this kind of conflict, why hadn't I attended an Adventist university instead?

5. Ford and Ford, *Adventist Crisis*, 83.

6. This contrast has now been vividly documented by Boyer, *When Time Shall be No More*. Boyer's survey of the history of apocalyptic interpretation clearly exposes the wild, bizarre, and frequently erroneous speculation emanating from historicist and futurist interpreters. So far as I am aware, Adventists and possibly Jehovah's Witnesses are the main contemporary practitioners of historicism. Futurism, with its idea of a secret Rapture and the Tribulation, has found a home particularly in the Fundamentalist movement, and there enjoys widespread popularity.

The Vanderbilt professors personal theological views, however, I carefully kept at arm's length. For their part, they didn't try to pressure me to change my mind. "We'd be disappointed if you changed your views," James Crenshaw, who would become my doctoral mentor, told me. Crenshaw was recognized as one of the world's leading authorities on Hebrew wisdom literature. "We only want you to demonstrate in research that you can use modern scientific methods in analyzing and interpreting the Bible. What you actually believe about these methods is your own personal business."

Fair enough, I thought, sitting there in his book-lined study on the third floor of the Divinity Quadrangle, where I'd come to ask about how to deal with the disturbing clash between my Adventist theological values and those taught at Vanderbilt. I would try to understand—really comprehend—what I was hearing, I determined, although I knew I could never accept all of it. I had chosen to write my dissertation under Crenshaw because the results of historical criticism, when used with Hebrew wisdom literature, seemed more compatible with traditional Adventist views. In a dissertation, I realized, I had carefully to thread my way between Adventist suppositions about the Bible and the contrasting conclusions of widely accepted historical-critical study. Briefly, however fleetingly, I flirted with writing on Old Testament apocalyptic literature, perhaps a topic from the book of Daniel, which was of great importance for Adventist theology. Just as quickly I gave up the idea. I was already having enough problems with the historicist mode of interpreting Daniel. What if my research failed to support the Adventist understanding of something in Daniel? That was altogether likely. Would I not risk professional suicide? Would I not likely bring to a swift end my career in the church? The denomination had published almost nothing about the wisdom books (e.g., Job, Proverbs, Ecclesiastes), and no primary doctrinal point as far as I was aware touched on them, so I felt relatively safe doing research in this area. It was thus that I came to develop a specialty in the Hebrew wisdom literature.

My dilemma over a safe topic for a dissertation may seem surprising, so a word of explanation is in order. Most Adventist scholars in theological or biblical studies in non-Adventist universities struggle with this issue. Typically, if they are serving on the faculty of an Adventist college, the employing college covers the tuition, books, and living costs associated with earning a degree at a non-Adventist (or Adventist) university. The college then expects such faculty to commit five years' service to the employing institution. The church also reasonably expects such sponsored scholars to remain loyal to the denomination, not only by living Adventist values while pursuing their degrees, but also by supporting, or at least, not openly criticizing denominational teaching in the form of a dissertation. What this says about the denomination's openness toward independent, objective research leaves much to be desired, but the church's position is understandable. Since universities typically publish dissertations, they eventually become public. Should an appointed Adventist leader get wind that a scholar has veered from official denominational teaching in a dissertation, serious consequences, including termination from denominational employment, could result. For an Adventist scholar working in an academic environment such as Vanderbilt, this threat—although unstated—loomed ever present.

Little more than five years after I had completed my PhD, an Adventist scholar fell victim to this danger. Ron Graybill, then an associate secretary at the Ellen G. White Estate in Washington, D.C., the archival institution that formally preserves and circulates the Ellen White writings, had been sponsored for a PhD in the History of American Christianity at Johns Hopkins University. When it was discovered that his dissertation, "The Power of Prophecy: Ellen G. White and the Women Religious Founders of the Nineteenth Century," portrayed Ellen White in a humanistic light, the White Estate promptly reassigned Graybill to the denomination's distance learning division, complaining that his work "creates an inaccurate impression of White, as it approaches her from the perspective of a secular historian."[7] When employed by the church, especially an institution like the White Estate, a person simply could not criticize or otherwise impugn Ellen White. The presence of such censorship has made many an Adventist scholar waver at the prospect of a dissertation. I refused to run the risk of deconstructing—even inadvertently—any of the church's teachings. Already I had invested too much of my life in the church to die on this hill, so to speak. I decided to work on the book of Proverbs, which seemed to be the safest of all the wisdom books for an Adventist.

Six years into my graduate program, Southern appointed me its scholar delegate to BRICOM (the Biblical Research Institute Committee of the Adventist denomination), a theological consortium of Adventist scholars from various theological disciplines. BRICOM essentially ran interference for the denomination, intercepting theological problems before they became major issues by providing scholarly, technical and popular defenses of Adventist teaching. BRICOM had originally been called the Defense Literature Committee. Despite its new name, it had yet to outgrow its narrow apologetic function. In its consortium meetings gathered the finest theological minds in the church. Gordon Hyde, a personal acquaintance of Laura's and my family, and one of my favorite college professors, was now the chair of BRICOM. I felt truly humbled to be in the presence of people I had long

7. *Southern Tidings*, "World View: White Estate Staffer Reassigned," March 1984.

respected, whose names graced many of the Adventist books I treasured, but with whom I'd never become personally acquainted. Finally, I thought, in this consortium, I'll get some help for the many doctrinal issues that were troubling me.

The more deeply I became involved in the work of BRICOM, however, the more disappointed I was. When the really difficult, intractable questions about Adventist doctrine arose, the committee turned to scholars who would defend—usually without flinching—the denomination's traditional teaching. The commission then published this defense in one of the church's journals, touting it as BRICOM's resolution of the problem. When someone dared to present a paper at variance with the church's teaching, it was quickly tossed into a dead file at BRICOM offices, never to resurface again. At Vanderbilt, in contrast, I'd discovered a much fairer, more evenhanded approach, especially when dealing with data that contradicted traditional religious faith. I found deeply, profoundly disturbing BRICOM's prejudicial way of handling such difficulties.

In one session of BRICOM, increasingly troubled by this prejudicial approach, I asked the presenter a difficult question about his research. Shock visibly spread across the room. Hyde, especially, glared at me menacingly, his eyes darkening. I had unwittingly committed a major faux pas. Later, when the meeting ended, a friendly BRICOM veteran pulled me aside. "You're a bright young scholar," he whispered. "I hate to see you ruin your career by posing such difficult questions. Don't rock the boat! Don't object when someone biases their research in favor of the denomination. When you're assigned a paper, you'll want to do the same yourself. Present in your best scholarly language a conclusion you know BRICOM and the larger church is waiting to hear. Embellish your paper with scholarly paraphernalia, footnotes, technical language, and so on. But don't *ever* write anything that contradicts the church's traditional theology. That way, you'll survive to fight another day."

How could such an approach be a search for truth? Wasn't it a sham? I wondered. Is this scholarly charade the best the denomination has to offer when it comes to dealing with some of the difficult theological problems? Why must the church shy away from basic theological evidence? Was the denomination even interested in research that might challenge its traditional teachings?

My conflict intensified and deepened. Where could I look for answers? Back on the Southern campus, I dared not confide my struggle with anyone—I mean *anyone*—save Laura. Outside our home, in the classroom or in any of the churches where I occasionally preached, to express my deepening apprehensions would be like setting the torch to the increasingly fragile timbers of my Adventist convictions. I struggled virtually alone in a silent, disillusioning world. Inner pressure kept building.

It erupted unexpectedly, not in an upsurge of pent-up feelings, but in a sigh, a quiet, reflective "Aha" moment, like letting the air out of a tire. Sitting in a threadbare, dark green stuffed chair, a remnant left over from a living room set we'd long since discarded, I was reading Rudolf Bultmann's essay, "Is Exegesis without Presuppositions Possible?" an assignment for a seminar I was taking on Bultmann (1884–1966), the well-known New Testament scholar. Bultmann astutely pointed out that no one approaches the biblical text without presuppositions, biases that have been left in place by many complex factors, religious upbringing, education, culture, and so on. In order to be as objective as possible, therefore, a person had carefully to identify and freely concede their own biases. One must get them out and onto the table, where they could be looked at carefully. Once they were deliberately brought out into the open they had less chance to skew interpretation. Admitting them lessened their impact.[8]

In that moment "the shoe dropped," as the expression goes! Through all the years of graduate education, it suddenly dawned on me, I had been relying on my Adventist biases to filter out any new, differing insights—particularly theological ones—I had come across. As a result, I hadn't seriously listened to *anything* I'd been studying at Vanderbilt! I had been blocking it out. I was in denial. Mortified at my closed-minded arrogance, and annoyed at my naiveté, I thought of one popular Adventist scholar who had taken a doctorate in theology from a well-known university. "For every page of non-Adventist literature in theology I'm assigned," he boasted, "I literally read one equivalent page in Ellen White to counteract it. As a result, I've come through my doctoral studies with my Adventist faith intact."

Of course! No wonder! He, as I, had deliberately ignored or closed his mind, permitting Adventist preconceptions to filter his thinking! If Adventists never listened seriously to other theologians, I reasoned, how could they honestly expect those same theologians—or anyone else—to take seriously Adventist claims? How could I expect my professors to read the Adventist books I'd been regularly offering them? The enormity of such a simple, obvious insight momentarily overwhelmed me. I really wanted to be a person of integrity. I wanted congruity—honesty—to be the guiding principle of my life. If so, I reasoned, shouldn't I at least listen, not only to Bultmann, but to all my professors as well? Ought not I to try to understand their points of view as honestly as I could? That seemed only fair.

---

8. Bultmann, "Exegesis without Presuppositions?" 289–97.

A genuine religious scholar, I believe, tries to be open and honest with the biblical text. But such openness sometimes goes against traditional ways of understanding, including those of Adventism. Ironically, although Adventism claims to be more open and honest with the text than any other denomination, it is probably guiltier than most of suppressing honest scholarship. Yet it is the task of a biblical scholar to study carefully the text, regardless of how closely the text may agree with church teachings. The church, at least in the Protestant tradition, is ultimately subservient to the biblical witness, not the biblical witness to the church. "It is the work of a serious theological interpreter of the Bible to pay close and careful attention to what is in the text, regardless of how it coheres with the theological habit of the church."[9] That is the only way to be faithful to the scriptural text. The church stands under the biblical text, not the other way round. Biblical scholars must be as open as humanly possible to the leading of the text, wherever it may take them.

Imagine how I felt when I came across the following description of a theologian's vocation!

> He cannot affirm any tradition and any authority except through a "No" and a "Yes." And it is always possible that he may not be able to go all the way from the "No" to the "Yes." He cannot join the chorus of those who live in unbroken assertions. He must take the risk of being driven beyond the boundary line of the theological circle. Therefore, the pious and powerful in the church are suspicious of him, although they live in dependence upon the work of the former theologians who were in the same situation.[10]

Twenty years of Adventist conditioning made me shudder at the personal cost of such authenticity. Horror stories of those who had drifted from the church after earning non-Adventist university degrees—particularly in the religious disciplines—flashed before me. Here I was, working toward a non-Adventist doctorate in Old Testament! The historical, religious, and theological problems I'd already encountered would require more than a lifetime to resolve, if even that was possible. I had encountered far more questions than ever before. I had no clue at this point how to formulate adequate answers. Yet I knew, if I really pursued the truth to which Adventism claimed it was committed, I *had* to take the risk. I had to get behind Adventist presuppositions to what one of my professors called "the question

9. Brueggemann, *Theology of Old Testament*, 107.

10. Tillich, *Systematic Theology*, 1:25–26.

beneath the question."[11] A quote attributed to Ellen White flashed into mind. "The greatest want of the world is the want of men—men who will not be bought or sold, men who in their inmost souls are true and honest."[12]

That spring afternoon, at the conclusion of my last semester of course work at Vanderbilt, I had reached a major tipping point. It was a metamorphosis that would lead me to look at my church in an entirely new—and disturbing—light. I had crossed my personal, intellectual Rubicon. There could be no turning back.

The fall semester I was asked to teach an upper level college course in the apocalyptic book of Daniel. Since Adventists draw their primary identity from such apocalyptic texts, it is common to find courses in apocalyptic literature in the denomination's colleges.

In the wake of my previous university study of apocalyptic literature, I began preparation for the course by carefully reexamining the traditional Adventist interpretation of passages crucial to Adventist theology in Daniel. With the lamp on my desk shining deep into the night, I pored over Daniel 7, 8, and 9, all critical, essential passages for Adventism. Adventists, true to the historicist manner of interpretation, claimed that these chapters pointed to a final work of divine judgment (known within Adventism as the *Investigative Judgment*) that began in 1844. William Miller, a New England farmer turned biblical interpreter and evangelist, had calculated that the chronology mentioned in these chapters culminated in 1844. And it was out of the Millerite movement of the nineteenth century that Seventh-day Adventism was formed. For this reason, no part of Scripture was dearer to the Adventist heart than Daniel.

Meticulously combing these chapters in the original Hebrew and Aramaic (parts of Daniel are written in Aramaic), I understood how incredibly difficult it was—if not impossible—to draw any specific, hard-and-fast historical or predictive conclusions from Dan 7–9. I realized again why many scholars had been baffled by the apocalyptic section of Daniel (7–12). Other interpretations than the traditional Adventist one were certainly possible, even unavoidable.

Frustrated by the dead end to which this research once more took me, I bleakly complained to Laura, who patiently listened, "The book of Daniel simply doesn't convincingly support the Adventist interpretation. I can't

11. The precise expression is "the problem beneath the problem of theological method" (Farley, *Ecclesial Man*, 3).

12. White, *Education*, 57.

find any compelling reason why the 'little horn' symbol of Daniel 7 must be identified with the Roman Catholic Church rather than the ancient Seleucid king Antiochus IV Epiphanes (175–164 CE), as most scholars think, nor why the 'two thousand three hundred days' of Dan 8:14 (KJV) pinpoint a final judgment that started in 1844. Other interpretations are certainly plausible, and there aren't any clear criteria in the text (or in the rest of the Bible, so far as I can tell) that make it possible to decide convincingly between the Adventist view and the other alternatives."

"What about Ellen White's support of the traditional Adventist understanding of Daniel?" asked Laura, who'd majored in religion in college. Ellen White, we both knew, had written extensively about Daniel 7–9.[13] Because Adventists accept Ellen White as a divinely inspired prophet and interpreter, they regard her support as decisive for denominational teaching.

"I don't know," I replied. Ellen White often based her doctrinal formulations on the writings of other Adventists, I realized, so an appeal to her ends up becoming circular reasoning. "If we cite Ellen White, the particular doctrinal teaching may not have been original with her. And if, as she insisted, we base our doctrine solely upon Scripture, then we can't use Ellen White to bail us out of an exegetical jam. If the doctrine of the Investigative Judgment in 1844 isn't compelling from the Bible alone, the church has no real justification for making it a central teaching; certainly not a requirement of membership."

"What you're saying is really disturbing! If you're right—and I don't doubt you—haven't you just undermined the main reason for the existence of the Adventist church? It grew out of the Millerite movement, based in large part on Miller's calculations about prophecy. I do hope you can find some solution for this before you walk into that classroom."

Her words jolted my memory. An Adventist minister, I recalled, had once casually asked me, almost in jest, it seemed, "If William Miller had known Hebrew, would there have ever been a nineteenth-century Adventist movement?" We were sitting around a campfire, deep in the interior of a Tennessee state park, planning to do some hiking the next day. His question was hypothetical. I now suddenly realized what my clergy friend had meant. The Hebrew of Dan 8, specifically, was even more obscure than in the English translation, on which Miller had unfortunately relied.

In this anxious state I began the class in Daniel. Deftly I maneuvered chapter by chapter through Daniel, trying to ignore, or at least minimize, serious discussion around the glaring problems. For the more astute, this ploy didn't work. Don, one of the best students in the class, usually sat in

---

13. See White, *Great Controversy*, 479–91.

the front row with his Bible open and notebook beside it. A recent convert to Adventism, he simply wouldn't back away from the problems. "How do Adventists get that the 'time that the word went out to restore and rebuild Jerusalem' [Dan 9:25] refers specifically to the decree of the Persian king Artaxerxes I in 457 BCE?" he pressed. "It seems to me Daniel is referring to the original decree of Cyrus the Great in 538 BCE, an excerpt of which is cited in Ezra 1:1–4."

Don knew that the 457 BCE date was absolutely critical to the Adventist claim that the prophecy of Dan 8:14, "For two thousand three hundred evenings and mornings, then the sanctuary shall be restored," ended in 1844 CE. If this 2300-year period, as Adventists interpret the "two thousand three hundred evenings and mornings," were to commence in 538 BCE, rather than 457, it would throw off the entire calculation by 80 years, making it end in 1763! That simply wouldn't work. And Don knew it.

"I can't really answer, Don," I replied, somewhat embarrassed, but also worried about his putting a finger on a gaping hole in the denomination's interpretation. "There is a decree promulgated by Artaxerxes I, cited in Ezra 7:12–26, but from the excerpt quoted it is hard to determine how it is anything more than a reactivation or perhaps an extension of the original decree of Cyrus that you mention. Even if this Ezra 7 decree is the one referred to in Dan 9:25, it should be dated to 458, not 457 BCE, which would also slightly throw off the 1844 date (to 1843), and mark as mistaken Ellen White and the early Adventist pioneers. I'm afraid the church has got to do some more research on this."

So it typically went the entire semester. I found myself saying again and again, "The church needs more research . . . the church needs more research." A few years later I would learn that in the late 1950s, about the same time I was converting to Seventh-day Adventism, the General Conference of the denomination had set up a special Daniel committee to investigate some of these problems. The work of this committee was kept hidden from the membership because the church's very identity was at stake. Frustrated by unresolved questions, the committee finally dissolved later in the 1960s without finding valid solutions. I could not have known then, but the whole issue was about to explode, creating a theological crisis such as the church had never experienced.

In that classroom with Don, however, no one realized there had ever been such a study committee. "We're working toward a solution," I tried to console distraught, questioning students, struggling at the same time to shore up my own flagging confidence. I felt hollow, insincere, and even evasive. Fearing loss of income, which I needed to support my family, I couldn't summon the courage just to say, "The text, as far as I can see, doesn't clearly support the Adventist view, and neither the church nor I have any answers to that." Instead of such courage, I bowed to economic and social pressure. I felt trapped in a world of illusions.

Little did I know that my internal personal struggle would shortly manifest itself throughout the wider Adventist community. And I would be stuck in the heart of the maelstrom.

5

Grace not Perfection

I do not at all understand the mystery of grace—
only that it meets us where we are but does not leave us where it found us.

—*ANNE LAMOTT*

During the next couple of years, I was busy with class preparation, usually teaching four or five courses per semester, commuting once or twice a week to complete my course work at Vanderbilt, sit for my comprehensive exams, and finally get to work on my dissertation, which I completed in late 1978 on the topic of retributive paradoxes or the difficulties with the so-called principle of retributive justice in the book of Proverbs.[1] When I took the final copy of the nearly four-hundred-page dissertation to the graduate school office, the dissertation secretary took out a small, six-inch ruler and carefully measured the margins of the typescript document and checked the arrangement of hundreds of footnotes, the title page, the bibliography, and the main text. I nervously watched. Only two or three days remained before the deadline the dissertation had to be turned in. "This looks fine," she said, as she carefully replaced the cover on the red and white box that contained the manuscript. I breathed a sigh of relief. Smiling, she looked up. "Congratulations! How would you like to lead the graduates from the graduate school into the commencement ceremonies by ceremonially carrying the black and gold university banner?"

---

1. My dissertation was titled "Retributive Paradoxes in Proverbs 10–29" (1978).

"I'd be honored," I gulped, completely astounded I'd been chosen for the distinction.

On a gray, overcast day on the broad, spacious green at Vanderbilt, I led all the graduate students from the schools of history, philosophy, psychology, religion, and education into the outdoor commencement along with more than seventeen hundred others, black robes, tams, and black and gold hoods flapping in the gentle, Nashville breeze.

Despite the festivity of that moment, representing years of hard study and the joy of finally achieving one of the major goals of my life, my internal struggle with the narrower, obscure points of Adventist theology persisted. The conflict was always there, like a dull ache. So far, I had somehow managed to keep my personal struggles to myself and out of public awareness. Bit by bit, too, I had been able to lessen the pressure of my growing uneasiness with Adventism by volunteering to teach Comparative Religions, Philosophy of Religion, and Old Testament Introduction, courses whose content was inherently less distinctively Adventist. I was thus relieved of having to deal openly with the more disputed matters for Adventism in Daniel and Revelation.

Yet neither keeping the theological difficulties to myself, nor focusing on basic religion courses proved sufficient. About this same time the first of three successive theological crises broke out in the local Adventist community and simultaneously spread throughout the larger North American Adventist world. It quickly became a roiling controversy, coming unexpectedly like summer storm clouds, rain beating down in torrents and running through the streets. It swiftly flooded into a full controversy—a war of words and ideas—over the nature of the gospel, what theologians call the doctrine of soteriology (salvation). This controversy then quickly swelled into a dispute over the Adventist interpretation of Daniel, and finally spilled over into a debate about the writings of Ellen White, the denomination's prophet. The three controversies were all linked in some way with the writings of Ellen White. Since all Adventist tenets and practices are influenced by Ellen White, it was to be expected that these three controversies would end up implicating her writings.

In the following chapters, I will discuss separately each controversy, although in actual experience they tended to merge and overlap. The three controversies and how the denomination mishandled them did much to undermine my already fading confidence in the denomination. The theological conflict publicly drew aside the curtain of secrecy and painfully exposed the inadequate biblical and theological basis for several of the key Adventist doctrines. Adventism finally would become fundamentally untenable for me. Following these explanations, I will describe how the church's devious approach to each of the theological trifecta finally led me to conclude that Adventism is simply wrong in several of its core doctrines. During the controversies, the denomination proved unwilling to acknowledge its wrongs—even in the face of overwhelming, convincing evidence.

The denomination has argued among its followers about law and gospel—the relationship of works to faith—since at least its General Conference session (a worldwide gathering) in 1888 in Minneapolis, Minnesota. The earliest Adventist statement of fundamental beliefs (1872) had fallen far short of a full acknowledgment that salvation comes through faith, as the New Testament teaches (see Eph 2:8–10). Instead, the earliest statement had placed heavy emphasis upon the observance of the Ten Commandments. This stress on the law or good works from that day to this has predisposed most Adventists, including many top influential leaders, to some form of legalistic moralism. This is the idea that one's meticulous obedience to the law counts toward divine acceptance. Before 1888, opponents of the church had quite correctly criticized Adventists as "legalists." "The law is spiritual, holy, just, and good," wrote Uriah Smith (1832–1903), the well-known editor of the *Review and Herald* (now *Adventist World*) only a few months after the 1888 session. "Perfect obedience to it [the Ten Commandments] will develop righteousness, and that is the only way anyone can attain to righteousness."[2] Such a statement, taken at face value, certainly sounds legalistic, at least to the church's critics.

In order to understand how Adventists arrived at this view of salvation, some background is necessary. In the early nineteenth century, along the East Coast from the southern states to New England, and through Kentucky, Tennessee, Ohio, and other Midwestern states, numerous religious revivals occurred, some inside rough-hewn churches, others spilling out into open fields and partially wooded terrain, or in mass camp meetings with thousands in attendance. Because these revivals spread all through the eastern United States, the region became known as the "burnt over district." Out of these revivals several new religious movements were born, including Seventh-day Adventism, which was, in turn, a direct result of the Millerite movement. Revival preaching of the day focused on three main themes: a personal encounter with God; the nearness of the Second Advent; and perfect holiness manifested in a sinless life. All the new religious movements that came into being in this period retained at least one of these themes.[3] Adventists have appropriated all three.

2. Smith, "Our Righteousness," 376–77. To his credit, Smith goes on to admit that a person acquires this righteousness through a synergistic obedience enabled by Christ. See Schwartz, *Light Bearers*, 183–97, for an account of the 1888 General Conference.

3. Corbett-Hemeyer, *Religion in America*, 147–48.

An origin in the "burnt over district" thus naturally inclined Adventism to perfectionism. The pursuit of spiritual perfection has, of course, been an important emphasis in Christianity down through the ages. It has biblical precedence. "I am God Almighty," said Yahweh to Abraham. "Walk before me, and be *blameless* [Heb. *tamim*, "whole," "perfect"]" (Gen 17:1). "Be *perfect* [Gk. *teleios*, "complete," "perfect"], therefore, as your heavenly Father is *perfect*" (Matt 5:48).[4] The end goal of Christian life is perfection, but what does this perfection mean? Much depends upon *how* perfection is defined. What is its measure? How high is the bar? Adventism has debated this question for over a hundred years. "God will accept only those who are determined to aim high," Ellen White put it in a late nineteenth-century comment. "He places every human agent under obligation to do his best. Moral perfection is required of all . . . We need to understand that imperfection of character is sin . . . those who would be workers with God must strive for perfection of every organ of the body and quality of the mind."[5]

Adventist thought about salvation may be plotted along a continuum. At the left are those who advocate salvation through total reliance upon God's generous grace through faith. On the extreme right are those whose final salvation depends upon attaining some kind of sinless perfection of character, as in the quote from Ellen White above. In between these extremes lie various shades of legalistic moralism or synergism (combinations of faith and works). To add to the confusion, Ellen White can be quoted in support of all these views.

It is hard to be precise here. The denomination, at least confessionally, teaches salvation through grace. This appears in all of its recent historical theological statements. The heavy emphasis in Adventism upon the keeping of the Ten Commandments, especially the Sabbath, however, tends in actual practice to overshadow an emphasis on salvation by grace, resulting in a kind of legalistic moralism or taken to an extreme, a hardline perfectionism. It is interesting that most of the new religious movements that arose in the nineteenth century burnt over district were Arminian in perspective.[6] Arminianism places emphasis upon human cooperation with the divine in the

4. The Lukan repetition of this dominical saying is quite different: "Be merciful, just as your Father is merciful" (Luke 6:36).

5. White, *Christ's Object Lessons*, 330.

6. This theological perspective developed with Jacob Arminius (1560–1609), and was adopted by John Wesley and the Methodist movement, whence it came into Adventism. Arminius opposed the strict predestination of the Calvinists and emphasized freedom of the will. Because it was freely chosen, by the same token, salvation could also be forfeited. Emphasis thus fell upon the believer's maintenance of the state of salvation through cooperation with the Holy Spirit.

process of salvation. Their heavy emphasis upon the Ten Commandments has led Adventism too easily to lose the delicate balance between salvation by faith and good works.[7] Legalistic moralism severs one's spiritual growth from faith in Christ and turns it into a moralistic attempt at letter-perfect performance of spiritual virtues. Although it pays lip service to justification by faith, in practice it actually denies it.

Throughout its history some Adventists have turned the doctrine of salvation into legalism in which human works—even though these works are believed to be empowered by the Holy Spirit—would finally elicit God's approval. Some have developed complicated forms of religious perfection. Only if a believer's life corresponds to a certain standard of perfection— usually left ill-defined—will one merit the heavenly reward. The goal of Christian life is thus a proven track record of perfect obedience to the will of God, without which one cannot finally be reckoned as blameless. According to this way of thinking, it is necessary finally to maintain a *sinless* life.

Let me put all this into perspective by reviewing the traditional Christian order of salvation, where divine grace is given a larger role. In the first place, a person becomes aware of the need for God. This is the work of the Holy Spirit, who draws and *convicts* a person of sinfulness. This leads to *repentance* and a turning from sinful behavior. God *elects*, or chooses to adopt a person into the redeemed community. The new believer is *justified*, forgiven, and put into a right relationship with God. At the same moment *regeneration* commences and initiates a lifetime of transformation, known as *sanctification*. Sanctification finally culminates in *glorification*, or the final restoration of the Christian at the Second Advent. From beginning to end this is a work of divine grace received by faith, although all along human cooperation is necessary. "The life that begins with conviction of sin, repentance, election, justification," summarizes John Macquarrie, "passes into the progressive work of sanctification, in which the Holy Spirit more and more conforms this life to Christ, deepening and extending it in faith, hope, and love."[8]

Bitter division over salvation marred the historic 1888 Adventist General Conference gathering of representatives from the denomination in Minneapolis, to which I referred above. Ellet J. Waggoner (1835–1916), a physician turned clergy, and then editor of the Adventist journal, *Signs of*

7. In spite of shifting denominational trends and unfortunate lapses into legalism, some Adventist leaders have gotten hold of the good news of the gospel of grace. E. J. Waggoner, A. T. Jones, A. G. Daniells (1858–1935), W. W. Prescott (1855–1944), Carlyle B. Haynes (1882–1958), Roy Allen Anderson, Edward Heppenstall, and Norval Pease, to name only a few, have trumpeted the gospel of God's grace.

8. Macquarrie, *Christian Theology*, 350.

the Times, teamed up with his associate, Alonzo T. Jones (1830–1923), to proclaim to the surprised delegates what they called "righteousness [justification] by faith," based primarily on the New Testament letters of Paul to the Romans and Galatians.

Interest in righteousness by faith continued into the 1920s, when A. G. Daniells published his landmark, *Christ Our Righteousness* (1926). By the 1930s, however, the denomination had settled upon an affirmation of the gospel that coincided essentially with the historic Christian view, summarized above. "We freely admit that we preach that men should obey God's commandments," thus wrote F. D. Nichol, then editor of the denomination's journal, the *Review and Herald*. "We also preach with equal vigor that a man's only hope of heaven is through the grace of God made available through the gospel."[9]

When I became an Adventist, I recall seeing stacks of the book, *Questions on Doctrine*, lying around the local church offices. Although the denomination would later quietly—not without controversy—rescind publication of this book, at that time (the late 1950s) it was heavily promoting *Questions on Doctrine* as an excellent defense of its theology. *Questions on Doctrine* stressed the church's claim: "According to Seventh-day Adventist belief, there is, and can be, no salvation through the law, or by human works of the law, but only through the saving grace of God."[10]

When Walter Martin published his critical review of Adventism, he agreed with *Questions on Doctrine*. "Adventists confess the basis of their salvation to be grace, and grace alone, the only basis upon which God deigns to save the fallen children of Adam." Having received salvation as a gift, however, a person then was "responsible for its maintenance and duration." This meant observing the commandments and, in Adventist thinking, a host of other mandates, such as avoidance of unclean foods such as pork and shellfish (Lev 11)—the kashrut laws. The pendulum thus shifted quickly and all too easily from faith to the ongoing life of obedience, which was required to maintain one's standing with God. "The Ten Commandments are still God's standard of righteousness and must be obeyed or salvation is forfeit," Martin bluntly put it.[11]

The Adventist teaching about salvation sounds a whole lot like what today is often called covenant nomism or synergism. *Covenant nomism* is the idea that once salvation (or election) has occurred, the individual redeemed status must be maintained by carefully keeping the law with God's

9. Nichol, *Answers to Objections*, 103.

10. *Questions on Doctrine*, 135.

11. Martin, *Truth about Adventism*, 204–5.

assisting grace.[12] *Synergism*, as the word implies, is similar: "working to-gether with" God in the process of spiritual growth and maturity. In this understanding, justification, where a person is put right with God on the basis of faith in Christ, consists primarily in the forgiveness of sin. A process of spiritual growth follows, called sanctification—a cooperative effort of the believer with the Holy Spirit—and must continue throughout life. Upon the success of this cooperative effort the final divine judgment declares one's eternal salvation.

How can salvation through grace by faith come as a gift, and then be made contingent on good behavior? Doesn't that render the gift-character of salvation null and void? Is it now to be made complete by good works? Does faith finally have to be supplemented by human effort? "Did you receive the Spirit by doing the works of the law or by believing what you heard?" Paul asked his Galatian audience (Gal 3:2) Paul was referring to the *gift* of the Holy Spirit which, like salvation itself, comes to the believer through faith, not through the successful performance of duty. The Christian tradition—not just Adventism—has struggled valiantly to understand this symbiotic relationship between faith and good works. In Adventism, as we have noted, the resolution of the tension all too often has taken the form of legalistic moralism or even perfectionism. Such a resolution extracts sanctification—spiritual growth—from the sphere of faith and turns it into moralism, with all its "attendant self-conscious pride or its nagging uncertainties." Sanctification is rooted in faith and justification, not the other way around. "In opposition to all synergism," Berkouwer notes, "even the very first beginning of the passage from darkness into light is possible and real only through the grace of God and by virtue of justification."[13] This delicate relationship between justification, being put right with God, and sanctification, spiritual transformation and renewal, formed the substance of the first crisis of the theological trifecta in Adventism.

I never remember a time in my Adventist experience when there wasn't some dispute going on about divine salvation.

---

12. E. P. Sanders, who coined the expression "covenant nomism" as descriptive of first century rabbinical teaching, defines it as the "view that one's place in God's plan is established on the basis of the covenant and that the covenant requires as the proper response of man his obedience to its commandments, while providing means of atonement for transgression" (*Paul and Judaism*, 75).

13. Berkouwer, *Faith and Sanctification*, 20, 90.

As a teenage convert, I was strongly influenced by Adventism's moralistic tendency, and tried (in vain, I must confess) to live the kind of Christian life it seemed to require. I severely reproached myself for lapses, however minor, because I wanted desperately to be a "perfect" Christian. In the plethora of rules, which seemed to grow beyond all bounds when I started seriously to read Ellen White, I often lost sight of what little of God's grace I had experienced. My Christian experience gradually turned into private misery. I experienced little peace or joy. A vague angst, an aching insecurity, continually troubled me. I obsessively scanned labels on canned food neatly arranged on the shelves in my dad's convenience mart (he had recently purchased the business) to make sure no animal products (especially pork) were used in preparation, scrupulously watched the minute movements of the clock on Friday evenings, as the sun set in the west, to ensure I didn't transgress even the opening seconds of the Sabbath. "We must guard the edges of the Sabbath," well-meaning Adventists explained. "It is in those opening seconds of the Sabbath we are most likely to become careless." In such rigor I wasn't alone. Most Adventists who take Christian living seriously admit to similar anxious experience. While giving lip service to salvation by grace, the Adventism I experienced at ground level was really a not-so-subtle legalism, a salvation purchased—or at least maintained—by a costly, spiritually exhaustive attempt somehow to obey perfectly the divine law. "Conflict after conflict must be waged against hereditary tendencies," I shuddered when I read such mandates in Ellen White. "We shall have to criticize ourselves closely, and allow not one unfavorable trait to remain uncorrected."[14]

Throughout my early pastoral experience, I struggled constantly with these thoughts. How many works? How much faith? How many laws? What kind of perfection? Absolute perfection? Flawless moral perfection? Relative perfection? In some of the painful, wan countenances of the men, women, and youth in the pews I'm afraid I sadly witnessed the effects of such a moralistic conception of Christian living. It turned seemingly normal people into judgmental critics of other people's behavior. I'm afraid there was little awareness of God's assuring grace in the congregations I pastored. It seemed to me Adventism was tailor-made for strong-willed people; people with weaker self-control quickly faded and dropped out of the church. Fortunately, I had inherited a strong determination, and so managed doggedly to keep at it, despite more failures than I care to admit. I took pride in never being a quitter. When I lapsed, I dutifully got back up and went at it again.

14. White, *Christ's Object Lessons*, 331.

Then a pastor friend, sensing my inner spiritual struggle, recommended James Kennedy's "Evangelism Explosion," a personal evangelistic program designed for churches. It laid strong emphasis upon salvation by grace. Kennedy's program (1962) approached personal salvation by asking two probative questions: Have you come to the place in your spiritual life where you can say you know for certain that, if you were to die today, you would go to heaven? Suppose, secondly, that were you to die today and stand before God and God were to say to you, "Why should I let you into my heaven?" what would you say?

I couldn't satisfactorily answer either question. I hadn't come to the place where I felt certain I would even be in heaven. I simply wasn't good enough—perfect enough. And here I was, preaching the so-called "gospel" every Sabbath!

When my pastor friend brought up the subject, I was co-pastoring a "district," in Adventist polity a cluster of three churches and a new developing congregation that met in a hotel ballroom in Somerset, Kentucky. Each Saturday morning, Laura and I started from our home near Corbin to lead worship in two of the four congregations, while my co-pastor, Terry Mc-Comb, served the other two. We tucked JoAnna, then barely a year old, into the back of our black Volkswagen, and drove past Cumberland Falls State Park along winding roads all the way to one of the tiny churches near Liberty, Kentucky. We enjoyed driving by pastures and cultivated fields, noticing the small well-worn farm homes and old, weather-beaten barns set back from the highway. We glanced in wonder at the tiny coal seams still visible in the hillsides where engineers had cut the roadway. Finally, we turned off U.S. Route 25 and onto a narrow, paved road that snaked through the low-lying hills to the small, white wood-sided rural chapel, complete with a coal-burning stove and a genuine outhouse. The small congregation, consisting mainly of two or three families and their kin, had not the slightest inkling of the personal struggle I experienced all over again every time I climbed into the pulpit.

After we moved from southeastern Kentucky to take the Adventist church in Madison, Tennessee, Elden Walters, an Adventist evangelist, began to promote his *New Testament Witnessing*, a program—manual and all—adapted for Adventists from that of James Kennedy. I implemented the program in my congregation, and in the process came to experience what it meant to confess Jesus Christ by faith. "If you confess with your lips that Jesus is Lord and believe in your heart that God raised him from the dead, you will be saved" (Rom 10:9). Gradually, through careful study of the Bible, especially with the guidance of several non-Adventist writers, I personally discovered the gospel of God's grace. I abandoned my quest for moral perfection, and began to trust in Christ. "For by grace you have been saved through faith, and this is not your own doing, it is the gift of God" (Eph 2:8). I started—cautiously, feeling my way along—to preach the gospel of free grace. Since there were always some in the congregation who were bound up in traditional Adventist legalism, such sermons usually aroused opposition. "If you leave us with only faith in God's love and grace," one frustrated, irritated, middle-aged church member challenged, after one of my sermons on the gospel, "What's to become of the law? What about the Sabbath?" He was afraid that without the restraint of the law, and thus the threat of it, people would entirely abandon morality.

My preaching during this period, I felt, actually conformed to official denominational teaching, at least that found in the church's formal doctrinal statements. "Salvation comes as a free gift of God's grace, accepted by faith in Christ," stated the *Seventh-day Adventist Encyclopedia*, published a year after I entered the ministry.[15] I even found support in Ellen White: "If you give yourself to Him, and accept Him as your Savior, then, sinful as your life may have been, for His sake you are accounted righteous. Christ's character stands in place of your character, and you are accepted before God just as if you had not sinned."[16] I thrilled at other indications of grace in Ellen White:

> The sinner must ever look toward Calvary; and with the simple faith of a little child, he must rest in the merits of Christ, accepting His righteousness and believing in His mercy . . . We are to accept Christ as our personal Savior, and He imputes unto us the righteousness of God in Christ.[17]

> Apart from Christ we have no merit, no righteousness. Our sinfulness, our weakness, our human imperfection make it impossible that we should appear before God unless we are clothed in Christ's spotless righteousness. We are to be found in Him not having our own righteousness, but the righteousness which is in Christ.[18]

By the time Laura and our family relocated to Collegedale and moved into our newly-built, green-sided, split foyer house in the low-lying hills beyond the University, I had renounced my earlier perfectionistic views and become an advocate of "righteousness [justification] by faith." Good works, I was convinced, were the *fruit* of salvation by faith, not in any sense the

15. *Adventist Encyclopedia* (1966), s.v., "Salvation," 1134.

16. White, *Steps to Christ*, 62.

17. White, *Selected Messages*, 1:384.

18. White, *Selected Messages*, 1:333.

basis of it. They did not sustain or earn salvation. Salvation was a gift. "We know," Paul wrote to the Galatians, "that a person is justified not by the works of the law but through faith in Christ Jesus" (Gal 2:16).[19]

This was my experience in the Seventh-day Adventist Church on the eve of the controversy over the gospel.

Exactly how and where the controversy over the gospel commenced in the 1970s, I'm not certain. It is impossible to pinpoint a single event. It happened more like an outbreak over there, then somewhere else, then taking hold almost everywhere throughout the denomination. No doubt a number of factors converged, not the least of which were the seeds of the continuous debate over salvation that seemed always to be going on in Adventism. Robert Brinsmead, a former Adventist lay theologian and erstwhile critic of the church, launched his widely read journal, *Verdict*, to emphasize his personal rediscovery of the gospel of salvation by faith as proclaimed in the Protestant Reformation. Jesus "took our sin and alienation upon Himself," Brinsmead, a former perfectionist, announced, and "reconciled us to God by His death on the cross, and by His resurrection restored the race to favor with God. The whole deed of our salvation was accomplished and finished in the Christ event."[20]

Brinsmead had unfortunately acquired previously a reputation as an agent provocateur of the denomination. His intriguing religious odyssey, like a meteor streaking across the night sky, had taken him from extreme perfectionism in his early career all the way to the Protestant Reformation *sola gratia* (by grace alone), and eventually would find him ironically settling finally into a secular agnosticism. At this juncture in his personal religious odyssey, however, he was a strong advocate of salvation by grace. Because of Brinsmead's previous opposition to the church on a range of issues, however, the church's administration had already condemned anything he wrote even before it was published. He was a persona non grata. That placed him off limits for the devout. His writings were contraband. Nonetheless, most

19. The expression, "faith in Christ Jesus" can also be rendered "faithfulness of Christ," thus more clearly indicating that the source of acceptance or justification is Jesus Christ. "Justifying faith," writes Emil Brunner, "means in fact that we should place our sole confidence in the Word of Christ, living entirely on the gift of grace, and making it the sole foundation of our life" (*Dogmatics*, 3:303).

20. Brinsmead, *Judged by the Gospel*, 23. In 1971 Brinsmead published the *Institute Syllabus 1971* in which he gathered together excerpts from various scholars on the gospel of grace. In light of what is discussed below, he highlights the differences between the Protestant and Catholic views of justification by faith (31–32).

of the Southern University religion faculty took notice of his articles and other publications, and on occasion referred to them (without naming the source!) in class. Finding them useful, despite the taboo, I collected two bulging file folders of Brinsmead's writings on the topic of the gospel.

Desmond Ford, a professor of religion at the denomination's Avondale College in Australia, and later, Pacific Union College in Angwin, California, became personally acquainted with Brinsmead and took credit for weaning Brinsmead away from perfectionism. Ford thus became an unwitting catalyst in the dispute. He had earlier been a delegate to the church's Palmdale conference on righteousness by faith, held in Palmdale, California, in April 1976. Nineteen church leaders from Australia and North America met to discuss righteousness by faith, and subsequently released the study documents from the conference.[21] Years before the Palmdale conference, however, Ford had been emphasizing in articles, college classes, and sermons the Pauline doctrine of justification by faith. He had agreed with the Protestant Reformer, Martin Luther that the great doctrine of justification should be set at the center of the church's theology. Justification, as Ford noted, "has been the central theme of the preaching in every movement of revival and religious awakening within Protestantism from the Reformation to the present day."[22]

Justification "touches man's life at its heart, at the point of its relationship to God," Berkouwer put it. "It defines the preaching of the Church, the existence and progress of the life of faith, the root of human security, and man's perspective of the future."[23] We will hear more of Ford in the following chapters when the crisis over the gospel spilled over into and merged with the controversy about the Investigative Judgment.

Fearing that this renewed emphasis on faith and justification would jeopardize the keeping of the Ten Commandments, the denominational leadership instinctively turned back to the older legalistic moralism and perfectionism. *Review and Herald* editors Herbert Douglass and Kenneth Wood[24] began confidently advocating perfectionistic views in the denomination's main journal, as well as in other publications. Douglass, the boldest, most outspoken of these neo-perfectionists, rejuvenated Peter Abelard's (1079–1142) moral influence theory of the atonement. The purpose of

21. These were later privately printed and circulated by Walker, *Documents from Palmdale.*

22. Ford, "Scope and Limits," 12.

23. Berkouwer, *Faith and Justification*, 17.

24. Wood emphasized a relative perfection, one of "constant growth . . . obtaining new victories for Christ, of conquering evil habits, of developing the positive Christian virtues" that continues throughout the lifetime ("Goal is Perfection," 3).

Jesus' death was not atonement for sin, according to Abelard, but rather a grand, cosmic demonstration of God's love. The tortured body of the crucified Jesus revealed to the world how far God was willing to go to save humankind. Rather than substitution and atonement, the life, work, and death of Jesus provided the Great Example of the God's generous love. Christ's moving Example, in turn, motivated humanity to love and respond to God. God forgives and accepts humanity on the basis of this love. Made visible in Jesus' self-giving, God's love wins people to God, and releases the newly-awakened love in people.

Douglass applied this moral influence theory to Adventist eschatology (doctrine of last-day events). Before the Second Advent, the final generation of Seventh-day Adventists would have to achieve spiritual perfection, claimed Douglass, and thus be safe (from spiritual relapse) for the Lord to "harvest." Hence, this view is often called "harvest theology." "Use your sickle and reap, for the hour to reap has come, because the harvest of the earth is fully ripe" (Rev 14:15). At the harvest, the spiritually perfected Adventist community would thus vindicate God's character.

> In the moral area of character development, *perfection is possible and expected . . .* To silence that last, lingering question—that Jesus was sinless because He was God and not truly a man who faced sin on the same basis as all the rest of humanity—Jesus now waits for His church to *reproduce* what He achieved, thus proving again that man with fallen human nature *can live without sinning.* This demonstration will complete the vindication of God's character and government and will settle the question of His justice and mercy forever.[25]

Much depends, of course, on what Douglass meant by "perfection." For him perfection was a life *without* sin or sinning. It was a "call to moral perfection."[26] Wood defined it in Wesleyan fashion as a person "perfect in his sphere by letting the principle of love control all aspects of life."[27] Douglass thought that the Adventist community, or at least major segments of it, would arrive at this sinlessness, namely, moral perfection, *before* the end of time. "That overcoming [sin] is possible constitutes an essential element in the uniqueness of the Adventist message," Douglass wrote. "Not only

25. Douglass, *Perfection*, 28–29, 53. Emphasis supplied.

26. Douglass, "Unique Contribution," 24. Many perfectionists believe that it is possible, with divine assistance, to come to a place where one no longer sins. Some believe, as did Douglass, that people would actually arrive at this perfection during their earthly existence.

27. Wood, "Role of SDA," 26.

is overcoming possible, it is expected by God of His people."[28] Elsewhere he wrote: "Even as the farmer must wait for his seed to mature, so Jesus must wait until the gospel seed has produced a sizeable group of mature Christians in the last generation prior to His return."[29] It was his locating of perfection *prior* to the Second Advent that distinguished Douglass's view of perfection from that of most in Christian history, and gave it a peculiar, Adventist spin.

Douglas didn't get this theory of perfectionism out of thin air. As we have seen, it had deep roots in Adventist tradition. One Adventist pastor, Preston Smith, earlier put it this way:

> When probation closes, the Christian will have reached the *state of mature perfection*. God has provided for this experience through the latter rain ministry of the Holy Spirit, which places the finishing touch on character. Just as the Holy Spirit kept Jesus from sin so He will keep last-day Christians from sin and enable them to stand the severest trials that men and devils bring upon the people of God.[30]

As I read Douglass' articles and editorials on the subject, I questioned, doesn't harvest theology essentially ignore the radical nature of sin, its deep-rootedness at the core of human personality? Doesn't imperfection characterize all earthly existence? The complete transcends this earth; we will never realize it in historical time, but can only hope for it in faith.[31] Isn't it naïve to claim that everyone—in the present life—*must* reach the place where they could live without sin in order to qualify for heaven? "Sin is not merely a particular action, even the attitude of an individual," Macquarrie rightly points out, "but a massive disorientation and perversion of human society as a whole." Only when we recognize this, can "we begin to perceive the really terrifying character of sin."[32] The Adventist perfectionists seemed to de-emphasize or even trivialize sin. Sinless living is a "willful choice *not* to rebel against God in thought word, or action," some claimed.[33]

---

28. Douglass, "Unique Contribution," 32. In the same vein, Wood imagined the Adventist people at the end of time, "They have the faith of Jesus—a faith that enables human beings . . . to be victorious over evil. They reflect the likeness of Jesus fully . . . They are safe to save" ("Role of SDA," 26).

29. Douglass, "God is Urgent," 23.

30. Smith, "Perfection in Christ," 10. Emphasis supplied.

31. See Brunner, *Dogmatics*, 3:304.

32. Macquarrie, *Christian Theology*, 262.

33. Priebe, "Real Gospel," 24.

It's simple—with Christ's help—just stop sinning! This, I recognized, was a hopelessly naïve view of sin and human nature.

Because of their prominence and influence as editors of the denomination's official journal, and combined with the church's ingrained opposition to Brinsmead, along with suspicion now building against Ford because of his relationship with Brinsmead, this made Douglass's and Wood's perfectionistic notion of salvation through moralistic character development appear to be *official* denominational teaching. I was never sure whether the top leadership actually embraced this version of perfection or whether they thought it was merely politically expedient to do so. I would eventually discover, to my dismay, that denominational leaders often exploited theology (and especially Ellen White) to shore up their authority. This juxtaposition of Brinsmead and Ford against prominent denominational leaders boded ill for those of us on college faculties. As we dealt with the theme of salvation in class, we were automatically tarred with heresy should we dare agree with the apostle, "We know that a person is justified not by the works of the law, but through faith in Jesus Christ" (Gal 2:15). For concurring with the New Testament, we were *ipso facto* called "Ford-ites," or "followers of Brinsmead," "Brismead-ites." Ours was the "New Theology." After all, Christian perfectionism was being advocated openly in the pages of the *Review*, the church's official journal, and affirmed and urged by top denominational leaders!

As this conflict infiltrated our classes, rumors quickly spread throughout the larger Adventist community that the religion faculty at Southern, because they were emphasizing salvation by faith through grace, were now teaching "heresy." They were teaching the New Theology! They were deliberately, intentionally misleading students. Irate fathers telephoned the school administration. "We sent our daughter there to receive a Christian education, not be duped into accepting false doctrine!" shouted one angry Alabama father. One University administrator, trying to be protective, sympathetically warned the religion faculty, "Avoid using the word 'gospel' in your sermons, especially when you preach in one of the churches here in the South, lest you be misunderstood. It is too loaded a term. Rumor is spreading all over the place that our faculty is teaching that, if you have faith in Jesus, it doesn't matter how you live. They're calling you 'Fordites'! I've heard it everywhere. Perception is reality!"

"I'm sorry," I answered, "that's ridiculous! 'Gospel' is a perfectly good biblical word. I don't see how I can preach from the Bible, especially the New Testament, without using it. The New Testament, as you know, has four books that are called 'gospels.' Should we stop referring to them?"

Seemingly oblivious to the confusing effect the *Review* was having in the churches, exacerbating tension between the religion faculty, the pastors, and the Adventist public, the *Review* kept obstinately promoting perfection-ism. Ford within and Brinsmead without urged salvation by grace through faith in Jesus. Douglass persistently asserted his perfectionistic harvest theology. In Jesus a necessary beginning was made, he insisted, but it was only a beginning. There must be something more. One must continue and finally attain the perfect sinless lives of end-time, last generation Seventh-day Adventists. God waits, he noted, for "His church to prove . . . that the life of faith that He [Jesus] lived and the character He manifested are possible attainments that all men may reach."[34] Adventists—not other Christians—will "demonstrate to the world that man need not remain a sinner, that man may attain a sinless, righteous experience by the same faith that Jesus exer-cised . . . The non-Adventist public is to 'come and see'" what Adventism has accomplished in the lives of its adherents.[35] Such grand, cosmic statements elevated successful character development and sinless perfection to the level of the gospel—actually equating them *with* the gospel—and set them forth as the central message of Adventism. This was what it meant to be prepared for the Second Advent.

As these editorials continued to roll out, it became apparent that Dou-glass had essentially gotten his perfectionistic harvest theology from Ellen White's writings. Clothing his ideas with Ellen White's authority, Douglass rained down upon gullible church leaders copious quotations:

> What Christ was in His perfect humanity, we must be; for we must form characters for eternity.[36]

> The Lord requires perfection from His redeemed family. He expects from us the perfection which Christ revealed in His humanity.[37]

> Through repentance, faith, and good works he may perfect a righteous character, and claim, through the merits of Christ, the privilege of the sons of God. The principles of divine truth, received and cherished in the heart, will carry us to a height of moral excellence that we had not deemed it possible for us to reach.[38]

---

34. Douglass, "Unique Contribution," 18–33.

35. Douglass, "Word Games," 37.

36. White, *Testimonies to Ministers*, 173.

37. White, *Child Guidance*, 477.

38. White, *Sons and Daughters*, 10.

One defect, cultivated instead of being overcome, makes the man imperfect, and closes against him the gate of the Holy City. He who enters heaven must have a character that is without spot or wrinkle or any such thing.[39]

Those who are living upon the earth when the intercession of Christ shall cease in the sanctuary above are to stand in the sight of a holy God without a mediator. Their robes must be spotless, their characters must be purified from sin by the blood of sprinkling. Through the grace of God and their own diligent effort they must be conquerors in the battle with evil.[40]

A spotless, sinless perfect character *in the present order*, prior to the Second Advent, for Douglass, was the goal of redemption. Faith in Christ was certainly the efficient means, but in the final analysis nothing short of *total* victory over inward and outward sin was required, nothing short of complete, unabashed sinless, righteous moral character.

As I read Douglass—and Wood—I tried to figure out what my reaction should be to this barrage of perfectionistic theology spewing from the denomination's official journal. Already students reading the *Review* had become more than curious. The professional Adventist theological community, however, was incensed over Douglass's and Wood's co-opting of the church's main publication, the *Review*, to teach this form of religious perfectionism. Helmut Ott, a member of Southern's religion faculty, fired off a letter to Donald John, editor of *Insight*, an Adventist youth publication. Ott complained that *Insight* had misleadingly called Douglass's perfectionism "Adventist." "Your readers deserve to be exposed to other Adventist views on this matter—views according to which salvation is understood as God's gift of grace, obtained through faith in the all-sufficient righteousness of Christ, rather than through character development and behavior modification"[41]

Amid the growing conflict, I couldn't help but recall how perfectionism had been embedded in the so-called gospel I'd heard from many Adventist pulpits from my earliest days. Should I momentarily lapse into a single, even "minor" sin, these sermons had led me to believe, God would rescind the forgiveness that had been graciously bestowed, throwing me back into a sinful, all-or-nothing "lost" condition. If I were to go to bed at night without remembering specifically—and confessing—*all* my sins one-by-one, and were to die unexpectedly, I would be eternally lost. Often it felt something

39. White, *Young People*, 144.
40. White, *Great Controversy*, 425. Cf. White, *Early Writings*, 48, 72, 280–81.
41. Helmut Ott to Donald John, 3 November 1980.

like walking around with an egg balanced on my head, nervously hoping I wouldn't let it fall and break. Forgiveness, to be retained, had to be accompanied by a conscientious, stubborn adherence to a whole range of dietary, religious, and spiritual mandates until I got to the place where I could successfully keep all of them without a single lapse. Only then did I stand a chance—and then only a slender chance—of making it through the final hurdle, the world's greatest, most troublous period, the time of the Seven Last Plagues, *without the benefit of Christ's heavenly mediation.*[42] Perhaps some of these fears were of my own making, or maybe I was just naive, but this was the underlying message I'd absorbed from too many sermons.

The senior minister, Jere Webb, invited me to preach on justification at the morning worship in the large Collegedale University church. My text for the sermon was from Romans: "We hold that a person is justified by faith apart from works prescribed by the law (3:28)." After reading the text, which in context represents a concluding note to Paul's argument in the opening chapters of Romans, I began. "This is one of the most radical conclusions ever drawn in the history of religion." I went on to sketch how justification mentioned in this text had been at issue in the Protestant Reformation, and what a difference understanding justification could make in our lives. "It saves us from nagging anxiety about how well we are doing," I said, relating my own experience. "We don't constantly have to pull up our own spiritual roots every time we think of it to see how we're growing. Our acceptance with God—our righteousness—is located outside us, outside our experience, in Jesus Christ."

Following the sermon, as the departing congregation filed by, Robert Francis, my esteemed professor and now colleague on the religion faculty rudely interrupted. "How dare you preach about justification?" he shouted, oblivious to the shocked onlookers. Francis was usually soft-spoken, composed and even-tempered. Not here. Not now. He was visibly upset. His face reddened. "We've got to stop all this talk about justification, this . . . this controversy going on, and focus more on sanctification and Christian growth!" he yelled. "Preaching on justification only emboldens people to keep on sinning! It encourages them to do whatever they want!"

---

42. The Seven Last Plagues are sketched in Revelation 16. Adventists believe these are still in the future, at which time God's mercy will have been withdrawn from the human race. Hence, there will be "no Mediator to plead their cause before the Father," Ellen White explains. "I also saw that many do not realize what they must be in order to live in the sight of the Lord without a high priest in the sanctuary through the time of trouble. Those who receive the seal of the living God and are protected in the time of trouble *must reflect the image of Jesus fully*" (*Early Writings*, 71. Emphasis supplied).

"I respectfully disagree," I replied, taken back by his sudden antagonism. Why was he so angry? "I don't believe preaching about justification necessarily leads to lawless behavior." Francis had spent his entire career teaching a perfectionism not unlike that of Douglass, as I well knew from my student days. He was heavily invested in the notion that Christians must achieve moral and spiritual perfection before they would be finally redeemed. It didn't surprise me he sharply disagreed with the premise of my sermon. "We've heard about sanctification—and perfection—so much it's running out our ears," I continued, thinking about Douglass and Wood and their torrent of editorials. "As a result, people have little or no assurance of God's love and acceptance. To the contrary, Bob, I think we desperately need to hear *more* about justification, not less. How can there be any sanctification—however one defines it—without justification?"

Significantly, this was the last time I ever preached in the University church. I would soon be labeled a heretic.

6

The Shaking of Adventism

Grace strikes us when we are in great pain and restlessness . . . It strikes us when, year after year, the longed-for perfection of life does not appear, when the old compulsions reign within us as they have for decades . . . Sometimes at that moment a wave of light breaks into our darkness, and it is as though a voice were saying: "You are accepted. *You are accepted*, accepted by that which is greater than you, and the name of which you do not know . . . Do not seek for anything; do not perform anything; do not intend anything. *Simply accept the fact that you are accepted*

—*PAUL TILLICH*

T he Adventist controversy over the gospel escalated dramatically the moment Geoffrey Paxton, an Anglican priest, published his master's thesis about Seventh-day Adventists, submitted to the University of Queensland in Australia. He had little idea his thesis, which he titled, *The Shaking of Adventism*, would land like a time bomb in the middle of an already raging Adventist debate. Paxton had become acquainted with the Adventist community in Australia, where the controversy over the gospel also smoldered. During his research, he'd personally gotten to know Robert Brinsmead as well as Desmond Ford. The title for his book is a double entendre. The "Shaking" is Adventist terminology for the final eschatological testing of the Adventist elect, when those insincere or pretentious will be "shaken" out of the church and doomed forever.[1]

1. "The mighty shaking has commenced and will go on, and all will be shaken out

Focusing on the history of Christian theology as manifested in the Protestant Reformation, in a deceptively simple argument, Paxton challenged one of the basic Adventist tenets: The denomination taught that it had been divinely set apart to carry on the reforming work begun by the Protestant Reformers. Adventists believed that they were proclaiming an equivalent theological message to that of the Reformation, the sixteenth-century religious break with the Roman Catholic Church. "The Reformation did not, as many suppose, end with Luther," Ellen White wrote of this Adventist notion. "It is to be continued to the close of this world's history. Luther had a great work to do in reflecting to others the light which God had permitted to shine upon him; yet he did not receive all the light which was to be given to the world. From that time to this, new light has been continually shining upon the Scriptures, and new truths have been constantly unfolding."[2]

For Adventists, Paxton noted, the Reformation continued steadily onward in the form of the mission of the Seventh-day Adventist church. An implication of this idea is that other Christian denominations have either failed to carry on the Reformation or have become derailed or corrupted and lost sight of the Reformation. Interestingly, the same criticism the Protestant Reformers invoked against Roman Catholics, Adventists now turned on their fellow Protestants (and other co-religionists). Other Christian churches, just like the Roman Catholic Church before them, have corrupted the faith "once for all entrusted to the saints" (Jude 3). Adventists thus understand the dire epithet "Babylon" in the book of Revelation to be descriptive of the rest of Christendom—except them, of course. Their main task is to call people out of the fallen, misguided churches, "Come out of her [Babylon], my people, so that you do not take part in her sins" (Rev 18:4). This gives them both a unique identity and an urgent mission, they believe. It is a role no one else can fill.

Instead of the customary opposition centering on problematic biblical passages like most critics of Adventism before him, Paxton simply set against this bold, broad Adventist claim one of the central doctrinal themes of the Reformation: the doctrine of justification. The Reformer Martin Luther (1483–1546) once called justification the "article with and by which

---

who are not willing to take a bold and unyielding stand for the truth and to sacrifice for God and His cause" (White, *Early Writings*, 50). For a discussion of the *Shaking* in Adventist eschatology, see Chaij, *Preparation*, 65–73.

2. White, *Great Controversy*, 148. This belief is stated even more strongly in the denomination's latest theological compendium (General Conference, *Adventists Believe*, 192–97).

the church stands, without which it falls."[3] What if, Paxton questioned, the Adventist church's teaching about justification contradicts this central emphasis of the Reformation? What if there is a fundamental difference between the Adventist teaching on justification and that of the Reformers? If Adventist teaching about justification—a doctrine crucial to the Protestant Reformers—contradicted that of the Reformation itself, how can Adventists then logically claim to be a *continuation* of the work of the Reformers? How can they say they are in continuity with the Protestant Reformation? This was the question Paxton insistently posed.

It was a simple, yet stunning inquiry. But it had never occurred to me. I had never taken the time to look for an actual, precise continuity between the teaching of the Protestant Reformation about justification and that of Adventism. Nor had it apparently occurred to any other Adventists with whom I discussed it after I'd read Paxton, including my colleagues on the religion faculty, although I felt certain there was an Adventist historian of theology somewhere who was aware of such an alleged conflict between the Adventist view and that of the Reformers. Were we—the so-called modern Reformers—embarrassingly unaware of the decisive issues in the conflict between Protestants and Roman Catholics during the Reformation? Had we somehow gotten wrong the central issue of the Reformation which, if we were truly continuing the work of the Reformation, we should be all about restoring to the church? The controversy between righteousness by faith versus moralistic perfectionism now narrowed semantically to a single word: *justification.*

In my home library, surrounded by floor to ceiling bookcases, I dug into the musty pages of history and carefully reexamined the Reformation period. Medieval Roman Catholicism, against which Martin Luther had revolted when he published the *Ninety-Five Theses* in October 1517, I discovered, had taught that God enables sinful humanity to become actually righteous through a divine, infused spiritual empowerment that comes from Christ. Grace initially draws a person to Christ; then, after baptism, grace begins to transform that person. Like a stream of water, this power flows into a person. It infuses. Perhaps it wouldn't be too crude an analogy to compare it to a hypodermic syringe that injects righteousness into a person. This divine act of *making* people righteous, Catholicism identified as "justification." Something more, however, must happen before the new Christian may be completely acceptable to God. After baptism, the person must continue by grace to live a life of faith and love. Two types of grace are essential. What is called "*actual* grace" brings about the forgiveness of

---

3. "*Articulus stantis et cadentis ecclesiae*" (Luther, *What Luther Says*, 2:704, n. 5).

sin; "*habitual* grace" enables a person to perform the necessary good works. Should one fall into sin—and who doesn't—the sacrament of penance helps a person recover a state of grace. In the final judgment only the Christian who has arrived at a required state of righteousness (from the divine point of view) will fully qualify for eternal bliss. A person then will be certifiably righteous because of having actually been made so by infused supernatural grace. God then crowns the transformation by bestowing eternal life as a final reward.[4]

For medieval Roman Catholics, in other words, justification involved not only forgiveness, or the pardoning of previous sin, but also the transformation of the inner person through grace. "We are renewed," Carl Peters put it, "by which we are not only reckoned just but are so in fact."[5] To me, this merging of justification and sanctification sounded suspiciously like what Adventists had been saying all along!

Martin Luther's own tormented, conflicted personal experience had taught him how misleading it was to think that a human being could ever attain—even with God's special help—the staggering levels of righteousness in word and deed sufficient to *merit* eternal life. Along with the other principal Protestant Reformers, John Calvin (1509–1564) and Ulrich Zwingli (1484–1531),[6] Luther made a critical distinction between justification and sanctification.

Luther abandoned the Catholic notion of impartation or infusion of righteousness in favor of a legal or forensic concept. *Justification* is the divine declaration or legal verdict that, on the basis of Christ's righteous life, atoning death, and resurrection—outside the person—God regards or considers a believer as righteous, thus meeting the high legal requirements of the divine law. It is the "declaration of God that one who trusts in Christ's atoning work, however sinful, is treated or accounted as righteous."[7] As Paul puts it: "There is therefore no condemnation for those who are in Christ Jesus" (Rom 8:1).

---

4. For this summary of the Roman Catholic position at the time of the Reformation, see Feiner and Vischer, *Common Catechism,* 569–70.

5. Peters, "Decree on Justification," 225.

6. Note Calvin: Justification "is the main hinge on which religion turns." The person "justified by faith is he who, excluded from the righteousness of works, grasps the righteousness of Christ through faith, and clothed in it, appears in God's sight not as a sinner but as a righteous man . . . it consists in the remission of sins and the imputation of Christ's righteousness . . . to be justified means something different from being made new creatures" (*Institutes,* 3.11.2).

7. Oden, *Justification,* 36.

Justification, a word Paul appropriates from the law court, Luther understood in a legal sense as a verdict or declaration of God. It is objective, something God declares on our behalf. Justification doesn't actually make righteous, transform, or perfect. It isn't an injection or infusion of righteousness that miraculously turns someone into a person who is now acceptably righteous. We don't actually become righteous as a result of justification. Rather, justification is an objective, judicial, or legal declaration of divine acceptance, analogous to a court declaring an exonerated defendant, "not guilty." To change the metaphor, we are "innocent," it proclaims. It is God's work for us—outside our own experience—mediated through the life, death, and resurrection of Jesus. On the basis of what Christ has done God declares and considers us to be righteous. "Therefore just as one man's trespass led to condemnation for all, so one man's act of righteousness leads to justification and life for all" (Rom 5:18). Luther liked to cite Rom 4:5: "To one who is not working [to earn God's favor], but believing in the One who *justifies the ungodly*, his faith is reckoned as righteousness" (lit. trans.). We—the ungodly—do not become inwardly, ontologically righteous through justification, Luther taught, contrary to the Catholic understanding. When we believe, God considers, counts, or reckons us to be righteous even though in our humanity we are not actually so. This is true because our righteousness is found in Christ, not within the self, even within the forgiven self. Luther's Latin motto has become famous: *simul iustus et peccator*, "always justified and [always] a sinner."[8]

Sanctification, as Luther and the other Reformers understood it, on the other hand, concerns actual, inner spiritual transformation. This process continues over a lifetime. Sanctification—not justification—is the divine process that *makes* us righteous. Sanctification is God's work *inside* us through the Holy Spirit. Justification and sanctification are thus logically distinct, one objective and external; the other, subjective and internal. Although forgiven and granted perfect acceptance with God, we still possess in our person a sinful or broken nature. Yet the legal state of justification ensures our righteous standing before God. It is complete, whole, and final. No human work or merit has any power here; justification is the ground of our acceptance. It is the basis upon which we are accepted through the whole lifetime. It is the foundation upon which sanctification is built.

---

8. In Romans 3:22–23, where Paul declares that the "righteousness of God through faith in Jesus Christ" is available to all, particularly those who "have sinned and continue to fall short of the glory of God" (lit. trans.), comes very close to Luther's formula, "at the same time a righteous person and a sinner." In Rom 4:1–6 it is evident that the righteousness from God that is accredited to the individual comes from outside the person. It may thus be thought of as an extrinsic or objective righteousness.

Sanctification—the transformation of the Christian—is always dependent upon and rooted in justification. Justification, in Luther's mind, isn't an infused, sanctifying grace, as Roman Catholic theology seemed to say. Upon justification a person must depend every day. The Reformers insisted that a person is thus righteous in this present life only by faith.

The Reformation understanding of justification, I realized, couldn't really be squared with legalistic moralism or its forlorn child, perfectionism, because no human work could really add to or supplement God's verdict. "Who will bring any charge against God's elect? It is God who justifies" (Rom 8:30). A synergistic, legalistic, or perfectionistic approach suggests the accumulation of a person's merit or qualification required to meet God's approval. The degree to which our basic sinful nature has been transformed during our life, which varies individually and depends upon a variety of other factors, does not modify, obstruct, or jeopardize our standing before God. Our personal salvation—from first to last—depends entirely upon justification, which is objective and complete in Christ, rather than sanctification, which is subjective, ongoing, and always incomplete.[9] For the Reformers, the gospel proclaimed the "good news," assurance of God's acceptance here and now. It was this that gave the Reformation such spiritual power.

As I read Paxton, I was astonished at the careful distinction between justification and sanctification, and how I'd entirely overlooked it. Eagerly I read on. Catholic theology of the sixteenth century indeed had essentially merged justification and sanctification. It appeared to fuse or even confuse them, Paxton pointed out, turning both into an internal, subjective process, even though both happened through divine grace. Sixteenth-century Catholic theologians blurred justification and sanctification, treating them as aspects of the same process. The practical implication is that since we start out with an incomplete, inward righteousness, but never seem in this life to get beyond that incompleteness, we can never be certain we are good enough to be accepted by God. Since in this life we are always "works in progress," we must try to live so that we may eventually lay claim to eternal life as our reward. Only thus will we qualify to face the divine judgment,

---

9. Again note Calvin: "It is very well known by experience that the traces of sin always remain in the righteous, their justification must be very different from reformation into newness of life. For God so begins this second point in his elect, and progresses in it gradually, and sometimes slowly, throughout life, that they are always liable to the judgment of death before his tribunal. But he does not justify in part but liberally, so that they may appear in heaven as if endowed with the purity of Christ" (*Institutes*, 3.11.11).

which may be compared to a final exam. We must grow spiritually to the point we can pass the exam.

In his lengthy biography of Martin Luther, the Catholic historian Hartman Grisar criticizes Luther's view of justification. Human beings in the Catholic faith have full freedom to do that which is good. God has supplied them with the necessary grace to enable them to "freely cooperate." Baptism and entrance into the church "makes a man a child of God by virtue of sanctifying grace." If a person sins after becoming a Christian, that person can "confidently hope to regain the state of grace through the merits of the death of Christ, provided he submits to penance and resolves to amend his life." Against Luther Grisar argues, "mere faith in the application of the merits of Christ is not sufficient."[10] I don't remember reading anything that so concisely captures the traditional Adventist view of salvation! Compare Adventist W. H. Branson:

> Perfection, then, is possible for us. The God who demonstrated His power by bringing Jesus from the dead can also make you perfect—perfect in every good work to do His will. How is this accomplished? It is by Christ working within us. He does within us and through us the things that are well-pleasing in God's sight . . . Thus we receive His righteousness. It still does not come by our own works but by what He does for us and through us.[11]

The Reformation view, as Paxton outlined it, because it emphasizes God's work in justification *for* us rather than God's work in sanctification *inside* us, offers immediate assurance of God's acceptance, and liberates us from the self-absorbing, introspective struggle for personal salvation, allowing us to engage freely in ministry for others. "Forensic justification has to do with what is *extra nos* [outside us], with the imputation of what Christ has done on our behalf. This was, indeed, the original disposition of the Reformation."[12]

Puzzled, I looked closer at the famous Council of Trent (1545–1563), the lengthy conciliar response of the Catholic Church to the Protestant Reformation. Not surprisingly, I discovered Paxton to be correct about the Catholic teaching of the time. The Council claimed justification "is not only a remission of sins but also the sanctification and renewal of the inward man through the voluntary reception of the grace and gifts whereby an unjust man becomes just." Not only are "we reckoned to be just but we are truly

---

10. Grisar, *Martin Luther*, 73.

11. Branson, "Lord Our Righteousness," 2:595.

12. Berkouwer, *Faith and Justification*, 91.

called and are just, receiving justice [righteousness] within us."[13] In Canon 11 Trent put it this way:

> If anyone says that men are justified either by the sole imputa-
> tion of the justice [righteousness] of Christ or by the sole remis-
> sion of sins, to the exclusion of the grace and the charity which
> is poured forth in their hearts by the Holy Ghost, and remains
> in them, or also that the grace by which we are justified is only
> the good will of God, let him be anathema.[14]

While Adventism thought it was in continuity with the themes of the Protestant Reformation, proclaiming a gospel consistent with that of Luther and Calvin, the magisterial Reformers, if I read Paxton correctly, Adventists were actually—perhaps unwittingly—advocating doctrine actually more similar to that of the medieval Roman Catholics, which the Reformers had opposed! Had Adventism been confused in claiming continuity with the actual theology of the Reformation? Had it glossed over important distinctions? I pondered. Were there other denominational teachings also historically or theologically misinformed? Paxton was important, I realized, not only because of his emphasis on the distinction between justification and sanctification—a correction the denomination sorely needed to counteract its dalliance with perfectionism—but because Paxton had spotted a critical defect in the Adventist claim.

It amazed me how quickly Paxton's message—despite its technical nature—spread across the country. Adventists everywhere, it seemed, bought copies of *The Shaking of Adventism*. Ministers, at first here and there, but then in significant numbers started to preach the gospel of the Reformation. A few clergy got so bold in their proclamation of the Reformation gospel they incurred the wrath of their traditional congregations or worse, that of denominational leaders. Some lost their pulpits. My personal files contain numerous letters from lay and clergy who announced they were leaving the Adventist church over this and other doctrinal issues. One local pastor, David Vandenburg, aroused the suspicion and ire of Desmond Cummings, the president of the Adventist Georgia-Cumberland Conference, but fortunately managed to hold on to his position because the congregation, which had warmly embraced this Reformation teaching, resisted his removal. In

13. Schroeder, *Canons of Trent*, 33–35. The Canons further point out that justification is *not the imputation* of Christ's righteousness, but the act whereby God *makes* the believer righteous. Furthermore, one can never be certain to have received this grace. Justification can also be increased by good works (ibid., 34–39). These ideas bear a striking resemblance to themes I had heard often repeated by Adventists.

14. Council of Trent, session 6, chap. 7, as quoted in Leith, *Creeds*, 411–12.

Florida, five members of the Boynton Beach Adventist Church, in a long, fifteen-page openly circulated letter, announced they were leaving the denomination over the doctrine of justification and some other doctrinal issues. Also in Florida, Phillip Wilson, who had been a classmate of ours when Laura and I were at Southern, after four years of harassment and innuendo, much of it coming from denominational leadership, was abruptly fired as Senior Minister of the large Central Seventh-day Adventist Church in Orlando. Wilson had followed the debate over justification into the next crisis that developed in the denomination, the controversy over its view of the Investigative Judgement. This is the topic of the next chapter.

In Idaho, Dennis Sellers and his wife Judy resigned from the ministry at the Coeur d' Alene church over the issue of perfectionism versus justification, claiming that they were aware of over a hundred ministers who had also resigned. Paul Crecelius, one of my former students, left Adventism and enrolled in Southern Baptist Theological Seminary. "At least I can preach the gospel with relative freedom," he cynically told me.[15]

At the Adventist seminary, several students, persuaded by Paxton's analysis, launched a new journal named *Evangelica*, which featured opinion editorials, mostly critical, of the church's main teachings in the light of the Reformation understanding of justification. Its initial issue contained an article on the scandal of the gospel. "The gospel may challenge our theological beliefs," Alexander LaBrecque wrote. "It will challenge every attempt to be justified by our personal righteousness before God, now or ever."[16] The journal quickly became controversial. Anyone caught openly reading *Evangelica* at Southern Adventist University was regarded suspiciously. Faculty and students joked about carrying copies around like contraband in "brown paper wrapping"! I made sure to read *Evangelica* in the privacy of my home with the blinds closed! The journal, unfortunately, didn't long remain in print. Within the next few years, when its voice was extinguished, most of the editors fled the denomination for the friendlier clime of other Protestant bodies.

Paxton toured Adventist college campuses throughout the United States, including Southern. While at Southern, he spoke to the Association of Adventist Forums, a controversial organization independent of denominational control and dedicated to free and open discussion of issues that concerned Adventists. Afterward, on our back lawn Laura and I hosted a reception for Paxton, where those in attendance enjoyed discussing

15. Paul Crecelius to Jerry Gladson, 20 July 1983.

16. LaBrecque, "Scandal of Gospel," 21. LaBrecque's denominational seminary scholarship was revoked because of his beliefs about justification by faith, *sola scriptura*, and the identity of the Adventist church.

justification, the Reformation, and how the Adventist church ought to respond to the furor in its ranks over the gospel versus perfectionism.

Because he came from outside Adventism, Paxton was a threat more dangerous than Brinsmead or Ford. Adventist leadership responded frantically in the pages of the *Adventist Review* (formerly, the *Review and Herald*), the *Ministry*, and in public gatherings in the larger churches. For the first time, I began to hear whisperings that the Adventist denomination actually stood in theological continuity with the Radical or Anabaptist branch of the Reformation rather than that of Luther or Calvin, and that this was what was meant when Adventism claimed to be advancing the work of the Reformation.

There were four principle branches of the Reformation: Lutheran, Reformed, Anglican, and Anabaptist. The Anabaptist movement, often called the Radical Reformation, led by Menno Simons (c. 1496–1561), didn't assent to justification by faith alone because the Pauline doctrine seemed to jeopardize the importance of the inner work of grace and Christian obedience (sanctification). Like Catholics, Anabaptists placed more emphasis upon transformation or sanctification. Adventists, we were now informed, were to be identified with the Anabaptist movement rather than with that of the magisterial Reformers, Luther and Calvin. Paxton had it all wrong. The Anabaptists were really our spiritual forebears. Somehow, I had missed this distinctive historical connection during my theological training, perhaps, my critics would say, because I hadn't attended the Adventist seminary. (I had, however, taken a course in the history of Christianity at Southern.) What is more, the church passionately argued, Paxton had failed to take into account this Adventist connection with Anabaptism. He overlooked entirely the historical Adventist linkage to the Radical Reformers, mediated chiefly to Adventists through Methodism. Methodism, whose soteriology and ecclesiology (doctrine of the church) had greatly influenced early Adventism, and had supplied the hierarchical organizational structure Adventists finally adopted. The Methodists, in turn, had been influenced by the Moravians, an Anabaptist sect, during John Wesley's theologically formative years.

Wesley, however, was closer to Luther and Calvin than to Anabaptism. I came across a sermon by John Wesley in which he distinguished justification and sanctification in much the same way as Luther and Calvin. "If any doctrines within the whole compass of Christianity may be properly termed fundamental," Wesley said, "they are doubtless these two: the *doctrine of justification*, and that of *the new birth*. The former relating to that great work which God does *for* us in forgiving our sins; the latter, to the great work which God does *in* us, in renewing our fallen nature . . . in the moment we are justified by the grace of God, through the redemption that is in Jesus, we are also 'born of the Spirit.'"[17]

Erwin Gane, a religion professor at the Adventist Pacific Union College, in a series of unpublished and widely circulated papers defending traditional Adventism, took strong objection to Paxton. Gane maintained that a close study of the New Testament revealed that justification is *both* a forensic or legal declaration of acquittal *and* an inner spiritual transformation. Gane pointed to Luther's unsystematic tendency of saying one thing here and another there. At times, he tended to be imprecise about justification, particularly in his earlier writings. For Luther, Gane claimed, justification was not merely a simple declaration that a sinner was considered righteous. Rather, a person was justified in a union with Christ that comes only by faith. In this, Christ's righteousness thus becomes the sinner's own. As Christ is joined by faith with the believer, Christ's righteousness comes to reside within the believer.[18]

The main point of the denomination's reaction to Paxton had validity, I had to admit. Adventists actually did have historically and theologically more in common with the Anabaptist movement than they did with the Lutheran and Reformed branches of the Reformation. In an unpublished paper, William Johnsson, a New Testament scholar at the Adventist seminary, clearly identified this flaw in Paxton's argument. Paxton had oversimplified the connection of Adventism to the magisterial Reformers (Luther and Calvin), he maintained. It elevated and made central only one model of salvation as depicted in the New Testament—justification by faith—ignoring the redemptive, reconciliation, forgiveness, and holiness models. Furthermore, Paxton failed to take into account Luther's own ambiguity about justification, and focused only on the final position the great Reformer seems to have adopted. At times Paxton's work is "simple, direct, logical, persuasive," Johnsson concluded, "but, on closer examination, it is flawed, narrow, distorted."[19] Johnsson, however, did credit Paxton with emphasizing the importance of the doctrine of justification.

Was this fine, somewhat meticulous distinction between external and infused justification and righteousness really so important? I asked when I

17. Compare Guthrie: "Justification-faith and sanctification-action must be distinguished from each other, but they can never be separated. They are two different aspects of the one gracious work of the same God" (*Christian Doctrine*, 332).

18. Gane, "Justification the Act," 46.

19. Johnsson, "Evaluation of Paxton," 32.

finished reading Paxton. Is it really worth all the uproar it was stirring up in the church? Was it not the dregs of a dispute over trivial semantical distinctions long since buried—and best forgotten—in the dust of history? Practical Christian life would really be different, I could see, should one live out of complete, generous divine acceptance rather than out of the slender hope of perhaps obtaining that divine acceptance someday. That justification was logically prior to sanctification, and not to be confused with it, seemed clear enough. Living *from* acceptance rather than *toward* it restored the joy of Christian living. "Beloved, we are God's children now" (1 John 3:1). By emphasizing justification in this way—in keeping with the Protestant Reformers—I realized that Paxton was talking about a truly revolutionary, liberating concept.

Paxton's real "sin," if I may use that term, was his formal accusation that Adventism had confused historical and theological realities. He had accused Adventism of *being wrong*, and that about one of its major claims! To suggest in print that the church might be historically or theologically incorrect, for most Adventists, was simply intolerable. Didn't the Adventist church have the "truth"? The church was just not open to a public airing of even alleged theological or historical errors.[20] Such open discussion would imply the church could make theological mistakes. Paxton had thus committed a grievous, unpardonable miscalculation. This more than any other turned him into a bogeyman for Adventists.

Herschel Lamp, MD, a missionary Adventist physician and ordained minister, left the denomination over the issue of justification. In an open personal letter circulated widely among the Adventist constituency he announced his departure by recalling his own conversion to the church:

> The East Pennsylvania Conference Bible worker gave my mother, my sister, and me Bible studies for about a full year and covered nearly every subject a new Adventist is supposed to be catechized, including health reform, wedding rings, other "Christian standards," etc.
>
> The first time I was ever in an Adventist church was the Sabbath in December of 1940 when I was baptized in the Harrisburg [Pennsylvania] Church . . .
>
> Upon returning home to Carlisle that December evening I went to the home of one of my high school classmates where I played table tennis with my three best friends. I stopped the

20. Paxton complains that, when he visited the Adventist General Conference in Washington, DC, church leaders tried to "play down" the conflict over the gospel. "A triumphalistic church and a triumphalistic leadership will not be quick to repent and to openly acknowledge mistakes" (*Shaking*, 152).

game after a while to tell them of my baptism. Knowing nothing of my religious studies, they asked me what this step meant. My answer is still vivid to me—to my shame! I told them that the significance of my becoming an Adventist was that I could no longer play pinochle, 500, and other forbidden card games, nor could I attend movies with them, nor could I go to the dance at the Junior Prom, nor could I ever again shoot pool with them at the local pool hall! I didn't mention vegetarianism, abstinence from tea, coffee, and cola drinks, the avoidance of fictitious reading, etc., but it was enough to persuade them that I had lost my mind! As a new Seventh-day Adventist, this was my testimony, my witness, my gospel presentation . . . Looking back I remember no Bible study on justification by faith in the atoning death and faultless merits of Jesus Christ that could give me the assurance of salvation apart from the works of the law. I was simply ignorant of the gospel.[21]

Lamp describes a type of Adventism similar to the one I experienced. Officially—on paper—the church professes a gospel of salvation by faith. In the day-to-day life of most Adventists like that of Lamp, however, the gospel is often little understood or appreciated.

Another Adventist minister, Dudley Nichols Jr., tells of learning about the gospel when he studied under the popular professor, Edward Heppenstall, at the Seventh-day Adventist Theological Seminary in the early 1960s. "If works save a person," Nichols remembers Heppenstall saying, "how many works does a person have to have to be saved? At what point may one claim salvation?" This is a common failure for all forms of Christian perfectionism. How is "perfection" to be defined? No one can point to anyone past or present who has attained it, whatever it is. Perfectionism leads to all kinds of misunderstanding, harsh judgments, and personal uncertainty.

When Nichols, a convert to Adventism, got into the parish, however, he discovered a different message. "The Gospel in Adventism must be understood in the light of the law of God," he writes in his exit letter from the church. "The Sabbath, the three angels' messages, the Investigative Judgment, Christ's High Priestly ministry, the state of the dead, the spirit of Prophecy, and many other minor points. That is why Christ has not yet returned a second time. To an Adventist this message is the saving message." Moreover, he heard the church saying that God—and the entire universe—is waiting upon Adventists to show that it is humanly possible to

21. Herschel Lamp to an anonymous friend, 20 February 1980, cited in Brinsmead, *Judged by the Gospel*, 17–18. Lamp left the Adventist church at about the time of this letter.

live without sin, to demonstrate once and for all that there can and must be a final group of sinless people upon earth. Listen to the anguish in his words:

> No wonder when I was in college the young people were talk-
> ing about how difficult it would be to live through the time of
> trouble [the last great crisis upon earth]. No wonder they were
> scared of it. They had absolutely no assurance of God's saving
> grace.
>
> No wonder Adventist members have so little assurance. No
> wonder they don't understand the Gospel. No wonder so many
> of them are discouraged. No wonder that I found many young
> people who had given up the church and attended no church at
> all. They were taught that they had to be perfect or sinless to go
> through the time of trouble and be saved.[22]

Nichols, who had served several large Adventist congregations during his career, resigned from the Adventist clergy, and with his wife Joyce, son Loren, and daughter Vivian, quietly withdrew from the church.

Dudley, Joyce, and their children were close personal friends. Laura and I had known them since college. Their sad departure left me with survivor's guilt. The evangelical publication, *Christianity Today*, posed the question whether there would be a "rash of defections" over this issue. "Tra-ditionally, Adventists are taught they can't be sure of heaven until they have lived lives good enough to have their sins blotted out during the Investiga-tive Judgment," Tom Minnery wrote. "That, in many cases, has spawned an attitude of 'perfectionism,' always striving to be good enough, but never sure just how good that is."[23]

As the debate over the gospel deepened, some like Nichols and Lamp resigned; others were fired, particularly in Australia. There were a few such cases in America. I began to fear I might be one of them. In class as well as in the pulpit I tried to make clear my acceptance of the Reformation doctrine of justification. Rumors hence spread that I had become a "Fordite" and thus, a *heretic*. Laura naturally became concerned. She had started a master's program in counseling at the University of Tennessee at Chattanooga. Since I had been identified by some in high places as heretical meant that Laura, once she had completed her master's and started on her doctorate, would never be able to teach at Southern, which she had really hoped to do. Al-though it is difficult for someone outside the denomination to understand, once a person within Adventism is associated with any teaching or person considered suspicious by church leaders, it is virtually impossible thereafter

---

22. Nichols to Seventh-day Adventist Church at large, 1984.
23. Minnery, "Adventist Showdown," 76.

to rectify one's reputation. Once besmirched, a person is thus marked for life. And so was Laura because of her personal association with me.

Our daughters, JoAnna and Paula, even though they were quite young when the gospel crisis erupted, intuitively sensed the building pressure. School classmates picked up the rumors. A friend one day brazenly asked JoAnna, "Is your dad a heretic?' Besides angrily denying it, she didn't know what to say. She had no idea what such a word even meant.

As this and other theological controversies swept over the denomination, it struck me that Adventism seemed to be experiencing all over again some of the doctrinal conflicts that had plagued the Christian church in centuries long past. The denomination was repeating that history. The striking parallels between Adventism and the universal church resulted from Adventism's isolation from the rest of Christendom, setting itself apart from other churches. The denomination had neglected to learn from common religious experience. From its beginning, Adventism had held in contempt other Christian denominations and basically refused much association with them. It started its own educational system because it believed public education too corrupting, published its own books and, in effect, primarily listened only to those within its own fellowship. It became obsessed with being right about every single theological issue. The result of such standoffishness was a kind of religious inbreeding. Adventism had thus unwittingly become a shining theological example of George Santayana's famous aphorism, "Those who cannot remember the past are condemned to repeat it."

As in all controversies within Adventism, Ellen White was inevitably dragged into the fray. White's perfectionistic, legalistic statements unfortunately seem to have gotten more attention than her contrasting evangelical ones. One of my colleagues, Adventist theologian Helmut Ott, labored to reconcile Ellen White with the Reformation view of justification. Unfortunately, the results of his efforts, published in book form,[24] have not enjoyed widespread acceptance within the denomination. For his apologetic contribution he too was branded a "heretic."

It is true that the New Testament, and especially the Old, can be cited on both sides of this matter, as we can see when the letter of James is set over against Paul's letter to the Romans. Usually, these tensions can generally be resolved when the circumstances of each author are taken into consideration. Might the same be true for Ellen White? White, however,

---

24. Ott, *Perfect in Christ.*

has inadvertently become one of the primary sources of the church's confusion about the gospel, a wax nose that can be turned in any direction. It
is safe to say, I think, that had Adventism set to one side Ellen White and
followed single mindedly the biblical witness, it probably would never have
experienced the confused semi-Pelagian emphasis on human works and legalistic moralism from which it has long suffered. As things stand, however,
all sides in the church's debate quote White for their respective positions.

Over the decades that have passed since this crisis over the gospel, I've realized
that drawing too sharp a distinction between justification and sanctification
goes beyond the biblical evidence. The two aspects of salvation must be distinguished logically and theologically, to be sure, but in practical experience
they occur simultaneously. When one is justified, declared righteous, instan-
taneously regeneration or the process of sanctification begins. Sanctification
is God's work *within*; justification, God's work *without*. Justification is the
ground of our acceptance with God; sanctification, the actual transformation.

Paul's references to justification, I think, can best be understood as
forensic, and thus convey that the justification or righteousness bestowed
is really external to the person, located in Christ, not infused within the
individual. Take Rom 3:21–22, for instance. "Now, apart from law, the
righteousness of God has been disclosed, and is attested by the law and the
prophets, the righteousness of God through faith in Jesus Christ." If "faith
in Jesus" is understood as the "faithfulness *of* Jesus"—a very plausible interpretation—then the sense of this passage is that God justifies the person
who accepts in one's behalf the faithfulness of Jesus. Jesus's faithfulness is
credited, as it were, to that person by faith.

I realize Paul may be read differently. Paul's use of the legal terminology of justification is only one way salvation is put within the New Testament.
It is only one model or paradigm of salvation. Salvation is also likened to a
ransom paid for slaves or prisoners (Mark 10:45; Gal 3:13). In another, Jesus
is seen as the powerful Victor who delivers us from the dark, satanic realm
(Col 1:13–14; 1 Cor 15:24--28). In still another, Jesus is the sacrifice who
sheds his own blood to make peace between God and humanity (John 1:29;
Rom 3:25). All these images—taken from first century social and religious
culture—are necessary to give greater understanding of what it means to be
reconciled to God. All, however, are agreed that salvation comes from God.

The Adventist controversy really boiled down to two competing views
of justification. Justification by faith in the sense that God not only accepted
and justified a person, but at the same time infused a righteousness within,

was set against justification as a forensic or legal declaration—outside the person—in Christ. In this case, the infusion of righteousness is not what renders the believer acceptable to God. The first view, in Adventism at least, often takes on a peculiar perfectionistic or legalistic hue. Accordingly, people are finally accepted on the basis of the level of moral perfection they have achieved together with divine assistance, of course. To add to the controversy, Ellen White could be quoted on both sides of the debate.[25]

For me, the forensic idea of justification is the model that most adequately captures the objective, apart-from-us, divine nature of salvation. Quite independent from anything that is happening within us—or will ever happen—God accepts us on the basis of Jesus Christ. Justification by faith indicates that it is completely a work of God. Whatever one thinks of justification, it is of grace, and not of merit. "By grace you have been saved through faith, and this is not your own doing, it is the gift of God—not the result of works, so that no one may boast. For we are what he has made us, created in Christ Jesus for good works" (Eph 2:8–10).

Where the Adventist church went wrong here was in not respecting different interpretations of the gospel and justification. The church, unlike what is evident in the New Testament, was not open to a variety of perspectives, even though these might seem contradictory. It did not approve or allow an ongoing discussion. Instead, out of fear about the implications, the church attempted to squelch the primary Reformation view of justification. In doing so, it inadvertently and defensively clung to a view similar to the sixteenth century Roman Catholics. In retrospect, it should have allowed—even welcomed—diversity on this point.

While few on the teaching faculty at Southern knew it at the time, Roman Catholics and Lutherans had already begun (in 1965) a little publicized series of bilateral talks aimed at reconciling their different understandings of justification. Twenty years later, as the Adventist controversy started to shift to other issues, Catholics and Lutherans issued the following joint statement:

> We emphatically agree that the good news of what God has done for us in Jesus Christ is the source and center of all Christian life and of the existence and work of the church . . . Our entire hope of justification and salvation rests on Christ Jesus and on the gospel whereby the good news of God's merciful action in Christ is made known; we do not place our ultimate trust in anything other than God's promise and saving work in Christ. This excludes ultimate reliance on our faith, virtues, or merits, even though we acknowledge God working in these by grace

25. See Herbert Douglass, "Righteousness by Faith," 1105–8.

alone (sola gratia). In brief, hope and trust for salvation are gifts of the Holy Spirit and finally rest solely on God in Christ.[26]

There is truth, too, in Hans Küng's conciliatory statement: "Protestants speak of a declaration of justice and Catholics of a making just. But Protestants speak of a declaring just which includes a making just, and Catholics of a making just which supposes a declaring just. Is it not time to stop arguing about imaginary differences."[27] While the differences aren't really as "imaginary" as Küng assumes, in his classic work on justification, John Buchanan expresses much the same sentiment: "All parties must be held to admit that, when a sinner is justified, he is, in some sense, both made and accounted righteous."[28]

These matters have never been resolved to the satisfaction of the Christian community. They have subsequently led to controversies over the gospel like the one in Adventism.

The gospel calls upon us humbly to admit that we are sinners. Not only do we do wrong, we are the kind of persons who are capable of wrong-doing, even of horrendous cruelties. We are "bent" toward evil. The Christian solution to our broken, sinful nature is embodied particularly in the doctrine of justification. We are forgiven and accepted through God's generously offered grace. We do not earn divine salvation. It comes as a gift. Good works are then evidence of a grace joyously operating in our life. Works aren't meritorious; they are evidence of our relationship to Christ. They are a working out of a salvation already present. The final judgment merely demonstrates or makes clear this connection.

As the controversy over the gospel waned, Adventist scholars persuaded church leadership to adopt the following conciliatory article of belief:

> In infinite love and mercy God made Christ, who knew no sin, to be sin for us, so that in Him we might be made the righteousness of God. Led by the Holy Spirit we sense our need, acknowledge our sinfulness, repent of our transgressions, and exercise faith in Jesus as Lord and Christ, as Substitute and Example. This faith which receives salvation comes through the divine power of the Word and is the gift of God's grace. Through Christ we are justified, adopted as God's sons and daughters, and delivered from the lordship of sin. Through the Spirit we are born again

26. Anderson et al., *Justification*, 16.

27. Küng, *Justification*, 221. Cf. Jas 1:12; 2:5, 8–12, 24; John 5:24; 1 John 3:1; Gal 3:25–29; Rom 3:28. For a concise summary of Protestant views of justification today, see Harink, "Setting Right," 20–25; Downing, "Justification," 298–317.

28. Buchanan, *Doctrine of Justification*, 228.

and sanctified; the Spirit renews our minds, writes God's law of love in our hearts, and we are given the power to live a holy life. Abiding in Him we become partakers of the divine nature and have the assurance of salvation now and in the judgment.[29]

Almost a decade after Paxton's book, the same scholars who crafted this statement prepared an expanded edition of Adventist theology under the title *Seventh-day Adventists Believe*. In Fundamental Belief 10, they presented a theology of salvation that is consistent with the common Protestant view of salvation by grace. "Neither Christlike [*sic*] character traits nor faultless behavior is the ground of our acceptance with God. Saving righteousness comes from the one righteous Man, Jesus, and is conveyed to us by the Holy Spirit." They steered away from the perfectionism advocated by Douglass and Wood, locating Christian perfection instead in the imputed righteousness of Christ. This book was reissued in a revised edition in 2005, but the article of salvation remains essentially the same.[30] It continues to stand as an endorsement of the classic Protestant view of salvation.

When I discovered these two editions of *Adventists Believe* and read the articles on salvation, I couldn't help but grieve for all those clergy and laity who had left, been driven out of the Adventist church, or had their reputations irreparably tarnished because they had accepted that "a person is justified by faith apart from the works prescribed by the law" (Rom 3:28). What terrible, senseless losses for the body politic!

Through the 1970s and 1980s, varieties of perfectionism thus ran virtually unchecked through the church. "Never before in the history of Adventism has it [perfectionism] received so much stress and such explicit expression," observed Geoffrey Paxton.[31] Due to the resurgence of these perfectionistic trends, which had been present in the denomination like a dormant virus almost from the beginning, the church tumbled into a genuine crisis over the gospel that spread into almost every nook and cranny of the church. Those who weren't enamored with moral perfectionism or other forms of legalism started to feel more and more uncomfortable about the direction in which the denomination appeared to be headed. As it turned out, the crisis over the gospel was only the opening salvo of three major crises of faith which, in rapid succession, engulfed the church and brought me to my own life-altering moment of crisis.

29. General Conference, *Adventist Church Manual*, 25–26. See also Ball, "Saving," 10–13.

30. General Conference, *Adventists Believe*, 129; cf. General Conference, *Adventists Believe*, 2nd. ed., 146. All further references to this book herein are to the second edition.

31. Paxton, *Shaking*, 144.

7

When Prophecy Failed

About that day or hour no one knows, neither the angels in heaven, nor the
Son, but only the Father. Beware, keep alert, for you do not know when the
time will com

—*JESUS*

The three crises centering on the gospel, the judgment, and Ellen White,
respectively, were indivisibly linked. Although I will distinguish them
here for the sake of analysis, given the complexities of the Adventist setting it is really difficult to separate them. One crisis overlapped and glided
almost seamlessly onto another. Like a telescoping instrument, each crisis,
thrusting deeper into the heart of Adventism, in turn, greatly escalated the
theological vulnerability both to the church at large as well as to individuals
within it.

I have already mentioned my continuing struggle over the Adventist
interpretation of certain apocalyptic passages in the book of Daniel. While
preparing to teach an upper level college course in Daniel, as mentioned
earlier, I carefully reexamined the traditional Adventist interpretation of
Daniel 7–9, and discovered an alarming number of discrepancies. I had
been vaguely aware of these for some time, but to discover them on my own
in the original Hebrew and Aramaic texts was really unsettling, to put it
mildly. These passages, especially Daniel 7–9, I knew, were absolutely crucial for establishing the identity of the Seventh-day Adventist church. The
whole movement, in a vital sense, rested squarely upon Daniel 7–9. Did I
really want to risk introducing the book of Daniel to students who expected

their study to buttress the traditional Adventist interpretation, knowing that, at the same time, I would have to alert them to these problems as well? Little did I know that a controversy over these very passages was about to break out in the church.

The doctrine you are about to read strikes anyone outside Adventism as a highly complex, confusing, and speculative interpretation of the biblical apocalyptic literature. I'm not sure how many Adventists even understand or could articulate the resulting doctrine, otherwise known in denominational jargon as the *Investigative Judgment*.

Apocalyptic literature, with its own inherent challenges, is especially confusing when read literally, as was generally the practice in nineteenth century religious speculation. This was the religious climate that gave birth to Adventism. The Adventist interpretation of Daniel is based on the *historicist* approach to apocalyptic literature. Historicism, as the name implies, assumes that predictions found in the apocalyptic books of Daniel and Revelation are continuously and steadily fulfilled during the ongoing course of history, particularly Western history, from the time of the original writing down to the present day and even into the future, climaxing in the end of the world.[1] In other words, according to the historicist mode, an apocalyptic writer predicts a future that unfolds continuously along the linear historical path, from the initial writing of the prediction to the very end of history, which is, of course, still future. Modern advances in the study of apocalyptic literature, spurred by the discovery of many more apocalypses from the period of early Judaism not found in the biblical canon, however, have rendered historicism obsolete as a mode of interpretation. Historicism, it is now recognized, seriously misreads the apocalyptic writings. So far as I am aware, it is advocated today only by Adventists and the Jehovah's Witnesses, and perhaps a few other smaller groups. Regrettably for Adventism, the church understanding of apocalyptic literature—and its self-identity—is completely dependent upon the historicist mode of interpretation. This means it is dependent, not upon the texts per se, but upon a specific *method* of interpreting those texts. Without this method of interpretation, one would not be able to arrive at the Adventist position.

Understanding the Adventist interpretation of biblical apocalyptic literature is thus essential for the grasping what Adventism is all about. The denomination's primary mission is centered in an *apocalyptic* theological vision, a vision, in turn, dependent upon a historicist interpretation of apocalyptic writings. Other denominations, while they don't completely

---

1. See Damsteegt, *Foundations*, 19, for a discussion of historicism in the hermeneutics of William Miller.

ignore theology, may be motivated more by other factors, as for example, a sense of community, a liturgical style of worship, or social service, like the Salvation Army. Adventism, on the other hand, lives or dies by its apocalyptic theology, by belief in its apocalyptic doctrines. It wins converts in large public evangelistic meetings by persuading them of the truth of its theology, anchored in the books of Daniel and the Revelation.

My struggle with Adventist apocalypticism began while I was a parish minister, as I have already mentioned, but now that struggle interjected itself like an unwelcome intruder into my teaching career. The struggle was, for the most part, intellectual, but there were practical implications. When it came to sermons and Bible studies, I focused on doctrines with which I could personally agree and tried to avoid those—like the church's interpretation of Daniel 7–9—with which I had difficulties. Instinctively, I guess I realized such compartmentalizing was inherently untenable with an organization so obsessed with theological conformity. It boded ill for my future. With Adventism, you were expected to swallow it whole. There were no halfway measures. You had to be all in. But how could you do that when some things didn't seem to fit?

The controversy over the gospel quickly morphed into a sharp dispute over the denomination's interpretation of Daniel 7–9 and its correlative doctrine known as the Investigative Judgment. This doctrine gets its name from a peculiar understanding of the final divine judgment. The final divine judgment, Adventists claim, will be devoted to the heavenly investigation of the life story of every human being. This judgment will determine who—past and present—is worthy of eternal life. Only those who successfully pass this divine scrutiny will be finally, effectively forgiven; all others will be lost and consigned to the fires of the "second death" (Rev 20:10–11). Moreover, no one really knows whether they will be lost or saved *until* this judgment has rendered its final verdict. The Reformation doctrine of justification obviously clashes with this idea. It is therefore easy to see how the controversy over the gospel led inevitably to a dispute over the Investigative Judgment. "A misconception of the great sanctuary truth [another name for the Investigative Judgment]," wrote R. A. Anderson, for many years a leading Adventist denominational administrator, "has robbed many of the very assurance they need when we will have to stand without a Mediator just prior to our Lord's return."[2]

Yet no doctrine among Adventists seems more sacrosanct, unless it is the prophetic ministry of Ellen G. White, which will be discussed in the following chapters. Adventists have repeatedly claimed that the doctrine of the

---

2. As quoted in Ford, *Daniel 8:14*, 1.

Investigative Judgment represents their *unique* contribution to Christianity. This doctrine, often called the "sanctuary truth," certainly is distinctive to Adventism: no other religious community in the world has ever taught it. But many outside the denomination and also within have boldly, openly challenged the doctrine.

Adventist New Testament scholar Desmond Ford, introduced in the previous chapter, was one of these. His understanding of justification by faith led him finally into direct conflict with the doctrine of the Investigative Judgment. The Investigative Judgment to Ford seemed to base human salvation on abiding in Christ, which meant above all keeping the commandments of God, and through divine assistance developing a perfect character worthy of transformation into God's everlasting kingdom.

Ford, a tall, slender, athletic man in his early 50s, a popular teacher and eloquent preacher, had an outgoing, charming personality. While teaching at the church's Avondale University in Australia, and later at Pacific Union College, he developed a significant following. That he was so popular, I think, really frightened Adventist leadership, especially when he began publicly to take issue with aspects of the doctrine of the Investigative Judgment.

In his teens, while still an Anglican, Ford had showed a precocious interest in the Bible, which naturally continued after he and his mother, who claimed at the time to be agnostic, converted to Adventism. He soon discovered Ellen White's major work, *The Great Controversy*, and read it voraciously, thrilling over its tales of the Reformers, John Wycliffe, John Huss, and Martin Luther. But also present in the *Great Controversy* was the doctrine of the Investigative Judgment.[3]

Trying to comprehend the doctrine, Ford noted that in Hebrews 9 the ancient Hebrew Day of Atonement (*Yom Kippur*) is said to have found its Christian fulfillment in the cross of Jesus. "Nor was it to offer himself again and again, as the high priest enters the Holy Place year after year with blood that is not his own," Ford read in Hebrews, "But as it is, he has appeared once for all at the end of the age to remove sin by the sacrifice of himself " (Heb 9:25–26). This passage compared Jesus' death to the high priest's ritual sacrifice offered annually on the Day of Atonement (see Lev 16:6–10). Adventists, like the writer of Hebrews, interpret the Day of Atonement as having typological or symbolic significance. The ancient rituals of this solemn day, one of the High Holy Days in Judaism, symbolically pointed forward to critical events in Christian history. The sacrifice of a goat specifically

---

3. Desmond Ford, interview by Jerry Gladson and Donald Wilkinson, May 23, 1999. Much of the following is based on this interview.

dedicated to Yahweh on the ancient Day of Atonement found its ultimate
fulfillment in the atoning sacrifice of Jesus.

There the comparison ends. The writer of Hebrews understood the
Day of Atonement to have been fulfilled at the cross. Ellen White, Ford noticed, instead placed the fulfillment of the Day of Atonement in 1844, at the
beginning of what Adventists call the time of the Investigative Judgment.
Despite his lack of theological sophistication at the time, even as a teenager
Ford could readily see that the book of Hebrews and White's *Great Controversy* presented two very different, mutually contradictory, interpretations
of the Day of Atonement. At fifteen, fresh from his baptism, Ford began a
lifelong quest to unravel the difficult and contradictory Adventist doctrine
of the Investigative Judgment.

Outside observers of Adventism find this doctrine, involving as it does
a novel interpretation of the ancient Day of Atonement, obscure and complex. Even within the church, few understand its significance. I also had
trouble with it. In my pastoral years, I could never get all the individual
pieces of the doctrine to hold together long enough to be intellectually convincing, even though I dutifully presented it in all the Adventist evangelistic
meetings I conducted. Afterward I wondered, if I can't get the doctrine to
hold together exegetically or logically, how can I expect someone else to
grasp its importance? And *this* is the church's unique teaching?

One weekend, James Crenshaw, my doctoral mentor at Vanderbilt, visited the Southern campus to speak at an event I was hosting, and stayed the
night in our home. That evening, while sitting around our kitchen table after
the dishes had been taken away, I tried explaining this doctrine and why it
had by then become such a maelstrom of controversy. In his inimical way—
Crenshaw always liked to challenge assumptions—he tersely responded,
"What difference does all this exegetical 'sleight of hand' possibly make?"
Despite its inherent obscurity, the controversy over the Investigative Judgment, initially troubling to a fifteen-year-old Adventist convert, eventually
was to have far reaching echoes in the greater Adventist world.

Let me try to explain the Investigative Judgment and why Adventists give it
such importance. Biblically, the Investigative Judgment rests primarily upon
Daniel 8, with some reference to Daniel 7 and 9, read in conjunction with
Leviticus 16 and the book of Hebrews. Daniel 8 contains an apocalyptic
vision that concerns a ram and a male goat, symbols of the struggle for military and political dominance on the part of the ancient Greeks versus the
Persians. Standing by the river Eulaeus (Ulai), usually identified with an

artificial canal that connected two rivers north of the ancient Persian city of Susa, Daniel sees a ram charging "westward and northward and southward" (Dan 8:3–4). This ram is a symbol for the "kings of Media and Persia" (8:20), the ancient empires of Media and Persia, the latter of which dominated the ancient Near East from the sixth through the fourth centuries BCE. A male goat, with a strange, bizarre horn protruding from its forehead, opposes the ram. "It threw the ram down on the ground and trampled upon it" (8:7). The male goat represents the "king of Greece" (8:21)—Alexander the Great (356–323 BCE)—who conquered Persia and the then-known world in the late fourth century BCE.

Following the triumph, the male goat "grew exceedingly great" (8:8). At the height of its power, the horn breaks off, and out of it arise four other horns, apparently representing the final four geographical divisions of Alexander's empire, distributed among his four dominant generals (8:22): Cassander (Macedonia-Greece), Lysimachus (Asia Minor), Seleucus (Syria-Babylonia), and Ptolemy (Egypt). One of the horns, called here "a little one [Heb. *qeren-'ahat*]," becomes so prominent it progresses menacingly "toward the south, toward the east, and toward the beautiful land" (8:9), or the land of Israel. It challenges the "host of heaven," and throws "down to the earth some of the host and some of the stars" (8:10). The vision goes on to tell how this entity finally concentrates its fury on the "sanctuary" (Heb. *miqdash*), the Jewish Temple in Jerusalem. "It acted arrogantly," throwing out the daily sacrificial ritual, and "overthrew the place of his sanctuary" (8:11). So hostile is it toward the Temple, Daniel hears a heavenly being desperately crying out, "For how long is this vision concerning the regular burnt offering, the transgression that makes desolate, and the giving over of the sanctuary and host to be trampled?" (8:13). The answer comes in a specific time period: "Unto two thousand and three hundred days; then shall the sanctuary be cleansed" (8:14, KJV). I have cited this verse from the King James Version because it is from the KJV of verse 14 that Adventists have laid the foundation of this doctrine.

We have to go back to the mid-nineteenth century to realize why. In the 1830s and 1840s, farmer turned lay revivalist William Miller (1782–1849) based his revival message on Dan 8:14. At the time, the book of Daniel had attracted great interest among those who, given the dark economic and political conditions of the Jacksonian era, were afraid that the end of the world was impending. They wanted to know when the end would occur. Miller approached this question from the book of Daniel. He differed from other interpreters of the day by taking the "sanctuary" in Dan 8 as a symbol for the earth. The "cleansing" of the sanctuary, mentioned in Dan 8:14 (KJV), therefore became a symbol to him of the final purification of the earth by the fires of God at the end of time (see 2 Pet 3:12). This purification would end civilization as we know it. Miller thus identified the "cleansing of the sanctuary" in Daniel 8:14 with the end of the world.

Miller was joined in the 1840s by a number of prominent clergy, including Joshua Himes, from the Christian Connection, a denomination that eventually would became a part of the United Church of Christ. Himes, who served as Miller's publicist and campaign manager, helped promote widespread, enthusiastic interest in the approaching end of the world. The oratory of the Millerite campaign grew so frantic that Horace Greeley, out of concern for the public, felt it necessary to issue a special edition of the *New York Tribune* to counter it. By the time of its demise in 1844, the Millerite movement numbered as many as fifty thousand adherents.[4] Seventh-day Adventism got its beginning from the followers of Miller.

Overly cautious at the beginning of the movement, Miller finally fixed the time for the end of the world in 1843; then, in January of that year, modified his calculation to embrace a period between March 21, 1843 and March 21, 1844. Adopting the "year-day" principle for interpreting biblical apocalyptic chronology, he interpreted the 2300 "days" of Dan 8:14 (KJV) as 2300 actual *years.*[5] Then fixing the beginning of the 2300-year period at 457 BCE, based on the date of the decree of the Persian King, Artaxerxes I, "to restore and rebuild Jerusalem" (Dan 9:25), Miller tidily calculated the 2300 years to reach from 457 BCE to 1843 CE. When Jesus failed to return to earth by March 1844, however, his followers persuaded the now increasingly wary Miller that the actual date should be adjusted to October 22, 1844. On that day, they were absolutely confident, Christ would return to earth, bring an end to human civilization, and usher in the kingdom of God.

The Millerites, as we would naturally expect, suffered a bitter, agonizing disillusionment on October 22. Clustering in small groups at their farms and homes, they anxiously awaited through the long day the sensational moment when the heavens would rend asunder and Christ appear. Midnight came. They looked into the moon-lit starry sky. There was no triumphant Christ. Their neighbors laughed at them, shaming many into recanting their faith. Ever afterward they spoke sadly of October 22 as the "Great Disappointment." Many of the leaders of the movement went back to the churches they had so abruptly left. Before his death in 1849, Miller himself admitted

---

4. Butler et al., *Religion in Life*, 425. Also note Ahlstrom, *Religious History*, 478–81.

5. Adventists still follow this "year-day" principle whereby a day in apocalyptic (or prophecy) stands symbolically for a year, usually thought of as 360 days rather than 365. This is based upon Ezek 4:6 ("I assign you, one day for each year") and Num 14:34 ("every day for a year"). Thus, the 2300 *days* are read in Dan 8:14 as 2300 *years.*

that he was wrong to have made 1844 the terminal point of the prophecy, but retained to his death the belief the 2300 days had something to do with the Second Advent that lay indefinitely in the future.[6]

A few of his more ardent followers—those destined to form the Seventh-day Adventist movement—set about reinterpreting Daniel 8. They remained convinced about the accuracy of Miller's calculations. *Something* had happened on October 22, 1844. They were sure of it. *What* had happened was the question. As is true of most millennial sects, they ended up reinterpreting their failed prophecy.[7] Painstakingly working through Daniel yet again, they concluded the "sanctuary" in Dan 8:14 wasn't the earth after all! Instead, it was the sanctuary *in heaven*, where Christ now ministers on behalf of his people, "the true sanctuary, which the Lord erected, not humanity" (Heb 8:2, lit. trans.). Turning to the book of Hebrews, they noticed that the Hebrew sanctuary or tabernacle, and the Jerusalem Temple, which succeeded the Hebrew sanctuary, had followed the same basic physical design. Both, they observed, had been patterned after the "true" sanctuary in heaven (Heb 8:5; Exod 25:8, 40; 1 Chr 28:19). This led them to a close study of the ancient Hebrew sanctuary, especially the rites that took place on the Day of Atonement, when a ritual "cleansing" of the sanctuary transpired (see Lev 16:15–19). Was this Day of Atonement cleansing, like the earthly sanctuary itself, symbolic of an event that was to happen in heaven on October 22? And was this what William Miller had actually inadvertently discovered?

On the tenth day of the seventh Jewish month, Tishri, corresponding to our September or October, occurred the most solemn of Jewish High Holy Days, the Day of Atonement. According to Leviticus, after offering an initial sacrifice for himself and his kin, and ritually carrying its blood into the inner sanctum of the sanctuary (the Holy of Holies or Most Holy Place), the high priest selected two male goats (Lev 16:1–14). He cast lots over the goats, designating one for Yahweh; the other for a mysterious 'Azazel, which because of its antithetic role in the ritual, represents the chaotic or demonic.[8] Yahweh's goat was then offered as a "sin offering," its blood taken into the inner sanctum of the sanctuary and lightly sprinkled on the Ark of the Covenant (16:15). This ritual act "reconciles," "atones for," or "cleanses," as these Adventists interpreted it, the people of God and the sanctuary, which

6. Nichol, *Midnight Cry*, 475.

7. Harvey observes when such sects experience a failed prophecy, their trust and ardor for the movement that produced the failure strangely does not falter, but often grows even stronger. Such was certainly true among the Millerites (*Jesus and History*, 90).

8. See my "Enigma of Azazel," 88–123.

had been ritually defiled by its presence in the middle of a sinful community (16:16).

The Azazel goat then became a scapegoat and ritually transported the uncleanness—here thought of in almost physical terms—away from Israel. The high priest confessed over it "all the iniquities of the people of Israel, and all their sins." He put them upon the head of the goat, and sent it away into the wilderness, where it presumably died (16:20–22).

Two of Miller's most devoted followers, Owen R. L. Crosier (1820–1913), a lay preacher and editor, and Hiram Edson (1806–1882), a farmer, were apparently the first Millerites to link this dramatic ancient Hebrew ritual with the 2300-day prophecy of Daniel 8. On the very morning after the crushing disappointment, following a period of prayer while kneeling on the hay-strewn earthen floor in Edson's barn, Edson and Crosier set out across a desolate cornfield, its wilted stalks cradling unharvested ears of grain abandoned months ago by disappointed followers of Miller, to offer encouragement to their disillusioned friends. In route Edson had what he later described as a "vision," although it was probably more of a sudden insight, an "Aha" moment. "Heaven seemed to open to my view," he later wrote, "and I saw distinctly and clearly that instead of our High Priest coming out of the Most Holy of the heavenly sanctuary to come to this earth on the tenth day of the seventh month, at the end of the 2300 days, He for the first time entered on that day the second apartment of that sanctuary; and that He had a work to perform in the most holy before coming to this earth."[9]

He and Crosier rushed to their Bibles and reexamined their previous interpretation of Daniel, Leviticus, and Hebrews. The younger, better educated Crosier, collaborating with Edson and another Millerite, F. B. Hahn, subsequently wrote an article summing up these two aspects of cleansing, the blotting out of sins and the final, eschatological disposal of sins, symbolized, they now believed, in the fate of the two goats. Building on Edson's visionary idea, Crosier reasoned by analogy with the Day of Atonement ritual, that in the heavenly sanctuary at the end of the 2300 years there would have to be the same two corresponding aspects of cleansing, one concerned with the blotting out of sins; the other, their final disposal over 2300 years later.[10]

Almost a decade later, J. N. Loughborough tried to clarify the eschatological blotting out of sins and the work of the final divine judgment. To cleanse the heavenly sanctuary of the confessed sins of people meant, in

9. Hiram Edson, as quoted in Nichol, *Midnight Cry*, 479.

10. Crosier, *Day-Star* Extra, February 7, 1846, quoted in Froom, *Prophetic Faith*, 4:889–90. Froom offers an account of Edson and Crosier (4:877–92).

effect, that God would finally have to engage in the formal act of judging the human race. By the end of the 1850s the essential ingredients of this doctrine were in place, leaving James White (Ellen's husband) only the task of rounding it out and furnishing the legal metaphor under which it has been designated ever since, the doctrine of the *investigative* judgment.[11] By that time, however, Crosier, one of the chief architects of the doctrine, had abandoned the interpretation, and joined the Advent Christian Church, the other denomination formed from the remnants of the Millerite movement. The Advent Christian Church does not accept the doctrine of the Investigative Judgment.

As taught today, the Investigative Judgment enlarges on these two phases of divine judgmental activity. The first phase, prior to 1844, involves the fate of the confessed sins of God's people. In the ancient Hebrew sanctuary, the daily confessed sins figuratively accumulated in the sanctuary, thus rendering it ritually unclean. This required an annual cleansing on the Day of Atonement. Similarly, as the people of God have confessed their sins down through the ages prior to 1844, these sins have accumulated, so to speak, in the heavenly sanctuary. Like the earthly sanctuary, the heavenly therefore requires some type of cleansing. "Thus it was necessary for the sketches of the heavenly things to be purified with these rites, but the heavenly things themselves need better sacrifices than these" (Heb 9:23).[12]

As in the earthly sanctuary, where sins were cleansed through the ritual offering of Yahweh's goat, so in the heavenly the blotting out of accumulated sins is accomplished by a process of cleansing. This cleansing, or clearing of the record, Adventists believe, requires the prerequisite work of investigation into the individual life stories of those in the community, just as did the ancient Israelite Day of Atonement. The people were to humble themselves before the Holy God as they with bated breath awaited the outcome of the atonement procedure (see Lev 23:24–32). Now, the corresponding heavenly procedure between October 22, 1844, and the Second Advent of Christ must determine who will finally receive eternal redemption and who will not. Ellen White explains:

> As anciently the sins of the people were by faith placed upon
> the sin offering and through its blood transferred, in figure, to
> the earthly sanctuary, so in the new covenant the sins of the
> repentant are by faith placed upon Christ and transferred, in

11. James White, "Judgment," 100. Later Adventists would distinguish this phase of judgment from the final disposal of evil. These are the (1) *investigative* and the (2) *executive* judgments, respectively.

12. For a fuller treatment of this doctrine, see General Conference, *Adventists Believe*, 347–69.

fact, to the heavenly sanctuary. And as the typical cleansing of the earthly was accomplished by the removal of the sins which it had been polluted, so the actual cleansing of the heavenly is to be accomplished by the removal, or blotting out, of the sins which are there recorded.[13]

This quotation indicates that *typology* offers the hermeneutical key in the doctrine of the Investigative Judgment. In typology, persons, places, events, and institutions, because of their array of similarities, correspond to future persons, places, events, and institutions. In the Investigative Judgment, the ancient Day of Atonement ritual prefigures or typifies the heavenly sanctuary and the process of final judgment. In 1844, this typology indicates, Christ began the second phase of his work in the heavenly sanctuary—the final judgment.

"He entered the second and last phase of His atoning ministry," Article 24 of the Fundamental Beliefs of Seventh-day Adventists puts it, for a "work of Investigative Judgment which is part of the ultimate disposition of all sin." The heavenly tribunal in 1844 began reviewing the cases of all who have ever lived, analogous to a human court reviewing or "investigating" the evidence, to expose the worthiness or unworthiness for eternal life. This investigation "makes manifest who among the living are abiding in Christ, keeping the commandments of God and the faith of Jesus, and in Him, therefore, are ready for translation into His kingdom."[14] To symbolize this new phase of activity, just as the high priest anciently did in the earthly sanctuary, Christ "moved" on October 22, 1844, from the Holy Place to the Holy of Holies or Most Holy Place in the heavenly. Although this judgment commences with the deceased, at some unknown moment it will pass to the living, making the present time one of ominous significance. Again, Ellen White:

All who have truly repented of sin, and by faith claimed the blood of Christ as their atoning sacrifice, have had pardon entered against their names in the books of heaven; as they have become partakers of the righteousness of Christ, and *their characters are found to be in harmony with the law of God*, their sins will be blotted out, and they themselves will be accounted worthy of eternal life.[15]

13. White, *Great Controversy*, 421–22.
14. General Conference, *Adventists Believe*, 347–48.
15. White, *Great Controversy*, 483. Emphasis supplied.

Since it is closely associated with the final events of human history, this doctrine confronts Adventists with a powerful sense of urgency. They are living in the very time of the final judgment, when their personal cases may suddenly come up before the heavenly court! The urgency in the Investigative Judgment also stirs up anxiety about personal salvation. Some Adventists now maintain this judgment is not really about personal assurance of salvation. It is intended rather as vindication to show the universe that God is right or just in saving God's people and that God's people deserve eternal life. But an individual's ultimate acceptance with God, if Ellen White is to be believed, seems to remain in abeyance until the divine investigation is complete. Personal sin is not finally removed in reality until the heavenly court has rendered its verdict. The forgiveness of sins is made contingent upon the development of a character comparable to that of Christ. Sinful records are not purged until the final verdict. "The heavenly sanctuary is cleansed by the final removal of the record of sins in the heavenly books," where sins have been stored during earth's entire history.[16] If this is true, isn't everything in the Christian's life dependent upon the menacing judgment always suspended over one's head? No matter how much a person may desire forgiveness, no matter how certain the forgiving grace of God, one can experience little relief because there is no decisive verdict taken in this life. We may hope for the best—even trust in the best—but we really don't know the outcome. Taken at face value, the Investigative Judgment robs a person of any real assurance about personal standing with God. "My main objection to the Investigative Judgment," Desmond Ford admitted, "has always been that it saps assurance."[17]

Since the Investigative Judgment developed out of a reinterpretation of the disastrous Millerite prediction that the world would end in 1844, many opponents of Adventism have criticized the doctrine as a "face-saving" device. In their influential study of movements that have advanced similar unfulfilled predictions, Festinger, Riecken, and Schachter pointed to the Millerite movement as the poster child of what such groups commonly do when grand expectations end in bitter failure. Often the group finds new explanations as to why their original belief was correct after all. Adventists, through the complicated doctrine of the Investigative Judgment, in effect, have shifted the anticipated divine action to the heavenly realm rather than

16. General Conference, *Adventists Believe*, 360–63. Quote on 355.

17. Ford interview, May 23, 1999.

to the earth.[18] By removing the anticipated event from the flow of history and transferring it to the heavenly realm, Adventists have at the same time exempted the doctrine from critical examination. It is literally an other-worldly event that has to be taken solely on faith. Who is to say what the Resurrected, Living Christ actually did on October 22, 1844?

Entirely unique to Seventh-day Adventists, this doctrine has come to identify the church's central mission. Adventists claim it reappears in the symbolic cry of the first angel in Revelation 14: "Fear God and give him glory, for *the hour of his judgment* has come" (14:7, emphasis supplied). For Ellen White, the Investigative Judgment represents the climax of the great controversy between God and Satan (hence the title of her work, *The Great Controversy*). She understands the entire biblical text as the story of an apocalyptic, dualistic controversy between the Lord of heaven and the archrival, Satan, a fallen angel. The whole of human history is understood in the light of this raging contest between good and evil.[19] At stake is a demonstration or vindication of God's true character: God is both loving and just. At the beginning of the struggle is the fall of Lucifer (Satan) from heaven; at the other end, the Investigative Judgment and the eschaton. At the end, God will finally be fully vindicated.

In 1889 Ellen White delineated the doctrines she considered "land-marks" for Adventists. Among them, in addition to the three angels' messages of Revelation 14, the seventh-day Sabbath, and the unconscious state of persons in death, she listed the "cleansing of the sanctuary transpiring in heaven"—the Investigative Judgment.[20] "Never, never seek to remove one landmark that the Lord has given His people," she emphasized to a troubled Adventist inquirer in 1898. "The truth stands firmly established on the eternal Rock—a foundation that storm and tempest can never move."[21] The denomination insists that this doctrine is the central feature of Adventist theology, its exclusive contribution to the Christian world.[22] The doctrine is interwoven with almost every major Adventist teaching, as Dale Ratzlaff notes:

18. Festinger et al., *When Prophecy Fails*, 28. This work develops the theory of cognitive dissonance, what happens when opinions, beliefs, or items of knowledge are "dissonant" or inconsistent with each other. Groups often reinterpret the offending items, as did the Adventists, simply forget the dissonance (amnesia), or try to increase proselytizing to surround themselves with more people who are convinced of the same thing. Adventists have employed all three strategies.

19. See Wood, "'We Must all Appear,'" 1–4.

20. White, *Counsels to Writers and Editors*, 30.

21. White, *Testimonies for Church*, 8:162.

22. See Adams, *Sanctuary*.

It is intertwined so tightly with other "unique" aspects of
Adventism that to cut out the "sliver" of the cleansing of the
heavenly sanctuary and the Investigative Judgment would require the removal of, or the painful separation from, a mass of
connected, theological tissue. Or, to change the metaphor, the
removal of this central pillar might cause the catastrophic crumbling of Historic Adventism.[23]

Yet today's Adventist, owing to its complex difficulty and abstractness,
scarcely pays any attention to the Investigative Judgment. More than a century and a half later, the church has had difficulty sustaining the relevance
of the doctrine, not to speak of its urgency. This is increasingly the case the
longer the ongoing heavenly investigation takes. For practical purposes, in
the day-to-day life of the average Adventist, the doctrine of the Investigative
Judgment plays no part. It rarely surfaces in sermons or Bible studies. In
my twenty-six years as an Adventist minister, outside the public evangelistic crusades where it is dutifully proclaimed, I probably preached on the
Investigative Judgment only once or twice in an ordinary worship context.
Some ministers privately admit to never preaching about it. One Adventist
evangelist—off the record—told me that he "preached the doctrine only
because it was considered essential in evangelistic preaching, not because
it made any sense."

Despite its receding role in Adventist life, Adventists still hail the Investigative Judgment as its distinguishing icon. As with many icons, it plays
a largely symbolic role, with little relationship to everyday life. Like an icon,
too, it is beyond tampering or removal. For Adventists, this doctrine has always been ironically the religious equivalent of the Holy of Holies or the inner sanctum of the deity. One may avoid it, keep it at a safe distance, but one
must *never* challenge it. To do so is to imperil one's eternal salvation. "Our
only safety is in preserving the ancient landmarks," Ellen White cautions.[24]
Here is a theological construct, in other words, that may never be altered
or revised. It is, in essence, regarded as infallible, despite its dubious origin
in a flawed interpretation of Daniel. That is why, throughout Adventist history, anyone publicly tinkering with the Investigative Judgment doctrine
has been quickly identified, quarantined, and eventually banished from
denominational life. Any criticism of this doctrine, in short, constitutes a
direct, frontal attack on the heart of Adventism itself.

Desmond Ford was well aware of all this. As he studied at Avondale
University, and later at Potomac University (now Andrews University,

23. Ratzlaff, *Cultic Doctrine*, 273.

24. White, *Counsels on Health*, 459.

Berrien Springs, Michigan), however, the problem of the relationship be-tween Hebrews 9 and the Investigative Judgment in Daniel 8 continued to weigh upon his mind. According to the Investigative Judgment, in 1844 Jesus moved from the outer apartment—the Holy Place—of the heavenly sanctuary to the inner, or Most Holy, to begin a work of investigative judg-ment. Yet Hebrews 9 clearly portrayed Jesus entering the Most Holy at his ascension, 1,800 years earlier! "For Christ did not enter a sanctuary made by human hands, a mere copy of the true one, but he entered into heaven itself, now to appear in the presence of God on our behalf" (Heb 9:24). In addition to this passage, Ford noted another in the same book. "We have this hope, a sure and steadfast anchor of the soul, a hope that enters the inner shrine behind the curtain [the Most Holy], where Jesus, a forerunner on our behalf, has entered" (6:19–20). Only one chapter in the entire New Testament discusses the typological significance of the Day of Atonement, he mused, and that is Hebrews 9. *There is absolutely nothing in Hebrews 9 about* 1844! Hebrews 9 is about the death of Jesus c. 30 CE, not about a far-off future event set for 1844.

One day Ford was confidentially sharing his concerns about the Inves-tigative Judgment with another minister who happened to be the president of the local Australian Adventist conference. "You might find it interesting to know I was elected president of the conference to combat the teachings of William W. Fletcher [1879–1947]," the minister confided. "As you know, Des, Fletcher was one of our evangelists and later a church administrator, serving in both Australia and India, but in the 1920s he started questioning the Investigative Judgment—just as you're now doing. Eventually, because of these doubts, he severed his connection with the church in 1930 and joined the Free Evangelical Association."

"You were elected conference president to combat Fletcher?" Ford asked, incredulous. "You then obviously know that Fletcher eventually came to the conclusion the Investigative Judgment was erroneous."

"Indeed so!" asserted the minister.

"After you had studied Fletcher's teachings, what was your conclusion?"

"I came to the conclusion that Fletcher was right, and that the church was wrong."

"And you're still the president of the conference! How?" blurted Ford, unable to restrain himself.

"Martin Luther said a lot of things that were wrong, and God still used Luther. I reckon that, even if Adventists are wrong about the Investigative Judgment, God can still use them."

When Ford returned from the Adventist seminary to take an academic appointment at Avondale University in Cooranbong, New South Wales,

Australia, he resumed the discussion with this same denominational leader. "There are several professors teaching at the Adventist seminary who don't believe in the Investigative Judgment. You know I have reservations. How am I ever going to teach meaningfully about this topic?"

"Carefully explain the problems, I mean, very gently, very pastorally, but try to come up with the very best solution you can," was the only advice he could give. Ford would later discover that similar suspicion about the Investigative Judgment had been rife among clergy throughout the entire history of the Adventist church.[25]

Ford took the conference president's advice and over the next decade tried to confront the problems in the Investigative Judgment by setting out some tentative solutions. This very effort—because he simply could not ignore the difficulties—turned Ford unintentionally into a controversial figure in the Australian Adventist community. He decided to pursue a PhD in rhetoric and speech at Michigan State University and, upon completing that, obtain a second PhD at Manchester University (Great Britain) in New Testament. The latter degree, taken under F. F. Bruce (1910–1991), afforded him a much more thorough examination of apocalyptic literature, the interpretation of which he now sensed lay at the heart of the Adventist problem.

During his study at Manchester University, Ford found out that the problems with the Investigative Judgment ran even deeper than he'd suspected. The doctrine flatly contradicted parts of the New Testament. If the Investigative Judgment was to determine who is finally worthy of eternal life, how could that be squared with the New Testament assertion "there is *now* no condemnation for those who are in Christ Jesus" (Rom 8:1)? Or the Johannine writings (in a saying of Jesus)? "Very truly, I tell you, anyone who hears my word and believes him who sent me has eternal life, and *does not come under judgment*, but has passed from death to life" (John 5:24).

Ford puzzled over these passages, wondering how the assurance offered in justification, as taught in Paul's writings, could be harmonized with the notion that the actual fate of the redeemed would finally be decided in 1844 or subsequently. If so, the illustrious persons of Christian history, such as Augustine, John Wesley—or even Paul and the apostles—could have had no real assurance of salvation because the judgment of God had not yet met to determine their fate. Ford was aware there had always been in Christian

---

25. In my interview with Ford, he mentions Adventist book editors, college, conference, union, and division presidents, "all of whom share my concern. It is very widespread" (Ford interview). In Ford's own later study of this question, he alludes to A. F. Ballenger, E. S. Ballenger, L. H. Crisler, I. Kech, W. W. Fletcher, L. R. Conradi, R. A. Grieve, all of whom left the denomination, and W. W. Prescott and L. E. Froom, who stayed with the church, but expressed deep concern over this doctrine (*Daniel* 8:14, 1).

theology an unresolved tension between the idea of a present justification—
a putting right with God—and a judgment according to works (see Rom
14:10; Rev 22:12). The entire tenor of the Investigative Judgment, however,
seemed to shift the main emphasis of the divine act of reconciliation on the
cross and in the resurrection to the critical event that happened in heaven in
1844 and the following years.[26] It appeared to rest the lion's share of human
redemption upon compliance with the moral law of God in clear contradic-
tion to justification and the gospel of grace.

Literally reeling from this huge difference between Adventist doctrine
and the New Testament, Ford decided to reexamine the biblical underpin-
nings of the Adventist teaching about the Investigative Judgment. His probe
struck further massive exegetical and historical difficulties,[27] as it were,
many of the same ones with which I had long been struggling.

Ford noticed there is simply no linguistic or semantical connection between Daniel 8:14 ("Unto two thousand and three hundred days; then shall
the sanctuary be cleansed" [KJV]), the passage on with the doctrine rests,
and Leviticus 16, which is used to link the two passages. The word translated
"cleansed" in the KJV of Dan 8:14 in Hebrew is actually *nitsdaq*, a passive
verbal form from *tsadaq*, "vindicated," or "restored [to its rightful state]," as
most modern translations render it.[28] Leviticus 16, on the other hand, consistently uses either *kipper*, "atone," or *taher*, "cleanse" when referring to the
actions of the high priest on the Day of Atonement (Lev 16:19, 27, 30, 32).
These two terms are not in the same semantical field as *tsadaq*. The early
Adventists would never have noticed this, because they didn't read Hebrew.
How likely is it that the two passages, from widely different literary genres
and social situations, one from a priestly ritual text, the other apocalyptic,
are talking about the same thing? And if they aren't, how can Adventists link
them on the slender basis of an English translation?

Examining more closely the literary context of Daniel 8, Ford now
noticed that the sinister agency responsible for defiling the sanctuary in
the text wasn't identified with the people of God, as Adventists taught, but
with a pagan power symbolized as "another horn, a little one, which grew

26. Early Adventist interpreters so accentuated 1844 they denied the cross could
be legitimately called an atonement. William Miller, for instance, argued that Christ's
sacrifice on Calvary was a "propitiary [*sic*] sacrifice to God," but the actual atonement
was made through the heavenly intercession of Christ (Letter to the editor, *Western
Midnight Cry* 4, December 21, 1844, 26). Unfortunately this confusion extends into
early Seventh-day Adventist literature and is even advocated by some today. It involves
more than semantics, as the *Adventist Encyclopedia* tries to claim (75).

27. Ford's critique of the doctrine is much too extensive to review here. I mention
only the major points, and refer the reader to the full 990-page text of his *Daniel 8:14*.

28. *KBL*, 794, renders this "be brought into its right."

exceedingly great toward the south, toward the east, and toward the beautiful land" (v. 9). This horn is usually identified by most biblical scholars as Antiochus IV Epiphanes, a Syrian king (175–164 BCE) known as one of history's most ruthless tyrants.[29] Antiochus desecrated the Jewish Temple in Jerusalem in December 167 BCE by deliberately placing an altar to the Greek god Zeus Olympus over the altar of burnt offering and offering sacrifices upon it. What is said about this power in Daniel 8 fits Antiochus' actions (see vv. 22–26), which is reason enough most scholars identify the ruler with Antiochus (see 1 Macc 1:41–64; Dan 11:31). Adventists, Ford mused, have strangely ignored the immediate context of Dan 8:14, and have therefore confused this pagan desecration of the Temple with the deposition of confessed sins of God's people throughout history. It is not God's people who are desecrating the Temple in Dan 8. It is the menacing "little horn" power (8:9–14).

As if this weren't enough, reading Dan 8:14 in the Hebrew text, Ford noted that the 2300 "days," as the KJV (King James Version) has it, crucial to the Adventist calculation that ends in 1844, could not actually be found in the text.[30] Instead the Hebrew literally reads: "For two thousand three hundred *evenings-mornings.*" This expression in Hebrew is *'erev boqer,* found only here in the Hebrew Bible. Being of singular occurrence makes it much more difficult to interpret. Most scholars think the expression refers to the regular evening and morning sacrifices, mentioned in Dan 8:13 as the *tamid,* the "regular burnt offering," and offered at the Jerusalem Temple on a regular, twice-daily schedule, like morning and evening prayer (see Num 28:3–8). Thus, the reference to 2300 evening and morning offerings, two offerings per day, would actually extend over 1150 days, not 2300, as Adventists claim. At least one modern translation renders this text accordingly. "It will continue for 1,150 days, during which evening and morning

29. This is "undoubtedly a reference to Antiochus IV" (Smith-Christopher, "Book of Daniel," 7:116); "the perverse Antiochus" (Lacocque, *Daniel,* 161). "The king of strong countenance can only be Antiochus Epiphanes" (Young, *Daniel,* 179). This view enjoys wide consensus among modern scholars. Adventists, in contrast, understand this power to be that of pagan and papal Rome, which they claim "obscured the priestly mediatorial ministry of Christ in behalf of sinners . . . by substituting a priesthood that purports to offer forgiveness through the mediation of men" (General Conference, *Adventists Believe,* 357).

30. The KJV appears to follow the ancient Greek Septuagint (LXX), probably translated from the Hebrew and Aramaic before the Christian era. This latter version has "until evenings and mornings, two thousand three hundred days." The Theodotian version of the Septuagint, produced near the end of the second century CE, has "until two thousand and three hundred evenings and mornings" (Dan 8:14). The Theodotian version became the standard Greek text for the book of Daniel.

sacrifices will not be offered. Then the Temple will be restored" (TEV).[31] The sense of the passage is apparently that the desecration of the Temple would disrupt the regular daily morning and evening ritual for 1150 days, almost the exact length of Antiochus' actual desecration (167–164). The Temple was rededicated in November or December 164, almost three years after its desecration.[32] If this is the case, the 2300 evenings and mornings could not extend to 1844!

Furthermore, Adventists date the interpretation of the 2300 "days" from 457 BCE, the date the Persian king Artaxerxes I authorized a return of the Jewish exiles from Babylon to renew and support the worship of Yahweh in Jerusalem.[33] Daniel specifies such a decree was intended to "restore and rebuild Jerusalem" (9:25).[34] Of the three decrees authorizing the Jews to return to their homeland, under the Persian kings Cyrus (538 BCE), Darius I (520), and Artaxerxes I (458–457), none clearly fits the criteria set out in Dan 9:24–27. "Know therefore and understand: from the time that the word went out to restore and rebuild Jerusalem until the time of an anointed prince, there shall be seven weeks" (9:25).[35] It is probable that the earlier decree of Cyrus is meant (538), but that date would throw off the Adventist calculation of the 2300 years, making it end in 1763 CE. Since there were actually several deportations and exiles, and several returns from exile,[36] however, it is impossible to be certain which return is intended by Dan 9:25.

31. The revision of this translation, known as the *Contemporary English Version* [CEV] (1995), reverts to the standard rendition of Daniel 8:14, "It will be two thousand three hundred evenings and mornings before the temple is dedicated and in use again."

32. Soggin, *History of Israel*, 301–4.

33. A portion of this decree, preserved in its original Aramaic, may be found in Ezra 7:11–26. Scholars debate whether this refers to Artaxerxes I (454–423) or Artaxerxes II (404–358); the decree, if dated to the reign of the former, historians commonly place at 458 rather than 457.

34. I leave aside here the whole question of whether Dan 9:24–27 is a key to interpreting the chronology in Dan 8:14, as Adventists claim. There is little warrant for seeing Daniel 9 as the interpretation of Daniel 8. Rather, the two passages are parallel in some way, as is common throughout the book (e.g., Dan 2 and 7), and only as parallels shed light upon each other.

35. As a subtext to the 2300 years, Adventists find in Dan 9:24–27 a prophecy reaching from 457 BC to the ministry of Christ (27 CE) and the mission of the early Christians to the non-Jewish world (34 CE). The "seventy weeks" in this passage are 490 days (= years). Thus 457 + 490 = 33 CE. Because this crosses over the imaginary 1 BCE to 1 CE line, where there is no zero year (0), a year must be added to compensate, yielding 34 CE. The remainder of the 2300 period, namely, 1810, is added to 34 to reach 1844. See Nichol, *SDABC*, 4:853–54.

36. See Bright, *History of Israel*, 360–402.

The Adventist attempt to pin down such a date, Ford concluded, is unconvincing; at the very least, uncertain.

Finally, Ford found himself turning back again to Hebrews 9, the passage that had originally sparked his life-long quest. This is the only passage in the New Testament, he reflected, that explains in christological terms the meaning of the Holy and Most Holy apartments in the sanctuary/Temple, the only place that directly reveals the Christian typological significance of the Day of Atonement. It is the only New Testament passage that talks about the "cleansing" of the sanctuary. According to Hebrews 9, at the cross the heavenly realities were purified by the blood of Jesus (9:23–26). Then at Christ's ascension, he entered into the Most Holy place, "once for all . . . obtaining eternal redemption" (9:12). Ford discovered eleven other New Testament passages where Christ is said presently to be at the right hand of the Father.[37] Moreover, Hebrews goes on to identify the so-called heavenly sanctuary with "heaven itself," and not a building or tent with two literal rooms (9:24). Within Hebrews, or in any other New Testament writing, there was no trace of a momentous judgment finally clarifying the fate of all humanity to begin far in the future *in* 1844. Instead, the New Testament writers expected the Second Advent—and the judgment—to occur at any moment, even suddenly in the first century CE.[38]

Ford concluded that there was no viable way to link Daniel 8 and Leviticus 16, or to show that the saints would be the ones who would "defile" the heavenly sanctuary. It was exegetically impossible to construct a timeline, using Dan 8:14, from 457 BCE to 1844 CE, or to find in the New Testament any awareness of the Christ assuming a new ministry of judgment in 1844. Ford was thus pressed to the disturbing conclusion that the doctrine of the Investigative Judgment had no real basis in the Scripture. The Adventist church was teaching an erroneous, unsound doctrine, and had been since the 1850s! One of the church's landmarks, its only unique doctrine, had collapsed. Prophecy had failed.

37. E.g., Acts 7:55–56; Eph 1:20–23; Heb 1:1–3.

38. See Mark 9:1; Matt 10:23; Luke 9:27; Rom 13:11–14; 1 Thess 4:13–18; Heb 1:2; James 5:8–9; 1 John 2:18.

8

Heresy Hunters

Truth is incontrovertible. Panic may resent it; ignorance may deride it;
malice may distort it; but there it is.

—*Sir Winston Churchill*

Desmond Ford's honesty about the Investigative Judgment had rendered him so polarizing and controversial for Adventists that Australian church leadership pressured him into taking a visiting scholar position at the Adventist Pacific Union College, in Angwin, California. I don't know whether the main church leadership "arranged" for this teaching position at Pacific Union College—to remove Ford from Australia—or whether the opportunity was genuine, unaffected by Ford's polarizing reputation. Perhaps the advice he was given contains a clue. "If you ever come back to Australia," tartly warned an Adventist official, "you'll never teach here again."

No sooner had he taken up his duties at Pacific Union College that a new book appeared, 1844 *Re-examined*, by none other than the perennial provocateur, Robert Brinsmead, who had been one of the major advocates of the gospel revival then sweeping through Adventism. Never one to use diplomatic words, Brinsmead described the Investigative Judgment as a "clumsy, immature understanding of ultimate reality without linguistic or exegetical support."[1] When some Pacific Union College students got hold of 1844 *Re-examined,* they challenged Ford. "Dr. Ford, this book is really

---

1. Brinsmead, 1844, 116.

disturbing. Is Brinsmead correct? Are Adventists *wrong* about the Investigative Judgment?"

"I had either to lie," Ford later confessed, "or candidly admit that
Brinsmead was right in most of his criticisms of the doctrine."

The controversy surrounding Ford thus didn't magically go away when
he crossed the Pacific and took up residence in California's Napa Valley. One
of the local leaders in the Pacific Union College Association of Adventist
Forums (a local chapter of the national Association of Adventist Forums),
asked Ford, "Would you discuss your views on the Investigative Judgment
at a meeting of the Forum?"

Ford hesitated, remembering why he'd left Australia. "If I do," Ford
replied, "I think it may cause problems for the Adventist Forum and the
College."

"Nonsense! It won't! At a Forum, as you know, you can say about
anything you like. No one will threaten you." Still skeptical, and against his
deeper instincts, Ford cautiously accepted. He had no way of knowing life
was about to change drastically.

Before a large audience at Pacific Union, on October 27, 1979, barely
135 years after the controversial October 22, 1844—an irony not lost on the
audience—Ford went public. One story tells that the astonished president of
Pacific Union College, Jack Cassell, at that time traveling in Japan, got hold
of a tape recording of Ford's Forum address the next day! General Conference leadership, stunned that an Adventist professor of religion would dare
make such bold, critical public comments about such a cherished Adventist
teaching, were at a loss to know what to do. They hastily dispatched Richard
Lesher, the new Director of BRICOM, to Pacific Union College to find out
exactly what had been said at the Forum. Once Lesher returned to Washington, DC, the church's headquarters, with his report, the General Conference
President, Neal Wilson, made the decision that Ford should immediately be
placed on "administrative" leave until his doctrinal views could be evaluated. He was then required to present his critique of the Investigative Judgment to a panel of church leaders and theologians for appraisal.

Thus Ford began almost a year of imposed silence. The address he gave
that October, however, spread via tape recording throughout the American
and Australian Adventist community. On every Adventist college campus,
it seemed, faculty and students popped the cassette into their stereo tape
decks and listened to Ford's now controversial lecture. In churches rural
and urban, clergy and church members hung on Ford's every word. The
Adventist community waited with bated breath to see how Ford would respond at the end of his administrative leave, and even more so, how the

denomination would react should the results of his research be unfavorable. As in the Investigative Judgment itself, ironically the church awaited the verdict.

For me, teaching the course in Daniel that year became almost un-endurable. Impatient students, as predictable, wanted immediate answers. I was pummeled in almost every class period by insistent questions about Ford. Students demanded to know how the church was responding to its critics of the Investigative Judgment. "Is Ford right?" they asked. "What do you think of Brinsmead's book?" "How can we exegetically get the Investiga-tive Judgment out of the book of Daniel?"

In an effort to defuse the crisis brewing in my course on Daniel, I orga-nized the students, mainly religion majors, into teams of three or four, and gave them the assignment of presenting to the class the various views—both Adventist and non-Adventist—on Daniel 8. One group compared Robert Brinsmead, Desmond Ford, and Ellen White on the Investigative Judgment. This strategy proved particularly effective. By allowing the students to grap-ple personally with the issues, it released some tension and yet provided direct, personal exposure to the difficulties that were plain enough for any-one who wanted to see them. Might some Adventist church leader wander through the halls and eavesdrop at the door? I worried. As the semester drew to a close, I realized I didn't really want to risk teaching Daniel again.

On August 10, at Glacier View, a denominational youth camp located high in the picturesque Rockies, near Boulder, Colorado, almost a year after Ford's controversial Adventist Forum address, Adventist church leaders and theologians assembled. They were there to debate, and more importantly, decide what the church should do about Ford's research. (This conference would ever afterward be called in Adventism simply, "Glacier View.") Ford's research had by now resulted in a dissertation-like document of almost a thousand pages. After nearly a week of deliberation, even though many church leaders who were called upon to make the final decision candidly admitted they had not actually read the document, the assembly acknowl-edged in a Consensus Statement the validity of some of the theological and exegetical problems,[2] but stopped short of accepting Ford's proposed reso-

2. For instance, the Statement concedes that further study is needed on the in-terpretation of Dan 8:14, that the year-day principle is not decisively recognized as a principle of prophetic interpretation, and that the atonement of Christ is all-sufficient and not compromised by the Investigative Judgment (see General Conference, "Con-sensus Document," 16–19). Jillian Ford, Desmond Ford's wife, took copious notes on

lutions. "I didn't need to read it," remarked one official. "I know already it's heresy." How he knew this without reading it, he didn't say. His attitude, unfortunately, was all too prevalent. As one administrator put it, "Only books that support the Adventist position do I read—certainly not works such as Ford's!" So much for critical thinking!

Ford proposed that instead of the single, unified denominational interpretation of 1844, which I have described in the previous chapter, the church look instead for multiple fulfillments of Daniel, as well as for other apocalyptic predictions, along lines of what he called the "apotelesmatic principle."[3] Denominational leaders flatly rejected this idea. They did agree, however, to set up a committee to study further the issues Ford had raised and recommend solutions more satisfactory to traditional Adventism.

In company with the Southern Adventist University religion faculty, I arrived at Glacier View just as the formal investigation of Ford drew to a close. The formal evaluative meeting was to be followed by a general consultation of Adventist theologians from all the church's colleges. I had no sooner entered the guest lodge when I caught sight of James Londis and Robert Zamora, friends from Washington, DC. Londis was senior minister of the three-thousand member Sligo Adventist church, situated near the General Conference offices. Zamora was chair of Columbia Union College's religion department, also near the General Conference, just outside Washington, DC. They were euphoric at the new openness they had witnessed even among church administrators gathered there for Ford's inquest. "It's a new day," Zamora exclaimed, as he warmly greeted me near the registration line. "Church leaders have opened up a real review of the Investigative Judgment doctrine. The winds of change are sweeping through the church!"

"They've also promised no one's employment is going to be jeopardized because of what they think about 1844," Londis added, addressing the raw, inchoate fear all of us deeply felt. Jim, Bob, and I spent the rest of the afternoon touring nearby Estes State Park. Between stops to take in the snow-capped mountain peaks stretching as far as the eye could see, they filled me in on the stirring events they'd witnessed the preceding five days.

---

the Glacier View conference, and published a transcription of these eighteen months later (*Adventist Crisis*, 55–76).

3. "This principle," Ford writes, "affirms that a prophecy fulfilled, or fulfilled in part, or unfulfilled at the appointed time, may have a later or recurring, or consummated fulfillment" (*Daniel 8:14*, 302). In other words, a prophecy may have many different fulfilments throughout history. The Investigative Judgment in 1844 may be considered one of these. The Glacier View delegates criticized the apotelesmatic principle on grounds it lacked external controls and could be used to make a prophecy mean many things, some of which may have no basis in the context of the original prophecy ([General Conference], "Statement on Ford," 20–22).

That evening President Neal Wilson addressed the delegates. "Despite the problems with the Investigative Judgment recognized during the Glacier View inquest," he assured the audience, "no minister or theologian will have their employment put in jeopardy over what they think about this doctrine." Whew! I felt enormous relief! What wonderful, blessed news! My anxiety melted away as I sat listening to the always articulate Wilson.

None in that audience knew, however, that Wilson had just come from a three-hour, confidential meeting with Desmond Ford and his wife, Jillian. Wilson and several other top church leaders, including K. S. Parmenter, the president of the Australian Division of the Adventist church, pled with Ford to disavow his research and abandon his conclusions. They emphasized that the delegates to the Glacier View conference had already vetoed most of them. Parmenter read from a letter he had carefully composed.[4] "Des," he began, "are you willing to acknowledge that there are several points in your present position on the doctrine of the sanctuary and related areas and the role of Ellen White that are out of harmony with the 'Fundamental Beliefs' of the church? Are you prepared to suspend these views, and even make a public statement to this effect?" Ford felt as though he had just been struck. Sensing Ford's bewilderment, Parmenter sympathetically paused, aware he was speaking, not just for himself, but in behalf of the entire delegation at Glacier View. "Are you willing, going forward, to ensure that your teaching and preaching will always be in harmony with the 'Fundamental Beliefs' of the church? Furthermore, will you acknowledge publicly that your Pacific Union College lecture, as well as your recent manuscript, presents some areas of doctrine that are out of harmony with the pillars of our faith? Will you suspend any discussion of these ideas unless at some time in the future they might be found compatible with the positions and beliefs of the Adventist Church?" *Was this a veiled threat of loss of employment?* Ford wondered.

Although it doesn't appear in the text of the letter, a final restriction demanded Ford renounce publicly Robert Brinsmead, with whom he had developed a cordial relationship. "Pray about these things, Parmenter urged sympathetically. "Think about them very carefully. We'll give you a week to reconsider."

"I don't need a week," Ford replied, utterly shocked at the demands being imposed. "I can respond *now* to all these conditions. The answer is *no* to all of them!"

---

4. These restrictions were stated in a letter to Ford from K. S. Parmenter, dated August 15, 1980, and were later incorporated in the minutes of Glacier View (see General Conference, "Parmenter-Ford," 10–11). I have paraphrased them here.

In a letter written a few days later to Parmenter, however, Ford did agree "to keep to myself the views that have brought perplexity."[5] Despite this, on September 18 church leaders took the final step of defrocking (canceling ordination) and firing Ford. By this decisive action, they apparently hoped to neutralize his influence by reclassifying him as "unofficial," "toxic"—a ploy that has usually worked with Adventists who rely solely and uncritically on denominational sources for moral and theological leadership. Later, alarmed that Ford was scheduled to speak in several Florida churches, Henry Carubba, the President of the Florida Conference, used this very ploy, "[Ford] has persisted in his erroneous views regarding the Sanctuary doctrine . . . [and] he is *no longer a bonafide minister of the Seventh-day Adventist Church* . . . Dr. Ford has been dispelled [*sic*] from the Adventist ministry and holds no such credentials."[6]

Six weeks following Glacier View, Ford found himself, coat in hand, defrocked and thrown out of the Adventist ministry. He had joined a long line of exiles whose "sin" was questioning this singular, unalterable church doctrine. Although there were further unsuccessful attempts to reach a compromise on the part of the General Conference,[7] Ford would go on to found an independent, parachurch ministry called Good News Unlimited. This ministry proclaims the gospel through seminars, lectures, tape recordings, and publications. Now in his eighties, Ford continues this work.

Adventist theologians and pastors, upon hearing of the private meeting and of Ford's subsequent dismissal, were outraged at this betrayal of honest scholarship. Returning to Southern Adventist University and only then learning what had subsequently happened to Ford, whose only error was in daring to ask honest questions, and seek to work them out responsibly, I was furious! I'm afraid I took Ford's rejection personally. My hopes that Adventism had come to a new era of openness, as my two friends had joyously announced, were crushed. The church's leadership, despite the promise glibly made at Glacier View, it appeared, intended now to put down all dissent. It was to be harmony—uniformity—at any price.

Aggrieved faculty at Andrews University, the church's main seminary, sent an open letter to the General Conference deploring the "rending asunder of Christ's body by what we consider to be the unjust recommendation that Dr. Desmond Ford not be employed in denominational service." Larry

5. Ford to Parmenter, 26 August 1980.

6. H. J. Carubba to Florida Adventist Churches, 19 February 1981. Emphasis Carubba.

7. One of these attempts occurred in San Francisco in 1982, but led merely to an intellectual standoff. The church leaders refused to budge from the traditional position on the Investigative Judgment (Ford interview, May 23, 1999).

Geraty, Professor of Archaeology and History of Antiquity at Andrews, accused the *Adventist Review* of trying to bias the outcome of Glacier View in the minds of its readers by a series of highly partisan editorials and articles leading up to the conference.[8]

The *Campus Chronicle*, student newspaper at Pacific Union College, splashed the headline: "Ford Defrocked," devoting its entire September 25 issue to the events swirling around Ford. John Toews, pastor of the nearby South Bay Seventh-day Adventist Church in San Francisco, set an example that would now be repeated many times by resigning from the Adventist ministry. At the same time, his congregation joined him in withdrawing from the denomination, changing its name to the South Bay Gospel Fellowship. "We feel we want to move into the mainstream of Christianity now," Toews insisted, "because we feel that Adventism is very definitely way off to the side."[9] A high level Adventist administrator minimized Toews' defection with the callous remark, "It would be worth losing 100,000 members to get rid of Ford and this problem." The Adventist clergy journal, the *Ministry*, in an effort to head off a stampede for the exits, dedicated its October issue to the topic, "Christ and His High Priestly Ministry," which included a full discussion of the events at Glacier View and a critique of Ford's research.

Four years earlier, I had reluctantly admitted to myself and to Laura that the Adventist doctrine of the Investigative Judgment, with all of what seemed to be its exegetical "slights of hand," wouldn't hold up under honest scholarly scrutiny. That was why, I thought then, no religious scholar outside Adventism had ever accepted it. Many of the exegetical difficulties Ford had encountered were identical to those I'd personally uncovered. Unlike Ford, however, I'd kept these misgivings to myself, confiding only in a few friends. Now I felt compelled to join my colleagues on other Adventist college campuses in expressing concern for Ford and for intellectual honesty. For Adventist theologians the implications of what had happened at Glacier View were chilling. We had hoped that the Glacier View conference would lead to a new, more open era for the denomination. We were deeply, bitterly disappointed at the hardline, rigid position the church's top leadership had taken.

An opportunity to speak out came when the Adventist Forum at Southern Adventist University invited the religion faculty to discuss the proceedings of the Glacier View conference at a public assembly in the University church. The eight of us on the panel that day divided predictably.

8. Geraty to Kenneth H. Wood (editor of the *Adventist Review*), 15 September, 1980.

9. Toews, quoted in Tom Minnery, "The Adventist Showdown," 77.

Religion chair Douglas Bennett, Robert Francis, Albert Liersch, and Frank Holbrook affirmed their loyalty to the traditional Adventist teaching about the Investigative Judgment. Lorenzo Grant, Ed Zackrison, Ron Springett, and I admitted reservations, insisting there were still many lingering, unanswered questions.

When my turn came, I pointed out to the audience of more than two thousand that the link between Daniel 8 and Leviticus 16, crucial for the traditional Adventist interpretation, "isn't at all obvious." "Furthermore," I continued, "all the references to the imagery of the Day of Atonement in the New Testament letter to the Hebrews claim that immediately upon his ascension Jesus entered the Most Holy Place, not the Holy Place, as Adventists claim. We really ought not to think of the mediatorial work of the ascended Christ in such literalistic ways as 'entering' various physical 'compartments of heaven.' Rather, we should recognize the symbolic or typological nature of such referents."

All tried to be pastoral. We carefully identified the difficulties and sorted through the proposed resolutions, but we refrained from any final decision on the traditional doctrine. Many who were in attendance, however, unused to the manner in which theologians handle disputed notions (by discussion and debate), weren't prepared for such subtle theological or exegetical distinctions. In their minds, the religion faculty of Southern Adventist University had now irrevocably capitulated and joined Ford in "attacking" the church! It was now a dichotomized "them" versus "us." The Forum discussion only enraged traditional Adventists.

A "town and gown" dispute erupted in Collegedale, whose population consisted mostly of Adventists. People branded the department of religion "Fordites," sympathizers with Desmond Ford, now a *former* Adventist minister. The label "Fordite"—as generally true of most labels—was patently unfair. Half of the department was clearly unsympathetic to Ford. The rest of us had acquiesced, I think, to a more realistic grasp of the theological difficulties, but even we urged caution and further study. Such neat, scholarly distinctions, at home in a rarified academic atmosphere, however, didn't really count for much among the populace. For many traditional Adventists, we were from that day forward considered nothing more than "Fordites." Therefore, like Ford, we ought to be eliminated from the faculty and even from the church. Every grocery clerk, baker, and auto mechanic in Collegedale suddenly turned into an amateur theologian. Douglas Bennett, Robert Francis, and Frank Holbrook, either because they really believed in the Investigative Judgment, or because they feared the rising tide of reprisal, began distancing themselves from Ford and even from those of us in the religion department who saw merit in what Ford had brought to light. The religion department at this time essentially fractured, split right down the middle. My personal internal struggle for intellectual integrity now merged uneasily with a new, but more immediate, practical battle for economic survival.

Not long after the Forum meeting, a middle-aged man and woman appeared at my office door. "We're here as members of the 'Committee of Concerned Adventists,'" the man announced. "We're interviewing college faculty about the Ford controversy, trying to find out what it is all about. May we ask you a few questions?"

It was dark and cold outside. I had arrived at the office about an hour before my first class, hoping to catch up on some paperwork. I was the only one there. I knew of the "Committee of Concerned Adventists." It was a group of well-intentioned, but misguided persons who had taken it upon themselves to investigate the Ford controversy and figure out whom to hold responsible. But this was my first encounter with any of the Concerned Adventists. Frequently, when I was out and about, students and community residents would stop to ask me about the debate, so their concerns weren't new, but I was very wary of what would happen should I say too much. Were they surreptitiously recording the interview? I had to be extremely careful. Now my livelihood, my ability to provide for my family, depended upon it.

Seating themselves in my office, the man got directly to the point. "Could you explain to us in simple, understandable terms the problem with the Adventist interpretation of Daniel 8?" It was a leading question. It was also a complex question.

Uneasily, I sensed this was a setup. "Do you read Hebrew?" I replied, looking for a possible way out. I thought of the long discussion in Ford's manuscript about the Hebrew word *tsadaq* (usually translated "restored") in Dan 8:14.

"No, I don't," he said calmly.

"Then I'm afraid I'll be unable really to explain to you 'in simple terms' the problems. They require some knowledge of the original Hebrew text." I refused to go any further than that. My answer basically was, "No further comment." This irritated the couple. Finally, they realized they weren't going to get anywhere, and so left. Such encounters soon became commonplace, but one never knew whether the inquirers were acting as surrogates for mistrustful church administrators, who themselves were reluctant to confront a professor directly.

The struggle wasn't limited to Southern. Church administrators all over the United States began cracking down on ministers and other church employees who showed any sympathy with Ford. Neal Wilson wrote in the October 1980 issue of *Ministry* (14–15):

> A minister who cannot conscientiously support significant
> doctrines of this church and who openly challenges the church,
> indicating that it is wrong in certain areas and always has been
> wrong, and who creates a divisive situation by drawing followers
> to himself and engaging in schismatic activities, should prob-
> ably expect to be questioned to determine whether it is wise or
> possible for him to continue as a minister of the gospel in the
> Seventh-day Adventist church.

Wilson's words, probably unintentionally, opened the door for an inquisition. Self-appointed "heresy hunters," like the Concerned Adventists,
seemed now to pop up everywhere, many using their official denominational positions to justify an assault on any would-be dissenter. Ben Leach,
president of Southwestern University, near Fort Worth, Texas, caustically
lambasted church scholars for wanting to "correct the mistakes in doctrine
we have made in the past."[10] Conference administrators interrogated pastors, trying to find out whether they had any sympathy with Ford.

In Northern California, the Adventist conference fired Robert Palmer,
pastor of the Meadow Vista, California, church; Norden Winger, pastor at
Fort Bragg; and John Zapara, pastor of the Woodside church in Sacramento,
all accused of holding views incompatible with Adventist theology.

In Central California, the conference forced academy (Adventist high
school) religion teacher Dale Ratzlaff to resign. At the time I didn't realize I
would later have to make the same decision. Two seminarians at Andrews
University, Ben Merrill and Al LaBrecque, both under denominational
sponsorship, had their scholarships suddenly revoked.

In Australia, Ford's homeland, church administrators fired Lorin
Jenner, Wayne Pobke, and Heinz Suessenbach when they refused to sign
a doctrinal loyalty oath. Within two years, Australian conferences would
dismiss fifty more ministers. Generally such sackings meant that these ministers had been emphasizing the Protestant understanding of justification
and that they had acknowledged, along with Ford, the difficulties with the
historic Adventist view of the Investigative Judgment. In short, they had
been caught up in the first two doctrinal crises that had so quickly overtaken the church. An undetermined number of Adventist ministers in the
United States, Canada, and Australia simply resigned, often under protest.
In Australia, almost two hundred ministers left their churches, one quarter
of all Adventist clergy in the country! Adventists had never known such
widespread clergy upheaval.

---

10. Quoted in *Evangelica News*, "Pastors, Scholars Under Fire," Winter 1981.

Why such turmoil and unrest over what looks to an outsider like an intramural quarrel over esoteric, obscure, and uncertain biblical texts? Why the tumult? Why the ruination of peoples' lives over vague apocalyptic texts? At the time I never took into account the political forces at play. I've always been somewhat naïve about church politics. Politics were always in play, of course. I just never gave church politics much attention.

The Adventist church is built upon doctrinal propositions, more so than many denominations. Its bold theological claims give the denomination its distinct identity. There is nothing wrong with making extraordinary claims or in staking out firm theological positions, so long as they are adequately supported and maintained with a degree of humility. Adventism does not adequately support many of its doctrines, nor advance them cautiously with humility. The downside is that doctrines often get frozen like glacial ice, impervious to alteration. They do not melt easily. Adventists are literally obsessed with being *absolutely correct* about every single theological point. This is especially true when Ellen White endorses any given doctrine; it is carved in stone from that point forward. And Ellen White regrettably endorsed the Investigative Judgment from the beginning.

The denomination doesn't get its unity through a sense of shared community, not so much through a common ethos, but through a unified field of theology that gives the denomination its identity. This theology, in turn, justifies church leaders' moral and political authority. When that theology is challenged, or the membership begins even to *think* the leaders are considering altering or reinterpreting some point of the theology, they quickly withdraw support from the leadership and then from the entire church. This is a domino theory: if one doctrine goes, all the others follow in quick succession. It is a slippery slope; to step over the edge with one doctrine is to slide down all the way into apostasy. This is where Ford fatally erred: he stepped over the line.

In retrospect, the theological crises that overtook the Adventist church at this time were never really about the quest for truth, as I mistakenly, naively believed; they were about preserving uniformity and political authority. Political power was all bound up with the theology. That the Adventist church claims to be the primary depository of the infallible, indisputable truth of Christian faith gives its leadership enormous power over the minds and hearts of the faithful. I mistakenly thought these were primarily theological crises; they were rather an intermingling of politics and theology. They could not be so neatly separated. The authority of the denomination and its leaders had to be maintained, whatever the cost. Prick one hole in the Adventist doctrinal balloon and the whole denomination might have the air sucked right out of it. Political chaos and anarchy! Obviously, there were exceptions to this attitude among the church's leaders. There were some courageous leaders who were truly interested in getting at the truth about the gospel and the Investigative Judgment. But they were few and far between, too few to make a real difference.

As confusion spread, Adventist scholars like Gerhard Hasel, Professor of Biblical Theology at Andrews University, went hither and yon trying to put out the doctrinal firestorm. Like me, Hasel had earned his doctorate at Vanderbilt University. I caught up with him when he gave a lecture in the Chattanooga First Adventist Church. Unflinchingly loyal to traditional Adventist theology—one of the few Adventist scholars who could be so identified—Hasel surprisingly admitted to the audience that Adventists had a problem with the translation of "cleansed" in the KJV of Dan 8:14, a key term in the doctrine of the Investigative Judgment. The word *tsadaq* in the Hebrew text should be rendered "restore" or "justify," not "cleansed," he said. So Dan 8:14 was about restoring or vindicating the sanctuary, not cleansing it from sin, as Adventists had long taught. He also admitted that several foundational dates involved in calculating the 2300-year time span to arrive at 1844 were suspect. What was the precise year of Jesus' birth? Was it 10, 6, 4, or 3 BCE? When between 27 and 34 CE did the crucifixion of Jesus take place? In what year did the 2300-year prophecy actually begin? In 458 or 457 BCE? "We must suspend our judgment until all the facts are in," he urged the audience of about four hundred.[11] I was amazed at his forthrightness. Not twenty miles away at nearby Southern Adventist University, the religion faculty had been accused of heresy and threatened with the loss of their livelihood for merely conceding the same difficulties.

At Southern, President Frank Knittel, leading a faculty now caught between trying to maintain intellectual honesty and mounting opposition in the constituency and the churches, urged tolerance and patience, like Hasel. "Differences of belief, even very serious difficulties," he passionately implored in one faculty assembly, "including theological ones, don't constitute anarchy or disorder per se." Referring to the problems with Daniel 8, he continued, "Arguments about the sanctuary in our church are as old as the church itself, and within these arguments are valid differences of opinion."

As I listened to Knittel, I thought about what might be learned from Adventist history. Was history repeating itself? There had been Albion F. Ballenger (1861–1921), an Adventist minister, editor, and administrator, whose earlier case strikingly paralleled that of Ford. Ballenger resigned from a dull editorial position with the Adventist National Religious Liberty Association (now the denomination's Religious Liberty Association) to

11. Hasel, "Daniel 8."

participate in evangelistic activity in Wales and Ireland. While there he ran into difficulty while trying to find the Investigative Judgment in the book of Hebrews (the same problem Ford would have seventy years later). The book of Hebrews did not know of a special ministry of Christ in the heavenly sanctuary in 1844, centuries later, Ballenger concluded. In Hebrews, Christ ascended directly into the presence of God (Heb 9:23–28). He didn't pass through the Holy place, then into the Holy of Holies in 1844.

When he submitted his views to a special review committee, the committee unanimously forbade him to publish them. "Keep your difficulties to yourself. Don't publicize them." Unlike Ford, who agreed to keep the problems to himself, Ballenger stubbornly refused. He was subsequently dismissed from the Adventist clergy. "If I accept the testimony of the Scriptures," he sadly wrote to the Adventist leadership, "I find myself under your condemnation; and you call me a wolf in sheep's clothing, and warn my brethren and the members of my family against me. But when I turn in my sorrow to the Word of the Lord, that Word reads the same." Heartbroken and crushed, he turned away from Adventism, where he had been ordained in 1893, with the sad confession, "I fear to reject God's interpretation and accept yours . . . I must go on my pilgrimage alone."[12] For a number of years afterward, until his death in 1921, he continued to proclaim his views primarily to Adventist audiences, but with little success.

In recent years there had been the case of Raymond F. Cottrell, longtime associate editor of the *Adventist Review*, and one of the associate editors of the seven-volume *Seventh-day Adventist Bible Commentary* (1953–1957). During the preparation of volume 4, which contains the book of Daniel, Cottrell became acutely aware of the difficulties in the Adventist interpretation. "There are no definite statements in the Bible which support the view of SDA [*sic*] on this point," he wrote in a summary of his conclusions. The doctrine of the Investigative Judgment appears to be "derived from the teachings of Mrs. White, which, in turn, are the result of *her interpretation* of the Bible." Boldly he confessed, "The [Investigative Judgment], to me, is the most colossal, psychological, face-saving phenomenon in religious history . . . [I] personally do not believe that there is a suspicion of a verse in Scripture to sustain such a peculiar position."[13]

Responding to Cottrell's concerns, the General Conference formed a special, confidential "Daniel" Committee, charged with resolving some of the difficulties. Cottrell labored faithfully on the committee, which disbanded a few years later without resolution. It gave up on solving the problem.

12. Ballenger, *Cast Out*, 111–12.
13. Cottrell, quoted in Ford, *Daniel 8:14*, 61–62. Italics in the original.

After he retired and could speak more openly, thus no longer under denominational constraint, Cottrell went public. He told audiences from coast to coast, particularly after the Ford condemnation at Glacier View, that the Adventist doctrine of the Investigative Judgment could not be sustained from the biblical text. Instead, it was derived from Ellen White, who played to role of an "inspired reinterpreter" similar to the New Testament writers' inspired reinterpretation of the Old.[14] Cottrell's view, as he admitted, leaves Adventism in the embarrassing position of having its signature, unique doctrine based entirely upon Ellen White's reinterpretation of the Bible. Inherently within the doctrine of the Investigative Judgment there was thus concealed a fundamental challenge to Ellen White's credibility. Ellen White's authority would now become the third theological crisis to overtake the church.

Cottrell and Ballenger were but two prominent Adventists I remembered that day in the faculty meeting while Knittel spoke. They had serious reservations with the doctrine of the Investigative Judgment. They were joined by many others, whose names have mostly been lost.[15] The denomination's response had been essentially the same in every instance: leadership initially tried to ignore the voices of dissent, and then, in some cases, drove the dissenters out of the church. Ironically, a denomination that had so frequently condemned other denominations for refusing to listen and change on the basis of Scripture had proven unwilling itself to alter its course when its moment of truth had arrived.[16]

By the time the Ford controversy had escalated into denomination-wide proportions, I was no longer teaching the course in Daniel, and so was not

14. More precisely, Ellen White in her early vision about the events connected with 1844 was merely following the interpretation of Hiram Edson (and O. R. L. Crosier) before her (*Early Writings*, 54–56). She would later elaborate this vision and set out in fuller detail what became the traditional interpretation of Adventism. See Damsteegt, *Foundations*, 122–23.

15. Ford offers a much more extensive list, some of whom have already been mentioned: O. R. L. Crosier, whose views helped create the doctrine, but who later repudiated it. James White (Ellen's husband), D. M. Canright, E. J. Waggoner, A. F. and E. Ballenger, W. W. Fletcher, L. R. Conradi, W. W. Prescott, L. E. Froom, Harold Snide, R. A. Grieve, R. D. Brinsmead, R. A. Cottrell, C. G. Tuland, Earl Hilgert, and D. Sibley (see Ford, *Daniel 8:14*, 25–67).

16. A careful reading of General Conference, *Adventists Believe* (2nd ed.) shows that, while some of the language has been modified to clarify the role of justification by faith as the ground of one's acceptance with God, the Investigative Judgment, based on Daniel 8, Leviticus 16, and Hebrews remains firmly in place (347–69).

so publicly exposed when the first wave of criticism swept across Adventist college campuses. However, in one of the classes I did teach—Christian Beliefs—a part of the curriculum dealt with the unique Adventist interpretation of Daniel 8. This beginning level course was in the college general education curriculum, so all religion professors were expected to teach it or an equivalent. My syllabus for the course was arranged along the lines of a systematic theology so that the topic of the Investigative Judgment, being an aspect of eschatology, appeared last among the topics to be studied. By that point in the semester students were weary. As I reviewed the topic in class, I recall intentionally using expressions such as "the church teaches," or "the church believes" that implicitly put a little distance between my own personal awareness and the church's official doctrines. I didn't make it personal by saying, "I believe." I honestly admitted to the class there were difficulties, however, but that more research needed to be done.

Was I upset by the all the gossip, the condemnation and threats? Obviously. These were scary, worrisome times to be an Adventist scholar. I constantly worried about my family. Laura was now in a doctoral program in counseling psychology at Vanderbilt University. School expenses for both her and our daughters (who were enrolled in private Adventist schools) were mounting and we were having a difficult time making ends meet. What if I lost my job over all this? I'd unwisely staked my whole career— my whole life—on Adventism. I had no backup plan. There was no plan B. Where would I go if I got fired? What would I do to make a living? What right had I to risk the future of Laura and our daughters, JoAnna and Paula, on account of my mounting concerns? Why should I "die on the hill" of an obscure, esoteric interpretation of Daniel? The hard knot of anxiety within refused to dissolve. I felt terribly conflicted.

With Desmond Ford, two integrally related theological problems now merged and coursed frighteningly through Adventist arteries: the denomination's traditional understanding of justification, and the church's unique doctrine of the Investigative Judgment. It was hard to avoid what most of the denomination's critics had been saying all along, that the intricate, complicated Investigative Judgment represented a fanciful, face-saving spin early Adventists had given to the embarrassing nineteenth-century Millerite failure. More than a century of silence, suppression, and cover up had finally borne bitter fruit. But the worst was yet to come.

9

Ellen White in the Dock

> Do not quench the Spirit. Do not despise the words of prophets,
> but test everything; hold fast to what is good.
>
> —*St. Paul*

Sometimes the struggle felt like pulling threads out of an old wool cardigan. When I pulled one thread, it was connected to still another. The whole Adventist theological cardigan seemed to be unraveling, thread by thread, going to pieces in my hands.

In Long Beach, California, veteran Adventist pastor Walter Rea, right on the heels of the Ford controversy, pulled loose still another thread.

Rea inadvertently discovered that Ellen White (1827–1915), Adventism's revered prophet and co-founder, while insisting that her extensive writings originated in inspired, divine revelation, had apparently surreptitiously borrowed a significant amount of her literary output from other authors. Rea's discovery sent shock waves through Adventism. Paxton had already pointed out the denomination's embarrassingly confused jumble of ideas about the meaning of the gospel. Ford had challenged the church's triumphal, unique eschatological claims about the Investigative Judgment. Now, by casting suspicion upon Ellen White, Rea had dared to rush in where angels fear to tread.

Ironically, Walter Rea had long been a passionate devotee of Ellen White. As a teenager, he'd learned to type by using her books as literary models. In college he had made extensive compilations of her comments on the Bible. Upon entering the pastorate, he had incorporated these compilations into a two-volume edition of Old and New Testament biographies, drawn exclusively from Ellen White. A third volume had followed on the apocalyptic books of Daniel and Revelation, again drawing entirely from White. Rea had up to now been unflinchingly loyal. He had sought in Ellen White's writings guidance for everything in his life.

Matters started to unravel a few years earlier when a member of Rea's congregation had given him a worn copy of *Elisha the Prophet*, a book written by the nineteenth-century scholar Alfred Edersheim (1825–1889). This copy was more than antique. Ellen White's signature adorned the flyleaf! Knowing that the book had once belonged to Ellen White, and that she had literally touched its pages and her eyes had fallen upon it, Rea clutched it reverently like a sacred relic. Eagerly he plunged into reading it. Because of his thorough acquaintance with White's writings, he couldn't help but notice scores of seemingly inexplicable literary parallels between Edersheim and what White had written in some of her major popular works.

Then he came across a two-volume history of the Old Testament also written by Edersheim.[1] He found that many of Edersheim's chapter titles, subtitles, and even individual page headings amazingly corresponded to those in White's *Patriarchs and Prophets* (1890). His curiosity piqued, Rea undertook a more extensive investigation. What he found astonished him. White had also used Edersheim's New Testament history[2] in the composition of her popular life of Christ, *The Desire of Ages* (1898). His search widened. He found other nineteenth century books from which Ellen White had apparently taken material, especially William Hanna's *Life of Christ*,[3] also used for the *Desire of Ages*.

Rea recalled that White's book, *Sketches from the Life of Paul*, published in 1883, had later been curiously withdrawn from circulation. At the time there were accusations that in *Sketches* White had liberally plagiarized *The Life and Epistles of Saint Paul*, by W. J. Conybeare and John S. Howson.[4] For Rea, discovery of such extensive borrowing on the part of Ellen White was unnerving. Some Adventist church leaders, it turned out, had apparently for almost a century known about such literary borrowing by Ellen White.[5] The church's traditional view of Ellen White—the one I had embraced along with Rea—was that she received her fully-formed ideas directly from God

1. Edersheim, *Bible History*, 2 vols.

2. Edersheim, *Life and Times of Jesus the Messiah*, 5 vols.

3. Hanna, *Life of Christ* (1863).

4. Conybeare and Howson, *Life and Epistles of Saint Paul*, 2 vols. For a discussion these allegations together with an Adventist response, see Nichol, *White and Critics*, 403–67.

5. See Nichol, *White and Critics*, 403–515, for other instances of such borrowing.

and, although she had literary assistants to help her put the manuscript into proper grammatical shape for publication, the actual content was original with her. "My views were written independent of books," White had insisted early in her career, "or of the opinions of others."[6] Did this assertion apply also to her later career (after 1867)? Did it apply to the books Rea now put in question? Rea had accidentally uncovered a more massive amount of borrowing than the church—or Ellen White—had ever admitted. White had borrowed theological ideas, exegetical insights, literary structure, section titles, and frequently individual words and expressions from sources she had at hand, without any acknowledgement. Here is an example with the exact borrowing in italics:

> *The Great Teacher*
> John Harris (1836, 1870)
>
> Having authoritatively announced his will, he [Christ] can carry it into all the recesses of the soul, and, in perfect harmony with our free volition, can *so identify it with our thoughts and aims, so blend* it with the stream and current of our consciousness, that in *yielding obedience* to his word we are only obeying the actings and *impulses of our own minds.*

> *The Desire of Ages*
> E. G. White (1898)
>
> All true obedience comes from the heart. It was heart work with Christ. And if we consent, He will *so identify* Himself *with our thoughts and aims, so blend* our hearts and minds into conformity to His will, that when obeying Him we shall be but carrying out *our own impulses.*

It is readily apparent that White's paragraph is based on Harris. Ellen White has appropriated ideas, phrases, and clauses, then shortened the paragraph. This type of resonance, as far as Rea could tell, extended through most of Ellen White's published material. With the exception of the editions of *The Great Controversy* (1884, 1888, 1911), she had never given any acknowledgment of her literary sources. In at least one known instance White attached a phrase she sometimes used to identify a direct divine

---

6. Ellen G. White Manuscript 27, 1867, quoted in Arthur L. White, *Ellen G. White,* 16. In one instance, faced with the similarity of some of her writings on the subject of health in other publications, she claimed that, after writing the articles, she discovered similar ideas in other publications, and so used these to develop her own work (White, *How to Live* [1865]).

revelation, "He [Christ, the Great Teacher] said," to material she appears to have borrowed.

> White, *Testimonies for Church* (1900), 6:58–59:
>
> We have the Great Teacher with us today . . . He said: "There is a great work before you *in this place . . .* "
>   *Here are themes worthy* of our contemplation . . . Here is *infinite wisdom, infinite love, infinite justice, infinite mercy. Here are depths and heights, lengths and breadths, for our consideration. Numberless pens have been employed in presenting to the world the life, the character, and the mediatorial work of Christ.*

> John Harris, *The Great Teacher* [from the introduction by Herman Humphrey (1836)]:
>
> *Here* then, Christian reader, is a *theme worthy* of an angel's pen . . . *infinite wisdom—infinite love—infinite justice—infinite mercy! Depths, heights, length, breadth—all passing knowledge! Innumerable pens have been employed in presenting to the world the life, the character, and the mediatorial work of Christ.*

Did Ellen White intend the words following the "Great Teacher" appellation to be taken as from Jesus Christ? This is unclear, as Ron Graybill has admitted.[7] This instance, however, remains a remarkable example of the type of borrowing at issue. It is easy to see that the White paragraph, written more than sixty years later, is heavily indebted to Humphrey.

"Although I am as dependent upon the Spirit of the Lord in writing my views as I am in receiving them," she had written in 1867, "yet the words I employ in describing what I have seen are my own." Evidently, this wasn't always the case, at least in her later writings. Without giving appropriate credit, she used the words, phrases, and ideas of others in her books and numerous articles.

Alarmed at what he had found, Rea appealed to the Ellen G. White Estate for assistance. The White Estate is the official denominational trustee of the White literary corpus, at that time located in Takoma Park, Maryland. The Estate typically advocates for Ellen White, so Rea supposed it might not be too eager to collaborate in his investigation. Rea therefore advised that either he, or preferably, an independent investigator play an important role in the analysis. The White Estate wouldn't agree to this condition. They felt, quite reasonably, that as the legal trustees of White's literary archives, such an investigation lay within their area of responsibility. Weren't they the

---

7. Graybill, "Did White 'Borrow?'" 7.

custodians of White's legacy? Exasperated by this refusal, Rea, who had a well-earned reputation for persistence, continued to press the issue. Unwilling to take "no" for an answer, he kept prodding the White Estate. After several repeated appeals, Rea gave up. He independently published his findings in a book significantly titled *The White Lie*.[8]

The White Lie was taken by church leaders as a full-scale assault on Ellen White. Typically, manuscripts written by Adventist authors for circulation mainly within the church or in public venues are carefully reviewed by the church's literary editors (censors?) to make sure that no ideas contrary to Adventist doctrine may be found in them. By going to an independent publisher, Rea bypassed this crucial review, and thus aroused the ire of the church's autocratic leaders. Perhaps feeling put off, like a jilted lover, by Ellen White herself, to whose legacy he had devoted much of his life, Rea hastily reacted. He brazenly challenged one of the central pillars of Adventism. No person in Adventist history is revered more than Ellen White. No one is considered more important. She stands head and shoulders above every other Seventh-day Adventist who has ever lived.

Here's why. In December 1844, just after the fortuitous demise of the Millerite movement, seventeen-year-old Ellen Harmon was humbly praying in the company of four other women, when she fell into some kind of a spiritual trance. In a vision she saw the beleaguered Millerites, spurned and scorned by all the established denominations, en route to the heavenly kingdom. She witnessed the glorious Second Advent of Jesus and the triumphal entry of the saints into heaven.[9]

Discouraged already by two humiliating failed predictions about the arrival of the Second Advent, the most recent having been October 22, a scant two months earlier, many Millerites welcomed this dream from the young Ellen Harmon. Several similar trance-like experiences followed, during which Ellen exhibited several remarkable physical manifestations. She lost all awareness of her surroundings, yet while in an ecstatic trance even the strongest person present was unable to restrain her physical movements. During one such experience that incredibly lasted more than four hours, she appeared not to breathe at all, although her heartbeat remained constant. Ellen went on to wed a young Millerite preacher by the name of James Springer White (1821–1881), and together they guided the founding and development of the Seventh-day Adventist church after the ill-fated breakup

---

8. Rea, *White Lie*. In five appendices in this book, Rea offers over a hundred pages that indicate White's literary dependence upon external sources (281–409).

9. This dream is recounted in White, *Early Writings*, 13–19.

of the Millerite movement. Their role in the early development has earned them the title of co-founders of the nascent Adventist movement.

Singularly impressed by Ellen White's experiences, early Seventh-day Adventists came to believe she had experienced an ecstasy similar to that of the biblical prophets.[10] They believed she had received the biblical gift of prophecy. New Testament scholars have since pointed out that prophecy in the early Christian church was more like what we now call fervent, spirit-filled preaching than ancient Hebrew prophecy,[11] but Adventists have consistently interpreted Ellen White's experiences as being in continuity with Old Testament charismatic, prophetic manifestations.[12] They believe she carried on the tradition of the great prophets of the Old Testament: Isaiah, Jeremiah, Ezekiel, and others. Of her visions, Ellen White wrote:

> In ancient times God spoke to men by the mouth of prophets and apostles. In these days He speaks to them by the *Testimonies* of His Spirit. There was never a time when God instructed His people more earnestly than He instructs them now concerning His will and the course that He would have them pursue.[13]

Her early public experiences, with their charismatic phenomena, called "visions," appear to have subsided over time, the last occurring in 1879 or 1884 (the date is disputed). They gave way to episodes known as "night visions" or "prophetic dreams," private experiences during the night hours. Most of her writings, she claimed, came out of these night experiences. Over her lifetime, it is estimated that she had approximately 2,000 visions.

Although she had only about three grades of formal education, over the next seventy years she preached extensively and wrote even more voluminously. She composed an incredible 4,600 magazine articles, 200 tracts, 6,000 manuscripts, 2,000 letters and journal entries, and more than 24

10. Note Balaam, who "falls down, but with eyes uncovered" (Num 24:4); Jeremiah, who "shakes" (Jer 23:9); Daniel, who says of his trance, "strength left me; and my complexion grew deathly pale, and I retained no strength," but whose vision was not perceived by those around him at the time (Dan 10:7–9). Such phenomena have sporadically appeared in Christian history (see Lindblom, *Prophecy*, 1–46). For the New Testament, see 1 Cor 12:10, 28; 14:1; Eph 4:11–12.

11. Thus Paul writes to the Corinthians, "Let two or three prophets speak, and let the others weigh what is said" (1 Cor 14:29). To the Thessalonians he counsels, "Do not quench the Spirit. Do not despise the words of prophets, but test everything; hold fast to what is good" (1 Thess 5:19–21). These Christian prophets were subject to evaluation by the congregation.

12. See Jemison, *Prophet Among You*, 33–75. This was a textbook used extensively in Adventist college classes, including the class I had taken in the writings of Ellen White while in college.

13. White, *Testimonies for Church*, 4:147–48.

books. She toured the United States, Europe, and Australia, until at least age eighty-one, when she preached seventy-two times in twenty-seven different locations. She commented on topics ranging from biblical interpretation and theology to health, church administration, pastoral life, and domestic relations. When she died in California on July 16, 1915, she left an enormous literary legacy that continues powerfully to influence the Adventist church today.[14]

Adventists reverently speak of her literary heritage as the "Spirit of Prophecy," a term drawn from the Apocalypse, "the testimony of Jesus is the *spirit of prophecy*" (Rev 19:10). The Adventist use of this particular passage reflects more than verbal affinity. By linking this passage with Rev 12:17, which employs the same terminology, "testimony of Jesus," Adventists stake out their claim of the gift of prophecy, along with the observance of the seventh-day Sabbath, as the singular marks of the final, last-day church. "The dragon was angry with the woman [the church], and went off to make war on the rest of her children, those who keep the *commandments of God* and hold the *testimony of Jesus*" (Rev. 12:17).

How did Ellen White go about writing so many books and articles? Adventists believe she received the basic ideas in visions or dreams. These she wrote out as carefully as she could.

Her writings abound in expressions like, "August 24, 1850, I saw . . . "; "God has given me a testimony of reproof for parents who treat their children as you do your little one . . . "; or "From time to time I have been permitted to behold . . . "[15] With such expressions she attributed her writings to a divine source. However, in matter written for non-Adventist audiences, like the *Desire of Ages*, her account of the life of Christ, because they would unduly prejudice the reader, she eliminated such expressions. But what lay behind the actual content of these more popular trade books, she claimed, was also revealed to her in vision.

Due to lack of education, what she laboriously wrote out in pen and ink often required editorial refinement. Consequently, others amended her manuscripts so that they would be editorially acceptable. Before his death in 1881, James White performed this role. In subsequent years various editorial assistants, such as Marian Davis (1847–1904) and D. E. Robinson (1879–1957), took over these tasks. Acting as copy editors, these assistants improved the literary quality, eliminated unnecessary repetition, sharpened

14. A chronological listing of all her writings appears in Fortin and Moon, *EGWEnc*, Appendix C, 1300–1465.

15. White, *Early Writings*, 59; *Great Controversy*, x; Ellen G. White, Letter 1 (1877), respectively. (The correspondence of Ellen White has been archived at the White Estate, and designated by number and year of origination.)

sentences, and otherwise shaped the passages with an eye for correct syntax.[16] Of Marian Davis' work, Ellen White recalled:

> She takes my articles which are published in the papers, and pastes them in blank books. She also has a copy of all the letters I write. In preparing a chapter for a book, Marian remembers that I have written something on that special point, which may make the matter more forcible. She begins to search for this, and if when she finds it, she sees that it will make the chapter more clear, she adds it. The books are not Marian's productions, but my own, gathered from all my writings.[17]

For certain volumes, like the *Desire of Ages*, in other words, Ellen White's editors compiled materials on specific themes drawn from her voluminous manuscript collection. They then arranged these in a cut-and-paste fashion in notebooks. This technically amounted to a new redaction of her writings. Moreover, White insisted, never were these literary assistants "permitted to add matter or change the meaning of the messages I write out."[18] White relied heavily upon this process especially in her later declining years. The editors carefully preserved White's content, always submitting it to her for approval before going to press.

After her death in 1915, her will authorized the trustees to prepare in timely fashion compilations of her published and unpublished materials.[19] So successful in this has been the White Estate until today these compilations equal or exceed in number the actual books produced during her lifetime.

Where in this process did the alleged borrowing occur? Adventists have consistently maintained that the content of Ellen White's visions, which she wrote out in longhand, closely mirrored the actual vision, not that of any secondary source.[20] As we have seen, Ellen White herself strenuously protested that her literary assistants added anything to what she had written. If we take her word for it, the borrowing must have occurred primarily at the point when she initially wrote out the vision, but before her editors got hold of it. This is precisely what Adventist historian, Donald McAdams, discovered. In 1974, a few years before Rea, in a less-publicized but detailed

16. Denton Rebok describes the process in *Believe His Prophets*, 197–200.

17. Ellen G. White, Letter 61a (1900), quoted in Nichol, *White and Critics*, 477.

18. White, "The Writing and Sending Out of the Testimonies to the Church," 4, quoted in Jemison, *Prophet Among You*, 331.

19. *Adventist Encyclopedia*, 1406–18; Olson, "Preparation," 663–68.

20. On this see Arthur White, *White Writings*, 79–105.

study of White's most widely circulated work, *The Great Controversy*, McAdams observed:

> What we find when we examine the historical portions of the
> *Great Controversy* is that large sections are selective abridgements and adaptations of historians. What Ellen White was
> doing was not just borrowing paragraphs here and there that
> she ran across in her reading, but in fact following certain historians page after page, leaving out much material, but using
> their sequence, some of their ideas, and often their words. In
> the samples I have examined I have found no historical fact in
> her text that is not in their text. What we have in the handwritten manuscript appears to be an account based so closely on
> other historians that it does not even seem to have gone through
> an intermediary stage, but rather from the historians' printed
> page to Mrs. White's manuscript, including historical errors and
> moral exhortations.[21]

The preface to the 1911 edition of *The Great Controversy* carried an
admission that Ellen White had quoted literary sources in cases "where a
historian has so grouped together events to afford, in brief, a comprehensive
view of the subject." This was done, she claimed, not "for the purpose of
citing that writer as authority, but because his statement affords a ready and
forcible presentation of the subject."[22] To the contrary, McAdams learned,
her dependence upon such historical sources was clearly more extensive
than this concession implied. Furthermore, she made only this single concession in all her extant 100,000 pages of writing.

McAdams's conclusion agrees with an anecdote related by Dudley
Canright, a former associate of Ellen White:

> One Advent sister who had been with Mrs. White for ten years
> told the author personally that she had seen her copying from
> a book in her lap. When visitors came in she would cover the
> book with her apron until they had gone, then proceed with her
> copying. Her works show that the sister told the truth.

---

21. McAdams, "White and Historians," unpublished manuscript, 19. See
Brinsmead, "Legend of Ellen White," 15. Earlier (1970), William S. Peterson had discovered inaccuracies in White's account of the French Revolution ("Textual and Historical Study," 57–69).

22. White, *Great Controversy* (1911), xii. This caveat also appears in the 1888
edition.

Canright calls this "literary theft," the purloining of "another's writings" and offering them to the public as one's own.[23]

It is precisely the general lack of acknowledgment, even denial of it, not the borrowing itself, that creates the problem. Nowhere in her writings, except in the preface to *Great Controversy*, does Ellen White give any hint that she was indebted to other authors. She leaves readers to think— whether intentionally or unintentionally—that she received her messages from God, but expressed them in her own literary style. What Ellen White apparently did to the contrary, were it a dissertation submitted to a modern university or book manuscript submitted to a modern publisher, would be called "plagiarism." Most likely it would disqualify the person at the university who dared to submit it. Plagiarism is the act of taking ideas, words, or thoughts from the writings of another and representing them as one's own. The *Guide to American Law* defines it as the "act of appropriating the literary composition of another, or excerpts, ideas, and passages therefrom, and passing off as one's own creation."[24] Yet Adventists categorically deny that Ellen White plagiarized.[25]

The whole issue reminds us of one of Ellen White's older contemporaries who also claimed prophetic inspiration. Founder of the Church of Jesus Christ of Latter-Day Saints (the Mormons), Joseph Smith Jr. (1805– 1844), claimed to have received the *Book of Mormon* (1832) and other writings through a process of prophetic discernment and vision. Shortly after the *Book of Mormon* appeared, however, it was noticed that its plot and literary style resembled that of a novel by Solomon Spaulding, so it was then alleged that Smith had borrowed his material from Spaulding. The Latter-Day Saints, of course, deny the "Spaulding Theory," as it is called,[26] but it is one of the interesting parallels between the Mormon movement and Adventism.

23. Canright, *Life of E. G. White*, 201.

24. *Guide to Law*, 8:207. Plagiarism is "copying the text of a work created by someone else and passing it off as your own" (Collin, *Dictionary of Law*, 2nd ed., 178).

25. The denomination retained Vincent L. Ramik of Diller, Ramik and Wight, in Washington, D.C., a law firm specializing in legal matters in publishing, to examine the matter. Using the *Great Controversy, Desire of Ages*, and *Sketches from the Life of Paul*, Ramik concluded that "Ellen G. White was not a plagiarist and her works did not constitute copyright infringement/privacy" (MEMORANDUM OF LAW LITERARY PROPERTY RIGHTS 1790–1915 [1981], 26–27); Kenneth Wood makes reference to this legal brief in "Ellen White's Sources," 3. Ramik was obviously using legal rather than ethical categories. In White's day, the crediting of one's sources was not rigorously maintained. In the light of legal precedents of the time, White may not be strictly guilty of illegal plagiarism, but even this is debatable. Her tendency to borrow freely and represent the results as her own, however, remains a serious ethical problem for White and the Adventist church.

26. See Chase, "Spaulding Manuscript," 602–4.

Now, thanks to Walter Rea, a denomination weary of controversy was learning that, not only had Ellen White "paraphrased" historians and theologians, she had often represented the "borrowed" phrases and ideas as revealed to her by the Lord. Rea's discovery forced from a surprised General Conference President Neal Wilson an admission that White had used far more sources in her writing than the church had ever been aware![27] Ellen White, seemingly prophet of austere, uncompromising morality, now stood accused of unethical practice in the very medium she routinely employed. It seemed to be an egregious betrayal, not only to Rea, but to other devoted followers as well.

Unsettling, painful questions about White's credibility now swept like blustery winds across the Adventist denomination. Did Ellen White really see visions or have dreams? Were her dreams or visions—charismatic experiences—misunderstood by her and the Adventist community? Had she fabricated such experiences, instead furtively copying material from other sources and claiming it for her very own? How credible was her denial that what she saw in vision she wrote down in her own words? Why didn't she enclose the words of other sources in quotation marks, or at least give credit, as should any author who legitimately borrows material? Why not throughout her writings admit indebtedness, instead of implicitly leaving the impression her work ultimately derived solely from divine revelatory experiences?

It gradually came to light that a small group of Adventist leaders close to Ellen White had known of her extensive copying almost from the beginning, but had deliberately withheld it from the general membership. Educator W. W. Prescott (1855–1944), then a secretary of the General Conference, for example, wrote to W. C. White, Ellen's son and trustee of her writings:

> The way your mother's writings have been handled and the false impression concerning them which is still fostered among the people have brought great perplexity and trial to me . . . it is no use to go into these matters. I have talked with you for years about them, but it brings no change. I think however that we are drifting toward a crisis which will come sooner or later and perhaps sooner.[28]

27. Wilson, "This I Believe," 8.

28. W. W. Prescott to W. C. White, 6 April 1915, as quoted in Brinsmead, *Judged by the Gospel*, 153.

That crisis had finally arrived. One day in class, while the dispute about Ellen White swirled all around us outside the classroom, I summarized a point I was making by quoting from Ellen White. From the back of the classroom of thirty students a deep voice sarcastically boomed, "From *where* did she copy *that*?" I had been looking down, reading from my lecture notes. Startled by the question, I quickly glanced up, but couldn't immediately determine the inquirer.

"I'm afraid I don't know," I said, and let the comment hang, unresolved, in the air.

Like many anxious church members, students seemed apprehensive about what was going on with Ellen White. She had alarmingly been called into question. And with her, the entire Adventist theology and mission that depended so heavily upon Ellen White was now suddenly put at risk. Ellen White now sat appallingly in the dock.

10

The Interrogation of Ellen White

Inquiry is human; blind obedience brutal.
Truth never loses by the one but often suffers by the other.

—*WILLIAM PENN*

C hurch leaders, convinced that Rea was essentially a disgruntled mal-
content, a gadfly who had no business continually pestering them,
impulsively reacted, just as they had done with Ford. Walter Rea, fed up
by months of delay on the part of the White Estate, leaked the scandalous
story of Ellen White's borrowing to the *Los Angeles Times*.[1] In so doing he
publicly exposed the White problem. Adventist leaders immediately fired
him. They then punitively voided his ministerial license. "Rea's action toward one of the denomination's highly respected pioneers," sharply rebuked
C. E. Bradford, president of the North American (Adventist) Division, "has
rendered him incapable of serving as an Adventist minister."[2]

Getting rid of the informant was only half the battle, however. The
Ellen White problem Rea had exposed was still there. Adventist leaders

---

1. Dart, "Plagiarism." This article preceded Rea's study, *The White Lie* (1982),
mentioned above. The article was reprinted the next day in the *Chattanooga [TN]
Times*, October 24, 1980.

2. Press release issued from the General Conference of Seventh-day Adventists, quoted in *Unlock Your Potential* 15 (1980) 23. In an interview with Walter Rea,
conducted by J. B. Goodner, Helmut Ott, Steven Zimmerman, and Jerry Gladson, on
September 20, 1981, Rea bitterly accused Adventist leadership of "stonewalling" about
White's literary borrowing. By publishing his findings independently he intended to
"force" the church to deal with the problem.

frantically now turned to Fred Veltman, a veteran New Testament scholar trained in source and literary criticism, methods used in biblical studies to detect external sources and evaluate the integrity of biblical documents, to investigate the validity of Rea's claims. Given the denomination's earlier opposition to historical and literary criticism of the Bible, this move in itself was remarkable. The denomination was now turning to contemporary historical criticism, an approach to the Bible that the church had widely condemned, for assistance in defending Ellen White's integrity. Veltman was on the religion faculty at Pacific Union College, the same denominational college at which Desmond Ford had once taught until he had been similarly fired. Veltman was to spend the next eight years (1980–1988) critically examining a fifteen-chapter sample of the *Desire of Ages* for traces of undocumented borrowing.

First published in 1898, Ellen White's best-selling biography of Christ, *The Desire of Ages*, is probably her most popular, full-scale work, especially among Adventists. It was compiled from Ellen White's articles, letters, manuscripts, and journals, both published and unpublished sources, in the years preceding the final redaction of the book. White had earlier written on the life of Jesus in her *Spirit of Prophecy*, volumes 2–3,[3] and in many articles and pamphlets. In the 1890s, while in Australia, she began the task of producing a major work on the life of Christ. White delegated to Marian Davis, whom she called "my bookmaker," the responsibility of assembling the materials. Either Davis or White collected far more than just White's own writings, as the Veltman study was soon to reveal.

Since we served on BRICOM during those eight years I had several substantive conversations with Veltman about this project. "Fred," I cautioned him once after a BRICOM session, "considering that the church has already terminated Walter Rea and Desmond Ford for uncovering things they weren't supposed to find, do you think it's sensible to go through with your project?"

Shaking his head, Veltman nervously waved me aside. "Many others have told me the same thing. But I really want to know the truth. I've been assured, however, that nothing like Rea experienced will happen to me. My project—unlike Rea's—is sponsored by the General Conference."

"So was Ford's. And you know what happened to him!"[4] I considered Fred a personal friend. And I was worried about him, given how the General Conference had handled the Ford situation.

3. White, *Spirit of Prophecy*, 4 vols.

4. In a postscript to his final study, Veltman candidly wrote: "In October 1980, soon after I accepted the responsibility for conducting this research into Ellen White's use of sources, I was advised to back out of my commitment. The project was described

eight years with the project, however, I remain confident that the evidence will speak

By the time he completed his massive, one-thousand-page study, I was then living in Atlanta and no longer employed by the Adventist church, but Fred and I were both partly right. Fred didn't lose his job; neither were his findings widely disseminated. For the most part, they have been generally ignored, which is perhaps the saddest, most disappointing outcome of all.

While Veltman quietly toiled in the bowels of musty libraries, the denomination sustained further damaging news about Ellen White. Sixty years earlier, Dudley Canright had advanced the claim that White's visions were actually the result of epilepsy or a similar physical condition stemming from an injury sustained in childhood. At nine years of age, Ellen had suffered a severe trauma when a playmate struck her on the head with a heavy stone.[5] Two Adventist physicians, Delbert Hodder and Mollerus Couperus, now reexamined this injury in the light of Canright's epilepsy theory. Their conclusion: White's visions were the result of *partial-complex seizures*—temporal lobe or psychomotor epilepsy.

Many symptoms White manifested while in a visionary state, Hodder and Couperus noted, were consistent with partial-complex seizures. During such a seizure, although victims appear not to breathe, breathing nonetheless imperceptibly continues. Words or even sentences appear to escape involuntarily from the mouth, and the victim keeps the eyes open, sometimes looking upward. In the middle of a seizure, the person often engages in

---

as a 'no win' situation. There was no way, so I was told, that I could please both the General Conference administrators who had commissioned the study and those in the church who were raising questions about Ellen White's writing methods. As I now draw the project to a close I am no closer than I was then to knowing whether my 'prophet' friend was correct in his prediction. We will just have to wait and see. After nearly eight years with the project, however, I remain confident that the evidence will speak for itself. Truth is at stake here. It is not a matter of winning or losing." ("*Desire of Ages* Project," 949).

5. Canright, *Life of E. G. White*), 99–109. White describes her injury in these words: "I was stunned by the blow, and fell senseless to the ground . . . When [after three weeks], I again aroused to consciousness, it seemed to me that I had been asleep . . . a great cradle had been made for me, and in it I lay for many weeks. I was reduced almost to a skeleton . . . For two years I could not breathe through my nose, and was able to attend school but little. It seemed impossible for me to study and to retain what I learned . . . My nervous system was prostrated, and my hand trembled so that I made but little progress in writing, and could get no farther than the simple copies in coarse hand. As I endeavored to bend my mind to my studies, the letters in the page would run together, great drops of perspiration would stand upon my brow, and a faintness and dizziness would seize me. I had a bad cough, and my whole system seemed debilitated" (*Life Sketches*, 17–19). These are symptoms of severe concussive head trauma.

THE INTERROGATION OF ELLEN WHITE

automatic movements, such as slow, graceful motion of the shoulders, arms, and hands, or even walking about. A person may repeat words or hallucinate, experiencing brilliant visual or auditory stimuli.[6]

During the approximately two thousand visions in her lifetime, beginning in her teens, White manifested many of these symptoms. She appeared not to breathe. She gestured gracefully, or made large sweeping motions with her arms. Repeating words such as "glory, glory" over and over, she wrung her hands, walking back and forth. Vivid scenes swept over her consciousness. More significantly, White tended to write copiously about her impressions. Patients with temporal lobe epilepsy also often display hypergraphia—excessive, compulsive writing.[7]

This particular variety of epilepsy was not identified before the invention of the electroencephalograph (EEG), so physicians in Ellen White's day had no reliable means of diagnosing the problem. Because it was an uncommon form of epilepsy, it might easily have been minimized or, since it occurred in a religious setting, interpreted as a supernatural experience or perhaps even as divine inspiration. Even the victims, unaware of the nature of their disorder, could simply have accepted their experiences as supernatural. Hodder concluded:

> Mrs. White seemed unaware that the content of the visual hallucinations she thought were "visions" were part of a seizure, unaware that her personality traits and deep interest in religion were produced by her injury, unaware that her ability to write was itself a manifestation of her illness, she did what any honest God-fearing person would have to do in a similar situation— she shared them with others and it was these others who labeled her as a "prophet" and made her the center of the developing Seventh-day Adventist Church.[8]

Ellen White has long been gone, so no one will ever be able to diagnose conclusively temporal lobe epilepsy. Adventists are now left to ponder, however, not only whether White copied much of her written material, but whether she was also victim of undiagnosed temporal lobe epilepsy.

Through the years I have often been asked how I would explain the Ellen White phenomenon. Hodder's theory of temporal lobe epilepsy has

6. Delbert Hodder, "Ellen G. White," 1–10. A shorter version of this privately circulated paper appeared as "Visions or Partial-Complex Seizures," 30–37. See also Bear et al., "Behavioral Alterations," 197–227; Couperus, "Head Injury," 17–23; Couperus, "White and Epilepsy," 24–25. The denomination's defense may be found in Peterson, *Visions or Seizures?*

7. Waxman and Geschwind, "Hypergraphia," 314–17.

8. Hodder, "Ellen G. White," 15.

always seemed to me—though, admittedly, I'm not a psychiatrist—a plausible, at points even compelling *scientific* explanation. But it is limited and reductionistic. Immediately after the Hodder and Couperus theory made its appearance, the White Estate nervously assembled a team of Adventist mental health specialists who with little coaxing gave White a clean bill of physical and mental health. They decided that there was no convincing evidence she suffered from any type of epilepsy or that the complex partial seizures could adequately account for the beneficial role she had played in the development of the denomination. Ronald and Janet Numbers, otherwise critical of White, admitted that although Ellen White may have displayed many of the symptoms consistent with this diagnosis, "her behavior also differed in significant ways from what might be expected of someone experiencing complex partial seizures."[9] This neurological explanation, however, doesn't preclude a theological one. Ellen White and those who followed her no doubt believed that her experiences were of divine origin. For the faithful, it is conceivable that God providentially used White's pathology to accomplish good. She was certainly a stabilizing influence in the early development of the Seventh-day Adventist church. There is mystery here. Nevertheless, the temporal lobe epileptic explanation must be carefully considered when Ellen White's total experience is assessed.

With a double-edged sword now hanging over Ellen White, those of us in the pulpit and classroom had to try to make some sense of her experience and writings. Confidence in Ellen White in the Adventist community had suffered a serious, perhaps fatal blow.

Questions of credibility have long hovered around Ellen White. Almost a decade earlier than Hodder, Couperus, or Rea, a former classmate at Southern Adventist University, now professor of the history of medicine at the University of Wisconsin published *Prophetess of Health: A Study of Ellen G. White*. Adventists frequently claim that White's views on health and medicine, which form the theological basis for their worldwide health ministry, represent notable advances in health science. That she seemed to be ahead of her time has been considered an evidence of her divine inspiration. In *Prophetess of Health*, however, Ronald Numbers, cited above, a fourth generation Adventist, son of an Adventist minister, grandson of another, and relative of a General Conference president (the highest office in the denomination), demonstrated convincingly from the historical record that

9. Numbers, *Prophetess of Health* (3rd ed.), 278. The first edition of this work was published in 1976. References here to this work are to the third edition.

her views could largely if not entirely be traced to the health concepts of the nineteenth century. Furthermore, it was clear White had freely derived most of her ideas about health from her own milieu, ironically, in a fashion not unlike that of her literary borrowing. A couple of examples must suffice.

One of White's nineteenth-century sources was L. B. Coles, a health reformer and associate of William Miller, who wrote *The Philosophy of Health* and *The Beauties and Deformities of Tobacco-Using*. Coles emphasized the importance of proper diet, sunshine, fresh air, rest, exercise, temperance, cleanliness, and sensible dress as ways to optimum health. White picked up these same remedies, referring to them as "pure air, sunlight, abstemiousness, rest, exercise, proper diet, the use of water, trust in divine power— these are the true remedies."[10] She also apparently borrowed Coles' mantra that just as it is a sin to violate one of the Ten Commandments, it is a sin to violate the laws of life. Parodying Coles, she wrote: "It is truly a sin to violate the laws of our being as it is to break the ten commandments."[11]

A popular view at the time, known as "vitalism," held that a vital force, placed in the human body at birth, controlled a person's form, development, and activities, including health and longevity. Lust or sexual passion diminished this vital force. Note the following:

Horace Mann:

Man *came from the hand of God so perfect in his bodily organs . . .* so surcharged with vital force, that *it took more than two thousand years of the combined abominations of appetite and ignorance . . .* to drain off his electric energies and make him even accessible to disease.

Ellen White:

Man came *from the hand of God perfect in every faculty of mind and body*; in perfect soundness, therefore perfect in health. *It took more than two thousand years of indulgence of appetite and lustful passions* to create such a state of things in the human organism as would lessen the vital force.

In thus accepting vitalism, Ellen White seems dependent on Horace Mann.[12] The White parallel makes only cosmetic changes.

10. White, *Ministry of Healing,* 127.

11. White, *Testimonies for Church,* 2:70.

12. White, *Testimonies for Church,* 4:29; Mann, *Life and Works,* 5:335–36. This is from a transcript of an address given in 1853. Quoted in Numbers, *Prophetess of Health,* 213.

When Numbers' book first appeared in 1976, it created quite a stir. Numbers encountered considerable opposition from denominational leaders, some of it hostile, especially during the research and writing process. Photocopies of a prepublication version of the manuscript, which Numbers had privately shared with some of his colleagues, were covertly circulated. Word of the manuscript got back to General Conference leaders. As a result, Numbers, untenured at the time, lost his academic position at Loma Linda University, making him one of the denomination's first casualties in the trifecta of theological crises.[13]

When the book was published, my confidence in Ellen White was still largely intact. Harold Metcalf, editor of the Adventist publication, *Unlock Your Potential*, asked me to write a couple of articles in Ellen White's defense.[14] Using the limited inerrancy model of biblical inspiration, I claimed that biblical authors also used extra-biblical sources for some of their material, and occasionally incorporated "minor" factual errors in what they had written.[15] It should be no surprise, I argued, to find a similar situation in Ellen White. Numbers read my articles and, in a letter to me, insisted that *every* health principle she advocated in her writings could be traced back to the health literature of the nineteenth century. His book, despite my objections, demonstrated this beyond a shadow of doubt. Invoking Occam's Razor—when a simple explanation suffices, there is no need for a more complicated one—he claimed there was no necessity for any supplemental theory of divine inspiration to account for White's views on health. She was clearly a person of her time.

Numbers was one of the first significant contemporary historical critics of Ellen White. His study laid the groundwork for the findings of Walter Rea. In one of his final lectures before leaving Loma Linda University, he related that "the ultimate cause prompting me to write what I did was . . . to discover the truth."[16]

13. "No faculty member or administrator in the university, or elsewhere in Adventist education for that matter, publicly protested Number's termination," opined Jonathan Butler ("Historian as Heretic," 19).

14. Gladson, "Battle," pt. 1, 6–7; "Battle," pt. 2, 25–30. At the time, I was unaware of the opposition Numbers had faced from top church leaders who desperately tried to suppress his research. Had I been aware of this antagonism, I never would have written. I owe Dr. Numbers a sincere apology for my haste in writing the articles naively critical of his work.

15. *Limited inerrancy* is the view that, although the Bible is generally reliable, it may incorporate minor errors in history, science, chronology, and so on, but not in theology. With the church's encouragement, I applied this model to Ellen White's writings.

16. Quoted in Numbers, *Prophetess of Health*, 15.

Those closest to Ellen White, her secretarial assistants, editors, and other prominent church leaders of the era, we have seen, apparently recognized that she had borrowed from other authors to fill in gaps in some of her major writings, such as the *Desire of Ages* and the *Great Controversy*. Knowledge of this, however, was not widely disseminated among the denomination's colleges and churches, where a view of Ellen White's inspiration prevailed that approached the plenary theory.[17] Not only did God inspire Ellen White, God also supplied her thoughts, and sometimes even the very words to express the revelation. Debate over the nature of her inspiration had earlier come up in the Bible Conference and Bible and History Teachers' Council, convened in Takoma Park, Maryland, on July 31-August 1, 1919. The transcript of this Conference was strangely either lost or misplaced until archivist F. Donald Yost in 1974 found two packages wrapped in paper, containing twenty-four hundred pages of typewritten manuscripts—the verbatim transcripts of the Conference.[18] Now this document appears on the web site of the Office of Archives and Statistics of the General Conference of Seventh-day Adventists.

Many of the participants in the 1919 Conference, which included several legendary persons in Adventist history, such as A. G. Daniels, then president of the General Conference, W. W. Prescott, former professor of religion at Andrews University, then a field secretary of the General Conference, and F. M. Wilcox, the editor of the *Review and Herald*, learned that Ellen White had directed her literary assistants to research and find appropriate historical and theological resources to supply details and fill in portions of her major popular trade books (*Desire of Ages*; *The Great Controversy*). Many of these resources Fred Veltman would later uncover. In 1883, Ellen White published *Sketches from the Life of Paul,* intended as a resource for the Sabbath school lessons (Adventist equivalent for Sunday school lessons) for the second quarter of 1883. She took approximately 12 percent of this work from W. J. Conybeare and J. S. Howson, *The Life and Epistles of*

17. René Pache defines plenary inspiration: "The original documents of the Bible were written by men, though permitted the exercise of their own personalities and literary talents, yet wrote under the control and guidance of the Spirit of God, the result being in every word of the original documents a perfect and errorless recording of the exact message which God desired to give to man" (*Inspiration and Authority*, 71). Ellen White wrote that "it is not the words of the Bible that are inspired, but the men that were inspired . . . He [God] guided the mind in the selection of what to speak and what to write . . . The testimony is conveyed through the imperfect expressions of human language, yet it is the testimony of God" (*Selected Messages*, 1:21, 26). According to Robert Olson, "This is the manner in which Ellen White believed that she herself was inspired" ("Was Ellen White Like Prophets?" 6).

18. See Couperus, "Bible Conference," 27–57.

St. Paul (1858).[19] When the cry of plagiarism went up, White's *Sketches* was withdrawn from public sale, and only reissued in 1974. Of *Sketches from the Life of Paul*, A. G. Daniels, chair of the Ellen G. White Estate (1915–1935), and also chair of the 1919 Conference, observed:

> There was so much of their book put into "The Life of Paul" without any credit or quotation marks . . . we got Conybeare and Howson, and we got Wylie's "History of the Reformation" [J. A. Wylie, *History of the Waldenses*], and we read word for word, page after page, with no quotations, no credit, and really I did not know the difference until I began to compare them. I supposed it was Sister White's own work. The poor sister said, "Why, I didn't know about quotations and credits. My secretary should have looked after that, and the publishing house should have looked after it" . . . She did not claim that that was all revealed to her and written word for word under the inspiration of the Lord.[20]

This was more than just negligence on the part of Ellen White. There apparently was a deeper problem.

The conferees in 1919 candidly admitted, furthermore, that Ellen White had made historical and theological mistakes. She had to ask others more knowledgeable in certain areas to help her "correct" her writings. The conferees wondered how they could ever communicate this fact to the general Adventist public, caught up as it was by an inerrant, plenary notion of inspiration. How could they avoid threatening peoples' confidence in Ellen White if the errors in her writings were openly admitted? Because it contained such forthright debate, the transcript of the 1919 Bible Conference was set aside (lost?) at the White Estate in Takoma Park, Maryland, while the church by default allowed its membership to remain in blissful ignorance. As a student at Southern, for instance, I never heard anything about the 1919 Bible Conference, nor about the literary borrowing. Ellen White was inspired of God and always spoke the truth, I was taught. In their defense, I don't think my professors had any awareness of the 1919 Bible Conference. Jack Provonsha, a Loma Linda University professor, put it a little more bluntly:

19. Nichol, who wrote before the transcript of the 1919 Bible Conference was rediscovered, claims only 7 per cent came from Conybeare and Howson, although another 2.5 percent of her book "might be considered loose paraphrases" (*Ellen White and Critics*, 424).

20. Quoted from the transcript in "Appendix 4: The Secret 1919 Bible Conferences," in Numbers, *Prophetess of Health*, 388–89.

This doesn't mean that everyone involved gets "off the hook" that easily . . . I feel a justifiable resentment toward those even well-intentioned people who concealed these "facts of life" from us all of those years out of a mistaken impression that we couldn't handle them. Those leaders who spoke so freely at that 1919 Bible conference and then went home with their lips sealed showed at the very least a lack of courage.[21]

Panic-stricken staff members from the White Estate now scurried all over the country trying to put out the fires Rea's claims of plagiarism had kindled. Most of these efforts aimed at shoring up the traditional understanding of Ellen White, but one staff member took a slightly different tack. Ron Graybill, an assistant at the White Estate and a doctoral candidate in American Religious History at Johns Hopkins University, courageously alerted the Adventist public to what was anticipated in the Veltman study. I got a brief glimpse of Graybill's candor when he visited Southern during an apologetic lecture tour.

Not only did her borrowing of sources undergird her major works, Graybill admitted, but in specific instances Ellen White even took literary content from other authors, then boldly prefaced it with her customary visionary claim, "I was shown," an expression equivalent in Ellen White to that of an Old Testament prophet, "This is what the Lord God showed me" (Amos 7:1, 4, 7; 8:1). As proof, Graybill cited Ellen White's diary (for November 30, 1890). She took an explicit statement from Alfred Krumacher, *Elijah, the Tishbite* ("God never leads His children otherwise than they would choose to be led if they could see the end from the beginning" [20–21]), but attributed it to an insight she had received in vision. The use of Krumacher, without the visionary claim, and without credit to Krumacher, also appears elsewhere in the White corpus.[22] Like the Synoptic Gospels, a saying in one place in White's corpus would often be repeated elsewhere in a new context. Graybill summarized the alarming, pervasive extent of her borrowing:

> The material borrowed by Mrs. White included historical, geographical and chronological information, as well as devotional reflections, theological concepts . . . She also borrowed extra-Biblical comments on the lives of various Biblical characters, often turning the speculation and conjectureds [*sic*] of her sources into statements of positive fact.[23]

21. Provonsha, "Ellen White a Fraud?" 22.

22. White, *Desire of Ages*, 224; *Ministry of Healing*, 479; *Prophets and Kings*, 578.

23. Graybill (lecture, Southern Adventist College [Southern Adventist University],

In defense of Ellen White, the denomination has tried carefully to make a distinction between White and the authority of the Bible. The church's BRICOM affirms that the "Scripture is the final authority in all matters of doctrine and practice." What is more, the church doesn't believe that the writings of Ellen White "have a different quality of inspiration than does Scripture," nor does it think "the writings of Ellen White are an addition to the sacred canon of Scripture" or that her writings "are necessary to originate or establish doctrine." The difference lies, not in the quality of inspiration, but in the function. The Bible is directed to humanity in general. It is the Word of God in human language, while Ellen White applies the teachings of the Bible "to the spiritual and moral life of Seventh-day Adventists."[24]

Despite these attempts at clarification, Ellen White's authority has steadily escalated since her death in 1915 until now in many Adventist communities, she occupies a position of authority approaching or even surpassing that of the Bible. The technical term for this is "para-scriptural." Ellen White's writings are *para-scriptural* texts. Such texts function as authoritative texts quite a bit above that of ordinary religious literature, yet only slightly below that of the Bible, the scriptural norm of Christian faith. The measure of authority is one of degree. Ellen White's writings are a "continuing and authoritative source of truths which provide the church comfort, guidance, instruction, and correction," states Article 17 of the Fundamental Beliefs of Seventh-day Adventists.[25]

In this respect, Adventism may again be compared to the Church of Jesus Christ of Latter-Day Saints (the Mormons). To Mormons, certain writings of Joseph Smith are regarded as supplemental scripture (para-scriptural) actually equal to the Bible, and superior in the sense they convey contemporary inspired information. Mormons have even added to the title of the Book of Mormon the words, "Another Testament of Jesus Christ." Mormons publish the entire Bible (KJV only) together with the writings of Joseph Smith Jr. under one cover, thus giving the impression that the latter are additional scripture. Latter-day Saints also leave the canon of scripture open for further revelation from its contemporary prophet, an elected

Collegedale, TN, 1981). As he began his research into White's sources, Fred Veltman said this about the expressions, "I saw," or "I was shown": "Perhaps the most serious question being raised . . . has to do with Ellen White's use of such expressions . . . Such expressions are usually taken to mean that what follows was actually seen in vision. When the content of some visions is described with quotations or paraphrases from uninspired sources . . . Is the reader being led to believe the source of the vision is heaven? Is this what the writer means to convey? Does the writer intend to deceive?" ("Report to PREXAD," April 23, 1981, 19).

24. Biblical Research Institute, "Inspiration of Ellen White," 2–3.

25. [General Conference], *Adventist Church Manual*, 28.

official who serves also as the president of the church. Mormons have insti-
tutionalized the office of prophet.

Although Ellen White isn't considered "Another Testament," in actual
practice the boundary sometimes gets blurred. Those Adventists who rate
Ellen White as equal or superior to the Bible, like the Mormons, reason
that since she is the most recent prophet, her revelation takes precedence
over older revelation represented in the Bible. Because Ellen White is more
current, she supersedes the older.[26] This isn't the official denominational
teaching, much less the view of Ellen White,[27] but to many Adventists this
is how Ellen White functions. She provides the perspective through which
an Adventist reads the Bible. She is the hermeneutical key unlocking the
meaning of Scripture.[28] An Adventist interpretation of a biblical passage
is expected to harmonize with the writings of Ellen White. Otherwise, the
interpretation is regarded as doubtful or worse, erroneous.

A student at Southern walked into my office on one occasion and just
blurted out, "Why don't you believe Ellen White is the third canon of Scripture?" Startled, I looked up. Steve stood there, arms folded snugly across
his chest, jaw set, blue eyes blazing, as though in this question his whole
religious world hung precariously in the balance.

"Why do you use the expression '*third* canon' when referring to Ellen White?" I responded. "Are you aware Ellen White never considered her
writings an addition to the Bible?"

26. I came across this line of argument in a newsletter, *Inspiration Reflections*,
published by Mirror Ministry, an independent Adventist ministry. In its April 1998
edition an anonymous author claims: "Sr. [*sic*] White was just as much a prophet of
God as anyone ever was, and therefore we must consider her writings as the Word of
God . . . The fact that she was a messenger from God especially for our time, *makes her
messages more important to us than those of any previous prophet of God.* This is no way
depreciates the work of the previous prophets" (5) [emphasis added].

27. "I recommend to you, dear reader, the word of God as the rule of your faith
and practice. By that Word we are to be judged," writes White (*Experiences of Ellen
White*, 64, as quoted in Nichol, *White and Critics*, 88). White emphasizes the relationship: "Little heed is given to the Bible, and the Lord has given a lesser light to lead men
and women to the Greater Light (*Evangelism*, 257).

28. One of the denomination's official publishers, the Review and Herald, Hagerstown, MD, has published (1993) *The Study Bible*, an annotated Bible for Adventists,
containing the text of the KJV together with notes and commentary from Ellen White.
This Bible refers to these notes from White as an "inspired commentary." By placing
these notes together with the biblical text, this edition is a subtle indication of the growing tendency to place White and the Bible on somewhat equal footing or, at least, to use
White as the primary lens through which Scripture is read.

"She was a prophet, just like Isaiah, Jeremiah, and Ezekiel. And if she was a prophet like them, her writings must be equal to theirs. Do you believe she was inspired?"

"That isn't the issue here. Inspiration isn't the only criterion for inclusion in the biblical canon," I chose my words carefully. For weeks, ever since the semester had begun, Steve had been seen all over the campus informally interrogating faculty, stopping them on the walkways between buildings and on the steps leading into the University library. "There were no doubt some writings, such as Paul's lost letter to the Laodiceans,[29] that may have been divinely inspired, but which were not preserved in the New Testament. The process of canonization is long and complicated." Steve remained there in the doorway, unblinking, still standing, ignoring the empty chair nearest my desk.

"Even if you could make a case for including such writings in the biblical canon because they are inspired," I continued, "Ellen White's writings haven't been around long enough even to have begun such a canonizing process, which might take hundreds of years. Anyway, she didn't see her writings as potentially canonical. She saw her writings as a 'lesser light' to lead to the 'Greater Light,' the Bible. Using the word 'lesser' to refer to her writings, and 'Greater' to refer to the Bible, shows she saw a difference between them."

"Someone told me before I came here this morning you'd try to muddy the issue by referring to such scholarly complications. I don't know anything about a so-called 'canonical process.'"

"Then may I suggest you look into how the biblical books actually became part of a canon, and probe a bit deeper into the writings of Ellen White before drawing the conclusion that her writings ought to be made part of the *Bible*?" I emphasized the word "Bible," trying one last time to get him to think about what he was proposing.

It was futile. He remained unconvinced. Nothing I could say could disabuse him of the opinion that I was a "heretic" because I wouldn't elevate Ellen White to canonical status.

The official theology of Adventism, I repeat, doesn't formally equate or raise Ellen White to the level of the Bible. But the tension in the church between the authority of Ellen White and that of the Bible has persistently troubled the denomination and dissuaded would-be converts, such as my father.

---

29. "When this letter [Colossians] has been read among you, have it read also in the church of the Laodiceans, and see that you read also *the letter from Laodicea*" (Col 4:16].

I became accidentally entangled in this tension when I published a short commentary on the book of Job with the Adventist Review and Herald Press.[30] Originally intended as part of a series of popular commentaries, each done by an Adventist scholar, the Review and Herald canceled the project for economic reasons shortly after my book was released.

As every biblical scholar knows, Job is notoriously difficult to place in a specific historical era, or to decide who may have written it.[31] Job never gives any direct information about its origin. Unfortunately for Adventist biblical scholars, Ellen White, again no doubt following the traditional opinion of her time, like she did in health matters, claims Moses as the author. The *Adventist Bible Commentary*, in an article written by Norval Pease, defends this view.[32] My research, however, did not turn up a single modern scholar who would entertain such an idea, even the most conservative.[33] Nor could I find any external or internal evidence that would adequately support this notion. In the original draft of the commentary, however, I briefly discussed the Mosaic view, but left the door open to other options.

Well aware of Ellen White's opinion on the matter and the controversy then churning around her, the Review editor advised me to take out of the commentary any discussion about authorship. As a result, my commentary on Job is conspicuous among such works: it is probably the only commentary that doesn't discuss authorship! Despite the fact the Bible nowhere indicates who wrote Job, I had either to be silent on the matter or accept Ellen White's word over both the Bible and the reasonable conclusions of historical scholarship.

30. My literary firstborn, this volume was published under the title, *Who Said Life is Fair? Job and the Problem of Evil.*

31. The provenance of Job is much too complex to be discussed here. Proposed dates range from the mid-second millennium to the fourth century BCE, and the book is generally considered to be of composite authorship with, at minimum, the prologue/epilogue (Job 1–2; 42:7–17) and the dialogue and speeches of Yahweh (3–31; 38–42:6) coming from different sources. Most regard the Elihu speeches (32–37) and the Hymn to Wisdom (28) as secondary to the original work, as well as other shorter passages throughout (see Irwin, "Job," 391–92; Crenshaw, "Job, Book of," 863–64; Fohrer, *Introduction*, 330).

32. According to Ellen White, Moses wrote Job during his exile in Midian, following his exile from Egypt (Exod 2:15–21). "Under the inspiration of the Holy Spirit, he [Moses] wrote the book of Genesis and also the book of Job" (quoted in the *SDABC*, 3:1140. For Pease's treatment of this view, see ibid., 3:493.

33. For instance, the leading conservative Old Testament introduction, by Roland K. Harrison, speaks of the "anonymity of the book" (*Introduction*, 1039).

11

The Legend of Ellen White

The Word of the Lord came to me. "Mortal, prophesy against the prophets who prophesy out of their own imagination: 'Hear the word of the Lord!'" Thus says the Lord God, "Alas for the senseless prophets who follow their own spirit, and have seen nothing."

—*The Prophet Ezekiel*

When Fred Veltman completed his long-awaited, eight-year-long study of the alleged "plagiarism" in Ellen White, his findings upset long-time devotees of Ellen White.[1] Although limiting his investigation to only a small section of the *Desire of Ages*, specifically 15 out of the 87 chapters, or about 17 percent—thus making it difficult to generalize from this to all her writings—Veltman concluded that Ellen White had definitely used sources without giving due credit and that she, at times, even denied doing so.

Of the 2,624 sentences in the 15 chapters, 823 (31.4 percent) showed literary dependence upon a number of other authors, none of whom were acknowledged in the *Desire of Ages* text. William Hanna's *The Life of Christ* was by far the most common source, with 321 parallels. Close behind was Daniel March, with 129, then John Harris, Frederic Farrar, George Jones, Alfred Edersheim, J. H. Ingraham, Francis Wayland, and John Cumming.[2]

---

1. He summarized his larger, 958-page work in two articles, written specifically for Adventist clergy: Veltman, "The Data," 4–7; Veltman, "The Conclusions, 11–15. See also Veltman, "Desire of Ages *Project*."

2. March, *Night Scenes of the Bible*; *Walks and Homes of Jesus*; Harris, *The Great Teacher*; Farrar, *The Life of Christ*; Jones, *Life-Scenes from the Four Gospels*; Edersheim,

All were mostly authors of popular "Victorian" lives of Christ, a popular genre in the nineteenth century.[3] J. H. Ingraham's *Prince of the House of David* is especially interesting.[4] While browsing in an antique book store in Johnson City, Tennessee, my wife Laura came across this particular book and casually noted that it seemed a lot like White's *Desire of Ages*, a book with which she was very familiar. Albert Schweitzer called Ingraham's work—intended for family devotional reading—one of the best "edifying" romances on the life of Jesus.[5] And Ingraham called his work a "historical romance," consisting of fictional scenes written in the form of correspondence by a wealthy woman living in Palestine during the time of Jesus. The use of such fiction suggests that White was apparently not as concerned about historical authenticity in retelling the life of Jesus as she was about the spiritual or devotional value of the stories about Jesus.

In addition to these authors, which Veltman designates "major sources," there were twenty-one "minor sources," who may have contributed as few as one or two parallels. Ellen White's dependence on all these sources varied from close to verbatim usage as well as loose paraphrase.[6] She selected, condensed, paraphrased, rearranged, deleted, and added elements from her sources. The dependency included descriptive, devotional, theological, and exhortatory material. As Donald McAdams had discovered in his earlier study of White's *Great Controversy*, mentioned above, White used source material to develop the literary structure of some chapter subunits. She borrowed chapter titles, literary structure, as well as individual sentences and paragraphs.[7]

Based on an analysis of Ellen White's own handwriting, from samples obtained from the White Estate files, Veltman concluded that Ellen White herself, and not her editorial assistants, had borrowed literary material from these other sources. The sole admission of the use of such sources in her writings occurs in the preface to the *Great Controversy*, which I cite here again for clarity:

The Life and Times of Jesus the Messiah; Wayland, *Salvation by Christ*; Cumming, *Sabbath Evening Readings on the New Testament: St. John*. The publication data on these were not available to me so they are not represented in the bibliography of this book. All these works were in Ellen White's personal library,

3. See Pals, "Victorian Lives."

4. Ingraham, *Prince of House of David*, ix–x.

5. Schweitzer, *Quest*, n. 1, p. 328.

6. Veltman used a complex system of dependency on sources, ranking them at the sentence level from "strict verbatim," with a value of 7, to "independent," with a value of 0. The overall average for the 15 chapters was 3.3 on this scale.

7. Veltman, "*Desire of Ages* Project," 858–958.

In some cases where a historian has so grouped together events as to afford, in brief, a comprehensive view of the subject, or has summarized details in a convenient manner, his words have been quoted; but in some instances no specific credit has been given, since the quotations are not given for the purpose of citing that writer as authority, but because his statement affords a ready and forcible presentation of the subject.[8]

Veltman considered this admission "too narrow and perhaps too vague" in its scope. "It minimizes the use of sources," he insisted, "and it does not cover her practice of paraphrasing her sources." The admission suggests that White only felt documentation necessary when the source was used to provide authority, and that the mere paraphrase of material did not require such documentation. Although this is understandable, it still leaves unanswered why she tacitly allowed readers to think that she was not in any way dependent upon other sources. Moreover, this statement applied only to the *Great Controversy*. It was not a general admission covering the entire White literary corpus. Ellen White probably used literary sources in *all* her writings. Only in the *Great Controversy*, however, did she admit doing so, leaving readers of her vast literary output the distinct impression that her work was original. The source of her information was God, not other fallible human authors. Veltman's research contradicted the earlier view of F. D. Nichol, which reflected the traditional Adventist understanding of Ellen White's literary process. "Mrs. White wrote many thousands of pages of manuscripts," wrote Nichol. "Of all this vast amount of matter only an insignificant part is borrowed from other authors. And the borrowed part is most certainly not central to the spiritual theme that distinguished her writings."[9] Nichol's assertion now proved inaccurate. Whatever else, this situation posed a terrible ethical dilemma for Ellen White and the Adventist church. "This is the most serious problem to be faced in connection with Ellen White's literary dependency," admitted Veltman. "It strikes at the heart of her honesty, her integrity and therefore her trustworthiness."[10]

Ron Springett, a colleague on the religion faculty at Southern, recalled how, as a student at the Adventist theological seminary, he had not been made aware of Ellen White's literary borrowing. "Folks remembered what they were taught, even in graduate school, and compared it with what was

---

8. White, *Great Controversy*, xii. This caveat was included as early as the 1888 edition of this work.

9. Nichol, *White and Critics*, 467.

10. Veltman, "Conclusions," 14.

the actual truth," he wrote. "The deliberate and organized deception is what alarms most people, not the fact she borrowed."[11]

Arthur White (1907–1991), grandson of Ellen White and late former Secretary of the Ellen G. White Estate, under whom at the seminary Springett had studied the writings of Ellen White, confidently wrote almost a decade before Walter Rea's alarming discovery: "I can assure you that when you read her counsels, when you read Ellen White's books, you may know, except for the purely biographical material, that what she has there set forth was based on the visions that God gave her."[12] Did Arthur White simply not know? Was he blissfully ignorant of the way at least some of the writings for which he was the chief trustee were produced? Did his expression, "based on the visions," leave out a vital link between her sources and the final version of her writings?

In a letter to the White Estate Board of Trustees on March 9, 1983, Robert Olson, then Secretary of the Ellen G. White Estate, sent a photocopy of the flyleaf of *Sunshine and Shadows*, a book Ellen White had in her personal library. There, on the flyleaf in White's own handwriting appears what Olson describes as "the only known statement by Ellen G. White herself where she indicates that she used the writings of others in the presentation of her devotional materials." The note reads: "This is a book I esteem highly. Never let it be lost at this time. I appreciate it. I shall be pleased to keep this book for *it has treasures of truth which I appreciate in presenting to many others*."[13]

Shortly after Veltman had begun his research, Adventist editor, Warren Johns, candidly admitted: "The view of Ellen White that is now coming into focus is that she was much more widely read than even her own family realized, and that she utilized material from outside sources for her writings on a much more extensive basis than the church has been aware."[14]

Veltman resisted categorizing Ellen White's borrowing as plagiarism, arguing that plagiarism is legally much more complicated than mere literary parallels. In Ellen White's case, it would be necessary to establish that she had legally violated the common practices of the culture in which she

11. Email message to author, April 13, 2000.

12. White, *White Writings*, 104.

13. Emphasis added. The book in question is Clarke, *Sunshine and Shadows* (1868).

14. Johns, "Ellen White Plagiarist?" 6. "We see the silhouette of a woman who must have been a diligent researcher," Johns goes on to say, "who investigated her sources meticulously and used them judiciously and effectively, a woman fully imbued by God's Spirit, and a woman who has left from her prolific pen a treasure of inestimable worth to the church" (11).

lived, a difficult matter to resolve.[15] In short, one would have to "prove" such a charge under nineteenth-century United States case law. It would be unfair to invoke anachronistically modern definitions of plagiarism and charge White with such literary theft.[16] However, she really did appropriate the plot, literary structure, and actual literary expression from other authors and—intentionally or unintentionally—represented them as her own. The moral and ethical question this poses remains unresolved. For the thoughtful Adventist, Ellen White's authority has inevitably been compromised.

The borrowing problem has compelled the church to reconsider what it means to be a prophet or to experience divine inspiration. "What was her view of inspiration and revelation?" Veltman asked. "What did her charismatic experience include or exclude? How would she probably have justified her literary practices to herself?" Any attempt to address this matter, he indicated, would have to involve a careful study of nineteenth-century views of inspiration, particularly as they came to expression within the Adventism of the period.[17]

In view of all this, I couldn't help but think about the critical research that had long been going on in biblical studies, my field of interest. The critical, scientific study of the Bible had actually begun with "source" criticism, or "literary" criticism as it was originally called. Scholars isolated sources within the biblical text that originally had been drawn upon by the biblical writers. The most celebrated case, which overturned the long-held tradition that Moses had written *all* the Pentateuch, was the detection in the Pentateuch of four major literary strands: the Yahwist (J Source), the Elohist (E Source), Priestly (P Source), and Deuteronomist (D Source). Although this Documentary Hypothesis, as it is called, has been challenged and modified in recent times, the Mosaic theory of authorship of the Pentateuch has vanished from almost all scholarly literature.

Adventists historically have firmly resisted such critical research when it involves the Bible, not only in the Pentateuch. I will tell later how my adoption of critical, scientific research eventually proved fatal to my career as an Adventist biblical scholar. Yet with Veltman one sees the beginning of such critical study of Ellen White. Only such a serious approach to Ellen White, in my view, has any chance of salvaging her efficacy for the denomination. After Numbers, Rea, and Veltman, Adventism will have to modify its

15. Veltman, "Conclusions," 14.

16. "The practice of borrowing from other authors without giving explicit or detailed credit was widespread among writers of the eighteenth and nineteenth centuries," notes Dennis Fortin. "Although by today's literary standards this practice is unacceptable, it forms the historical context of Ellen White's own practice" ("Plagiarism," 1029).

17. Veltman, *Desire of Ages* Project," 953.

view of divine inspiration, because its understanding of inspiration has been modeled too closely on the phenomenon of Ellen White.[18] After Numbers, Veltman, and Rea, Adventists will no longer be able to read Ellen White uncritically. To its credit, the *Ellen G. White Encyclopedia* claims that the older "apologetic" approach to Ellen White must now give way to "a more open acknowledgement and discussion of Ellen White's use of borrowed sources."[19] If Ellen White is approached with critical methods, what about the Adventist approach to the Bible? Some Adventist doctrines, such as the Investigative Judgment, are dependent upon "pre-critical" or historicist approaches to Scripture, as we have seen. As the denomination realizes that the appropriation of Ellen White is dependent upon the contextualizing of her writings, it will also have to re-evaluate some of its other doctrines in the light of that same historical research. But such revision, I fear, lies in the far distant future. The present-day Adventist church is too frightened to undertake it.

Although Veltman conveyed his study much more tactfully than Rea, whose work had a sharp, acerbic tone, it essentially confirmed Rea's basic claims. Ellen White's literary output was enormous. No one knows what might be found in the depths of it should someone painstakingly examine all of White's writings rather than just a short cross-section of the *Desire of Ages*. Such an investigation would be so lengthy and complex the complete story will probably never be known. We will doubtless have to be content with only specimens or samples of such research. With only a portion of the *Desire of Ages* meticulously analyzed, and the vast body of her writings as yet untouched by source criticism, the church is condemned to nagging uncertainty about White's actual literary sources and to the ethical problem this now creates. For many Adventists, the unsettled situation will probably only further erode her authority. Some, like Veltman, are still able to say that "belief in her inspiration is not seriously compromised" by these findings. He justifies this stance by drawing attention to the Bible: "We don't have all the answers to questions on the text of Scripture."[20] For many others, however, the integrity of Ellen White's inspiration has been put into serious question; at least, she will forever be left under a cloud of suspicion. "If an

18. In a letter to Walter C. Utt, referring to Ron Numbers's discovery of Ellen White's sources for her health message, Ron Graybill states that, unless Numbers is credited with "some genuine points, people will never see any need to adjust their concept of inspiration accordingly" (Graybill to Walter C. Utt, 7 July 1976, as quoted in Numbers, *Prophetess of Health*, 17).

19. Fortin, "Plagiarism," 1035.

20. Veltman, "Conclusions," 15.

author is once detected in borrowing," according to William Hazlitt, "he will be suspected of plagiarism ever after."[21]

Veltman's study is now online at www.adventisarchives.org/docar-chives.asp, so those interested may examine it. Yet, even though his two *Ministry* articles have had wide circulation, most rank-and-file Adventists have essentially ignored what Veltman uncovered.[22] Today most Adventists go about their religious life with little or no awareness of what lies beneath the surface of Ellen White's writings. Evidence of this may be noted in the general church journal, the *Adventist Review*. Sandwiched between a report on some independent ministries and the Adventist Health System, its chain of hospitals and clinics, there appears this disingenuous note:

> The eight-year study of Ellen G. White's possible borrowing of materials from other writings for her book, the *Desire of Ages*, ended this year with researcher Fred Veltman concluding that her book does contain some ideas and phrasing similar to those of other writers but that it is independent of verbatim borrowing.[23]

Old legends die hard!

21. Quoted in *World Book Dictionary*, 2003 ed., s.v. "Plagiarism."

22. A good summary of Veltman's research also now appears in Veltman, "*Desire of Ages* Sources," 766–70. "There can no longer be any doubt," he writes, "that she used sources regardless of subject matter" (770).

23. *Review*, December 29, 1988, 10. Veltman's actual claim about White's indepen-dence runs in the opposite direction than this notice: "A fair assessment of the evidence would not deny or underplay the degree of dependence, but neither should it overlook or depreciate her independence" ("The Conclusions," 12).

12

Death of a Legend

Do not believe every spirit, but test the spirits to see whether they are from God;
for many false prophets have gone out into the world.

—*LETTER OF* 1 *JOHN*

The legend of Ellen White had already suffered what was in effect a mortal wound in the eyes of some of her nineteenth-century contemporaries.

One such was John Harvey Kellogg, MD (1852–1943). When Ellen White published the first edition of *Great Controversy* (1884), Kellogg, the Adventist physician and founder of the Battle Creek (Michigan) Sanitarium and brother of W. H. Kellogg (1860–1951), who launched the breakfast cereal industry, noticed that *Great Controversy* had relied heavily on J. A. Wylie's *The History of Protestantism*.[1] John Harvey Kellogg questioned W. C. ("Willy") White (1854–1937), Ellen White's son, confidant, and personal assistant after James White's death, about this.

"Don't you think that when Mother reads things that agree with what she has seen in vision, that it is all right for her to adopt it?" Willy White answered.

"No, not without giving due credit for it," Kellogg rejoined. "It may be all right for her to quote it and make use of it, but she ought to put quotation marks on [it] and tell where she got it.

"She had no right to incorporate it with what she had 'seen' and make it appear that she has seen it first of all," he continued. "The preface says this

1. Wylie, *History of Protestantism*, 4 vols.

book has been written by special illumination, that she has gotten new light by special inspiration; so people read things here, read those paragraphs, and they say, 'Here I saw that in Wiley's [sic] book.'"

Then Kellogg challenged, "That will condemn your book, detract from the book and the character of it, and it never will do; it is wrong. I simply won't stand for it, and I want you to know that I won't, and that this thing ought to stop."[2]

Little wonder that John Harvey Kellogg left the Seventh-day Adventists in 1907, the culmination of a long-standing dispute over authority with Ellen White herself.

My next door neighbor and colleague on the faculty at Southern, Ed Zackrison, made an exhaustive study of White's literary borrowing, and so had opportunity to consult personally with Walter Rea, under whom he had previously served as an assistant pastor. Zackrison accumulated a massive private photocopied collection of most of the sources relevant to the case of Ellen White's borrowing. With such evidence in his possession, he challenged those who tended to minimize the problem: "The borrowing is much more extensive than even Veltman's study has shown. If you don't believe me, I urge you to visit my study and take a look at the data, then make up your own mind!" I accepted his challenge, and spent several hours in Zackrison's book-lined study rummaging through file drawer after drawer. There simply was no doubt that the borrowing was much more serious and extensive than most Adventists had believed, more extensive even than Veltman had identified in his sample study. It simply was not true, as White claimed, "My views were written independent of books or of the opinions of others."[3]

Looking back on the whole controversy, Zackrison now sarcastically reflects, "One must look at the claims and then examine them. When she says, 'I saw,' we now know she saw it in a book. When she says, 'The Lord showed me,' we now know he allegedly directed her to a book . . . [This is] certainly not what we were taught in school."[4]

Adventists have been quick to defend Ellen White's plagiarism by pointing to the practice of some biblical writers who borrowed essential material from other biblical writers or even extra-biblical sources and incorporated it in their writings. There are numerous instances of this. Isaiah (2:2–4) and Micah (4:1–3) share a virtually identical oracle about the nations coming up to the "house of the God of Jacob" and learning the paths

2. Quoted in Brinsmead, *Judged by the Gospel*, 146–7.
3. E. G. White Manuscript 27, 1867, quoted in Arthur White, *Ellen G. White*, 16.
4. Email to Jerry Gladson, March 1999.

of peace. It is not certain whether Isaiah borrowed from Micah, or Micah from Isaiah (they were contemporaries), or whether both took this oracle from still another unidentified source. The gospels of Matthew and Luke made use of almost the whole of Mark, who had written earlier (c. 70 CE). The use of expressions, thoughts, and language from earlier or contemporary biblical works, as well as from extra-biblical materials, does occur often throughout the Bible.[5] Luke, in fact, acknowledges this practice, claiming to have referenced previous "orderly accounts of the events that have been fulfilled among us," and the oral narratives of "eye-witnesses" in the preparation of his book (Luke 1:1–4). John Robertson, in his defense of Ellen White, cites this passage: "Luke establishes the principle that inspired writers may draw upon sources other than visions from the Lord even in writing what later became the Holy Bible."[6]

To cite all of this in defense of Ellen White misses the point. It is not that both Ellen White and the biblical writers made use of borrowed material not original with them; this should be acknowledged. It is rather that Ellen White borrowed from other writers, neglected to give due credit to them, and merged their material into hers, leaving the impression that her writing was solely her own. This is the ethical problem raised by White's literary borrowing. In Ellen White's day, it was generally considered important to reference one's sources when citing or quoting. In biblical times, when documents were usually generated in and by the community, often with many persons, and not just individual authors, at work on them over a period of time, it was customary—even expected—to utilize the preceding literary (and oral) traditions. The communal and scribal nature of biblical literature, however, meant that such sources did not have to be acknowledged.[7] The sources, oral or written, as it were, belonged to everyone. They were community property! This is why most biblical books are anonymous. Even though Ellen White may have acted as though her sources—many of which were in her private library—were community property, this was not a

---

5. The appendix to the modern critical edition of the Greek New Testament lists the instances where the New Testament writers cite or allude to Old Testament or deuterocanonical (Apocryphal) and pseudepigraphical literature (see Nestle and Aland, *Novum Testamentum*, 772–808). The *Apocryphal* or Deuterocanonical literature refers to the early Jewish writings found in Roman Catholic and Orthodox biblical canons, but not in the Protestant or Palestinian Jewish canons. Pseudepigrapha is a catch-all term for all the other early Jewish writings that do not appear in the deuterocanonical literature or the Palestinian canon. There are allusions to both the Deuterocanonical and pseudepigraphical literature in the New Testament.

6. Robertson, *White Truth*, 29. See also Rice, "How to Write," 4–7.

7. See Ellis's study of the communal nature of biblical authorship (*Making of New Testament*).

widely accepted idea even in the nineteenth-century literary world, nor is it today with our stricter laws about plagiarism. In this respect, Ellen White's social situation and that of the Bible differ widely. To compare her singular practice with that of the biblical writers and editors simply does not justify or condone her copious use of unacknowledged sources.

Moreover, why would someone who received visions and auditory messages under inspiration from God go looking to other authors who would not have had the same divine experiences for the best way of expressing these singular visions and auditory messages? This would appear to be an exceedingly cumbersome way of noting one's visions. It wasn't that Ellen White lifted a word or idea here or there, but that she took whole sentences and paragraphs out of other works and offered them up as her own, without acknowledging or appropriately crediting the sources.

Faced with such these questions, I desperately tried to reconcile the enormity of White's borrowing with the denomination's claim that Ellen White was a prophet similar to those in the Bible. Paul's advice to the Thessalonian church seemed to offer a possible solution. "Do not despise the words of prophets, but test everything; hold fast to what is good" (1 Thess 5:20–21). Apparently, at the time Christian prophets were wandering rather freely around the eastern Mediterranean world. The apostle didn't want the churches to accept what these prophets were teaching without scrutinizing it. Neither was the church to ignore as contemptable these Christian prophets. Rather, they were to listen to them, but do so critically (Gk. *dokimazo*, "prove, examine, test"). The Christian prophets in his day were evidently advocating such confusing, contradictory notions that it became necessary to examine their messages critically. His advice a few years later to the Corinthians is similar: "Let two or three prophets speak, and let the others weigh what is said" (1 Cor 14:29). Paul's comment about prophets suggests that is it altogether possible to possess a spiritual gift like prophecy and yet misuse or abuse it. If Ellen White had the gift of prophecy, we must therefore ask, did she abuse it—at least some of the time? Didn't James White, Ellen's own husband, warn that spiritual gifts could get out of control and end up turning into a curse?[8]

After James' death in 1881, however, little could slow the gradual elevation of Ellen White's influence. Eventually—with personal encouragement—her authority became pervasive, almost canonical, at least in the

8. James White, "Gifts," 13–14.

Adventist culture in the United States. In other countries, due to the language barrier (her writings are yet to be translated into most languages), her authority has been less influential. In the United States, Adventists tend to quote her as the final word on about everything from the doctrine of God to whether one ought to eat two meals a day rather than three! What the plagiarism controversy demonstrated to me was that I needed to give closer heed the Pauline warning and be very cautious about accepting at face value anything White wrote.

For most of my more than thirty years as an Adventist, I had accepted that Ellen White's writings were divinely inspired. I had certain reservations, however. I harbored a deeply felt, yet inarticulate suspicion I couldn't quite put into words. Even though at the outset of my ministerial career I had determined to read all Ellen White's published writings, I refused to base sermons, Bible studies, or lectures on them. I regarded her writings as *secondary* to Scripture, and did not use them as corroboration for any theological observation. I sought to ground my sermons, Bible studies, and lectures in the biblical text. Ellen White's writings I regarded as primarily devotional or inspirational.

Then Numbers, Rea, and Veltman came on the scene. The careful research of these scholars convinced me that Ellen White was less credible than Adventism traditionally had assumed. When my family of origin was first learning about Adventism, my dad had seriously considered joining the denomination. My mother, sister, and I had become members. My dad had totally refused. What kept him outside the Adventist church for the rest of his life, he confessed, was Ellen White. "I just can't believe in that woman," he had admitted to me.

Perhaps some of his suspicion had rubbed off. When I read her writings—even before Rea—they seemed time and again to miss the essential spirit, the rhetorical tone and texture of the biblical text. They often missed the *kerygma* or essential message of scripture. Intuitively, I sensed White had often moved in an entirely different theological direction than Scripture. Her perspective was sectarian or narrowly confessional, more a buttressing of Adventism than a broader, common expression of Christian faith. She seemed to bend or exploit Scripture to an Adventist end, which is understandable, given her background and theological orientation. At the same time, this also meant she didn't provide a dispassionate guide for the reader of the Bible. The person who depends upon Ellen White for insight into specific biblical passages seldom becomes aware of any other perspective than that of Adventism. Ellen White's vision of the Bible is a narrow, biased Adventist one. The more I studied the Bible in depth, the more alarming for me became the conflict between the biblical text and what Ellen White had to say about it.

Since I was a religion scholar, this troubled me greatly. Then one day a faculty colleague in another academic discipline admitted to me, "A specialist in any field of research in the Adventist church will have difficulty with Ellen White, particularly in the area of their professional specialty."

There can be no doubt that Ellen White's influence, in large part, has been constructive for the Seventh-day Adventist church. She literally held life and limb together in every area of the church's thinking. I don't think the denomination would have survived, at least in its present form, without her. From her influence emanated the denomination's extensive educational system, from kindergarten to the university level, and its world-wide medical and humanitarian ministry, embodied in Adventism's many hospitals and clinics. Without Ellen White's influence the personal health of most Adventists would undoubtedly be the poorer. Through the practice of sound health principles—mediated by Ellen White—longitudinal studies have shown that Adventists as a group live an average of seven years longer than the general public. She shaped the church's doctrine of the Sabbath, the Second Advent, justification, sanctification, and so on.

The church, however, must now also honestly acknowledge the darker side of Ellen White. Her secret literary life has now been brought into the open. When the denomination reprints her works, as it frequently does, wouldn't it be prudent now to indicate her sources, if known, rather than perpetuate the myth that all or most of her material comes from God? Throughout the years, in order to safeguard Ellen White's reputation church leaders have regrettably concealed important facts that would have given greater clarity to her life and ministry. Her writings have usurped the primary role of the Bible, especially in many of the right-wing, closed Adventist communities. Her words over time have come to assume canonical authority and have stifled theological creativity. They have often bred unchecked fanaticism. Ellen White in one way or another has dominated and literally oppressed church life, from what goes on the dinner table to how people read and interpret the Bible. Ellen White, at best, has been a dubious, double-edged blessing to the church.

So it was that in the space of five short years, the Adventist community had seen three key tenets, "legitimating structures," as Peter Berger identifies them,[9] fiercely assaulted and undermined. The cumulative effect was traumatic. The North American Adventist community seethed in controversy. Frenzied discussion of justification by faith, of Daniel 8 and the Inves-

---

9. Berger, *Sacred Canopy*, 3–51.

tigative Judgment, and of Ellen White escalated into bitter, open theological warfare. Churches and colleges took sides; battle lines were drawn. Neutral ground—the leisure of scholarly reservation—became increasingly hard to find. The Adventist community churned, roiled, and broke into open conflict around the trifecta—Ellen White, the gospel, and the Investigative Judgment.

Facing the disclosures about Ellen White as honestly as I could, just as I had done with the issues raised by Paxton and Ford, I found myself once more unable to affirm, without reservation, a crucial traditional doctrine of Seventh-day Adventism. Could I really consider myself a genuine Adventist if I could no longer accept some of its most important doctrines? How could I remain clergy in a denomination the theology of which I was increasingly unable entirely to embrace? Could I pick and choose which doctrines I supported, and leave the others aside? Try as I might, I couldn't shake the importance of these questions. I felt hollow, weary, and insincere. Professionally, I felt required to support the church and its teachings. At the same time, paradoxically my thinking was divided. I was of two minds. My personal moment of truth, my moment of decision, relentlessly approached. I could feel it in my bones.

13

Purge

Curse the gossips and the double-tongued, for they destroy the peace of many.
Slander has shaken many, and scattered them from nation to nation; it has de-
stroyed strong cities, and overturned the houses of the great . . . Those who pay
heed to slander will not find rest, nor will they settle down in peace. The blow of
a whip raises a welt, but a blow of the tongue crushes the bones. Many have fallen
by the edge of the sword, but not as many as have fallen because of the tongue.

—*Jesus ben Sira* [*Sirach*]

E very generation or two," a wizened Adventist minister, veteran of many
denominational internecine theological wars, once confided to me,
smoothing his snow-white hair, "the church has to purge itself in order to
feel like it is right, and its critics all wrong."

"Purge" is the best overall descriptor for how the Adventist church
central leadership acted in reaction to the three theological controversies
that had all of a sudden overtaken the denomination. The initial strategy began with an attempt merely to silence those who dissented, usually through
some kind of informal personal agreement against discussing publicly the
disputed ideas, as in Ford's case. Then, if that failed, the church would terminate the dissident from employment and thus remove their source of
income, as with Walter Rea. The final spiritual step was expulsion from the
church community. Once the purge began, however, there followed thousands of voluntary defections, hundreds of clergy firings, and a few hasty
heresy trials that led inevitably to excommunication. All told, estimates of

membership loss to the Adventist church during this period run as high
as one million, although that is probably excessive since the controversies
were mostly confined to Australia, New Zealand, Canada, and the United
States. Without following a strictly chronological order, I'm going to relate
a number of incidents that occurred over the decade 1980–1990. These will
illustrate the theological climate in the Adventist church during these decisive, tumultuous days.

Southern Adventist University lost little time in readying itself for
what was predictably to come. As the trifecta of controversies, like waves,
crashed over the University, all three of the key protagonists in the disputes
held public meetings on or near the campus. Geoffrey Paxton spoke to an
audience of more than five hundred, mostly faculty, students, and community residents. Ford also visited the campus, although his visit came prior
to his infamous lecture challenging the church's teaching about Daniel 8.
Walter Rea also visited the community. By this time, however, University
officials—now running scared—wouldn't allow Rea any campus venue. Instead, Rea spoke at nearby Covenant College, a Presbyterian school located
on the crest of the well-known Lookout Mountain. There he shocked both
the Presbyterians and Adventists about the magnitude of Ellen White's
copying. Report of Rea's lecture spread so quickly through the Southern
Adventist University community that, for all the good the University's ban
had accomplished, it might have been better had he publicly spoken on the
campus. The appearance at and around the University of Paxton, Ford, and
Rea merely served to fan the embers of controversy.

The dizzying effect of three major doctrine debates, one upon top of
another, greatly worried me. Already, as a result of my doctoral studies and
further personal investigation, I was finding Adventism less and less intellectually, theologically, or spiritually satisfying. Adventists often boast that
people "read themselves into the Adventist church." My experience was now
the opposite. I was reading myself out of it. If Adventism was like a map, the
map for me no longer corresponded to the terrain.

I didn't know what to do. The denomination's official attempts to deal
with the theological problems, even at best, seemed far too inadequate. *If
this is the best we can do*, I often thought after reading still another official
article or paper about the debated issues, *we're in a lot of trouble.*

Religious communities like Adventism, which cling obsessively, even
desperately, to their peculiar, idiosyncratic interpretations of the Bible, often
lack even the most rudimentary processes for dealing with honest dissent.
Since at least the time of General Conference President, George I. Butler
(1834–1918), who boasted that the General Conference was the "highest
authority of an earthly character among Seventh-day Adventists," Adventists

have fostered a long, shameful, martyr-strewn history of dealing with dissent. A threat to any theological doctrine, however minor, is considered a threat to the whole church community. Since theology provides the raison d'etre of Adventism, the challenges to theology are ultimately challenges to church leadership. Disagreement with theology is equated with disloyalty to the church and quite simply, bad faith. In place of orderly discussion, debate, and compromise—the usual means of resolving conflict—Adventist leaders tend to "politicize" dissent, label it seditious, and go about trying to suppress or eliminate it. Theological conflict, Adventist leaders seem to think, somehow undermines the comprehensive truth claim of Adventism. If the church already has in hand correct theology, how can there ever be disagreement about even one point of it? If the theology is already flawless, how can one criticize it? So in the name of unity leaders try to suppress or eliminate dissent. They appear to have never grasped that a church community can have unity *within* diversity.

The Bible presents a multiplicity of theological perspectives through which the revelation of God has come to light. The gospels of Matthew, Mark, Luke, and John all diverge in specific instances, as does Paul, not to speak of the various Old Testament writings. No one common denominator brings these diverse writings together.[1] Adventism, which boasts of carefully following the Bible, has tragically become blinded to the diversity in the Bible itself. Adventist leaders generally try to isolate and purge the body politic of any who publicly disagree with the official dogma. Threatened on three cardinal doctrinal fronts, Adventism now stood poised to repeat its history of opposing honest dissent.

It was not the occasional appearance of a Paxton, Ford, or Rea that kept the fires of inquisition smoldering at Southern, but rather the persistent, determined agitation of one layperson, Florence Woolcock, who suddenly appeared in the community designating herself a "concerned" Adventist. It all started at a prayer meeting at the University church. Professor Gerald Colvin, chair of the psychology department, was at that moment leading a discussion on the Christian view of human sexuality.

"Dr. Colvin, what do you think about masturbation? Is it a sin?" The question in the back of the auditorium came from a rumpled little lady with a thin, wavering voice. That night, no one really recognized Woolcock, although she would go on to become notorious in the Adventist community. She was "concerned" about the theological "heresy" being taught at the University, she said. Woolcock had no official relationship to the school,

---

1. Emil Brunner notes that, while the biblical documents present diversity and a common denominator cannot be identified, the biblical documents "none the less find their unity in the one Jesus Christ to whom all bear witness" (*Dogmatics*, 3:242).

other than the fact her children were students there. Yet she had absolutely
convinced herself that Southern was drifting far away from the church's traditional moorings.

Colvin warily hesitated. As an Adventist psychologist, he was acutely
aware of the numerous, puzzling Ellen White comments about masturbation, which White called the "secret vice."[2] He also was aware of the plagiarism crisis now whirling around White. Choosing his words carefully, he
replied, "We have no psychological evidence that masturbation is harmful,
unless it becomes obsessive. Nor is there any indication in the Bible that it
is a sin."

Furious, Woolcock got up, turned and petulantly stalked out of the
meeting, convinced Colvin had not offered adequate support for Ellen
White's view of masturbation and by his tentative response had actually
undermined Ellen White. A few days later, Woolcock launched a frenzied,
somewhat disorganized, personal attack on the whole University. She declared ideological war on the faculty. Although she started with the topic of
masturbation, she quickly turned her wrath specifically on the theological
faculty, emboldened especially by Kenneth Wood's recent cavalier editorials in the *Adventist Review*, the church's general magazine, asserting that
Adventist colleges were all guilty of teaching false doctrine. The theological
crises, in her view, were nothing more than examples of the encroaching lib-
eralism and modernism taking over the church. Her protest letters quickly
turned up in the mail of almost every church leader, from the General Conference to the local churches.

Other disgruntled laity soon joined her fanatical rant. John Felts, a
tall, rotund, white-haired Adventist printer, helped her compose, edit, and
publish a series of broadsides that Woolcock and her supporters personally distributed to the doorstep of almost every home in the small village of
Collegedale. These *National Inquirer*-style tabloids, dubbed the *SDA Press
Release*, bitterly accused Southern in general and the religion faculty in
particular of specious "heresies." The word "heresy" appearing in the same
sentence as the University, for a closed community like Collegedale had
much the same chilling effect as calling a person a "witch" must have had
in seventeenth-century Salem, Massachusetts. The claim of heresy evoked
panic, particularly in the context of the ongoing theological controversies
in the larger church over Ellen White, the Investigative Judgment, and
the gospel. Like the so-called witches at Salem, accused heretics in such a

---

2. White's view of masturbation clearly reflects the influences of the nineteenth
century. She thought masturbation during the teenage years led eventually to paralysis
of the brain [dementia?], cancer, lung and spinal difficulties (*Testimonies for Church*,
2:409; *Child Guidance*, 444).

religious environment threaten the fabric of the community. Frightened, horrified, but well-intentioned people began ripping into students, faculty, clergy—anyone who had a different opinion than they on any religious issue. Collegedale began to act like the Salem witch trials of 1692, where the accusation itself was proof enough of guilt.

Fearing for their livelihood, University faculty and employees went cautiously home each evening, drew the blinds, ignored the phone, and walled themselves off as best they could from the rest of the community. Everyone suddenly became suspect—especially so the theologians. No one trusted anyone. Trust collapsed.

Another independent tabloid newspaper, *Pilgrim's Rest*, published by Vance Ferrell, joined the *SDA Press Release* in denouncing Southern. From a serious, journalistic perspective, neither *Pilgrim's Rest* nor the *SDA Press Release* had any real grasp of the serious theological problems confronting Adventism. Preying on peoples' widespread fears, they printed rash, unfounded allegations that ridiculed sincere, earnest people—administrators, theologians, and pastors—who were under pressure to find quick, satisfactory solutions to the denomination's theological woes. Woolcock, Felts, and Ferrell exaggerated, overstated, misquoted, and circulated rumors about anyone who dared publicly comment about the theological issues. Gossip spread like wildfire. What astounded me, however, was how eagerly—how ravenously—the Adventist public and the church administrators at every level accepted the dubious claims of this new right-wing, Adventist fundamentalist movement.

"Where there's smoke," touted Al McClure, Southern's Chair of the Board of Trustees and President of Adventism's Southern Union Conference, the judicatory which governed Southern Adventist University, "there's bound to be fire."

When I visited the Adventist General Conference headquarters, then located at Takoma Park, Maryland, whom did I come across but Florence Woolcock, standing like a sentry at the main entry, handing out fliers denouncing Southern? At an important General Conference theological consultation, attended by more than two hundred religion professors, the president of the General Conference, Neal Wilson, angrily waved a copy of Vance Ferrell's latest edition of *Pilgrim's Rest*. "Now we have the truth!" he fervidly exclaimed through clinched teeth.

Following the meeting, in company with Douglas Clark, another Adventist religion professor, I made my way to the front of the auditorium to speak privately with Wilson. I challenged the *Pilgrim's Rest* claims. "You can't take the claims of *Pilgrim's Rest* seriously," I objected. "They're inaccurate and misleading."

"I strongly disagree," Wilson brusquely responded, waving us aside. "The church has got to put a stop to this. I stand by the comment I made today."

How do you fight for a rational, objective search for truth in such an irrational, paranoid atmosphere? I brooded later. Top ranking church officials are quite convinced you are out to undermine and "get" the church? They see you as the enemy. The accusation is proof of guilt.

"Parents of Seventh-day Adventist youth," Woolcock implored, in a reprint of one of her earlier editorials from the *SDA Press Release*, this time mailed as a circular to hundreds of parents of Southern's students, "do you care about what is happening to the youth of our Church? . . . This insidious work [heresy and modernism] continues on steadily, month after month, year after year. It will go on without stopping unless you and I do something to see that it IS stopped!"

Surreptitiously, Woolcock gained access to a room adjacent to a classroom where Ed Zackrison was lecturing. A thin plastic folding divider curtain separated the two rooms. Quietly surveilling, she recorded the lectures, the student discussion, and Zackrison's comments. On another occasion, just as the class was dismissed, she came out from behind the partition and directly interrogated Zackrison. "Where do you stand on Ellen White?" From the notes made from these two visits, she wrote several articles for the *SDA Press Release*. Such intrusions into the privacy of the classroom turned Zackrison into the most frequently (mis)quoted faculty member. After hearing Woolcock's relentless attacks—but without checking them out— Adventist leadership grew deeply suspicious of Zackrison. Some prominent denominational leaders, also without bothering to check the accuracy of the rumors, urged he be immediately fired.

A life-long Adventist of Scandinavian ancestry, light-skinned, tall, blond, Zackrison had come to the University from a pastorate in California. From his large, spacious study, lined wall-to-wall with books, he vigorously dashed out class lectures, papers, and a doctoral dissertation in systematic theology from Andrews University, with a furor that amazed me. Before the heresy rumors began to hover around him, Zackrison, was very popular, not only as a professor, but also as a preacher in the Adventist community.

Lorenzo Grant also came under intense fire from the critics of the University. In his late forties, after a career in youth ministry, Grant had attended Howard University for his doctorate (DMin) in Christian ethics. He then joined the faculty at Southern, interestingly the only African American on an otherwise all white faculty.[3] His ethics courses drew large

3. Although it was never openly discussed, there was a strong undercurrent

enrollments. Intermingling fascinating, humorous story-telling with solid instruction, Grant was easily the most popular professor in the religion department. Also a popular speaker in Adventist churches across the country, Grant combined popular wit with a deep dedication to the church. But he didn't hesitate to speak his mind. "Theologians are an endangered species in Adventism," he famously quipped. Although there were others, Zackrison, Grant, and I took the brunt of the right-wing criticisms.

Professors at Southern now found themselves open targets for anyone who, for whatever reason, decided to invade their classrooms, publicly denounce them in print for heresy, or carelessly misquote them. Faculty were cautioned not to try to defend themselves. That only added fuel to the fire, it was claimed. Neither did their critics need offer proof of the accusation. As in the Spanish Inquisition, the accusation itself was proof enough.

Arriving early one day for a morning class, I found Florence Woolcock at the door, eagerly distributing a newly-issued broadside of right-wing propaganda to the students. She was dressed in a dumpy, gray overcoat, hair carelessly coiffed. "Why are you standing here at the door of the classroom?" I demanded, visibly quite annoyed. "Do you have permission to hand out your literature here?"

"No, I don't. But I think it's extremely urgent students be warned about your class."

"How do you know *what* I teach? Have you ever attended one of my classes?"

"No, I haven't. But I know you're just like Grant and Zackrison. You're friends with them. You're an associate. And, like them, you're teaching heresy," she stubbornly insisted. Guilt by association!

Later that afternoon I complained to the University administration about Woolcock's incursion into my class. "We really can't do anything about it," I was told. "This is a free country. Freedom of speech, and all that! We can't restrict our constituents from visiting the campus, talking to students, or even giving out fliers." Libel and slander thus became daily fare for most religion faculty members. We were fair game for even the most ridiculous, unfounded accusation. I was accused of being an undercover Roman Catholic Jesuit priest, intent on subverting the church. The source of this rumor appears to have been a black turtleneck sweater I wore to class one day. It must have resembled a clerical collar worn by a priest. I never wore the sweater again after that.

of racism in the criticism leveled at Grant during the theological crises. At the time, Southern had a long-standing reputation for minimizing the enrollment of persons of color. Today, fortunately, Southern is fully integrated.

In the University administration offices a few days later, I stopped in to talk with William Allen, the newly appointed academic dean. Allen lived next door to us. "I think you'd like to know that I and some others here are trying to curb what Florence Woolcock is doing on campus. We put it on the agenda for the last University board executive council. When we got to the meeting, however, the item had been mysteriously removed."

"Why?" I asked. "Do you think the chair, Al McClure, doesn't want to deal with this problem in the executive council?"

"The answer to that is one you probably know but don't want to hear," Allen grinned wryly.

"Which is . . . ?"

"The union president agrees with the right wing that some faculty ought to be fired. That's why he's not interested in restricting Woolcock. He agrees with her! She plays right into his strategy." I couldn't believe Allen would admit this so openly. There were listening ears in nearby offices.

"If you ask me," I volunteered, "here is the source of our problem. We have a board chair who doesn't really support us. He expects absolute loyalty but doesn't reciprocate. A union president—who is also chair of the Board of Trustees—must support the institution! That's a given in any polity I know about!"

Denominational pressure to stamp out dissent nevertheless continued unabated. In the face of constant agitation by Woolcock and her followers, I sought legal relief. It had become evident by now that no denominational official—at any level—would support me or any others on the faculty. My attorney, Harry Burnette, sent Woolcock an official, certified letter warning her of the legal consequences of public libel and slander. The letter demanded she "cease further publications which would tend to harm or threaten Dr. Gladson in his profession and calling."[4] Frightened by it, I don't think Woolcock referred again to me in print after the letter.

Vance Ferrell, another local right-wing critic of the University, joined forces with Woolcock by grouping the Protestant gospel emphasis, along with Ford and Rea, under a pejorative category he labeled the "New Theology." The significant part of the label—"New"—was the important element. Ferrell contrasted the debate over Ellen White, the Investigative Judgment, and the gospel emphasis with what he considered "historic" Adventism. Ferrell's description of both historic Adventism and the controversial issues, although widely accepted by many, was flawed and inaccurate.

"Live life as you find it out in the world," he satirized, accusing Ford in particular of antinomianism, the abandonment of all moral values, "and

4. Burnette to Florence Woolcock, 16 June 1986.

let your future be as dark as you want to make it . . . Sin, and you needn't be sorry for it was meant to be." Ferrell reprised the old Adventist perfectionism. Ferrell insisted on the resignation—or rather, the immediate firing—of most of the faculty at Southern, particularly the president at the time, Frank Knittel, Lorenzo Grant, Ed Zackrison, Ron Springett, and me.[5]

Frank Knittel, perhaps the most progressive president in Southern's history, held a PhD in Renaissance literature, and as the son of a teacher relished classroom teaching. Fiercely loyal to his faculty, he had helped Southern climb from a parochial, isolated college into a leader among Adventist institutions of higher education. Knittel, almost singlehandedly, had literally brought Southern into the modern era.

Ron Spingett, studious and erudite, was quite the opposite of the energetic Knittel. When he came from the United Kingdom to attend the Seventh-day Adventist Seminary in Berrien Springs, Michigan, he had no idea he would spend most of his academic life guiding Southern's religion majors—many howling and screaming—through two years of New Testament Greek. With a PhD in New Testament (Manchester University, United Kingdom) and a masterly British wit, Springett took great pride in witnessing his students regularly excel on their seminary Greek placement exam.

Attacks on Knittel, Zackrison, Grant, Springett, and me grew more determined. The evangelical journal, *Christianity Today*, alarmed at the spreading theological crisis, reported that several Adventist faculty members had already been fired and that the denomination was moving "closer to schism."[6] At Pacific Union College which, like Southern, was literally under siege from constituent, right-wing critics, trustees forced the resignation of the president, Jack Cassell. The *St. Helena Star*, an Angwin, California, newspaper, emblazoned, "PUC Caught in Middle of Adventist Schism."[7] Smuts van Rooyen, one of the denomination's most popular preachers and professors, resigned under pressure from Andrews University allegedly on grounds that his religious views differed from traditional Adventism.[8]

Southern, however, remained pretty much at the eye of the storm. How humiliating to come out of worship services on the Sabbath only to find the

<hr>

5. Ferrell, "New Theology," 1–2. The New Theology, he claimed, is characterized by the notion the "2300-day prophecy refers to something other than 1844" [Ford]; "subtle attacks on the Spirit of Prophecy [Ellen White] that undermine confidence in it" [Rea]; the "idea that the believer cannot stop sinning, and that God's Commandments cannot be kept in this life by anyone, with or without God's help [Ford and Paxton]."

6. Hefley, "Adventist Teachers Forced Out," 23–25.

7. *St. Helena Star*, "PUC Caught in Adventist Schism," March 17, 1983.

8. Lori Poppajohn, "Smuts Van Rooyen Resigns under Pressure," Andrews University *Student Movement*, May 27, 1981, 1–2.

latest *SDA Press Release* denouncing the faculty as guilty of heresy, attached
to the windshields of several hundred automobiles, or go out in the morning
to retrieve the newspaper and find the *Press Release* littering the front yard!

Let me be clear about one thing. No one—not Grant, Zackrison,
Springett, nor I—actually taught anything that, from an Adventist perspective, constituted heresy or deviation from orthodox Adventism. Despite my
personal uncertainties over the theological debates, I made sure the content
of my courses—what I taught in the classroom—lay within the established
parameters of the church's official doctrine. My lectures were "orthodox," in
other words. When students asked sensitive questions about the theological
controversies, I invariably supported and defended the denomination's official positions. Exceptions to this practice were unintentional, I believe, and
few and far between. A steady stream of students, it seemed, dropped by my
office unannounced to discuss the issues in confidence. In these conversations I supported—without fail—the denomination and urged the curious,
troubled student to have patience with the church while it worked through
the problems. "Hang in there. Don't give up. Go with the church," I repeatedly urged.

Rumors persisted that there were "plants," "moles," or "undercover
spies" in University classes to bait teachers into saying something that could
be used against them. Fielding impromptu student questions in religion
courses was to enter dangerous, uncharted territory. One religion professor, according to a student in his class, decided the best procedure was not
to take any questions at all. The students were to listen to the lecture, take
notes, and exit the class without any discussion.

"What do you think about Ford's interpretation of Daniel 8:14?" I
remember a slender, brunette student asking. In class she generally didn't
often participate in the discussion, so her question caught me by surprise.
Was she an infiltrator? A spy?

"Ford has said many things about Daniel 8:14. Do you have in mind a
particular issue?" I parried, trying to figure out her motive.

"No, I don't. I just wondered what you think about Ford's views?"

"Well," I began slowly, thoughtfully, cautiously. "You're probably aware
of the discussion that's going on at the General Conference level about the
Adventist interpretation of Daniel 8. Adventists believe that Daniel 8 predicts 1844 and the Investigative Judgment. Have you read the special issue
of the *Ministry* (October 1980) devoted to the Ford investigation?"

"No, I haven't," she admitted. By now her tone had convinced me she
was apparently asking an honest question. She wasn't a spy.

Questions about Ellen White surfaced persistently. "We know Ellen
White borrowed some of her material," I repeatedly commented when in

class. "Some church leaders have always known this, although the public hasn't been as aware. What we don't know at present is the *extent* or the *significance* of the borrowing. Fred Veltman, a New Testament scholar, under General Conference patronage, is looking into these questions and will render a full report."

What continually mystified me, however, was the fact that no church leader—not Al McClure, Neal Wilson, or any other church administrator—ever tried to find out what any Southern professor was actually teaching. As administrators, were they fearful of academia? No one ever asked me for a copy of my course syllabus. No denominational official ever sat down across from me in my study and personally discussed any of the controversies that were going on. Instead, almost all denominational leaders—from the highest to lowest—simply *assumed* that the right-wing accusations were accurate. No one in the church's upper echelons offered any defense of the beleaguered Southern faculty. It seemed as though they *wanted* us to falter and break under the pressure.

A Christian denomination such as Seventh-day Adventism has a responsibility to make sure that its higher educational institutions support in theory and practice the values and theology of the denomination. No one disputes this. Faculty within such institutions is rightfully expected to adhere to these values. At the same time, when a college or university enjoys public regional academic accreditation, as did Southern and all the other Adventist colleges, it must allow faculty reasonable academic freedom. This is a delicate balance, to be sure, but it can be achieved. A classroom in an academic Christian college is not a propaganda center where students are to be brainwashed. Rather, it is a forum to study Christian values in dialogue with other broadening viewpoints, while respecting and supporting the values of the sponsoring denomination. This was exactly what the religion faculty at Southern were committed to doing.

At the same time, whenever there are accusations against faculty for teaching contrary to the church's values, a church-sponsored university has an obligation to see that these accusations are adjudicated in a judicious and fair manner. Due process must be insisted upon. The faculty should have the right to face their accusers. The religion faculty at Southern was never given this opportunity. For us, there never would be due process. Church administrators simply took the word of our accusers without bothering to investigate or listen to our side of the debate. Accusation, again, was sufficient proof of guilt.

As the onslaught of propaganda from the church's right wing continued, it soon became clear that the University board chair, Al McClure, had essentially united with the school's critics. He was probably pressured by certain powerful, wealthy benefactors of the University to do so. At least one benefactor, on whose largess the University depended, had personally joined in distributing the literature of the right wing and calling for the resignation of the religion faculty. Rumor had it that this individual would drop a million dollars into the coffers of the University were it to get rid of Grant, Zackrison, and Gladson. It became evident, given the influence of such wealthy supporters, that we would get no real support from our Board of Trustees.

Frank Knittel summoned the entire religion faculty to his office for an emergency meeting. He informed us he would go over McClure's head and arrange an appointment with Neal Wilson, the President of the General Conference, to see what could be done at the church's highest level to halt the vicious and disturbing insinuations leveled against the school. "We'll get a University van—all of us," Knittel declared, eyes sparkling, voice crackling with anticipation that he'd at last found a plausible resolution to our dilemma, "and drive to the General Conference headquarters and present our case directly to Wilson." When Knittel tried to set up the appointment, however, to his utter amazement, Wilson obstinately refused. "I won't meet with *any* faculty from Southern, under *any* circumstances," Wilson emphasized. "You have a lot of people upset about what's going on at the University, so you'll just have to deal with it. I won't help you!" The General Conference President, the most powerful and important leader in the church, coldly turned his back on Southern Adventist University, leaving it to its fate.

How do you teach in such an atmosphere, where every word—or rumor—is pondered, analyzed, dissected, and parsed to see if it (hopefully) contains even the tiniest hint of unorthodoxy? Class sessions felt like trying to lead credulous students gingerly, cautiously through a minefield, with powerful IEDs buried in the ground all around, hoping no one would carelessly detonate one. Since students are naturally curious and acutely aware of what is going on around them, the trifecta—the gospel, the Investigative Judgment, and Ellen White—popped up frequently in religion classes, no matter what the assigned topic. There was simply no way as faculty to avoid controversy, no way to keep it entirely out of the discussion. There was no mute button.

In spite of the onslaught of church's right-wing propaganda, and despite my growing uneasiness with the church's doctrines, I still clung to hope that reasonable explanations could be found for the embarrassing theological discrepancies the denomination faced. Was there a way—an authentic way—for the church to continue to affirm the disputed doctrines?

What might that way be? I hadn't a clue. My advanced theological training utterly failed me. Instead of helping, all the research and study I'd done in Old Testament, New Testament, philosophy, and theology seemed to point in a contrary direction. The disquieting truths Paxton, Ford, and Rea had uncovered were valid. But the denomination stubbornly refused to face them. "Kill the messenger!" shouted the right wing. Adventist administrators everywhere, it seemed, were set to do just that.

In such a paranoid atmosphere, after several years of intense struggle, I'm afraid I gave up looking for resolution. Instead, I concentrated on mere survival. I tried to walk the narrow ledge between Adventism, on the one hand, and the principles of genuine scholarship on the other. I was torn between the "yes" and the "no." Deep within I could sense, against all the determination I could muster, that Adventism was spiritually and theologically slipping away from me. Its grand myth—once the passion of my life—was slowly dying inside. The church's fundamental dishonesty had spiritually dealt me a mortal blow.

Every time I walked into a classroom and looked into the eyes of the young, inquisitive, eager students, I trembled. How could I help these students in this turbulent, unsettled, confusing atmosphere? Would this class session be my last? Would there be a proverbial knock at the door and denominational leaders suddenly appear to escort me out?

My interior conflict shoved almost every other consideration aside. The struggle to bring together my professional life and my conscientious reservations inevitably had its impact on our home life. Conversation around the dinner table invariably began and ended with the theological problems. When not talking about them, we obsessed about them, and then lapsed into miserable, despondent silence. Laura and I seemed to be growing more and more apart. Every Saturday (Sabbath) morning, I reluctantly—by sheer determination—attended worship at the University church, convinced that whatever was going to happen I still needed the spiritual connection of worship. Laura preferred to stay away, averse to facing the community's suspicious, hostile eyes. We had literally become pariahs in the small community. When Laura did attend, she perfunctorily sang the hymns or joined in the litanies, but seemed aloof, far away. The Adventist myth had also long been dead within her.

JoAnna and Paula, our daughters, suffered most. Looking back, I believe the religious indifference our daughters have at times reflected since stems from the spiritual trauma inflicted upon our family. They passively bore the painful strangling of the spiritual and professional lives of their parents, all in the name of a self-righteous, judgmental orthodoxy. I realize now that they—as well as Laura and I—were experiencing what psychologists call "spiritual abuse" or "toxic faith." We were victims of spiritual trauma. How were we going to fight back? How were we going to get out of this mess? Such religious inquisitions, whatever they may be called, poison the minds of both victims and perpetrators because they deny the fundamental sanctity of what it means to be a free human being. They dehumanize.

The University chair of the Board of Trustees made no attempt to quell the widespread rumors. Instead of defending the beleaguered faculty, as was his stated duty, McClure quietly implemented a purge. In a faculty meeting, emboldened by the University's wealthy benefactors, he signaled that he intended to make Southern an "Adventist" college again. McClure bought into the right wing's frightening domino theory expressed by W. B. Quigley, of the Ministerial Department of the General Conference: "The kind of evangelicalism which is being promulgated will eventually destroy the Sabbath, the state of the dead, the imminent coming of Jesus, as well as the Investigative Judgment, and responsible Christian living."[9]

Scholars in the church's North American colleges and universities all grew more and more uneasy. Watching events at Southern Adventist University and Pacific Union College, the front lines of the battle, they feared that a similar purge could easily be touched off in their institutions. Top-level denominational officials firmly rejected any plea for patience or tolerance.

Instead of cowering in the corner and waiting for the proverbial knock at the door, as most of us seemed wont to do, Lorenzo Grant aggressively took action. Adventist scholars, he realized, were isolated from each other on campuses scattered across the nation. They could too easily be picked off one by one. They needed to organize in some manner, and converse with each other about the growing suspicion in the church regarding all theological scholarship. They also knew that denominational leadership, already nervous and antagonistic, would never sanction such organizational efforts. Grant therefore scheduled a meeting of representative scholars to take place in Atlanta, a convenient air transportation center. Delegates, who were expected to cover their own travel and expenses, should attend only with the blessing of the chief executive officer of their respective institution. Seventeen Adventist theologians, I among them, gathered in a Howard Johnson Hotel near Hartsfield-Jackson International Airport in Atlanta on a Friday and Saturday in early June.

9. Quigley to Lee F. Greer Jr., 19 August 1981. "State of the dead" in this letter refers to the church's belief that the dead "sleep" unconsciously in the grave until the resurrection, rather than go immediately into the presence of God at death.

Our overriding concern was the hardline, oppositional stance taken against Adventist theologians by most denominational leaders. Already several professors and clergy had been fired, including Desmond Ford and Smuts van Rooyen. Severely polarized was the North American Adventist community. Schism seemed ominous. The crisis pitted theologian against denominational administrator. We worried about the castigation of loyal, honest scholarship, scholarship that had heretofore provided the denomination its greatest resource during such theological crises. "Whereas some institutions pursue a policy of 'publish or perish,'" Charles Teel of Loma Linda University ironically encapsulated our dilemma in an adage that persisted in our minds long after the meeting, "we pursue a policy of 'publish and perish.'"

Fred Veltman was in attendance. Eagerly we listened to a preview of his research into the sources of Ellen White's book, the *Desire of Ages*. Our mouths fell open as he revealed that White had borrowed from novels as well as theological works. I described the painful events that had taken place at Southern Adventist University, while others related the struggle on their respective campuses. Larry Geraty shared a paper written by his colleague, Fritz Guy, a theologian from the Adventist Theological Seminary, who was unable to attend. Significantly, the paper was entitled, "The Future of Adventist Theology: A Personal View." Guy, long very active in denominational theological circles, conceded that any breakthrough in the church's stubborn attitude toward theological scholarship was now altogether unlikely. "I've resolved never to write another paper for the denomination," he sadly admitted. "A community can only properly function if it has honesty," he wrote. His closing words painted a bleak, depressing future. The horror was that the future already seemed to be unfolding before our eyes:

> Can the community accept and even encourage theological development? If not, Adventist theology has no actual future, even though it has the necessary theoretical qualifications. For if the community does not support the activity of theology, those with the educational equipment and the personal interest to engage in this activity will decline to do so, and the activity will cease. The end of theological activity would not, of course, signal the end of the community itself, but only the end of its theological growth.[10]

On Saturday, the Adventist Sabbath, the group drew up a conciliatory document emphasizing our determination—as theologians—to "work with church administrators in their efforts to unify the church through

---

10. Guy, "Future of Adventist Theology," 13.

theological dialogue, Bible study, fellowship, and prayer." We called upon church leaders to cease punitive action against church employees without due cause, and urged denominational leaders to foster instead an attitude of mutual trust, confidence, and collaboration in dealing with the Adventist theological crisis. The document became known as the "Atlanta Affirmation." The collaborative putting together of this Affirmation infused us with more confidence than we had felt in a long time. We were convinced this was a major step toward reconciling discordant voices in the church.

Church leadership, to our bewilderment, took precisely the opposite view. They misinterpreted the gathering in Atlanta and the resulting conciliatory document as conspiratorial, aimed at undermining the authority of the church. "The minutes [of the Atlanta gathering]," angrily wrote Kenneth Wood, editor of the *Adventist Review*, "provide clear evidence that an organized effort is being made to undermine the historic doctrines of the church."[11] That scholars had taken the initiative in organizing this meeting—without approval from the General Conference—further antagonized denominational leaders. (Keep in mind the pyramidal, or top-down, administrative structure of Adventism.) Such independence, despite its conciliatory tone, came across to church leaders as an act of defiance. We who affixed our names to the "Atlanta Affirmation" didn't realize it, but we had signed our denominational death warrants.

11. Kenneth Wood to Lee F. Greer Jr., 24 August 1981. To show how badly Wood misread the gathering, I place alongside his remark the exact words of the Atlanta Affirmation: "We are confident in the providential origin and distinctive message and mission of the Seventh-day Adventist Church . . . [scholars will] take frequent opportunity to express confidence in the truthfulness of the Adventist message." Wood's hasty remark reflected the general consensus among top church leadership.

14

Inquisition

The real and fatal cost of fundamentalist doctrine and ideology, as a system of life, is not its inner logical inconsistency, but rather its personal cost: it can be sustained as a viable way of life only at the cost of unchurching and rejecting, as persons, thinkers and scholars, and as Christians, all those who question the validity of the conservative option . . . they have . . . to be eliminated from the scene altogether.

—*JAMES BARR*

In May of that year, the graduating seniors at Southern generously selected me "Teacher of the Year," an honor that, under the circumstances, took me completely by surprise. I was humbled, but gratified, particularly since the honor had come when I was under such suspicion and criticism by church administrators. It was encouraging that I was effective as a teacher.

Laura, JoAnna, and Paula, and I vacationed in New England in August with close friends, Linwood and Fran Robertson. We visited Philadelphia, toured the historic district and Independence Hall, where the American Declaration of Independence had been signed, and then made our way to Boston. There we stopped at the sites associated with the American Revolutionary War. At Plymouth, Massachusetts, we stood at Plymouth Rock and imagined how the cold and bleary refugees from the *Mayflower* felt upon finally making land in December 1620. We camped for several days on beautiful Cape Cod. These were sacred sites to us because they all played a role in the long American struggle for freedom of speech, assembly, and religion.

We returned home on a Sunday afternoon. As we were unloading our yellow Plymouth station wagon, Ed Zackrison whirled into our driveway in his small Volkswagen. Jumping out, without bothering even to close the car door, he blurted out, "I have some terrible news! You, Lorenzo Grant, and I are slated to be fired tomorrow morning at the University Board of Trustees!"

My heart sank. Had the dreaded moment finally come? Was this the proverbial "knock at the door"? "Why? Why now? Why all of a sudden? Why without any warning?" I exclaimed.

"That's not clear. According to [Frank] Knittel, evidently the University board chair, McClure, has decided that we're all guilty of heresy and wants us out. He's convinced that the three of us are the real source of the controversy going on around here."

Zackrison's warning—miraculously, it seems—proved premature. McClure took no action to fire anyone that day. "I refuse to terminate anyone," said a defiant Knittel earlier to McClure, "without following proper University grievance procedure!" Was that why McClure didn't terminate anyone? In his notes for future action, we learned later from inside sources, McClure scribbled the word "urgent" by Knittel's name, thus adding Knittel to the list of persons to be eliminated. There is reason to believe McClure's list included other faculty who were not professors in the religion department. Melvin Campbell, the Dean of Students, was surprised to learn that he was on the list because his wife, a devout, loyal Adventist, allegedly didn't believe in Ellen White.

I had unfortunately long been included on McClure's list along with the other alleged "heretics" that the right wing had so designated. By now I was widely considered one of the most notorious dissidents. But up to now, no dismissal had occurred. With this aborted last minute attempt at firing, however, I entered a more intense period of insecurity. For the next six years the proverbial sword of Damocles dangled menacingly. A knot of anxiety constantly gnawed at me. I'm amazed I didn't develop an ulcer. The early elation I'd experienced with my unanticipated teaching career gave way to excruciating, persistent torment. Each morning dutifully I went to the office, not really knowing whether by day's end I would still be on the faculty. Whenever the University board met, I worried until I got news of what had transpired. Laura, the girls, and I tried to get away almost every weekend to the cabin we'd built at Ellijay, in the North Georgia mountains, about sixty miles distant. We even named the cabin the "Hiding Place," thinking about Corrie ten Boom's home in Holland, where her family had hidden

Jewish refugees from the Nazis. There, in the heavily wooded, mountainous terrain, it seemed, we felt we could leave Southern behind for a few restful hours, and find a little peace and quiet.

While teaching, it had long been my practice to revise my lecture notes and materials as the class unfolded, always with a view toward the next time I would teach the course. But now I had no real assurance I would ever teach any particular course or even be employed beyond the current week. So I began to neglect such revision. Under the incessant, ill-defined, gnawing pressure, my teaching, I'm sure, suffered. When will the sword fall? I pondered. When will I get the word, "Clean out your desk and vacate the premises"? If that happens, where would I go? What would I do? I'd regrettably now staked my whole career on *this* church, *this* university. How could I fight this? I felt hopeless, helpless, and alone. The crushing, inner turmoil, of being torn between visceral, almost instinctual loyalty to my church of origin and the growing awareness of its theological blunders, weighed heavily.

The same student I mentioned earlier—Steve—seemed to be everywhere on the small campus confronting faculty, visiting church officials, and other clergy, interrogating them about the issues under dispute. Snippets of his interviews started appearing in the *SDA Press Release* and *Pilgrim's Rest*. Was Steve secretly recording conversations, and then turning over the notes or transcripts to the University's critics? I wondered. Recording someone without consent, then making public what was said, I reflected, was unethical, if not illegal. Since Steve was majoring in religion, what he was up to was naturally of concern to the religion department. Having endured Steve's indirect assault for several months, the religion faculty called him in for a meeting.

Attired in a dark blue sport jacket, white shirt, and red-striped tie, Steve nervously took to a seat directly across from me at the long table around which we'd gathered. The religion department was then housed in historic Lynn Wood Hall, a large, three-storied, wine-colored, wooden structure that dated to the 1920s. It had been constructed of wood because the founders expected Christ to return soon, so there was no need to use brick or stone in its construction. Its ancient pine floors creaked with foot traffic, and in cold weather the radiators hissed and pinged. The high-ceilinged room where we met had once served as the office of the academic dean.

Our inquiry started indirectly. We hoped by such an indirect approach, if possible, to get some idea of Steve's motives. Why had he come to the University? Why, instead of studying for his classes, did he spend most of his time interviewing faculty and students? What was he looking for? What did he intend? For twenty or thirty minutes questioning continued.

Abruptly, Ed Zackrison asked, "Steve, have you been recording people's conversations without getting permission?"

"Yes, I have," he admitted.

"Don't you realize that's illegal, not to speak of unethical?" Zackrison pressed.

"Yes. I'm aware of that, but I think in view of the deadly heresy being taught around here by this faculty, I'm justified in doing it."

"In other words, the 'end' justifies the 'means,' or something like that?"

"You might put it that way." The overcast, gray skies outside grew darker as daylight slowly began to fade.

"Steve," Zackrison paused, like Perry Mason deliberately choosing his words, "while we've been sitting around this table, are you recording this interview—without our consent?"

"Yes, I am," he again answered smugly. His response fell onto absolute, stunned silence. Steve reached inside his coat and slowly extracted a tiny microphone, attached by a long, thin wire to a small tape recording device he wore on his belt. The equipment appeared to be of professional quality. "This is what I'm using." We glanced at Zackrison, then Steve, then at each other. We sat there, at a loss, speechless, for a moment or so.

"Steve, would you wait out in the hall while we discuss what you've just told us?" politely asked Douglas Bennett, the department chair.

While Steve waited in the hall, we were unable to reach agreement on what action to take. Assuming that Steve may have been surveilling under the direction of a denominational leader, or more likely, a wealthy, influential board member, some in the department were very fearful of interfering. "It's a free country, after all. We can't object when a student tries to gather information in this way. After all, we allow students to record our classes," they argued. Consequently, trepidation prevailed; no decision was made.

On learning about Steve's concession and the department's fearful reaction, a livid Frank Knittel sent word to the University Admissions Office that Steve was categorically not to be readmitted for the coming term. Steve was, in effect, expelled at the end of the semester and told not to return. What actually happened to Steve, however, surprised everyone. When the spring term ended, the Ohio Adventist Conference immediately hired Steve as a pastor, by-passing the usual denominational educational requirements for clergy. Steve, obviously, had no seminary training. He had barely a year of undergraduate study. The Ohio Conference president, although an alumnus of Southern, had publicly allied himself with the denomination's right wing. The president was ecstatic that he could employ someone who had taken such a bold stand against the "heresy" at Southern. By hiring Steve as a pastor, he typified the growing opposition of denominational leaders to the religion faculty at Southern.

In spite of the doomsayers, and the "heretical" buzz, the student enrollment in religion at Southern defied the odds and continued to increase. It is worth considering that the rumors of heresy were, in part, factors in stimulating this growth. People are attracted to controversy. Reinvigorated by this increased enrollment the religion department decided to add a much-needed faculty member to handle the burgeoning enrollment. After we'd decided on the new faculty position, and determined the academic discipline this person should represent, however, the University abruptly withdrew the budget for the position. Financial support was suddenly, inexplicably unavailable.

As the fall term approached, however, the university administration again abruptly shifted ground. We were going to get new faculty after all: Gordon Hyde. Hyde had agreed to come out of retirement to join the religion staff. In January, just as the winter term began, a second faculty position was also added! Jack Blanco joined the staff. Our eight-person department now suddenly had three specialists in systematic theology: Norman Gulley, Ed Zackrison, and Jack Blanco; and two in homiletics, or preaching, Douglas Bennett and Gordon Hyde! We had quickly gone from too few faculty to too many. What was going on?

Jack Blanco, formerly academic dean at Columbia Union College (now Washington Adventist University), near Washington, DC, had most recently served as a pastor in southern California. With a doctorate (ThD) from the University of South Africa, Blanco had wanted for several years to return to college teaching. In his early 50s, he also brought with him a very conservative reputation.

Blanco would later confirm his traditional Adventist loyalty by publishing *The Clear Word Bible*, an interpolated and loosely paraphrased scriptural text of the entire Bible that, where feasible, gives strong emphasis to Adventist doctrine. For instance, here is the way Blanco renders Dan 8:14, the key passage in the doctrine of the Investigative Judgment: "After two thousand three hundred prophetic days (which represent actual years), God will restore the truth about the heavenly Sanctuary to its rightful place. Then the process of judgment will begin of which the yearly cleansing of the earthly Sanctuary was a type, and God will vindicate His people."[1]

---

1. Blanco, *Clear Word*. Blanco acknowledges this "should not be considered a study Bible" (vii).

Unlike Blanco, Gordon Hyde, a tall, angular man in his mid-60s, formerly director of the denomination's BRICOM, the general church committee on which I had served all during the decade, brought a very different legacy. Almost twenty years before, when he had been the head of the communications department at Southern, Hyde had left the University to become chair of BRICOM. Hyde gradually came to think of his mission at BRICOM as that of identifying, neutralizing and, if possible, uprooting all suspicious, dissident thought from the church's theological community. The Adventist theological community subsequently came to dread what seemed like Hyde's overreach. His main concern, I'd long realized from my service on BRICOM, wasn't Ellen White, the gospel, or the Investigative Judgment. It was the method of biblical interpretation known as historical criticism, which scholars of all denominations virtually everywhere utilize in the study of the Bible.

Historical criticism is really an umbrella term covering a host of literary and historical methods that essentially apply a scientific approach to literary works, such as the Bible.[2] No true, faithful Adventist scholar, Hyde adamantly insisted, could utilize historical criticism. "There is no place for the vertical, for transcendence, in historical method or the historical-critical approach to biblical studies," he told the Biblical Research Institute Science Council (BRISCO) in Utah in 1977.[3] I was in attendance when he read this paper. The historical-critical method, he claimed, was a slippery slope that inevitably spiraled down to spiritual and theological oblivion. Once utilized—even in the slightest degree—it swiftly led to the complete, total rejection of biblical authority. The deep irony here was that Hyde was not by professional training a biblical scholar; his doctorate (PhD) was in Speech and Communication. Although undoubtedly a competent scholar in rhetoric and speech, and a gifted communicator, his focus was not theology or biblical studies. His denunciation of historical criticism thus came from outside the scholarly guild. Yet Hyde deftly wielded the authority of BRICOM against any scholar who dared openly to employ the historical critical

2. *Historical criticism*, to reiterate what was said above, may be defined as the attempt to understand the biblical text in its historical setting, taking into account the time and place of writing, the sources, events, persons, dates, places, things, customs, and so on, with the aim of determining the text's original meaning in its original, historical context (Soulen and Soulen, *Handbook*, 79–80). Hyde's underlying fear here may have been an intuitive awareness that historical criticism would spell trouble for some of Adventism's peculiar doctrines, such as the Investigative Judgment (see Chapter 7, "When Prophecy Failed").

3. Hyde, "The Divine and the Human in Revelation" (working paper, Biblical Research Institute Science Council, Price, UT, May 12, 1977), 4.

method. As chair of BRICOM he seemed to be in possession of enormous denominational power.

Hyde's strategy was disarmingly simple. By inviting to BRICOM various Adventist scholars to present academic papers on controversial topics, Hyde could subvert the presentations into an opportunity to gauge the scholar's personal attitude toward historical criticism. The regular proceedings of the BRICOM for Hyde thus became a way of flushing out sympathizers of historical criticism. Hyde appears to have maintained some sort of private list, like Senator Joseph McCarthy in his anticommunist crusade in the early 1950s, of all Adventist theologians and biblical scholars about whom he had reservations. In the years Hyde had been at BRICOM, the list had never stopped growing longer. Zackrison, Grant, and I had been added, although we didn't yet realize it.

Hints of Hyde's investigative strategy surfaced when I first joined BRICOM, but I was too naïve at the time to recognize it. At a Society of Biblical Literature convention (the world's largest professional society for biblical scholars) plenary session in St. Louis, I was seated alongside Hyde and Gerhard Hasel. Since I was then a novice at such professional gatherings, Hyde took me under his wing and began to point out the various Adventist scholars among the hundreds entering the hall, many of whom I'd never met. "That's X," he would calmly say. "He's a liberal and a historical critic. There's Y. He's loyal to the church." Hyde neatly placed everyone there that night into two categories: conservative = loyal; liberal = disloyal and critical. It didn't take many sessions of BRICOM before I caught on to Hyde's strategy. Now he had arrived on Southern's campus as member of our faculty! He was in our midst, on our team. He was now departmental chair. He had come straight from the denominational headquarters to set matters right.

That spring, under the board chair McClure's escalating pressure, Frank Knittel "resigned" the University presidency. Knittel was the first casualty from the school. Like Frederick, the Duke of Saxony, Martin Luther's protective monarch during the Reformation era, Knittel had been accused by the right wing of "harboring" heretics. The academic dean at the denomination's Union College in Lincoln, Nebraska, John Wagner, was selected as Knittel's replacement, and under his brief but troubled administration three significant events transpired.

Enrollment at the university—always a barometer of institutional health—now inexplicably started to decline. Although the drop could logically be attributed to the economic downturn then occurring throughout the United States, the University's critics hastily blamed it on the theological controversy, especially the hidden presence of heretics among the faculty, the "Achans in the camp" (see Josh 7:16–26). In a tuition-driven institution, fewer students translated into less tuition dollars. A five hundred thousand dollar deficit resulted. The new administration had no choice, it argued. It had to start retrenching faculty and staff. Overstaffed with eight faculty members, now including the newly arrived Hyde and Blanco, the religion faculty suddenly seemed particularly vulnerable. Had a faculty surplus been artificially created in religion so that retrenchment there would seem a logical place to begin? Was this a circuitous way of justifying the dismissal of the accused faculty without going through a normal grievance process? Had the budget crisis been artificially manufactured as a way to remove suspected faculty legally without the danger of litigation? The retrenchment process, whatever its actual intent, came to focus primarily on the religion faculty.

In November Wagner circulated a letter listing the eight members of the religion staff. Attached was a not-so-subtle announcement: "Please check names of the six people you believe would work most successfully as a team." The letter, in the interest of mere popularity, blatantly ignored tenure rights. Every member of the religion staff—except Blanco and Hyde—already had tenure. Later that month, in a lengthy, tense, controversial faculty meeting, several professors angrily demanded that the administration apply objective, generally accepted criteria in the retrenchment process. After two hours of bitter, heated dispute, Don Runyon, from the music department, blurted out, "We have talked for an hour or so about all this without getting to the bottom line. Some of us suspect this is simply old business under a new name—to get rid of Ed Zackrison and Lorenzo Grant." Without denial, Wagner indicated, sheepishly, "The letter probably intensified that point of view."

In January, a second letter appeared that listed the criteria to be used in the retrenchment. Length of service was listed as a consideration, but not as the most important, with "length of service to the Seventh-day Adventist Church in general" as another. On this basis, Hyde and Blanco couldn't be retrenched, although they had been at Southern only a short time and didn't officially have tenure; they were older than the rest of us, with more denominational experience. Was the board whimsically about to pick and choose among the criteria used to remove faculty?

Were we headed for a showdown? In a surprising move on February 1, Wagner reversed this position and indicated that *no* religion faculty would be terminated. Instead, the University would retrench only those who negotiated termination settlements involving reassignment, retraining, or resignation. The crisis passed without explanation. The sudden withdrawal was evidence of a devious plot that lay behind it.

15

Final Confrontation

When faith is in the mouth rather than in the heart, when the solid knowledge of Sacred Scripture fails us, nevertheless by terrorization we drive men to
believe what they do not believe, to love what they do not love, to know what
they do not know. That which is forced cannot be sincere, and that which is not
voluntary cannot please God.

— DESIDERIUS ERASMUS

L orenzo Grant, weary of the unrelieved pressure and uncertainty of
week-to-week employment, and despite having achieved academic tenure, decided to resign. He left to assume a position as a university chaplain
in the Washington, DC, area.

With Grant, who had initiated and organized the Atlanta Affirmation conference, and who had long been at the center of controversy, out of
the way, the University administration next stepped up the pressure on Ed
Zackrison.

At ten o'clock one morning I got a call from the academic dean, Larry
Hanson. "Are you free for about an hour?" He asked.

"Yes, I suppose so. I don't have another class until one."

"Let me come by and get you. Let's take a little ride. We need to talk."
Puzzled, I replaced the phone carefully and leaned back in my chair. I
glanced at my appointment book spread out on the desk in front of me.
Pens and pencils stood in a wire mesh, circular container. On the left sat a
tiny stone-carved Buddha—a gift from a student missionary—I kept there

as a reminder that God was at work among all peoples of the earth, not just Christians and Adventists. One student had sharply criticized me for having a sculpted Buddha on my desk. What could this sudden auto trip be about? I'd become suspicious about such telephone calls.

Hanson drove up in front of the religion building and called out, "Jump in, let's go for a little spin."

We headed out of Collegedale into the rural backroads, roads I knew well from a summer spent in door-to-door sales of Adventist literature in the rural countryside around the University. "Let's drive over to the Georgia-Cumberland Conference Camp Center, near Cohutta Springs, Georgia. I'd like to take a look at it." The local Conference had just built a luxurious, state-of-the-art camp and conference center in Murray County, nestled in the valley below Grassy Mountain, the highest peak in that corner of north Georgia. "We can talk as we go."

I remained silent, content to wait for whatever he wanted to say. For several miles we rode in silence. Then Hanson spoke.

"You've noticed what's happening to Ed Zackrison, haven't you? The board chair has instructed the University administration that he has to go. The pressure from all the Conferences and local church leadership has just gotten too great. McClure's taking steps now to fire Zackrison at the end of this semester. The University has received numerous complaints. You've heard them before. Ed isn't considered a 'true' Adventist. He doesn't believe in Ellen White. He's agitating in his classes and spreading dissent. Some powerful, wealthy patrons of the school—I leave you to guess who they are—have laid down an ultimatum: *Get rid of Zackrison, or else!*"

I wanted to ask what "else" meant, but instead said, "I'm aware of the pressure building against Ed. I'm also very close to Ed. He lives just across the street from me, as you know. I'm also aware of the complaints. I've been accused of many of the same things. There's no substance to them, Larry. They're all based on rumor and innuendo. Instead of firing Ed, the board should come to his defense and give him a chance to respond to the criticisms."

"I appreciate your concern," Hanson said. "That's why I've asked you to come with me today. You're a valuable member of this faculty, and I want you to stay with us. Let me see if I can put it plainly: The University administration has asked me to appeal to you to separate yourself as far as possible from Ed. Don't defend him. Don't support him. Give him a wide berth. If there is a hearing, don't testify on his behalf. Don't come to his aid in any way when the board fires him. Let him go. If you don't pull away from him, you'll suffer the same fate, I can assure you. You'll also be fired! If you back away, I'm pretty certain we can save your position."

By now the camp and conference center had come into view. The blue waters of the newly sculpted lake glittered in the morning sun. The conference center main auditorium looked inviting, nestled among the trees that gradually ascended the low-lying hills that led up the slopes of Grassy Mountain.

I was surprised at Hanson's candor. At first, I didn't know what to say or how to respond. The handwriting on the wall glowered above me, as though written across the clouds. I paused to collect my thoughts. "I appreciate your giving me warning," I told Hanson, "I really do. But you have to know that, whatever the consequences, I must do what I think is right." Larry Hanson was a good friend, and I truly appreciated his counsel. I also knew he was absolutely right. Should I continue to support Ed, as I had been doing up to now, my termination from the faculty would inevitably follow.

"I figured you'd say that," Hanson said, as he dropped me off at the religion building. "But don't say I didn't warn you."

Zackrison's attorney wasted no time in preparing for a lawsuit against Southern Adventist University on grounds of a civil rights violation. He eventually amassed an incredible five hundred pages of documentation, letters, bulletins, *SDA Press Releases*, *Pilgrim's Rest* numbers, even articles from the *Adventist Review*. Zackrison, his dilemma weighing heavily upon him, appealed to the University grievance process. When the University suddenly became aware that thirty-six faculty—including me—were ready to testify in Ed's behalf, the president and the board nervously negotiated a financial settlement. The agreement mandated Zackrison sell his home to the University, collect his family, and leave town. "I was given twelve days to get out of Collegedale," Zackrison reflects, looking back on the incident. "If I did not move in that time, the agreement would be void."[1]

The right-wing charges of heresy against him were never proven. As part of the agreement, the board canceled the $70,000 that Zackrison had been advanced for his doctoral expenses, a mere "paper figure," Wagner said.[2] Ironically, no mention was ever made of the University $500,000 deficit of the previous year. Had one of the wealthy patrons of the University, one who actively supported the right wing antagonists, subtly taken care of it? Or did the deficit never really exist? Was it a mere ploy to justify another agenda? We would never know.

Internally torn and conscience-stricken by his complicity in the clandestine University inquisition, a disillusioned Wagner resigned after only a year in office, helpless in mediating the vicious battle between the church's

1. Email to the author, January 13, 1999.
2. *Adventist Currents*, "Glad Tidings," February 1984, 28.

administration and its beleaguered faculty theologians. Wagner always seemed to me an honest person who really intended to do what was right but, in the highly polarized political atmosphere of the day, felt trapped in a no-win situation. Don Sahly, who had been in Asia during the years of crisis in North American Adventism, and thus had no "feel" for its context, succeeded him.

Knittel, Grant, Zackrison, and Wagner were now history. The guns of the critics suddenly became silent, the fog of battle lifted. The conflict seemed, strangely, to have been settled. Pressure against me miraculously appeared to lessen. For the next two years I managed to hang on in what felt like an uneasy cease-fire, a calm before the cannons roared once more.

I used this lull in the conflict to probe the theological problems ever more intimately, for there had not yet appeared any viable solutions. Conviction continued to deepen that, as far as I could determine, there was no resolution of the disputed issues about the Investigative Judgment or Ellen White short of a revision of key elements in traditional Adventist theology. Adventism was going to have to change theologically and structurally if it were honestly to face up to these problems. The church would eventually have to reassess its doctrine of salvation, its teaching about final events and the judgment, and its understanding of Ellen White.

My confidence in the historical critical method, which Hyde, now the new religion chair, stubbornly opposed, continued to grow. If hypotheses were to be tested by how well they accounted for the data, I reasoned, some form of critical approach was necessary to explain the development and present form of the Bible. As Leander Keck correctly put it:

> It is fundamentally wrong to regard biblical criticism as a threat to the Bible, because it is biblical criticism that has given us the Bibles we actually do read. Every Bible we can read rests on someone else's judgment about what the right wording is. This is as true of Hebrew and Greek Bibles as it is of any version.[3]

The Bible didn't just fall out of heaven in its present form! I was finding it impossible to go back to a pre-critical view of Scripture, such as Adventism seemed to require, and which I had in my formative years naively adopted. Excruciatingly, I was slowly realizing—against all hope—that the denomination would probably never change enough for me to live with integrity as a biblical scholar within it.

Our family was experiencing emotional turmoil, too, groping about in such a fog of uncertainty. Friends confronted JoAnna and Paula, "What's

3. Keck, *Bible in Pulpit*, 76.

the matter with your dad? Is he a 'heretic,' like everyone says?" One religion teacher at the Adventist high school, with JoAnna sitting there in the class, referred to me as a person a faithful Adventist student should avoid. "Dr. Gladson is guilty of heresy, and everyone knows it!" Mortified, JoAnna immediately got up, left class and came home crying (we lived only blocks away). Laura, having finished her doctorate (EdD) in counseling psychology, had nurtured hopes of teaching at the University. She applied for an adjunct faculty position, received immediate and enthusiastic support from the chair of the education and psychology department, Cyril Roe, but was firmly rejected by the University administration. She never found out why, but one faculty colleague, who claimed inside information, told us it was because "Laura was married to the wrong person."

I noticed that none of my remaining religion department colleagues, overtly at least, appeared troubled by any of the actual theological problems that had stirred up such controversy. "Too hot to handle, best to stay clear of them," seemed to be the watchword. Fear paralyzed the religion faculty. Since Zackrison's firing, everyone was on red alert. The chilly foreboding of a hasty dismissal made staying under the radar a priority for survival. Everyone hunkered down, eyeing others warily. The need for survival, as it usually does, crowded out every other impulse. What had once been a contented, progressive department—one of the denomination's finest before the crisis—now had become an emotionally dreary, cold place. Genuine, heartfelt communication ceased. The department of religion—once pride of the University—became increasingly dysfunctional. Don't talk, don't feel, don't rock the boat, be strong, good, right, and perfect—all the symptoms of a dysfunctional family—ruled supreme. Anger wasn't tolerated. The appalling transformation of a once-vibrant religion faculty was almost completely demoralizing.

For my students' sake, I dutifully attended to my teaching, but the spirit had gone out of me. Were it not for the support of sympathetic friends on the faculty in other departments and in the community, I don't know how I would have made it. Within the religion department, I struggled alone in my agonizing intellectual and religious pilgrimage. I lived for the weekends and the blessed escape they brought.

Two years later, the pent-up pressures exploded in a dizzying series of events that were finally to eject me entirely out of Seventh-day Adventism.

William Allen, Southern's newly-appointed Vice-president of Academic Affairs, and now our next door neighbor, telephoned. "I hate like everything to be the bearer of bad news," confided the slightly balding, former science and chemistry professor, "but I need to tell you about a meeting over the weekend in which Gordon Hyde, Al McClure, Jack Blanco, and probably Gerhard Hasel, although I'm not certain he was present, drew up proposed guidelines for the newly endowed chair in religion." O. D. McKee, an Adventist, owner and retired CEO of the well-known Little Debbie Bakery had contributed funds to endow a special Ellen G. White Memorial Chair in Religion. This endowed university chair was full of irony in view of the dark shadow then looming over Ellen White. An ad hoc committee had been appointed to develop the qualifications a potential nominee for the chair would have to possess. Jack Blanco had already unofficially been selected to assume the chair of the religion department once Hyde retired, and hence was a participant in the committee. Gerhard Hasel, whom I mentioned earlier, was the Dean of the Seventh-day Adventist Theological Seminary. He was serving as a consultant to Southern in the setting up of the endowed chair. A close friend and ally of Gordon Hyde, Hasel, an Old Testament scholar by training (PhD, Vanderbilt), had a dreadful reputation among scholars in the denomination because of his strong, aggressive, sometimes ruthless opposition to those employing historical critical methodology.

"This committee is considering making it compulsory that anyone appointed to the endowed chair must oppose *all* forms of historical criticism," Allen continued. "Don Sahly and I are very concerned about this trend. Hyde apparently wants to transform Southern Adventist University into the 'stronghold of orthodoxy' for the Adventist church. But Sahly and I think to ban all forms of historical criticism would discourage any progressive faculty from joining our staff. Eventually it would make it extremely difficult to attract qualified theologians. We would send a message that Southern had taken a step back into fundamentalism."

I felt nauseated. Was this yet another plot ultimately aimed at getting rid of me? I couldn't help thinking this. Obviously, such a person as I would be forever barred from accepting such a chair. Under the circumstances, I really wasn't interested in becoming an "Ellen G. White" chair of anything. If someone who utilized the historical-critical method could be automatically barred from holding this endowed chair, could they also be barred from teaching religion at Southern? Was Hyde manipulating the setting up an endowed chair as a thinly-veiled strategy to eliminate me? I was instantly suspicious.

Most Adventist scholars, it should be emphasized, accept historical criticism as a valid methodology. Most of these same scholars are also firmly committed to the Adventist tradition. Most biblical scholars of whatever denominational stripe regard it, in modified form at least, as consistent with the integrity of Scripture. But within the Adventist church's highest administrative echelons, for which Hasel often acted as theological spokesperson, there remained a powerful, long-standing antipathy—born primarily out of ignorance and fear—toward anything that smacked of historical criticism. This inner circle of leaders, which included the domineering General Conference President, Neal Wilson, considered anyone sympathetic to historical criticism as a traitor to Adventism. I look back on this paranoia now as badly misinformed, appallingly regressive, and intellectually lethal. I wonder now why I ever thought I could do scholarly work in such an environment. Gordon Hyde, of course, had long vigorously championed this reactionary viewpoint. Unduly influenced by the writings of the ultraconservative Francis Schaeffer,[4] he regarded historical criticism as the malevolent crossing of the Rubicon into skepticism. Accept historical criticism, and the death of Christian faith would inevitably follow, he believed. Naturally, Hyde and Hasel would now join forces to insist on opposition to historical criticism as a criterion for the endowed chair.

"What can I possibly do?" I asked Allen, quickly running through all this in my mind. "You know I stand accused of heresy. I'm already a marked person. I have no real influence in the matter, least of all in the religion department, and definitely not with Hyde."

"I realize it may be difficult," said Allen, "but all we ask of you is to use what influence you can muster to oppose Hyde's attempt to make the rejection of historical criticism a criterion. If you can do this, we'd appreciate it."

Allen had approached me unofficially, "off the record," I realized. Scientist that he was, Allen realized that should Southern adopt such a reactionary policy regarding the critical study of religion it would inevitably move the school out of the mainstream of academia and would, in the end, prove disastrous, perhaps even academically fatal. It would turn Southern into a fundamentalist backwater. Historical criticism in essence is the application of scientific method to Scripture.

Allen's phone call troubled me for several days. Soon classes and other routine duties pushed it out of mind. As arranged, Gerhard Hasel arrived to present the inaugural lectures—as luck would have it on the controversial topic of Daniel 8—celebrating the founding of the Ellen G. White Memorial Chair. No criteria for the potential holder of that chair had yet been announced, however, nor had any person been officially appointed. As part of the celebration, and to welcome Hasel, the religion faculty gathered for

4. On several occasions, both before I arrived to teach at Southern, and while I was with BRICOM, Hyde referred to the writings of Francis Schaeffer as a basis for his thinking. Like Schaeffer, Hyde seems to have operated with an inerrantist view of the Bible. See Schaeffer, *God Who is There*, 92–99.

pizza in the departmental conference room. After plates and cups had been cleared away, from his black leather attaché Hyde pulled out a thick sheaf of official-looking documents. "These documents have just arrived from the General Conference," he announced proudly. "These are the new guidelines for biblical study in our denomination. They have been in development for more than a year. The General Conference is extremely anxious that our religion faculty review and approve them."

Rumors had been floating around for months that the General Conference had been preparing a loyalty oath, a creedal statement of some sort that all religion faculties would be required to sign. I had heard enough about the proposed loyalty oath to know it probably contained a not-so-thinly-veiled condemnation of historical criticism. Was this set of papers the denominational loyalty oath, intended to silence dissent, make dissent a crime against the church? Was this a creed? Were Adventists not historically a creed*less* denomination?

"Although this is a celebration, tonight we have some urgent business," Hyde spoke cautiously, hesitantly, as though bracing himself for resistance. Holding up the document, he went on, "This is the latest version of 'Guidelines for Biblical Study.' The General Conference wants our *immediate* approval—without further delay. There has already been far too much dilly-dallying around on this." He passed copies around the table. Allen's telephone call now leaped suddenly into consciousness. *This was what Allen had warned!* With Hasel sitting there, I instantly sensed, Hyde was going to try to pressure the faculty into endorsing the Guidelines and thus pave the way for an anti-critical plank to be hammered firmly into the criteria for the endowed chair. I realized I had to act swiftly. But how?

I tensed, then suddenly found new resolve. I hastily scanned the fourteen-page document, like an attorney getting ready to cross examine a witness. My entire life I'd avoided confrontations like this. I would do almost anything to evade them. Some people relish conflict, especially with authority. I don't. This has often worked against me, rendering me more compliant than aggressive. Through all the Adventist controversies up until now I'd usually responded compliantly. I had cowered like a scared victim. I had kept absorbing the abuse, like a battered spouse, and tried somehow to keep going in spite of it. I desperately wanted the "marriage" to work. I was willing to sacrifice almost anything to make it so. Now—in this moment—that approach had to stop. I could avoid confrontation no longer.

"This is a complex document with a number of serious implications," I began deliberately, choosing my words carefully. "Have any of us seen this version before?" I made a sweeping motion toward those seated around the table. "I don't see how we can effectively deal with these Guidelines tonight, not before we've had a chance to read carefully what's here. The Guidelines address important issues that must be carefully evaluated. Only then can we give them a fair, honest appraisal. We dare not sign onto anything without knowing what's really in it, and what it all means."

A painful silence hung ominously over the room. Everyone looked at me as if to say, *don't you realize what's going on here? Are you dense?* Ignoring their stunned, stone-faced expressions, I persisted. "Notice here," my finger traced down the page to a paragraph I'd briefly detected a moment before, "this document implies that those who use historical criticism in the study of the Bible and theology have abandoned or, at least, endangered the historic Christian faith. Would that accusation apply to someone like C. S. Lewis?" He was the only example I could think of at the moment. "A literary critic by training, he utilized critical methods of biblical study in his writings. Yet his books have inspired—and converted—thousands."

Another bewildering stunned silence. *Don't you get it,* warned the grave stoic expressions around the table.

Hasel broke the palpable tension. "The historical-critical method, I don't have to remind you, Jerry, is based on the Enlightenment view that God never interferes with human history. There can't be miracles, supernatural intervention, or even divine inspiration—the very thing that lends power and authority to Scripture. If we buy into that presupposition, which historical criticism implies, the Adventist faith, which affirms miracles and divine inspiration, will be lost."

Now it dawned on me why Hasel was in this meeting. Long had he championed the denomination's effort to crush critical study in biblical and theological research. He had been Hyde's go-to person in BRICOM's campaign to expunge critical study from the church's scholarly ranks. Hasel was the denomination's champion, a formidable, even implacable foe. Now I had to go up against him, one-on-one.

"But Gerhard," I objected, "is it necessary to accept without question that presupposition? Isn't it possible to benefit from at least *some* of the insights of the critical approach without adopting all its original presuppositions? Don't we handle any theory that way? Few hypotheses hold up in every detail over the long haul. They're constantly revised as scholars make use of them. Historical-critical scholars now concede that miracles aren't necessarily excluded by the method. 'The theory and practice of the historical-critical method,'" I tried to recall Terrence Fretheim's exact words, "'is not bound to an understanding which views history as a closed continuum in which there is no room for divine activity.'[5]

5. Fretheim, "Source Criticism," 838. Carl Armerding puts this point even more

"Let me simply ask you, Gerhard, if you are opposed to any degree of historical criticism, how will you salvage Ellen White?" I paused, letting the question sink in, then continued. "We all recognize she borrowed heavily from contemporary authors and didn't give proper credit. The General Conference has commissioned a study, specifically using *source criticism*, to analyze how and why she borrowed these materials. Without source criticism—one of the original, primary methods of historical criticism—there is no way of accounting for what Ellen White did. Unless we can show that Ellen White's appropriation of the ideas, literary structure, and expression was consistent with her view of inspiration, her authority will certainly be compromised and seriously weakened. In other words, without some form of historical criticism, at minimum, source criticism, won't you have eventually to abandon Ellen White as a theological authority? Is there any other way to save her for Adventism?" I turned the arguments of Hasel and Hyde back upon them, knowing this was my only option.

Hasel looked at me coldly through steely eyes. Whether anyone else at that table grasped the significance of what I was saying, Hasel certainly did. He had no answer to my argument. Then, strangely, as though conceding the point, he changed the topic. "In Europe [Austria], where I grew up, we really didn't take Ellen White as an authority like Americans do. I was instead taught to ground my faith in the Bible, so Ellen White's plagiarism hasn't really bothered me. She isn't a final authority for me."

Astonished at Hasel's remarkably frank admission, Hyde unobtrusively put down on the table his tightly-clutched copy of the Guidelines. Frustrated and seemingly defeated, he backed away from the issue. Somehow, I felt, I had managed to avert a crisis. I had won a victory! I had given Allen and Sahly the support they requested of me. Little did I realize the price I would ultimately pay. I had openly—publicly—opposed Adventist authority vested in Gerhard Hasel and Gordon Hyde. It was just as though I had gone up against the whole denomination. No one who does such a thing could ever expect to survive professionally.

Yet again the dust of controversy settled, at least for several months. Things once more seemed to drift back into routine, the never-ending cycle of classes, staff meetings, papers, and grades. Hyde didn't mention the General Conference Guidelines again, nor were we ever to see another copy. My

---

forcefully: "Is it possible to employ critical method, but reject some of the assumptions which lie beneath it? I suggest that it is—that conservative theology both permits and even demands the use of the best critical tools" (*Old Testament and Criticism*, 3–4).

opposition appeared to have stalled the latest General Conference effort at a loyalty oath—at least at Southern.

Then occurred another weird, baffling telephone call. Sahly summoned me to his private residence, a block and a half up the street from our home. When I arrived, puzzled as to why he'd asked me to his private residence on such short notice rather than to his university office, I discovered Allen present together with Sahly. No one else appeared to be around. The house was ominously quiet. This was not a friendly, get-better-acquainted meeting!

"I've asked you come here rather than to my office because what I have to say concerns both you and Bill Allen," Sahly said, peering from behind his dark glasses, which he always seemed to have on, shielding his eyes from direct view. "It seems that a 'head of steam,' if I may put it that way, is building against you, Jerry. We need to see what we can do about it so what happened to Ed Zackrison three or four years ago doesn't happen again."

"I've received a number of complaints about you from students, several important church administrators, and a few pastors here in our area. Gordon Hyde especially has been sharply critical. He keeps coming by my office or, failing that, persistently telephones. He's very disturbed about your theological views." Sahly paused, slowly gathering his thoughts. "In view of all this pressure from students, clergy, and denominational leaders, Hyde has adamantly made it clear you will have to seek another faculty position. I'm not telling you to resign," he reassured politely, "but possibly the best solution for all concerned would be for you to move on to something else."

For a moment I didn't know quite how to respond. What Sahly—and Hyde—were suggesting was that I resign and leave! Like Zackrison I was being urged to "get out of Dodge." This was the opening salvo. If I persisted in stubbornly holding on—I would be summarily fired. Despite reservations about some of the key doctrines of Adventism, as I've said several times, I had remained faithful to teaching—and preaching—only orthodox, traditional Adventist theology, or at the very least, avoided making public comments that contradicted Adventist theology. What I got for such stubborn commitment was a chronic ache inside. The painful, internal split at times became almost unbearable. All I wanted was to be left alone—without Hyde's continual harassment—to work through the problems on my own and hopefully find some kind of personal resolution, or at least a stable place, a stasis of sorts. Was this too much to ask? Was this desire merely a dream, a fantasy to which I desperately clung? My thoughts went back to the celebratory dinner where I'd confronted Hasel and Hyde—on Sahly's behalf. That act of opposition now stood as a check mark against me. Hyde was once more riled up. There in Sahly's spacious living room I felt really abandoned by the university and all alone. Even Sahly was distancing himself. There was now nowhere to turn.

Where was the denomination that idealistically claimed it was committed to the pursuit of truth—uncovering, proclaiming, and trying to live out of it? The Adventism I was experiencing, obstinate in its refusal to concede even a single theological failure, was just as guilty as any of the other denominations it so freely condemned. Adventism was wretchedly, deeply mired in its own internal theological difficulties and dogged refusal to change. Politics had once again trumped theology. The whole miserable Adventist situation seemed hopeless.

Paradoxically, as misery washed over me while I sat there, I started to feel a strange, almost inexplicable sense of relief. A rocky road inevitably lay ahead. Was I coming to the end of the painful spiritual dissonance literally tearing me spiritually and emotionally apart? Soon, one way or another, would it be over? Adventism, it was clearly but painfully evident, had chosen to go in the direction of a hardened, frozen traditional dogma. Instead I had chosen the progressive path of fresh, exciting new discovery. The denomination and I were headed in different, opposing directions. The distance between us could only inevitably widen.

The next day I drove into Chattanooga to contact my attorney, Harry Burnette, who was well acquainted with Southern Adventist University. Since Hyde seemed to be the principal source of the complaints, Burnette advised me to meet privately with Gordon Hyde to sort out matters, and follow up the meeting with a carefully-worded summary of the conversation. For legal purposes I was to summarize the meeting in a letter, like an affidavit, written to Hyde.

Following Burnette's advice, I set up the appointment, but asked Laura to go with me as a witness to the interchange. By now I'd learned that one never goes to such meetings alone. Hyde seemed surprised I had initiated the meeting. When I told him we were there on the advice of my attorney, he appeared visibly shaken. "In that case," he said, "I don't think we should be having this meeting."

"I beg your pardon, Gordon," I protested. "It's obvious to me you're the person primarily responsible for the efforts to get me fired. You want me off the faculty. I deserve—Laura deserves—some explanation as to why you're doing this. My impression is that things have been going fairly well within the department and among our constituency for at least a couple of years. Your abrupt pressure on me to resign comes as quite a shock. It appears to come out of nowhere. There seems to be no reason for it. Why do you want me to resign?"

He ignored the question. Leaning back in his chair, he looked pen-
sively out the window, and then spoke somewhat condescendingly. "Given
the direction in which I want to take the religion department, you will eventually feel more and more uncomfortable here."

"What do you mean?" I insisted.

Hyde folded his hands, tenting them under his chin as though in the
act of praying, and observed coolly. "Well, you should be aware the University itself has embarked on a new direction." I was totally unaware of any
such "new direction" that had been decided upon. This new direction was
probably Hyde's own imaginary dream. It sounded too much like McClure's
aim to make Southern "Adventist again." I remained silent. Hyde continued.
"We now have a new president. We want to move the University away from
the course it has followed in the past few years. Given this new philosophy—
which I would specifically designate as 'conservative'—you're going to have
to ask yourself whether you would want to be a part of it."

"Isn't that a decision I should make for myself rather than having it
forced upon me?"

"Your theological orientation is at odds with this new direction! Why
can't you see that? It's diametrically opposed to what we have in mind. You're
headed in the opposite theological direction! For instance, you advocate use
of historical-critical methodology. The new philosophy of the university
simply doesn't allow for historical criticism. However you figure it, that puts
you at cross-purposes with what we're trying to accomplish here."

"Do you still not realize," I shot back, "that most Adventist scholars
today use some form of historical criticism—including our colleagues here
in the religion department? Don't you know that if you push Southern Adventist University in this so-called 'conservative' direction, as you put it, it
will eventually become isolated, even in the Adventist educational system?"
Allen's conversation a few months came again to mind. "I've had this discussion with every member of our department, and *all* of them think historical
criticism has a place in theological scholarship."

"That simply isn't true," Hyde countered. "I've talked with all of them,
too, and they assure me they're all opposed to historical criticism. They've
told me they flatly disagree with you on this point. So does Gerhard Hasel. Don't you get it, Jerry? You're out of step with the religion department.
You're out of step with the University. You're out of step with the Adventist church!" His adamant words contained truth, I realized. Over the past
decade, I recognized, the Adventist denomination had been intentionally
moving in a conservative, even fundamentalist direction. I was not—and
could never be—comfortable with that. I couldn't go back.

Hyde's expression hardened. "That's precisely the problem. You see yourself as something of a 'bridge' between liberal and conservative scholars. You see yourself as a link between not only one group of Adventists and another, but between Adventists and other Christian denominations. You even dared to invite *non-Adventist* Christians into your Comparative Religions class! How reckless and dangerous is that? Doesn't that expose young Adventists to the errors of the other churches? Welcoming diverse viewpoints is a fatal, unacceptable flaw in your teaching style. This became evident to me as far back as Price, Utah. Don't you remember?"

Laura and I looked at each other, utterly bewildered. We couldn't believe Hyde had hung on to that incident for over ten years.

The Committee on Science and Religion (BRISCO), a subsidiary of the Adventist BRICOM, of which Gordon Hyde was then the director, had held its annual geological field trip eleven years earlier in Price, Utah, near the Cleveland Lloyd Dinosaur Quarry and the Book Roan Cliffs. BRISCO customarily met in such exotic locations to study the vexing conflict between evolution and creationism through actual field observations of geological formations and their fossil evidence. Adventists take the first Genesis account of seven-day creation literally (see Gen 1) and go to considerable lengths to find geological and biological evidence that tends to support this creationist view. They represent the "creationist" side in the "creation science" debate. Historically, in modern times, at least, they were the *original* creationists. As a new member of BRISCO, on this trip I'd decided to bring Laura and the girls along for a vacation in California afterwards. We had driven leisurely across the country—our first family transcontinental automobile trip—enjoying the varied countryside.

A few days into the week-long meeting, as the sun dipped toward the desert horizon and the temperature started to plummet, Laura and I were standing outside our hotel room in the gathering dusk, and casually talking to two Adventist geologists we'd just met at the conference. We weren't chatting about any of the theological or scientific issues that had been discussed earlier. We were simply exchanging pleasantries and getting acquainted. One of our new geologist friends abruptly remarked, "You shouldn't be talking to us."

"What do you mean?" I asked, bewildered.

"Gordon Hyde just walked across the other side of the parking lot. He paused when he noticed you and Laura talking to us. I could tell from the knitted eyebrows and dark narrowing of his eyes he wasn't very thrilled."

I ignored the comment, thinking it odd and completely irrelevant. You can't be serious! Why would it matter to whom we talked? Surely no one could find fault with our being civil, for making some new friends, particularly new *Adventist* friends.

Now, eleven years later, that innocent conversation came back as the final nail in the coffin of my Adventist ministerial career.

16

A House Divided

> Every kingdom divided against itself is laid waste,
> and no city or house divided against itself will stand.
>
> —*Jesus*

My thoughts were still back in Price, Utah, in the parking lot of the hotel. Hyde's words shattered my reminiscing. "You were talking to some Adventist 'liberals.' I don't know what you were discussing. I don't really care. But such socializing and bridge building—such toleration of people with diverse viewpoints, even though they're nominally 'Adventist'—simply won't be tolerated at Southern now or in the future. You're hanging around with the wrong crowd, Jerry. For your own good, you have to *resign!*"

I went blank for a few seconds. I could hardly believe what I was hearing. Hyde sounded medieval, as though he was literally living back in the days of the Spanish Inquisition! This seemed like an absurd, paranoid reaction to what had only originally been a casual, friendly conversation. Yet Hyde saw it as conspiratorial, and had carried that impression, like a grudge, for eleven years. This was like McCarthyism all over again, "Are you a Communist?" "Are you a *liberal?*"

Why in heaven's name was I still sitting here in the office of the chair of the religion department at Southern Adventist University? The decision whether I left or stayed had been made long before—and by someone else. Hyde was either the instigator or the tool of more powerful forces bent on my elimination. If I'd had to hazard a guess, I'd say Hyde was the instigator. Talking to Hyde this morning was simply futile, a waste of time. The gap between us had become huge, like a vast, ever-widening chasm. We weren't even on the same page, much less in the same book. He was right about one thing. I would never fit into his narrow Seventh-day Adventist world. And since he held all the power, he would make sure I was permanently blacklisted—like the many other scholars he'd so branded.

It was hard to grasp how so trivial an exchange of social pleasantries in a parking lot in Price, Utah, had been given such a diabolic, conspiratorial interpretation! I had to remind myself I was dealing with someone who seemed completely paranoid. I had witnessed Hyde's dark side during the several years I was on BRICOM. Now that paranoia had me in the crosshairs. I had suddenly moved to the top of his legendary "hit" list. I suddenly felt like a complete stranger in my church of origin. Only now I wanted out!

A few days later, Sahly summoned me to come to his office. He was in a conciliatory mood.

"I heard about your meeting with Hyde," he said. "For months now Hyde has been complaining about you. A little while ago he urged, 'We might as well as go ahead and get Gladson out of here.' He then showed me a thick file of complaint letters about you he'd written to Al McClure."

"I wasn't aware Hyde was doing all this complaining," I replied. "He's never said a word to me about any problem with either my teaching or behavior. The meeting Laura and I had a few days ago was solely at my initiative."

"When I realized Hyde hadn't talked with you about any of this, I decided to call a meeting of the religion department—without you or Hyde being present—to find out what the other members of your department thought."

"About me?" I was incredulous! Clandestine departmental meetings! I shuddered at what was coming next.

"When I asked them whether you, as Hyde likes to put it, were the 'odd man out,' they became very wary," Sahly continued. "However, they agreed there was friction between you and Hyde. 'He shouldn't have challenged Hasel in that meeting,' one said. 'That was very unwise.'

"I asked them whether we could just let the situation remain as it is until Hyde retired a year from now. 'We can't do that!' said another. 'Sooner or later the church has to confront historical criticism, and we might as well do it right here and now. We totally support Hyde!'"

I took a deep breath and exhaled slowly, once more desperately struggling to stay calm. I suddenly felt mortified. The colleagues who claimed to be my friends, who had assured me repeatedly in private of their support, were now abandoning me, one by one, as they had previously deserted Grant and Zackrison. I guess I couldn't really blame them. If they opposed Hyde by supporting me, they would sooner or later find themselves in exactly the same quandary. But what about integrity? "The greatest want of the world is the want of men," I recalled a familiar Ellen White quote, "men who will not be bought or sold, men who in their inmost souls are true and honest."[1] All these men had, in private, agreed with me about the appropriate use of historical criticism. Now they were pulling back, retracting. I was as disillusioned that moment about humanity as I had ever been before.

"Jerry, I don't need to tell you," Sahly interrupted my jumble of confused thoughts, "if Gordon Hyde decides he wants you out, he has McClure and Wilson, the General Conference President, on his side, and there's very little I can do to stop him."

"You could tell Hyde to back off. As *president* of the University," I emphasized the word, "you have that kind of authority." Did this mean Hyde was really the power behind the throne? How much authority did Hyde have over Southern, indeed, over the whole denomination, or at least its higher educational institutions? I realized Sahly was acting under pressure from someone else, possibly McClure or, more likely, Wilson. Sahly was trying to comply with his superiors, who were solidly allied behind Hyde.

"True. But should Hyde still decide to move against you, he'll just go over my head to get it done." I sympathized with Sahly's political impotence. He seemed genuinely apologetic.

"Don, there is no real problem in the religion department unless Hyde wants to manufacture one."

"I agree."

During that month I had four more such meetings with Sahly. At times, he was sharply critical; then again, he would seem conciliatory. Several friends from the community, a few students, and even some faculty approached Sahly, urging him to put the brakes on Hyde's escalating assault. This annoyed Sahly. He took these supportive gestures as evidence that I was intentionally stirring up faculty sentiment against him. In the Adventist church a person is never supposed to criticize church leaders, at least publicly, lest it damage the "unity" (uniformity) of the church.

In the middle of March rumors surfaced about a top-level meeting in Atlanta, at McClure's Southern Union Conference office, that was aimed at resolving my fate. Hyde, Sahly, and McClure met privately.

---

1. White, *Education*, 57.

That semester I was teaching comparative religions and as a feature of the course had arranged for several guests from different faith communities to meet my 8:00 a.m. class. Although Hyde frowned on this approach, the students had responded enthusiastically about getting acquainted with these non-Adventist guests, and the religious communities they represented. I wondered, after my earlier meeting with Hyde, whether Southern had kept the comparative religions course in the curriculum merely to impress the accrediting body, the Southern Association of Schools and Colleges (SACS), to show that the University wasn't as narrow-minded as Hyde seemed intent on making it.

The morning after the confidential meeting at Southern Union Conference headquarters, I arrived on campus early to greet Mary Radpour, a representative from the Bahá'í faith, who was to be that day's guest. The cloudy, overcast sky made the early morning hour seem colder than usual. I waited for Radpour in front of the University administration building, the easiest place on campus for a visitor to locate. Sahly drove up, parked, and got out of his car. He then noticed me in front of the building. Briskly he walked over. Clutching arm loads of books, students were dashing off to early morning classes. Secretaries and administrative staff, inhaling the crisp March air, scurried toward the red brick administration offices to begin another day's work.

"Good morning, Don," I greeted him pleasantly, despite my growing apprehension. "Could you tell me what happened at the meeting yesterday with McClure and Hyde?"

He ignored my question. "Rumors about your being fired are all over campus! Who started them? Who fanned the flames? Why can't you stop talking publicly about this?" he insisted angrily.

"Don, I didn't start any rumors. Since my career is at stake, can you blame me for talking to a few people—in confidence—about what is happening?"

"*You* are the problem!" he shouted. People all around abruptly stopped, as if frozen, staring in amazement. "That letter you wrote twisted and turned every phrase of our conversation."

On my attorney's advice, I'd written a response to the previous conversation with Sahly, giving my perception of the interview. I had thus documented the interview as a precaution, just in case matters turned into litigation.

Sahly's face turned livid. "You should never have brought an attorney into this!" By now a small crowd of students and administrative staff had gathered around, wondering what was going on. We were exposed, right out there in public view. It was embarrassing.

"Look, under the circumstances"—I interrupted him—"I'm going to have to follow the advice of my attorney!" I knew that Southern had retained its own attorney, but didn't mention it.

If only Southern could get rid of me, I remembered, thinking back over the last few months, it could finally shed its unwanted "liberal" reputation (the constant right-wing theme), recover its reputation as a school of high Christian (conservative) standards, and reclaim equilibrium. I had sadly become, as in a dysfunctional family, the "scapegoat," the person now responsible for the institution's ills. Getting rid of me was never more urgent.

The dispute abruptly ended. Sahly and I arranged to meet later that morning where we could discuss matters in private. When I entered his office a few hours later, Sahly had recovered a calmer demeanor. "Al McClure, Hyde, and I discussed your situation," he began, describing the meeting at the Southern Union offices. "I told them that, as far as I was concerned, there was no problem. There was not enough evidence to convict you of heresy. So we decided to leave matters right where they are for now. You need to be aware, however, that everywhere I travel in the Southeast you are mentioned as a 'liberal,' or worse, 'heretic.' I don't see now how you can ever salvage your reputation in this denomination. As far as I'm concerned, you're one of our finest professors. What we need more at Southern, however, is not excellence, but solid, conservative Adventist orthodoxy. Mediocrity in teaching doesn't matter so long as one is perceived as orthodox. You need to decide whether the new direction on which the University has embarked—which Hyde has outlined—is one with which you can feel comfortable. In all honesty, you would find it best to try to get a faculty position somewhere else." This was the eighth time Sahly had made this statement—I had counted.

"We'll even help arrange such a move," he placated, obviously trying once more to be conciliatory.

Nothing had really been resolved, obviously. The University was only trying to find a convenient way to ease me out the door without facing litigation. That's why Sahly bristled at the thought of an attorney. A painful weariness oozed through me, filling every cell. My fate, from which I could no longer turn back, seemed inexorably written on the walls of the hallway of the administration building outside Sahly's office. It was only a matter of time. I was emotionally and spiritually exhausted. With great difficulty I made it through my classes that day. I found it hard to stuff deeply enough all my inner turmoil and assume a politically correct demeanor before my classes. I had become a pariah.

Although Sahly had finally convinced McClure there was no real problem, Hyde obviously didn't agree. He continued to agitate. In hallways

outside classrooms or on the walks leading from his office he kept solic-
iting information from students who'd had my classes, searching for any
flaw or tidbit of dissatisfaction he could use against me, which he promptly
reported to Sahly. One student related how Hyde had summoned her to
his office and asked specifically about one of my classes in which she had
enrolled. "I have a problem with a religion professor," she told him, "but it
isn't Dr. Gladson." When she mentioned the name of the other professor,
Hyde abruptly terminated the conversation, she said.

At the next religion department faculty meeting, Hyde announced
that Ron Springett would address the upcoming assembly of religion majors
on "some matters among biblical scholars and the Missouri Synod Lutheran
situation." He was referring to the furor that had broken out in the 1970s at
the St. Louis-based Missouri Synod Lutheran Seminary, Concordia, over
the question of biblical inerrancy. Many professors and students who could
no longer accept the idea of biblical inerrancy, the theory that every religious or secular fact, however incidental, in the Bible is totally accurate,
had literally walked out of their classes and offices to found a new seminary
and eventually, a new denomination, the Evangelical Lutheran Church of
America.[2] That dispute had significantly centered on the historical-critical
method. Hyde was constantly fond of citing the Concordia incident as a
cautionary tale for Adventism.

"The president of Southern, Don Sahly, wants us to position the religion department to give strong support for the official Fundamental Beliefs
of Seventh-day Adventists," Hyde said, as he later opened the religion department convocation. "This chapel assembly today is only one of a series
aimed at doing this very thing."

In the refurbished auditorium of the former music department recital
hall, with seventy-five eager, attentive students in the audience, Springett
began. He traced a series of alternative philosophical worldviews that were
obviously unacceptable to Adventists. "We must begin to ask what people
do not mean when they say they believe the Fundamental Beliefs of the
church. They may be merely using Christian language. They may be simply
saying what they think is the right thing, the politically correct thing, to say.
They may actually assent to an alternative worldview and yet use familiar
Adventist terms to refer to it.

"Modern historical criticism stems from one of these alien worldviews.
It is based on a naturalistic understanding of reality. No divine miracles, no

2. John Tietjen tells the story of this controversy, eerily similar to the conflict
at Southern, and the solemn withdrawal procession of the faculty and students from
Concordia's campus to nearby Eden Theological Seminary, which would become the
temporary home of the new seminary (*Memoirs in Exile*, 209–12).

divine intrusion into the world is possible, according to historical criticism. Much of the historical criticism we find today is based on these assumptions." Springett's opening remarks astounded me. Was this language really Hyde's? Was Springett merely the spokesperson? Two years earlier, Springett had confided to me, "We need to sweep all our doctrines onto the floor and start over!" Why was he now parroting Hyde? What was going on? I grabbed a notepad and started furiously writing down as much as I could. He seemed to be speaking directly about me.

Springett held up a book by the British scholar, Horton Davies.[3] He read Davies's observation that many "fringe" groups, such as Adventists, actually sabotage themselves by sending students to outside universities where their thinking starts to change. Then they come back to teach in their church's colleges, use familiar language, but fill it with alien, subversive content. "This practice polarizes the faculty, ministers, and laity," he emphasized.

He then produced a document telling of some of the personal interviews at Concordia Seminary. "These interviews show the need for answering questions of belief with a firm 'Yes' or 'No.' Concordia Seminary wouldn't tolerate equivocal answers about the Bible. This is what the Missouri Synod Lutherans had to do. They did what we must do here as well!

"If you think Adventists aren't involved in such a subversion of our faith, think again. A recent *Spectrum* article [the journal of the Adventist Forums] stated that it really doesn't matter whether Adam and Eve actually existed! I had an Adventist seminary professor who taught me it wasn't necessary to believe in the virgin birth so long as you believed in the incarnation. Inevitably such doubts filter down to the pews. Source, form, and tradition criticism—the heart of historical criticism—often disagree with each other. We have to repudiate historical criticism before it destroys us!"

I couldn't believe what I was hearing! Springett—a self-confessed historical critic—had been trained in the method at Manchester University. Up to this moment, he had privately admitted, he had been as persuaded of historical criticism as I. I was realizing at my expense Jonathan Butler's perceptive remark. "The only way to survive in so precarious a position was by way of complete discretion. Almost anything could be said in private. But Adventist academics who publicly dare to break the informal code of silence on controversial issues did so on their own,"[4] usually by paying a heavy personal and professional price.

3. Davies, *Challenge of the Sects.*
4. Butler, "Historian as Heretic," 21.

"We're beginning today a review of the Fundamental Beliefs of Seventh-day Adventists." Springett droned on. I felt like all eyes were suddenly on me. "We want to spell out what we do and do not believe. The religion department has embarked on this project today. This meeting is the first step. Now go to your professors. Confront them. Find out what they really do and do not believe."

Some years later, after both of us had long since vanished from the Southern faculty, Springett confessed in email messages to me (February 11, 1999; April 12, 2000) that the text of his address that day had actually been written by Hyde himself! Hyde also furnished Springett the book by Davies, the material from the Missouri Synod seminary, and a paper by Hasel opposing historical criticism, and insisted he draw from these as preparation for the address at the religion assembly. "I knew it was useless to argue," Springett reflected. "At the time I was reading Bonhoeffer's *Ethics*. His dilemma was similar to ours.[5] Do you oppose the Nazis openly and get hanged, or stay within the ranks and try to change things for the better? Some in Bonhoeffer's day chose one thing, others another. Who was right only God knows. It was a gut-wrenching experience. Almost every day we were asked to betray our friends and co-workers, spied on, misinterpreted, misquoted, and generally held under suspicion. We should never have been put in positions like that."

What few outside observers understand is that working in an authoritarian, hierarchical organization that makes absolute truth claims like the Seventh-day Adventist church puts enormous pressure on people inside it to conform, not only to its doctrinal views, but also to the whims of its leaders, which are usually put forth, in turn, as based on its doctrine. It is absolutely crucial that someone teaching at an Adventist educational institution, especially a theologian, mimic more or less the current official opinions of the denomination's leaders, who themselves often have little awareness of the real theological issues at stake. Hyde is a good example. He'd had very little actual experience with the historical-critical method because he wasn't by training a biblical or theological scholar. He held an earned doctorate (PhD), but in an entirely different, secular discipline. Yet failure to agree

5. Writing of the Nazi regime, Dietrich Bonhoeffer states: "Even in cases where the guilt of the government is extremely obvious, due consideration must still be given to the guilt which has given rise to this guilt. The refusal of obedience in the case of a particular historical and political decision of government must therefore, like this decision itself, be a venture undertaken on one's own responsibility" (*Ethics*, 308).

with powerful leaders like Hyde, even "perceived" failure to do so, could lead to professional disaster. Dissent—public dissent—wasn't tolerated. A few years later, Southern Adventist University also fired Springett. Today he is no longer active in the Adventist church. Springett's perceptive comment a decade later speaks volumes:

> Hyde and Hasel exploited their [the administrators'] fears to further their own agenda. The administration did not take time to analyze this situation. They did not stop to see that the right wing fringe was talking about something totally different to what Hyde and Hasel were pushing. It was all presented to them as part of the same thing.[6]

This comment explains why the whole controversy around me had shifted from the gospel, the Investigative Judgment, and Ellen White, to a whole new, albeit related set of concerns: the methods of biblical interpretation.

In the afternoon following Springett's chapel talk, one of my students asked to see me. He sat on the opposite side of the small light-colored oak desk in my office. Outside, the skies remained gray and overcast. "What do you think," he began slowly, "of teachers who skip over important theological themes in their classes?"

"Could you give me an example of what you mean, John?" I flashed back to Springett's urging students earlier in the day to confront their professors. I grew uneasy at where this seemed to be headed.

"Well, uh . . . like the 2300-day prophecy and the Investigative Judgment."

"Have students been saying this about me—that I omit important topics?"

"Yes," he emphasized firmly, then paused briefly. "Uh . . . You have been accused of leaving out important topics because they're controversial. Some say you do it because you don't agree with Adventist teaching."

"John, you're in my Old Testament introduction class. The purpose of that class, as you are well aware, is to survey the content of the Old Testament, excepting the book of Daniel, which in this University is studied in another, separate course. In our class, due to time constraints, I can only make passing reference to Daniel. Tell me, how should I work the Investigative Judgment doctrine into an Old Testament introduction class that doesn't include Daniel, where that doctrine is alluded to, without neglecting the other Old Testament books?"

"I see your point."

6. Ron Springett, email message to author, February 11, 1999.

"In any class where the Investigative Judgment is part of the curriculum, I try to deal with it. But in classes where it isn't—such as Old Testament and comparative religions—I leave it out. In a specific college course you generally study only the subject matter that is germane to it."

He seemed satisfied with my explanation. Then he continued. "You're also accused of being 'ecumenical'—too friendly with other denominations." Where had I heard this before? Had Hyde supplied John these questions, and then asked him to interrogate me? Would John then report back to Hyde?

"I see myself as a 'bridge-builder,' John," I replied, using the same words Hyde had used against me, "not a 'wall-builder.' I try to build bridges because I think that's the most effective way for Adventists to relate to the world around them. If we don't try to help others see what we have in common, if we don't reach out to them, how are they ever going to listen to us? We don't want to isolate ourselves completely from the rest of the world, do we? We have to find some common ground. My first instinct is to look for the common ground."

When he left, I considered what could happen should more student conferences like this occur as a result of Springett's mandate to uproot "heresy." While director of BRICOM, Hyde had utilized this identical strategy. He tried to turn people into informants against each other.

In April, responding to negotiations initiated by Sahly, Walla Walla University, an Adventist institution in Walla Walla, Washington, expressed interest in my joining their religion faculty. The psychology faculty was also interested in Laura. So we flew to Walla Walla for a three-day interview process. Although the three days were chocked full of activities, including my presenting a lecture on Hebrew wisdom in one of the Old Testament classes, we had opportunity to enjoy some of the countryside, lush with wheat fields and fruit orchards, which produce the famous Washington apples. The rich, loamy volcanic soil yields some of the nation's tastiest, most nutritious fruits and vegetables. The religion and university staff couldn't have been more gracious. Walla Walla had over the years become sort of a haven for harassed religion faculty fleeing from the rest of the denomination's colleges, and prided itself on its ability to "rehabilitate" these persons, as John Brunt, chair of the religion department put it. Their offer was highly tempting.

Several considerations kept us from accepting. The chair of the Walla Walla College Board, Bruce Johnston, who had been one of my favorite professors when we'd attended Southern Adventist University, had already started an investigation of my theological orthodoxy. I could imagine a repeat of what we'd experienced at Southern. If Johnston was already suspicious, what future would we really have there? I would once again be on permanent probation, only as good as my last class.[7] Then, too, the city of Walla Walla, compared to that of Chattanooga, was quite small, some forty-five thousand in population. That meant for every eight non-Adventists, there was one Adventist. Neither Laura nor I was entirely comfortable with that ratio. In our growing suspicion, sharpened by fifteen years in Collegedale, surrounded by Adventists, many of them of the right wing variety, it seemed like we'd be subjecting ourselves to an even more dangerous, paranoid Adventist climate. At least where we were, we could escape to Chattanooga or Atlanta. At Walla Walla, isolated as it is from the larger cities, there'd be little opportunity for escape. We felt like we'd be under constant scrutiny. We didn't want that kind of life. At this point, also, I wasn't even sure I wanted to continue working in an Adventist environment. A few days after we'd returned to Collegedale, Laura and I graciously declined the Walla Walla offer, thanked the school for its hospitality, and turned dejectedly back to our troubled, uncertain future.

Matters now seemed to be coming to a head. Frustrated and concerned, I decided again to meet with Hyde privately to see if there was any way matters might be resolved. We were torn. We had been here for fifteen years. This was our home. Our daughters had grown up here and now were on the verge of becoming young women. These were reasons to stay.

The morning of the appointment, Laura and I drove to a parking lot not far from Miller Hall, the newly renovated religion department facility. I felt tense, like I had to face even more, unexpected alarming news. The trees and flowers were just beginning to leaf and blossom after a cold winter, a winter that was far colder emotionally than the weather. We walked past the stately white columns at the portico of Miller Hall and through the double doors into the familiar building. Down the beige carpeted hallway we anxiously walked, past my office on the right, then those of Douglas Bennett, Norman Gulley, and Jack Blanco, finally into Hyde's at the far end of the corridor.

After we were seated, I began hesitantly, "Gordon, we're here to see if we can't find some resolution to the turmoil and confusion generated over the past few months . . . "

7. A few weeks later, a letter from Alden Thompson, academic dean at Walla Walla, confirmed my impression. "I will admit," he wrote diplomatically, "that the experiences through which you have gone in recent years, do place you in a certain jeopardy relative to the [Walla Walla Adventist] community" (Alden Thompson to the Jerry Gladson, 25 May 1987).

"Before I answer," Hyde interjected. "I think Don Sahly ought to be here for this conversation." Shadows darkened Hyde's face. The wrinkles outlining his forehead deepened.

"It isn't necessary that Sahly be here," I answered. "I've had all the communication I need with him about this matter. Since it seems that you're primarily behind the effort to have me dismissed, we've come particularly to talk to you."

Hyde ignored me. Picking up the telephone, he dialed Sahly's office. "Could Don come up to my office immediately?" Then he summoned Jack Blanco, the designated soon-to-be religion department chair after Hyde's impending retirement. The alacrity with which the two men rushed to Hyde's office, some two blocks away for Sahly, indicated they'd already been forewarned about the meeting. This was not to be a private meeting after all. A few awkward, embarrassingly silent minutes passed, with Hyde sitting there, silently trying to avoid our gaze. First Blanco and then Sahly entered.

Hyde now oddly lapsed into complete silence, along with Blanco, who sat mutely fixed in his chair. The three of them faced us like a panel of judges. I realized Sahly and Hyde feared a lawsuit and obviously wanted witnesses to what might happen.

"You *know* why you must leave," Sahly began, after perfunctorily greeting us. "Why do you have to ask all over again? You're regarded around here—and throughout the denomination—as someone fundamentally disloyal to the church. It isn't that you have actually *taught* anything contrary to Adventist doctrine. We have no evidence of that. It is that you are *perceived* as teaching heterodox ideas, and thus as unfaithful to the church. Our concern really isn't what you've taught; it's what we think you think. We can't read your mind. But several students have come to me complaining about you. They've accused you of raising questions that you never bothered to answer, and of giving tacit approval to people like Ford and Rea." Sahly was repeating what I'd heard him say at least a dozen times. It was the same thing the right-wing press had been saying. It was futile to try to dissuade him. He rambled on.

"Had you not retained an attorney, it might have been possible to work all this out. Instead of negotiating, however, you spread rumors all over campus that you were about to be fired. That did it as far as I was concerned! Your situation became impossible to resolve after that. Even so, I don't think that from the beginning of the controversy we could have ever saved you from your inevitable fate. You've brought all this down on your own head!"

So that's it, I thought. *I was to blame for the controversy.* Sahly really fears a lawsuit. Did they really expect me to remain absolutely passive about the machinations it seems they'd initiated and not confide in a single person? Did they really think I would just take it and do nothing to defend my reputation and career?

"What you need to realize," I countered, tasting my bitter, rising anger. I had a hard time remaining calm. I fought for control. "Your entire faculty is up in arms about what you're doing. The morale around here is lower than I've ever seen!"

"That's not true!" Sahly interrupted. "Only a small fraction of the faculty feels that way!"

"I've been here fifteen years, Don. And I've never known such a discouraged, disheartened faculty. They quietly talk to me in the hallways, in phone calls, at lunch in restaurants—off campus—and behind the closed doors of my office. I think I have a better sense of how the faculty at ground level feels about all this than any of you," I motioned toward Hyde, still sitting silently, relieved and pleased he'd managed to corner a heretic and was on the verge of ridding the church of at least one more.

Anger and frustration surged, almost overwhelming me. I fought to remain calm. *Here goes*, I thought. *Why hold back now? You've lost it all anyway.* I paused in mid-sentence, and then plunged in.

"The secretive manner in which you, Don and Gordon, have treated me, never giving me an opportunity to confront my accusers or even the accusations made—dismissing my entire twenty-year career in the Adventist ministry because I've been "perceived" to be disloyal by persons unknown to me—and never telling me what the specific charges were, has brought terrible emotional and spiritual anguish to Laura, JoAnna, Paula, and me. Your actions have turned us into pariahs, although we've lived here and been a part of this community longer than any one of you.

"Having never been given the opportunity to defend myself, I guess I'll just have to be content here and now to try to do so. You've heard it before but really haven't listened. Are you listening now? Or are your minds made up? For the record's sake, let me repeat where I stand in all this."

Hyde, Sahly, and Blanco sat in stunned silence, shocked I would speak to them in such tone.

"In my classes, it is a matter of honor to me that I never teach as fact, or reach as a conclusion, *anything* that is contrary to official Adventist belief. I have intentionally, deliberately, operated pedagogically within the parameters of 'orthodox' Adventist theology, to use your term. I challenge any one of you to show where—in a single instance—I have violated this principle. You've never offered me one single shred of tangible evidence that I've taught 'heresy.' Of course, I've made students aware of the questions that have been raised about certain doctrines, and of the continuing study going on around them. How could I leave my students in total ignorance about such matters and call it 'education'? What would a student do, having received a degree from Southern, after having gone out somewhere into one of our churches, and then been confronted with the questions raised by Paxton, Ford, or Rea? What would they have said? 'Well, I never studied anything about that in college, even though I took courses that dealt with these disputed doctrines.' What a weak, insipid response that would be! How valid would an Adventist college degree look then?

"Eventually, maybe our denomination will learn that respect and open discussion when people disagree are the only healthy ways to deal with conflict. Truth has a way of winning out in an atmosphere of openness and dialogue, not while whispered in secrecy and shadows. But until the church learns this, there can only be more 'witch hunts' such as the one you, Gordon, have started here. I'm not the first, nor sadly will I be the last, to be hunted down and eliminated. I feel the utmost sorrow and pity for a denomination that keeps repeating these same mistakes over and over, destroying in the process some of its finest, most loyal people."

"Take Gordon Hyde," I looked from Sahly to Hyde, sitting behind his desk, his hands steepled in familiar pose. "Gordon actually is a longtime friend of both Laura's and my family. He has known me since I was a teenager. He was one of the professors I most admired when I was a student here. Somehow, in his zeal to hold onto and impose his notion of traditional Adventism, he has tossed that longstanding friendship out the window. Nothing matters more to him now than my elimination from this faculty. He is obsessed with it. Can't you begin to see what this 'witch hunt' has done to all of you? Friendship, compassion, and pastoral concern mean absolutely nothing. All you're only interested in is calming some of your important, wealthy patrons and church leaders who haven't a clue as to what has really been taught in our classes. To satisfy them, you'll do just about anything. What's another faculty member? Grant, Zackrison, Ford, Rea—the list goes on. Now you are about to add my name to that list.[8] But the problems with church doctrine will still be there once I'm also gone. You haven't solved them. You have no idea how to solve them. You have only managed to silence—officially—another voice." I was furious!

"Our family has been hurt and scarred beyond measure. We have been traumatized. You have no idea that what you have done here has damaged Adventism far more than any sympathy I may have shown for Rea and Ford.

---

8. Most of the persons most intimately associated with the trifecta of crises in Adventism no longer are employed by the church—William Peterson, Herold Weiss, Ronald Numbers, Donald McAdams, Jonathan Butler, Desmond Ford, and Walter Rea—and many are no longer active church members. Now I would be added to this list.

Gentlemen, you should be ashamed of yourselves! I'm horribly angry and upset. You have ruined my life and career!"

"That's not true!" blurted Sahly. "*You* are the problem! *You* will have to take responsibility for what you have taught, what you have said and done. You've mishandled this whole matter!"

"You mean by consulting an attorney? Most of the faculty now has attorneys. That's the price of remaining employed here."

That abruptly ended the discussion. "I think there is nothing further to be accomplished in this meeting," I said, nodding to Laura, hinting it was time to leave. "This meeting is over." We got up and abruptly walked out, leaving Hyde, Blanco, and Sahly sitting there stunned. I've often wondered what they must have said once we'd gone.

As Laura and I walked to our car, past the McKee Prayer Garden, with its large stone monument engraved with the menacing Ten Commandments, symbol of Adventist legalism, overshadowing a stone altar designed for private prayer, symbolizing grace in a community devoid of it, I shook in rage. "Laura," I exclaimed, "it's all over! Let's get out of this toxic, horrible place!" Then, motioning toward the pleasant, green valley stretching down below us, framing the University shopping mall and the two large, red brick dormitories, tears forming in my eyes, I poignantly whispered, "We really aren't welcome anymore!"

17

Adventist in Exile

Though the Lord may give you the bread of adversity and the water of affliction,
yet your Teacher will not hide himself any more, but your eyes shall see your
Teacher. And when you turn to the right or when you turn to the left, your ears
shall hear a word behind you saying, "This is the way, walk in it."

— THE PROPHET ISAIAH

I left Southern Adventist University at the end of July 1987 to become
Academic Dean and Professor of Biblical and Integrative Studies at the
Psychological Studies Institute in Atlanta, Georgia (now known as Richmont Graduate University), a private graduate school specializing in the
training of licensed professional counselors. After sending out what seemed
like scores of résumés to colleges and universities with openings in biblical
studies, I discovered there wasn't really any demand for a castoff Adventist
religion scholar. Even at Richmont, questions had already arisen about my
Adventist connection, but the president, James Powell, quickly calmed the
board's fears by telling about the ordeal through which I had just passed. I
felt extremely fortunate to get the position at Richmont, which is how I will
henceforth designate the graduate school, even though the change in name
would come much later.

As Laura, JoAnna, Paula, and I drove south out of Collegedale, down
Ooltewah-Ringgold road, our yellow Plymouth station wagon and dark
blue Oldsmobile jammed with lamps, computer equipment (which I was
hesitant to put in the moving van), pillows, and dishes, past the site where

ended the famous Andrews' Raid, the daring Union theft of the locomotive known as the *General* from the heart of the Confederacy during the Civil War, I sighed in relief. Unlike the Union raiders, who were promptly captured, imprisoned, and executed by the Confederates, I was now free. My intense, agonizing struggle had finally, mercifully come to a close. Yet leaving Adventist employ after twenty-two years, ironically, was one of the hardest decisions I've ever had to make. It meant for my family the end of the only way of life we'd ever known. We were now on our own, outside Adventist culture.

My new academic position involved both administration and teaching. I taught graduate courses in biblical studies, theology, and hermeneutics. In this new, ecumenical Christian environment, I found the work gratifying. Students came to Richmont from all over the nation and some foreign countries to take their MS in Counseling through an affiliation Richmont had with Georgia State University and, at the same time, take the supplementary graduate curriculum in theology and biblical studies offered at Richmont. Eventually, Richmont would become independent, undergo a name change, and offer its own accredited graduate degrees in counseling and pastoral studies. Located in newly renovated facilities in the Family Life Center of the Mount Paran Church of God—one of Atlanta's premier mega churches—Richmont was directed by its hard-working president, James Powell, who was both an ordained United Methodist minister and licensed psychologist. Powell's thoughtfulness, along with that of Sylvia Lebby, the Registrar and accountant, and Julie O'Meara, who headed admissions, began to restore my faith in people and provided a safe refuge where I could begin to recover from my spiritual and emotional trauma. The faculty, especially Henry Virkler, Evalin Hanshew, Joyce Webb, Paul Mauger, and many others, supported me in ways I'd never experienced in the narrow, rigid Adventist world.

Now, however, I was an Adventist minister *in exile*. What did that mean? How could I now live out my vocation in ministry? Despite the entire reprehensible, disgraceful trauma my family and I had endured at the hands of Adventist leadership, still I hadn't reached the point where I felt I could just walk away from Adventism. Most everyone, had they been so treated, would have cut the ties and escaped long before. I was "too firmly addicted to the superstitions of Popery to be easily extirpated from so profound an abyss of mire," John Calvin once admitted.[1] Substitute "Adventism" for "Popery" in this comment, and you have a pretty good idea of where I was

---

1. John Calvin, "Author's Preface," 26, preface to the *Commentary on the Psalms*, as reprinted in John Dillenberger, *John Calvin*, 26.

at the time. The word "addicted" would also be accurate; Adventism truly had an *addictive* hold on me. Only with great difficulty, like someone trying to break an addiction, would I be able to come out of "so profound an abyss."

I struggled to understand what was going on inside. Sociologist Anne Wilson Schaef helped me recognize how I had become so addicted to Adventism that I would have difficulty breaking the ties. "An organization becomes the addictive substance for its employees," she writes,

> when the employees become hooked on the promise of the mission and choose not to look at how the system is really operating. The organization becomes an addictive substance when its actions are excused because it has a lofty mission . . . When this lack of congruence exists, it is more probable that the organization will enter into a rigid denial system with concomitant grandiosity . . . grandiosity is one of the characteristics of the addictive system.[2]

Putting all this into religious terms, R. Yao referred to such systems addiction as having a "fundamentalist mindset." It is "authoritative, intolerant and compulsive about control, an absolutist all-or-nothing, either-or, us against them." It sees no "grays" in life, and boasts, "I've got the truth and you don't." The Adventism I had experienced for thirty years certainly encouraged this kind of mindset. Consequently, when the strain of believing or practicing the church's tenets became too onerous, the entire belief system tended to crumble. That had now happened to me. I was attempting an "addictive withdrawal from a totalistic church system," but what painfully lingered, in Yao's words, was a "shattered faith syndrome."[3] I now had serious reservations about the Adventist teaching about salvation, the Investigative Judgment, the role of Ellen White, the Sabbath, and in fact, Adventist eschatology in general.

While I want to refrain from indicting an entire denominational constituency, there is no question that Southern had fostered so toxic a religious environment that it had probably adversely, even though subtly, affected every person who worked there. Its damage was so pervasive and unnerving that I clung—pathologically, addictively, I admit—to the denomination,

2. Schaef and Fassel, *Addictive Organization*, 123. Later I would find LeBron McBride's work, *Spiritual Crisis*, also to be valuable in understanding my recovery from an Adventist "addiction."

3. Yao, quoted by Thurston and Seebobin, "Psychotherapy for Evangelical Protestants," 139–40.

with its authoritarian ecclesiastical structure and absolute truth claims, like an abused spouse in a miserable, controlling marriage.[4]

Despite all, again like an abused spouse, as strange as it may seem, I still wanted to find a way to make the "marriage" work. To put it a little more positively, I wanted to find a way to continue my vocation as a bonafide *Seventh-day Adventist* minister—a theologian of the church—while working professionally outside the denomination in a new, broader ecumenical environment.

With this goal in mind I set about getting acquainted with the Adventist community in Atlanta. I wrote articles for some of the church's more progressive journals, and conversed with several Adventist pastors who themselves were exhausted over the denomination's never-ending quarrels. Some of these pastors had once been my students at Southern. An exciting opportunity to preach serendipitously opened up at the Atlanta North congregation of the Adventist Church.

The Atlanta North congregation was then meeting in temporary quarters in Dunwoody on the northeast side of Atlanta, anticipating a new building in the rapidly growing, upscale section of the city. Since selling its older church property, the congregation had changed its name and, like many other churches, migrated to the suburbs. The minister, Ralph Lefave, sympathetic toward the revival of the gospel in Adventism, with openness toward the issues Ford and Rea had raised, eagerly welcomed me to the pulpit.

After two or three sermons over as many months, I began to feel comfortable with this new relationship with Atlanta North. Lefave and I agreed that I could preach there on a monthly basis.

When Lefave sought consent for this arrangement from his church board, however, he ran into resistance. Harold Metcalf, the Southern Union Conference Ministerial Secretary, the supervisor of Adventist clergy in the southern United States, and member of the Atlanta North congregation, indignantly demanded an explanation. "You surely aren't going to allow *that* man to preach here, are you?"

Several board members, dimly aware of the controversy that had gone on at Southern, joined Metcalf. "Gladson's charm might sway some of our more gullible members," one said. "Southern Adventist University recently asked him to leave because of his sympathies with Des Ford," Metcalf continued bitterly. "He's even dared publish an article in the *Adventist Review* calling for denominational reconciliation with the polarized, heretical

4. While I do not consider Adventism a cult, the symptoms of leaving I experienced compare with those of persons leaving cults. See Hassan, *Cult Mind Control*, 168–98.

factions in the church. Surely we don't want his ilk in here! If you want my advice, we ought to put this kind of person out of the church. I've urged that for years. The Bible says there can't be any compromise with heretics!"

"The answer does not lie in a stricter enforcement of externals or a sharper focusing of orthodoxy, as important as these may be," I had written of the church's crisis in the article Metcalf mentioned. "The answer comes when we turn to the Center of our faith, learning from that Center what it is like to be supremely loved, and then reflect that love toward others inside and outside the church."[5]

When I had written these lines, some months before I left Southern, I still cherished hope that denominational leadership would seriously try to bridge the widening breach between conservative and progressive factions. Gradually, I had painfully realized, church leaders were much more interested in preserving their brand of orthodoxy, and in the political power that gave them. They wanted to get rid of perspectives that didn't quite square with their definition of Adventism. After all, in a theologically-oriented denomination a perceived theological rectitude provided the source of executive power over the church. The leaders weren't about to give it up. Despite my intention, the words of my article seemingly had the opposite effect. Each side grew more entrenched.

Harold Metcalf had been the Ministerial Secretary of the Southern Union Conference since I had entered the ministry in Kentucky more than twenty years earlier. He had been on the ordination council that examined me for ordination. Of medium height, a portly man with a full head of gray-white hair, he'd been a very successful itinerant evangelist, thundering Adventist doctrine in a loud, deeply resonant voice throughout a hundred Midwestern and Southern cities. Thousands of converts to Adventism owed their denominational allegiance to Metcalf. For many he symbolized traditional, conservative Adventism.

When Samuele Bacchiochi, a professor of church history at Andrews University, had published the idea that the reference to the "Sabbath" in the New Testament letter of Colossians was to be understood as the seventh-day Sabbath of the Ten Commandments rather than one of Israel's annual festivals, as Adventists had always insisted,[6] it had been Metcalf who had

5. Gladson, "Recipe: Love," 23.

6. In order to blunt the effect of Col 2:16–17 ("Do not let anyone condemn you in matters of food and drink or of observing festivals, new moons, or *sabbaths*. These are only a shadow of what is to come, but the substance belongs to Christ" [emphasis supplied]) on their strict observance of the seventh-day Sabbath, Adventists claim "Sabbaths" in this passage stands for the annual Hebrew festivals, not the weekly, seventh-day Sabbath. Bacchiochi is the first Adventist, so far as I am aware, to break with this view.

challenged Bacchiochi. He wrote several letters bitterly denouncing Bacchiochi's "heretical" views. Metcalf was the founding editor of a journal for
clergy called *Unlock Your Potential*, and didn't hesitate to use its pages for
promoting his conservative version of Adventism.

Metcalf's opinion prevailed that night in the North Atlanta board.
When I telephoned him a few days after Christmas, however, Metcalf denied his opposition. "What did you say in the board that caused Atlanta
North to retract my invitation to preach there?" I insisted. I was incredibly
weary of such picayune controversies.

"I didn't say anything incriminating about you," Metcalf snorted. *So
it's Ralph Lefave's word against yours*, I thought. Déjà vu. "I kept my mouth
shut. I wanted you to have the chance for a fresh start. I supported you."
Metcalf sensed I knew he was being evasive because, without pausing, he
went on, changing the subject. "Do you remember your sermon at the Stone
Mountain, Georgia, Adventist church?"

In October I'd preached at Stone Mountain, where Robert ("Bob") Hunter,
a friend from Kentucky days, was pastor. My sermon bore the title, "Find
the Center—Make it Known," and focused on the resurrection of Jesus.
"Adventism, in my opinion," I told the three-hundred-member congregation, "has often failed to emphasize the resurrection, a central teaching of
the New Testament." I referred to a Lutheran minister who, astutely noting
that Adventists didn't celebrate Easter like his church, once asked me, "Do
Adventists believe in the resurrection?" His question troubled me, because I
had always painfully missed an emphasis on Easter in Adventism.[7] "In my
own experience," I admitted, to stress the point. "I don't ever recall hearing
an Adventist minister preach on the resurrection of Jesus."

After church, Bob invited Laura and me to lunch. His wife had tragically died a year earlier, leaving him with the sole care of two small sons. To
his congregation's alarm, Bob had begun dating a *non-Adventist* woman,
something forbidden for Adventists. Adventists frown upon dating or marrying outside their faith—especially for clergy. They quote 2 Corinthians:
"Do not be mismatched with unbelievers, for what partnership is there between righteousness and lawlessness? Or what fellowship is there between

---

7. Adventists tend to downplay the celebration of Easter because it has incorporated many pagan elements, such as the hiding of Easter eggs, and the celebration of
the resurrection on Sunday. The latter was one of the practices that led the early church,
according to Adventists, to abandon the Sabbath. Adventists do believe in the resurrection, but disparage the trappings of Easter celebration.

light and darkness?" (6:14). Using this proof text, Adventists identify themselves as the "believers"; non-Adventists, however Christian they may be,
are the "unbelievers."

"Because of the recent theological controversies I've become uncertain
about the Adventist church," Bob confided. "I'd never marry an Adventist
now. Due to my new friend, I've started re-examining my personal relationship to Adventism—and going to her church on Sunday."

"As I re-examine things," he continued, "would you be my dialogue
partner? You might as well know—I don't think it's any secret—that Roy
Caughron (Ministerial Secretary for the Adventist clergy in Georgia and
eastern Tennessee), a former classmate of yours at Southern, warned me
when I asked him about this, 'You're aware of Jerry's heretical reputation,
aren't you?' he said."

Metcalf's reference to my October sermon brought all this back. He
hadn't been at the Stone Mountain church on that particular day, but his
awareness of even the details of the sermon reveals the power of Adventist
gossip that had done so much harm at Southern. With growing apprehension I was once more jolted into awareness that once you have been labeled
"heretic," or worse, "liberal" within the denomination, there is little chance
of ever finding your way back into the good graces of the leadership. I'd
heard of Adventists who, after being called heretical, had migrated to more
progressive environments like Loma Linda University in Loma Linda,
California, or Walla Walla University in Washington—schools more open
to new ideas—where they'd managed to piece together the semblance of a
new beginning. Denominational leaders, even in these instances, however,
remained perpetually suspicious. After being labeled liberal, these "tainted"
persons were rarely asked again to contribute theologically to the denomination's life. Desmond Ford was at this very moment in such a situation.
Although he'd never officially left the denomination, he'd been relegated to
the sidelines, never again actively to participate. Eventually, he too would
leave the denomination. Would this be my fate? Was I finished, permanently
disgraced, and isolated as an *Adventist* theologian?

"Harold," I controlled my anger, frustration rising. "You must realize
that while I was at Southern I never taught publicly anything that could
be considered unorthodox. I tried my best to work in harmony with the
church."

"Yes, I agree. But there have been lots of allegations—from students—
that you weren't 100 percent an Adventist. And where there have been so
many accusations, there has to be some substance behind them. You know
the old saying, 'where there's smoke, there's fire.'" Al McClure, Metcalf's
"boss," had quoted this very aphorism to the religion department during

the height of the crises. Metcalf was merely echoing his denominational superior's viewpoint.

"Once more I repeat, Harold, as I've told McClure, many of the allegations were trumped up charges made by people who had no real understanding of the theological issues involved, or how university classes are normally conducted. They're frivolous accusations. No one has ever offered any tangible proof of them."

"It doesn't make any difference," Metcalf shot back. "Any accusation is sufficient to put a person under a cloud of suspicion. And you're definitely under some pretty dark clouds."

I was getting nowhere. We finally agreed to part ways in disagreement, but remain on friendly terms. He would continue to oppose me until his untimely death a few years later. Despite some last-ditch efforts by Ralph Lefave, I never again preached at Atlanta North. My occasional appearance in the pulpit of the larger Adventist congregations had come to a sudden, abrupt end.

This painful, unfair rejection caused me to double down upon my conflicted relationship with Adventism. I suppose this often happens when people invest a lifetime in a denomination, whole-heartedly accept its theology, and then become more and more disillusioned. Would I ever be able to use my scholarship and pastoral skills in a significant way? Was I permanently excluded from meaningful fellowship—relegated to the fringe—within Adventism? I rediscovered the lines written by Paul Tillich about the cross a professional theologian inevitably must carry. Because a theologian is obligated to be critical of "every special expression" of theology, Tillich indicates, "he cannot affirm any tradition and any authority except through a 'No' and a 'Yes.' And it is always possible that he may not be able to go all the way from the 'No' to the 'Yes.' He cannot join the chorus of those who live in unbroken assertions. He must take the risk of being driven beyond the boundary line of the theological circle." The next lines fell like stone. "Therefore, the pious and powerful in the church are suspicious of him, although they live in dependence upon the work of the former theologians who were in the same situation."[8] As one Adventist pastor remarked, "Doing theology in Adventism is risky, dangerous business."

What was I to do? Give up? Walk away? Should I just allow the denomination quietly to take away—unopposed—my clergy license, in effect "defrocking" me, and sit in the back pew like an outsider each week, with little or no active part in church life? That way I could certainly remain a Seventh-day Adventist. But how would I function professionally? How

8. Tillich, *Systematic Theology*, 1:25–26.

could I do what I believed God had called me to do? Should I leave Adventism and join another denomination? If so, which? How would I deal with theological uncertainties that, as a former Adventist, I'd be bound to encounter in any denomination, matters like the seventh-day Sabbath and the nature of death? That would mean starting over at age forty-five and rebuilding my professional life among strangers. Should I become independent, obtain a ministerial license from one of several, quasi-legitimate, independent religious organizations, and become essentially a minister-at-large? If I did that, would I ever become a pastor again? Worse, should I quit attending church altogether, as had many former Adventist clergy who had been caught up in the denomination's theological wars?

Sitting in the heavy traffic on Interstate 75 the seventeen miles to and from my Atlanta office every day, I mulled over these confusing options, unable—even paralyzed—to pick any of them I thought might conceivably work. To add to my confusion, over the next few months several Adventist colleges contacted me about re-entering Adventist culture in what they advertised as a friendlier religious climate than that of Southern Adventist University. Atlantic Union College, near Boston, inquired about my becoming academic dean. Southwestern Adventist University, near Fort Worth, Texas, Walla Walla University in Walla Walla, Washington, and even Loma Linda University, all approached about faculty positions. These offers indicated that the denomination was now experiencing a shortage of veteran theological scholars. Loma Linda University's offer—a division chair in religion—strongly tempted. When I responded favorably to the initial contact, Loma Linda arranged a telephone interview conference. During the interview, with the entire religion faculty present, Steve Dailey, the university chaplain, asked, "You've been out of the Adventist work environment for a little while now. Are you now willing and anxious to come back into it?"

That was the wrong question! "I'm sorry," I responded, surprising even myself. "I can't think of anything more demoralizing than once again being in Adventist employment." That killed the interview and my chances of becoming the next Division Chair of Religion at Loma Linda! I hadn't resolved the integrity issue still roiling inside me. How could I submit again to Adventism when I was still very troubled about some of the denomination's basic theology? On the staff at Loma Linda—and at other Adventist colleges—were faculty whose conflict with the church ran far deeper even than mine. But I couldn't live that bifurcated life any longer. I couldn't act and speak one way in public and think another in private. I had come too far for that.

In this struggle Laura and I found we weren't really alone. In the Atlanta area, just as had been true at Collegedale, there were a number of individuals struggling with the same theological and political problems in Adventism. For a few months after we moved into the city we met with some of these persons on Saturday afternoons and shared personal stories. Fearing a permanent break with Adventism, all agreed not to allow ourselves to develop into a full-fledged, breakaway congregation. Our fellowship and study, we agreed, should merely supplement what we found in our respective congregations. The fellowship, if it served no other purpose, enabled us better to cope with the turmoil in Adventism. There was some solace in just commiserating together.

Months slipped by swiftly as I got used to the routines of a major metropolitan area, but they brought me no closer to a solution for the problem Adventism had become.

18

Preacher without a Pulpit

> With what shall I come before the Lord,
> and bow myself before God on high?
> He has told you, O mortal, what is good;
> and what does the Lord require of you
> but to do justice, and to love kindness,
> and to walk humbly with your God?
>
> —THE PROPHET MICAH

D espite the ordeal through which I had now passed, my ordination as an Adventist minister remained unaffected, or so I mistakenly thought. In Adventism, the local or regional church judicatory grants official clergy licensure. The Adventist Southern Union, comprising Kentucky, Tennessee, North and South Carolina, Alabama, Mississippi, and Florida, governs Southern Adventist University. The Southern Union therefore issues clergy credentialing to the ordained University staff for five-year renewable terms. My credentials were thus good for another five years. Adventism, however, made no provision for credentialing clergy whose work lay outside the denomination, with the exception of military and institutional (hospital) chaplains. Since I was no longer employed by the Adventist denomination, I had thus to begin the process of making sure my clergy license would be continued after that five-year period.

Why was I so concerned about such legal credentialing? Why now, especially since I had such deep-set misgivings about Adventist theology and ecclesiastical polity? Holding a valid ministerial license would mean I was formally authorized to conduct the affairs of a church, to preach, teach, administer the sacraments, and offer spiritual guidance. I would have official ministerial standing in the larger community outside the denomination. From the beginning of my college years, I had never wanted anything else than to be an ordained minister. That had always been my lifetime goal. For me, proper, legitimate ministerial credentials thus held great significance. They were just as important to me as similar official credentials are for physicians, nurses, attorneys, or other professionals. I had worked long and hard to achieve ordained ministry, and wanted to maintain that level of certified, official ministry—whatever happened to me in the future.

So I began the process of securing the future of my credentials. I didn't realize that the instant I left denominational employment, I had ceased to be a *licensed* Adventist minister. Unbeknown to me, I no longer held valid credentials. I no longer had ministerial credentials of any kind. My struggle would therefore be to *restore* my credentials, not to *renew* them. I was literally starting over, but didn't realize it.

The unfriendly, even hostile staff of the Southern Union Conference, which under Al McClure had aided and abetted the purge of Southern, would be of absolutely no help. I decided to go over McClure and contact "Bud" Bracebridge, the director of Adventist Chaplaincy Ministries, at the church's world headquarters in Washington, DC. Credentialing through the chaplaincy division that granted such standing to clergy working in military or hospital settings outside the local churches and institutions seemed the most logical place to start. Bud, a gentle, six-foot-three giant in his late fifties, with whom I'd gotten acquainted while teaching Southern's extension class in Columbia, South Carolina, some ten years earlier, was extremely helpful. He agreed to support my appeals process. Bracebridge had to refer the matter to Charles Bradford, President of the North American Division, the judicatory over Adventist churches and institutions throughout the United States and Canada. Bradford was one of the rare African-Americans in the church's top-level hierarchy. Bracebridge also enlisted the aid of Gary Patterson, the Assistant to the President of the North American Division.

Patterson, the middle-aged former senior minister of the Southern Adventist University church, and I had shared carpooling from Collegedale to Vanderbilt University, in Nashville, while completing our doctoral degrees. During the three-hour drive, we shared the secrets of our lives, divulging some of our deepest personal struggles. These trips had forged a strong bond of friendship that had outlasted the denomination's theological crises. Patterson had risen rapidly in the denominational ranks and had now become the personal assistant to the North American Division President.

Months slipped by after I had filed my initial appeal for the renewal of my credentials. On a Friday afternoon in February, I received a letter marked "North American Division, Office of the President." Slipping into my Richmont office, I sat down in the brown, high-backed executive chair, tightly gripping the letter that presumably would spell out my fate. Noise from student conversations in the hallway outside filtered in. Before opening it, I slowly pondered the sealed contents of the letter. For several minutes I hesitated. Then a sudden surge of hope welled up. Would it be favorable? Of course it would! How could it be otherwise, with all these friends working in my behalf?

I slowly opened the envelope. It was from Patterson. "I think I should devote myself to church administration," Patterson, who was no mean scholar himself, once quipped teasingly as my red Volkswagen chugged along the long interstate highway toward Vanderbilt, "so I can speak up in behalf of you theologians when you're under fire."

That time had oddly come, at least for me. "Your request for credentials," the letter began, "has been scuttled as a result of the same craziness that has dogged all of our steps for the last several years. I have done my best to plead your case, but it has not been successful."

The words stung like sharp needles. The breath suddenly went right out of me. I felt totally and irrevocably rejected. I had been denied! The door slammed in my face!

At some level I guess I realized this day would eventually come, but nothing had prepared me for the initial shock. Somehow, I had naively believed, I would eventually find justice and fairness, perhaps even a measure of vindication, rather than final condemnation and rejection, especially at the highest judicatory level of the church.

For a few minutes I sat there, numbed, my thoughts confused. Rage, anger, bitterness coursed through me. Had I been dreaming of the impossible? Was I quixotically tilting at windmills? Harsh, cruel reality came crashing in. Was there really no longer any place left for me within Adventism, my church of origin, my spiritual home? I felt horrible loss, the bitter relinquishing of a lifetime dream. I stared into the widening gulf that separated the unknown future from me. What if—because I no longer had ordained credentials—I lost my position at Richmont? How could I continue in professional ministry? Must I give up the struggle, resign from Richmont, and look for a small, out-of-the-way parish in a distant Adventist conference, out of the limelight—in obscurity—where I might quietly serve out my days? Would such a parish even be available for me after I'd been permanently stained with the taint of heresy? What about personal integrity? Could I conscientiously serve *anywhere* in Adventism? I felt miserable.

On Monday I telephoned Patterson. He was in California, but returned my call on Wednesday. "Gary, I want to know something about the thinking of the committee in denying my request."

"Quite a few people have actually talked about the merits of your case," he told me. "Bud Bracebridge has worked tirelessly on the matter. He consulted both Neal Wilson and Charles Bradford. Unable to come to a decision, Wilson finally referred the matter back to the Southern Adventist University board chair."

Oh, no! The Southern board chair, Al McClure! My old nemesis! I stiffened for what was coming next.

"In the final analysis, Al McClure killed your chances. His decision represents the same biased attitude that has followed all of us who, unfortunately, were at Southern Adventist University. There's still a slender hope, however. Wait until after the General Conference session this summer. If we get a sympathetic North American Division president, such as Ron Whisby, now president of the Columbia Union Conference (the Mid-Atlantic states), or even myself, you'll be in the clear."

"Isn't Al McClure the leading candidate for the North American Division presidency?"

"He is. But Ron Whisby is also a strong contender and I'm even in the running. If Al McClure gets the position, all hope is lost, of course. But hang tight until the election, and let's see what happens."

With this stinging rejection still smoldering, family tragedy struck. Laura's father, V. W. (Wilson) Hayes, died on March 29, following a stroke he had suffered three weeks earlier. Wilson, or "Papa," as we affectionately called him, had during the Great Depression studied for the Adventist ministry at a time when pastoral positions were extremely limited. Failing to secure an appointment upon graduation, he eventually settled on a dairy farm in Greenwood, South Carolina. There he and Pansy, his wife, raised six children, including Laura, the youngest. Through the years he had kept up with his theological studies. He blended in his person practical know-how about machinery, construction, and agriculture with an intricate understanding of theology, biblical studies, history, and philosophy. Papa loved sitting in his handcrafted, wooden chair, with its spacious arm rests, poring over a new book, busily marking in the margins. He seemed to remember almost everything he read. He was one of the last "renaissance" persons. I deeply admired him.

While Papa's breadth of knowledge left me in awe, his generous, universal acceptance of people endeared him far and wide. From the start, when Laura and I were dating, he welcomed me as a son—not merely a future son-in-law. Seemingly devoid of racial prejudice, he and Pansy hosted city and county dignitaries, traveling missionaries, itinerant preachers, and groups of professional tree-planters en route through the Carolinas while replanting forests that had been logged for pulp wood. From his abundant and well-tended gardens, he garnished many tables all over Greenwood County. A bronze plaque on his living room wall quietly heralded his selection as Greenwood's "Man of the Year."

Whenever Laura, our girls, and I arrived for a visit, he and I launched into a vigorous, nonstop conversation that invariably began with some topic in theology and then ranged over many branches of human knowledge. What a college professor he would have been, this Jeffersonian gentleman farmer! Converted to Seventh-day Adventism in his teens, over fifty years Papa had gradually become disillusioned with the denomination. He carefully followed the theological difficulties with which the church struggled, but abhorred the tactics Adventist leaders were using to suppress discussion. He grew even angrier as Adventist leadership stepped up the pressure on Laura and me. We were family! He sensed his own confidence in the Adventist church and its theology slipping away. "If I knew of a better alternative," he confided in me a few weeks before his death, "I'd leave the Adventist church."

Papa influenced me deeply. His sudden death broke my heart. In the future, I'd sorely miss his wise counsel and support. At his memorial service, I told the standing-room only audience, "Wilson Hayes was a great man— one of the greatest men I have ever known."

The General Conference of Seventh-day Adventists met in Indianapolis, Indiana, that summer. The world-wide gathering of Adventists included some ten thousand people, garbed in turbans, dark suits, and bright dresses. Totally unanticipated, the assembled delegates firmly rejected the re-election bid of the General Conference President, Neal Wilson, who'd been in office for the better part of two decades. His autocratic leadership style had apparently turned most of the denomination against him. Wilson's heavy hand had been lifted! The church's beleaguered theologians heaved a collective sigh of relief. Then they learned that Robert Folkenberg, president of the Carolina Conference, had replaced Wilson. As a member of Southern Adventist University's Board of Trustees, Folkenberg had earned the approval of the denomination's right wing because of his persistent criticism of Southern's religion department. For the Adventist theological community, then, Folkenberg would likely offer little relief from the polarizing forces that threatened to rip the denomination apart. An omen of this emerged a few days later when the General Conference overwhelmingly voted to deny clergy ordination to women. "Well, that's it," one dissatisfied lay delegate said. "This church has just officially said women are unequal. I'm not treated this way anywhere else. Why should I cooperate . . . with an organization that makes women victims of official discrimination? A church, no less!"[1] This vote derailed almost twenty years of theological investigation and study that had set the stage for the full and equal acceptance of women into the ordained clergy. It was just further evidence of the denomination's lurch to the hard right.

Laura and I learned of Wilson's shocking defeat and Folkenberg's equally unexpected election when we arrived in Indianapolis for an afternoon seminar we had been invited to present at the Association of Adventist Forums that was meeting simultaneously with the General Conference. Because Bradford had now retired, the presidency of the North American Division, the second highest office in the denomination, was now vacant. The Southern Adventist University Board of Trustees chair, Al McClure, it seemed, stood the best chance of being elevated to this office. McClure was elected hands down.

Extremely disheartened by this political turn of events, a few days later I sent a carefully worded appeal to the newly elected McClure about my ministerial credentials. Instinctively I realized it was really an exercise in futility. McClure had opposed me for years. This time nothing happened. Silence. The telephone never rang. No one, not even an assistant in his office, responded to my letter. Desperate, I wrote again, pleading with McClure at least to tell me something. I set a deadline. I told him I needed to know something by the end of October. By fixing a definite date I hoped to prompt him toward some action. If I had not heard by the end of October, I emphasized in the letter—tactfully, I hoped—I would have to explore other arrangements for clergy credentialing. I had no idea what that meant.

Months dragged by. October came and went. Again, silence. No communication. McClure was ignoring me. Not a word. Meanwhile, the gender discrimination of the General Conference in denying well-qualified, seminary-trained women a place in the ordained clergy weighed upon my

1. *Indianapolis* 1990, 39.

conscience. Should I succeed in getting my own clergy credentials renewed, how could I justify such credentials for myself when equally qualified women were denied the same? This was open, blatant sexism, cloaked by a thinly veiled, pious, self-righteous conservatism. Denominational leaders insistently cited what are known as the "house codes" in the New Testament that seem to subordinate women in the church community.[2] Most biblical scholars—including Adventists—had repeatedly pointed out to the denominational leadership that these passages were actually a reflection of the culture of the Roman world, not permanent, universal restrictions, and certainly not the final liberating word of the gospel. They were no more universally binding than the New Testament's condoning of human slavery in passages closely bound up with these same house codes. But the male church leadership had dug in its heels, even twisting to its own advantage earlier favorable studies that had endorsed the ordination of women. Ordained clergy in Adventism would be exclusively male for the indefinite future.[3]

Paradoxically, while the church affirmed women in the prophetic office (Ellen White was considered a prophet), it denied women ordination to the ministry. This never made sense to me. I couldn't find any biblical or theological justification for making such a gendered distinction. As far as I could tell, the New Testament placed no gender requirements on any of the gifts of the Spirit.[4] Such blatant sexual discrimination stirred up my anger all over again. In my irritation, I committed a fatal blunder that doomed forever my receiving clergy credentials from the Adventist church.

Having heard nothing from Al McClure, the man who ironically now held my ministerial fate solely in his hands, I wrote a third time. Only now I also expressed my disappointment over the denomination's decision to deny the ordained ministry to women. I protested the decision because it discriminated on grounds of gender, not actual ability or qualifications.

Still McClure didn't budge. Through the entire appeals process—from beginning to end—he never once acknowledged any of my correspondence. I don't possess a single scrap of correspondence from him (this was before the internet). Rudely he maintained total silence. I wondered if he feared putting anything in writing. Others had threatened lawsuits; rumors were rife.

2. See 1 Cor 14:33–36; Eph 5:22—6:9; Col 3:18—4:1; 1 Tim 2:11–12; Tit 2:3–8; but see Gal 3:28.

3. The Adventist General Conference Session of 2015 voted once more to withhold ordination from women.

4. See 1 Cor 12:4–11; Eph 4:11–13.

On January 16, exasperated over the whole affair, again I telephoned Gary Patterson, who had amazingly remained in office after the election as the division president's assistant—as he had with McClure's predecessor, Bradford. "Your appeal is scheduled to come for a vote before the council of Union Conference presidents in February," he assured me. "You should know something by March 1."

On March 1, one year after my original appeal had been first denied by the North American Division, and five months after the October deadline I had set, I again telephoned. "I simply had to know something," I told Patterson.

Patterson answered. "A lot of 'foot dragging' has gone on about your case," he explained. "The letter you wrote about the ordination of women really annoyed McClure. You got under his skin! After he read it, he took your name off. He didn't even put your appeal on the agenda. It wasn't even brought up."

Stunned, I guess deep down I'd really expected something like this.

"Something else you need to be aware of," continued Patterson. "As you may have heard, Bud Bracebridge, who was one of your strongest advocates, has tragically succumbed to leukemia, which he had been fighting for a long time. Your 'champion,' so to speak, is dead, your case abandoned." I sank deeper in my brown leather chair, gazing blankly at the pale green walls of my office. I felt numb, like I'd been struck. But I wasn't ready for what he said next. The words stunned.

"You had better see what you can do elsewhere." Patterson was subtly encouraging me to leave Adventism! His words struck like iron. They intimated there was no longer any room in Adventism for me! The highest tribunal in the church to which I could appeal had spoken by its rude, unprofessional silence, ignoring my pleas. It proclaimed as though in flaming letters: *Get out! You aren't worthy of even so much as a reply. You aren't wanted!*

For days I mourned, moping around. Without valid license, I had literally become a minister without a denomination, without a pulpit. Ministry had all my adult life defined me. It was who I was. All else revolved around this central life purpose. Since the age of seventeen, when I first felt God's call in the stockroom of my father's small grocery market, surrounded by hundred pound sacks of chicken feed and boxes of canned food, ministry had been my passion. Now the church I'd grown deeply to love and to which I had dedicated my entire life had irrevocably slammed the door in my face. I had been condemned and rejected without a hearing. No longer just an exile, I had now become a "church-less" refugee. I guess I felt much like John Tyler, the American president who was thrown out of the Whig party because of his resistance to the National Bank issue of the 1840s. I'd been reading his biography. Oddly, after being tossed out of his party, he became a political pariah, a president without party support. I was a minister without a church or denomination. I, too, was now a pariah.

Why not simply go to another denomination? I asked myself. People change churches every day, and think nothing of it. Adventists, however, consider leaving Adventism as virtually unpardonable. The denomination thinks other churches constitute the corrupt, mystical Babylon in the book of Revelation. The mission of Adventism is essentially to call people out from these other corrupt denominations. "Come out of her, my people, so that you do not take part in her sins" (Rev 18:4). When a person abandons Adventism—for whatever reason—and dares to join one of these corrupt, "Babylonian" churches, in cold black ink beside their name in the Adventist church ledgers is often inscribed the single, glaring word: "apostasy." For Adventists it represents virtually a taking leave of Christ, a forsaking of the one true God. There is little hope for those who leave—in this life or the next. They are almost considered infidels. Unless they repent and come back to the Adventist church, they will probably be lost forever.

When a person withdraws from Adventism, an informal type of "shunning" commences. By this time in my career, I'd written five books, all published by denominational presses. These would now suddenly disappear off the shelves of Adventist bookstores as though they were contraband. Friends I had known all my life would lapse into silence and speak to me no more, I pessimistically thought. Although they couldn't avoid contact, Adventist relatives would treat me as though I had a dangerous infection. I would painfully sense their unspoken pity. "How are the mighty fallen?" they would think, if not boldly ask. "I wonder how one so highly-educated could become so confused?" One by one my social network across the denomination would blink out like the lights of a city in a power outage. I would become as one dead among the living. "They are waterless clouds carried along by the winds, autumn trees without fruit, twice dead, uprooted" (Jude 12).

For JoAnna and Paula, it would bring the loss of the only church community they'd ever known. Although they had borne it in silence, they too had been severely damaged by the traumatic rejection Laura and I had experienced for the alleged "crime" of dissent. Unfortunately, they were ill-prepared—at twenty-two and nineteen—to distinguish God from the church that considered itself to be the primary locus of God's final revelation in the world. Going forward they might mistakenly blame the church's rejection and abuse on God, thus destroying their own nascent spirituality.

Thousands of Adventist students I had taught for over fifteen years would now be inevitably tainted with the stain of my defection. They would be treated as though they had contracted some kind of deadly spiritual virus while sitting in my classes. All their lives they would be carefully scrutinized for any signs of the dissent that had led to my demise.

Yet in my pain—suddenly and mysteriously—I sensed anew the Presence of God. "Happy are all those who take refuge in him" (Ps 3:11). "Though I walk in the midst of trouble, you preserve me against the wrath of my enemies" (Ps 138:7). God was strengthening me for the decision I now had to make, for the journey on which I had unwillingly already embarked. I started to feel a strange new kinship with the universal, ageless church. Christians through the ages had unhesitatingly followed Christ. The flow of the mighty river of the Christian faith enveloped me, carrying me down its silently moving, deep and tranquil waters toward the future.

PART THREE

Aftermath

19

Discovering the United Church of Christ

I ask not only on behalf of these, but also on behalf of those who will believe in me
through their word, that they may all be one. As you, Father, are in me and I am in
you, may they also be in us so that the world may believe that you have sent me.

—Jesus

On Wednesday, March 6, 1991, still reeling from the final rejection by
Adventism, I hesitantly dialed Roger Knight, the Conference Minister
of the Southeast Conference of the United Church of Christ. I had gotten
acquainted with Roger and his wife, Beth, at Pilgrimage United Church of
Christ, in Marietta, Georgia, where Laura and I had attended frequently
over the past two years. During the appeals process with the Adventist leadership, I'd purposely kept Roger apprised about my struggle over ministerial
licensure and the possibility that I might need to turn to the United Church
of Christ.

When Roger picked up his extension at the Conference office, abruptly
I began, "Roger, does your denomination accept 'refugees'"?

"Do we accept refugees! Come on over!" he shouted with an eagerness
that sent a tingle all through me, especially after the long years of struggle
and groping about within Adventism.

"Adventism has finally, completely terminated me," I explained. "I'd
like to begin immediately the process of the transfer of my ordination to the
United Church of Christ."

My first contact with the United Church of Christ had occurred four
years earlier. One morning, while confiding my ongoing struggle over

Adventism with Jim Powell, president of Richmont, he asked, "Have you ever considered the United Church of Christ? I understand they're quite sympathetic with ministers who desire—or need—to change denominations."

The next Sunday found Laura and me worshiping at Pilgrimage United Church of Christ, only a few miles from our home in Kennesaw. Located a quarter mile off busy Sandy Plains Road in a rapidly growing suburb of Marietta, the two-hundred-member congregation met in a single story, brown-sided building designed initially for educational and social events, with church offices situated on its western side. Anticipating the future addition of a worship center, by setting up folding chairs, the congregation worshiped temporarily in the spacious social hall.

That morning, Helen Pearson, a faculty member at Emory University and former member of the Communities of Christ (previously known as the Reorganized Church of Jesus Christ of Latter-day Saints)—thus a "refugee" herself—preached in the pastor's absence. I really appreciated the liturgy, the reverent emphasis on the public reading of Scripture, and the friendliness of the people. The simple Confession of Faith, which the congregation recited that morning, was impressive. Its profundity, expressed in the form of a doxology, rhythmically articulated, felt like cool water to my conflicted soul. "We believe in you, O God, Eternal Spirit, God of our Savior Jesus Christ and our God," it ran. "You seek in holy love to save all people from aimlessness and sin . . . In Jesus Christ, the man of Nazareth, our crucified and risen Savior, you have come to us."

Astonishingly, I spiritually resonated with almost every line of the Confession of Faith. Even more reassuring, I found that the Confession was not considered mandatory, but was only a witness to the common faith of the church. It represented a consensus, in other words. People could freely interpret this—and any other confession or biblical passage—according to their own personal understanding. In sharp contrast to Adventism, the United Church of Christ was firmly committed to theological diversity. For a brief time that morning, I could imagine myself free from the entanglements and addictive power of Adventism and worshiping in this peaceful environment.

Returning home, I looked for information about the United Church of Christ (not to be confused with the "Church of Christ"). It originated in 1957 as the result of the historic union of four denominations—the Congregational, the Christian Church, the German Reformed, and the Evangelical Synod.[1] Congregationalism went back to the English Puritans, of course, and the Christian Church to the early nineteenth century religious

---

1. See Gunneman, *United Church of Christ.*

movement of Abner Jones and Elias Smith, and before them, that of James O'Kelly. The German Reformed traced its ancestry to John Calvin and Ulrich Zwingli, while the Evangelical Synod came from the Lutheran tradition. Together these four denominations brought into the United Church of Christ every major strand of Protestantism, making it the most ecumenical body ever formed. Even part of my limited, Adventist Protestant heritage was therefore represented. James White, the husband of Ellen White, had been a member of the Jones and Smith version of the Christian Church, known as the Christian Connection in the New England of his day.

Could I be content in the United Church of Christ? I pondered. Liturgically, I found the worship quite engaging. I would enjoy the intellectual caliber of its theology. Helen Pearson's sermon had been intellectually and spiritually several notches above any Adventist sermon I had heard in a while. If the commitment to individual, theological pluralism was genuine, with provision for transfer of ordination, it was a definite possibility. In its fellowship, I sensed, my theology could grow and develop. Furthermore, if I had to change denominations (far more difficult than changing banks!), it was going to have to be a mainstream denomination. I was considering others, including the Presbyterian Church (USA), the Protestant Episcopal, the Lutheran (Evangelical Lutheran Church of America), and the Christian Church (Disciples of Christ). Whichever I decided, I was determined no longer to live in isolation from the Christian mainstream.

I arranged to meet Mark Cole, the senior pastor at Pilgrimage, for breakfast in at a small, cozy restaurant in Vinings, a northwest Atlanta suburb, not far from Richmont Graduate University.

"I'll be more than happy to assist you in making the transition," Mark assured. I decided then and there to attend Pilgrimage on a fairly regular basis to see what it felt like to be a congregant of the United Church of Christ. There I became acquainted with Roger and Beth Knight.

For weeks after the telephone call to Knight, the enormity of the decision to transfer to the United Church of Christ weighed heavily upon me. Had I done the right thing? Would I eventually regret the move? Could I—should I—have done more to resolve matters with Adventism? What more could I have done? Should I just abandon the struggle to maintain my clergy standing, give up my lifelong dream to be an ordained minister, and just be content to live as a lay person?[2]

2. Later I learned I could have continued as an ordained minister in Adventism, but I would no longer be licensed to function in that capacity. I could not conduct

What I had experienced in Adventism, I knew, "could only have happened in America," as the saying goes. European Adventism was evidently different. More progressive, more open to new ideas, it was less tied to Ellen White and the pioneers of the denomination. What if American Adventism were to move in a similar, progressive direction? What if, after I had broken with it, Adventism began to open up and become more tolerant? Once some of the more rigid, reactionary leadership passed off the scene, the issues that had finally snuffed out my religious life as an Adventist—the gospel, the Investigative Judgment, Ellen White—might conceivably be loosened a bit. That might make life as a theologian more tolerable, perhaps even feasible. I knew that Adventism would eventually change. All organizations change. The sheer force of sociological trends, over time, would eventually bring modifications in belief and lifestyle, as they do in even the most rigid of religious communities. It was already happening in Europe and in California. Even if these changes took root in most of the United States, how long would it take before I could function effectively as a scholar in Adventism? Would it happen in my lifetime? Would I live out my days, retire, and grow old waiting for a change that might never come?

As time went by, however, it became increasingly clear to me that to continue the struggle with Adventism would be futile. I had to make a decision based on *where* I lived and upon Adventism as it *now* presented itself. Already, while living in Atlanta, I had squandered almost three years in a pointless, frustrating battle with Adventist leadership. I had become bitter and angry at the injustice of it all. Laura, JoAnna, and Paula had silently endured my struggle, but the uncompromising, hardline attitude of the Adventist leadership, after the years of turmoil at Southern, had finally embittered them against not only Adventism, but against *any* church. Their estrangement now ran so deep that on Sunday—or Saturday—they chose to be absent from worship. I usually attended church alone. Totally absorbed in my own inner conflict, I had yet to recognize the toll my struggles were exacting on my family. The road of Adventism had come to a sudden, bitter dead end.

The process of transferring ordained ministerial standing from another denomination to the United Church of Christ involves the consent of the Association Commission on Church and Ministry. In my case this was the Georgia-South Carolina Association of the Southeast Conference of the United Church, to refer to the official names.[3] This Commission

weddings, administer the sacraments, or preach in most churches. This would have the equivalent to a suspension of my clerical calling.

3. Although it follows an essentially congregation style of church polity, the United Church has three geographical jurisdictions: the Association, usually a state or

evaluates the candidate's academic, professional, and personal background, verifies previous ordination, and implements a process to assist that person in understanding the history, theology, and polity of the United Church. Usually this requires some seminary classes or formal academic papers that are then reviewed by the Commission. Periodically during this process, the candidate meets with the Commission for evaluation and review. The entire process can take up to two years.

On Sunday, April 14, I awoke about 5:00 a.m., gripped by bitter, uncertain anguish. More reluctantly than I had hoped, Laura had agreed to join me that day in becoming members of the United Church of Christ. Membership in a local United Church, of course, was prerequisite to obtaining ordained ministerial standing. Although this prospect should have been gratifying, I still felt the pangs of guilt about turning away from the church community that had given me spiritual birth, nurtured and educated me, and provided long-lasting friendships. Adventism had been literally everything to me—too much, I suspect. I had given it the most vigorous, creative years of my life and career. Tossing and turning in bed, I tormented myself like a frightened lover plucking the petals from a rose. *Do you love me? Do you not? How can I do this? How can I not!* Six weeks had passed since my telephone inquiry, and still I had received no written confirmation regarding the rejection of ministerial standing by the North American Adventist Division. All I had to rely on were Gary Patterson's words, "You had better see what you can do elsewhere." No documentation of any kind. No telephone call. No personal contact. It would be four more years before I would discover in an article written by Patterson himself the reasons my ministerial standing had been denied. Commenting on my defection, he wrote: "It was not, however, his views on ordination [of women] which caused concern, but his expression of views on the Investigative Judgment and the ministry of Ellen White."[4]

When I read these words, I wondered how church leadership had managed to conclude, in the absence of any public statements by me, in or out of the classroom, on either the Investigative Judgement or Ellen White, that I was seriously deviant enough on these points as to warrant the removal of my credentials. Of course I had issues. Who didn't? At a deep level I had doubts about both Ellen White and the Investigative Judgment doctrine. But unlike Desmond Ford or Walter Rea—both of whom also lost their ministerial credentials—I had never gone public with them. Sometimes I

part thereof; the Conference, embracing several Associations; and the General Synod, which attends to the whole.

4. Patterson, "Difficult Times," 9.

wished I had. It might have been more honorable than all the smoke-and-mirrors I'd had to deal with.

Nothing was clear that April morning. I had been left dangling. The Adventist leaders didn't really care, or else they were afraid to put anything in writing. I was now totally insignificant, like a gnat they'd been able to swat. The denomination had finally achieved what it had determined to do at Southern Adventist University—remove me from Adventism and thus have one less "dissident" scholar to contend with. I'd been abandoned. I was now, not just an exile, but a refugee. I hadn't left Adventism. It had left me. Now I must seek refuge elsewhere, find a new spiritual home. My thoughts raced in the twilight hours that morning. Should Adventism through some miracle change and adopt a more pluralistic outlook, should it become more democratic and willing to welcome me back, I could probably return. As long as it remained the dysfunctional, addictive organization it had become, I must leave. I don't really have a choice.

At Pilgrimage United Church of Christ, Laura and I went forward at the close of worship to be received into membership. As the minister pronounced the words of the liturgy, "Let us unite with the church in all times and places in confessing our faith in the triune God," my uncertainty lifted and I felt a glow of satisfaction. Laura and I had now officially joined the great historic stream of Christianity, the church universal. We had become a part of a progressive, open-minded church, one that would challenge and encourage us to grow spiritually and theologically. No longer an irritant, a life stressor, our church community would now be a resource and strength for daily living. The members at Pilgrimage welcomed us happily. We had begun a new journey in a new place of refuge and joy.

A week later the United Church of Christ Association Commission on the Ministry scheduled my first interview regarding transfer of ordination. It was the day before my birthday. Once again the nagging uncertainty had returned, and I was feeling uneasy about my decision. I bargained with God that, if this move were not God's will, God would somehow block it. I decided to lay everything before the Commission, holding nothing back as I'd had to do so many times while in Adventism. When I explained my theological views, which no doubt appeared somewhat conservative in the setting of the progressive United Church of Christ, one of the Commission members, John Gunneman, a faculty member at Emory University, remarked, "Your personal views are no problem. There's room for you in the United Church. You'll meet people who represent other viewpoints, but you'll also be free to follow your own." I'm at a loss to express how much his comment meant. For the first time in my professional life, I began to feel truly accepted by a Christian community. It was wonderful.

The Commission found no problems with my academic background, my ordination, or references, and so decided to accept me into the process for transfer of standing. I was on my way! Two months later, following the completion of a series of formal papers on denominational history, theology, and polity, and after a two-hour oral examination that probed my theological understanding of baptism, the Eucharist, worship, and other matters, the Commission recommended me for "privilege of call." That made me eligible to accept a ministerial position within the United Church. All that remained was final approval by the Ecclesiastical Council of the Georgia-South Carolina Association of the United Church. That happened a few weeks later.

"The departure of Dr. Jerry Gladson from the teaching and pastoral ministry of the Seventh-day Adventist Church," Gary Patterson reflected four years later in the article mentioned above, "was not only the loss of one of our most outstanding Bible scholars, but a personal sorrow to me . . . The pain of these events is yet strong with me."[5]

At the Fourth of July celebration in Peachtree City, near Atlanta, I spent a delightful evening with another *former* Adventist minister who had also been denied his ministerial standing—Desmond Ford. Ford was the guest of Robert and Gloria Hale. The Hales had invited Laura and me to spend the evening of July 4 with them. With fireworks bursting in the night sky, illuminating trees and houses with a ghostly radiance, Ford and I talked long into the night.

Desmond Ford, I think, represents a tragic figure in Adventism. His ministry in the church spanned thirty-four years—mostly as a religion professor at Avondale University in Australia. A lifelong student of the book of Daniel, Ford tried vainly to alert denominational leaders about the difficulties of the Adventist interpretation of Daniel, as we have seen (see chap. 7). In retaliation for his efforts, church leaders removed him from the ministry and took the almost unprecedented further step of defrocking Ford, which rescinded his ordination.

Yet that night, remarkably, Ford betrayed no bitterness. "Hope springs eternal," he said when I questioned him about whether he thought the Adventist church could change. "You must understand," he went on, "Adventist leaders are acting in ignorance, and they must be forgiven for not really understanding. They're so busy tending to the business of the church they haven't time to explore theological matters." His graciousness toward those who had so wronged and condemned him was very moving, even Christlike. "Father, forgive them, for they do not know what they are doing" (Luke 23:34).

5. Patterson, "Difficult Times," 9.

That summer I gradually started to feel better about where my life was heading. We had broken away from Southern Adventist University. I had passed through the crisis of leaving Adventism and, although beginning over again in another denomination, had hope for a significant future ministry. My work at Richmont was exciting and promising. I had no idea that the most terrible crisis—the most terrible damage Adventism had inflicted—lay just ahead, before that summer ended.

20

Winter of Discontent

I am convinced that neither death, nor life, nor angels, nor rulers, nor things present, nor things to come, nor powers, nor height, nor depth, nor anything else in all creation will be able to separate us from the love of God in Christ Jesus, our Lord.

—St. Paul

On a Friday evening that September, I sat on the sofa in the living room reviewing a sermon I was to preach the next morning at the Hiram, Georgia, Seventh-day Adventist church. This event requires some explanation. Even while I was in the process of transferring my clergy standing to the United Church of Christ, a former student from Southern, Charles Jenkins, occasionally—boldly—defied the unwritten "ban" the denomination had placed upon me, and invited me to preach in the small, struggling Hiram Church, of which he served as pastor. He was fully aware that I was transferring to the United Church of Christ. That's why his invitation for me to preach was so audacious.

I noticed Laura seemed unusually sad and despondent. "Is something the matter?" I asked.

"I have something important to give you," she replied. Without saying anything further, she got up and went into our bedroom. She returned with a letter that she handed to me. "I was planning to give this to you earlier, but I guess I got scared."

Puzzled, not knowing what it was about, I took the letter. The opening lines clutched at my throat like a vise. "I've been waiting to tell you this for some time, but the occasion has never presented itself," the letter began.

"I've been unhappy for some time, and want out of the marriage. I can't give you all the reasons, but my reasons are valid to me. I don't want to hurt you in any way, but I no longer want to be married to you."

It felt like I'd been bludgeoned. For a moment, the room grew dim. I seemed to be a thousand miles away. This was not happening! I couldn't believe it!

I followed Laura to the bedroom. "Is this final?" I asked, sudden anger now jolting me out of shock. "Are you willing to talk about this?"

"I'm willing to talk about it, but you need to know I'm 99 percent certain this is what I want."

"Would you be willing to see a marriage therapist?" I asked. I remembered how for years I'd stubbornly refused to go into therapy, even when Laura had asked. "We can't afford it!" Now I bitterly regretted it.

"Yes, I'm willing to go to therapy, but I don't believe it would do any good. You and I are not suited for each other, and it would be better if we went our separate ways."

"You say that after twenty-six years! It surely took a long time to figure that out!" Outrage overwhelmed me. The old judgmental attitude, honed by years of practice in Adventism, surfaced. "What about the vow you took twenty-six years ago, 'till death do us part?' Doesn't that mean anything?"

"No! It doesn't. And it hasn't for a long time. My love for you died years ago." Anger suddenly ebbed, and the tears freely came. I wept bitterly on and off for days afterward. I dearly loved Laura. The pain seemed unendurable

The next morning at Hiram, somehow I got through the sermon, although I'm not sure what I said. How do you preach from the heart when the music has suddenly been sucked out of your life? Laura didn't go with me. She never attended church with me again.

I made an appointment with a female psychologist at a nearby counseling center. Four sessions followed, each ending with the same results. The therapist and I tried to persuade Laura to work on our relationship. Laura repeatedly emphasized she wanted out of the marriage and saw no possibility of changing her mind. I became desperate, out of my mind with fear. Yet I managed to keep the desperation within. No one—not even our closest friends—realized we were having this marital struggle. That only increased the tension under which I now worked at Richmont, because I foolishly felt I had to maintain an appearance of normalcy even while our marriage was crumbling—another woeful legacy from Adventism. The month of October, while we were in therapy, I appealed again and again to Laura. It was pure emotional hell.

We argued repeatedly. This was something we'd never done before. I insisted she work on the marriage. "You owe us that!" I argued. Just as stubbornly, she insisted, "I want out!"

November arrived. One Friday evening I had begun work on my installation service scheduled for Pilgrimage Church the following Sunday evening. The ceremony was to celebrate my becoming a fully authorized minister in the United Church of Christ. The telephone rang. I'd been expecting a call from Laura when she had finished work. Perhaps, I'd been thinking, we might do something that evening, something that could revive a little of the old romantic spark.

"I want you to go into the dining room," Laura began. "There's an envelope I want you to open." Clutching the cordless telephone, I slowly, fearfully made my way to the dining room. There indeed lay an envelope. Tearing open the envelope, I read words that marked our doom as a family. *Laura wasn't coming home.* She was moving out and would spend the weekend with a woman friend. Her mind had not changed. It would not change. She wanted out of the marriage. Her decision was final. There was no turning back. We argued. The telephone conversation degenerated into an angry, icy exchange.

That morning, I learned later, she had told JoAnna and Paula that she was leaving. They burst into tears. Gathering some things into a suitcase, Laura turned away and walked out, leaving the girls sobbing in their rooms, with photos of our now shattered family all around.

True to her words, Laura didn't return. For three weeks there was almost no contact. I fell into a deep depression. My emotions seemed to bounce off the wall, cycling through weeping, denial, despair, bargaining, hope, and back again. My whole world, it seemed, had suddenly been ripped apart. It was all I could do just to get through the day. I went to my office, perfunctorily did what I had to do and then, once alone, wept all the way home. I plopped down in front of the TV, or went to bed early and cried myself to sleep. Our girls came from school, and without saying anything, closed their bedroom doors and mourned in solitude. My sister, Deena Pett, who lived in Orange, California, offered to fly Paula out to stay with her for a while. Paula unhesitatingly accepted. JoAnna poured herself into her nursing classes at Kennesaw State University. She and I frequently commiserated and wept together, holding desperately onto each other, wondering how we would get through it. Deena, realizing the depth of my depression, phoned daily, trying to encourage me. I don't know what I would have done without her. Somehow, JoAnna, Paula, and I had to face the future—without Laura—as a broken family.

Not only was I miserable, at the same time I was furious at Laura. I blamed it partly on the influence of her psychological studies, partly on the strain of her psychological practice, partly on the Adventist church.

Just before Thanksgiving, Laura and I talked personally for the last time. The night before, I had slept only about three hours, worried over the encounter that was about to take place. I had never felt so low, so despondent. I seemed to be buried in some deep chasm with the light shut out and only the black, damp walls around me. Yet I clung to the dim, slender hope that some last minute change of heart on Laura's part—some miracle— would save our marriage.

Again I was bitterly disappointed. Laura repeated what she had said all along. "I have no more feeling or love for you. And I'm not going to change my mind! I want out!"

I probed for specifics, anxious for a way to understand why she wasn't willing to work on our relationship, why she would "throw away," as I put it, all our years together. "Why are you turning your back on a lifetime?" I pleaded.

"I can't fit into your lifestyle," she responded. "You wouldn't want a wife who takes a drink every now and then." She knew this was a sore point with me. Due to Adventism, I was committed to abstinence from alcohol. Up until then I had insisted she also refrain.

"I'm not opposed to a social drink every now and then," I tried to answer as calmly as I could, "although I'll never drink myself. What I can't handle is alcohol in the home."

"Then that's a huge difference between us."

The conversation was going nowhere, I could see that. The unspeakable horror of our broken marriage suddenly overwhelmed me. In desperation, I appealed, "When we came to Atlanta, I was as hurt and embittered about the Adventist church as you. I know that I had to make a choice about whether to release that bitterness or give up my faith. Engulfed then in bitterness, I decided to seek God. My study had taught me there was more to religion than rules. So I started every day, as you know, with prayer, meditation, and reading the Bible. Eventually, I think, I found my way to the Center and to a peace that sustains me. I rediscovered the real God, not the God of Adventism."

"I'm aware of your experience," she said, looking me directly in the eye. "But I'm not interested anymore in seeking God."

"How often I've wanted to come to breakfast and share what was happening spiritually in my life, but I didn't because I thought you wouldn't be interested."

"You're correct. I wasn't. I'm not. Spiritual things now leave me cold." Her cold, icy comment sharply reminded of how deeply Adventism and the crisis at Collegedale—toxic faith—as well as my own moralistic attitude, had injured her soul. The ordeal with Adventism had put the finishing touches on our marriage. I groaned inwardly.

"There's nothing that would cause me to break up our family," I said, self-righteously.

"That's another difference between us," she glumly responded. "I don't think that way anymore. I gave up on us five years ago. Do you remember our trip back from New Orleans? I tried to get you to talk about our relationship, and you shot back, 'Don't put me on the analyst's couch!'"

I remembered, ruefully. "I don't feel that way now. I'm willing to talk about anything you want to discuss. Give me a break! I think I've changed a bit since then."

"You just don't get it, do you! Can't you see? *It's too late!*"

She walked over to the antique, white marble top end table, a gift from my mother, and gathered up the pictures of the Hayes family that were sitting there. She began to weep. Then she turned and came toward me. We held each other, weeping, for several minutes. Holding on to her, grief-stricken, I sobbed uncontrollably. Finally, I got myself together enough to speak, again self-righteously. "Laura, you are the one who wants to end our marriage. It's a burden you'll have to carry the rest of your life."

"I know. I'm ready to assume that responsibility." Then she turned, walked out the door, and hurried down the walk, weeping as she went. She never looked back.

Laura filed for divorce in late December. After the required two-month waiting time required in Georgia, the divorce became final. Shortly afterward, JoAnna and I moved in with my brother, Michael, who was also divorced. Mike, a psychiatrist, had just purchased a spacious, rambling five-bedroom house in an upscale Atlanta suburb, complete with swimming pool, Jacuzzi, and fountain that stood near the pool entrance. His gracious gesture of inviting us to live with him touched me deeply. I took it as an act of God's grace through Mike. My entire family, Deena, Mike, Raymond, my other brother, and mother, were also extremely supportive.

Through the days and months following, I became obsessed with finding out why Laura had decided to divorce. If I could only figure out why, perhaps I could somehow fix the problem or, at least, get through it. I could also self-interestedly, I admitted, deflect some of the blame away from me. Her precipitous action, it seemed, was totally out of character. She had been raised with the ideals of the permanence of marriage just as I. I realized that my parents, Howard and Laura, had occasionally contemplated divorce but, although their marriage wasn't happy, stayed together. I always appreciated the fact I'd grown up in a home unscarred by divorce. That had also been the goal of my life. Laura's parents, Wilson and Pansy Hayes, strongly adhered to the permanence of marriage and were models of it. In one of our conversations about divorce, Laura admitted, "What I'm doing goes against everything I've been taught, but I have to do it anyway." At one level I understood her action as a revolt against parental and ecclesiastical authority. The oppression we'd suffered in Adventism, it seemed, had now born its bitter fruit in finishing off our marriage.

Was this Laura's way of finally rejecting the hell we had been through in the Adventist church? Perhaps the divorce was a way of reacting to that. I understood that traumas, such as the death of a child, often lead to divorces. I could think of other couples who had ostensibly weathered the Adventist crisis but whose marriages had finally broken up. Had the spiritual abuse inflicted by the church weakened our marriage to the point that Laura felt she could follow no other course than divorce? On and on I ruminated.

I realized Laura wasn't completely at fault. Seldom is it that only one partner in a divorce is entirely guilty. Alone and single, I had a lot of time to reflect on my part and what I might have done differently. Laura was right. I hadn't been willing to talk about our relationship. I didn't communicate well how I felt nor, worse, did I allow her freely to do so. Arbitrarily, I insisted she "toe the line" when it came to the inflexible rules of Adventism. I had insisted she give unstintingly of her time and abilities to the Adventist church, regardless of how she felt about it. These reprehensible actions on my part, given the peculiar set of circumstances under which we had lived, proved fatal. "What would have made a difference?" I asked her just before the divorce became final. "If you had talked more," she shot back.

I was now alone and single. Shattered spiritually and abandoned by my church of origin, rejected and divorced by the only woman I had ever really loved, I turned wearily to face a winter of discontent.

21

Yearning for a Home

By faith Abraham obeyed when he was called to set out for a place that he was to receive as an inheritance; and he set out, not knowing where he was going.

—*Letter to the Hebrews*

I sat in my room, brooding. Outside, the white wild dogwood blossoms sprinkled among the pines and oaks in the nearby woods rustled in the warm spring breeze. The blue sky was mirrored against the serene waters of the pool below. The pool fountain murmured with clear, soothing water. I looked around the baby blue, neatly decorated room in which most of my worldly possessions were now arranged. In the room across the hall I had set up my computer, file cabinets, and a couple of bookcases. The remainder of my library was stored in boxes in the attic. JoAnna, whose room was down the hall, had gone for the day to her college classes. Far away, in California, Paula was living temporarily with my sister, Deena. Tears filled my eyes. Our family had been shattered into pieces and literally scattered across the continent. I couldn't get that thought out of my mind. I had failed them all in some way. How could this have been prevented? How could I fix it? Although my brother, Mike, had graciously invited us to share his spacious northeast Atlanta home, its comfortable accommodations felt utterly strange. Spring, with new life bursting forth, had come outside. Inside, I felt dead.

Where was I to turn? I didn't know how I would go on. I seemed to be adrift. The problems with Adventism and my recent move to the United Church of Christ now took a back seat to these pressing family difficulties.

Every morning I got up, ate breakfast, drove down the busy Georgia 400 to Interstate 285, turned southwest toward Atlanta, got off on Mt. Paran Road, and headed into Richmont Graduate University. I went through the motions of my work as academic dean; inside, I was numb.

A sense of desperation foisted itself on me. Somehow, I told myself, I had to do something to establish a new, secure home for JoAnna and Paula. Laura still had regular contact with them, but I found it hard to endure watching them suffer what felt to them like a huge betrayal. Although I knew it would never be the same, I believed I had to try to make a new home for them.

Desperation drove me more than the loneliness. Reluctantly, fearfully, I entered the social dating scene. I dated several women, determined to find someone who would be a surrogate mother for my young, adult daughters, and also partly fill the void within me. Many of the women I dated sensed my desperation, and so quickly—and wisely—backed away. I seemed to be getting nowhere. I felt like I was falling into a deep, bottomless pit and didn't know when I would hit bottom.

Paula and JoAnna grieved in their own way. Laura, too, must have mourned in hers. Divorce wreaks havoc in any family. Its ripples don't end with the divorce decree, but extend outward for a lifetime, echoing painfully again and again through generations. Divorce is the death of a once-living relationship. Things are never the same. I painfully understood the strong language attributed to God in the book of Malachi, "I hate divorce" (2:16).

Paula remained in California with my sister, Deena, for six months, and then returned to Atlanta. Still trying to escape from her shattered, wounded family, she then decided to stay for a while with her cousins in South Carolina. She and I had little direct contact except by telephone. JoAnna buried herself in studies at Kennesaw State. She and I had many long talks and, during these, developed a very close relationship that continues into the present. Yet nothing seemed to soothe my tormenting guilt that they had been permanently hurt by the breakup of the family. I had failed them at a crucial point in their life passage into adulthood. I had failed Laura, too. I accepted the blame for our failed marriage.

Then began what I can only describe as a continuous, palpable awareness of the divine Presence. I regarded this experience as the spiritual presence of God because it seemed more than merely emotional or psychological. It was profoundly spiritual, and difficult, even impossible, to put into words. The mystics in various religions told of similar experiences. Not that I had suddenly become a mystic, but the spiritual realm seemed to be immanently present to me. Prayer appeared perfectly natural, almost like breathing. It was as though I was in continuous communication with the Spirit of the

Living God. I could pray driving along the highway, sitting in my university office, or in the classroom, and felt that I had been heard—and answered. An incredible peace passed over me and seemed to abide deep within. I resonated with Paul's experience, "We do not lose heart. Even though our outer nature is wasting away, our inner nature is being renewed day by day" (2 Cor 4:16). Was I experiencing some sort of spiritual transformation, a new conversion? Life for the Christian is really a series of mini conversions. Was this one of them? I don't know. I only knew that, despite all my troubles and losses, I experienced an incredible peace. There came to me a sense of humility and compassion such as I had never known before. I felt closer to God than I'd ever felt in my entire life. This incredible experience lasted for almost a year before it finally subsided. I took this as a sign that God was with me through it all.

A former student, Claire Knudson, who had been in one of my classes at Southern, happened to see an article I had recently published and decided to telephone me. Claire lived in California, where she was a nurse at Loma Linda University Medical Center, the large Adventist hospital near San Bernardino. "I've followed your career and the problems at Southern for a long time," she told me. "Like you, I've become disillusioned with Adventism and have joined another denomination, the Evangelical Lutheran Church (ELCA)."

Sensing I had a sympathetic ear, I poured out all my pain and loneliness, as people coming through a divorce often do. Claire couldn't resist the opportunity to play matchmaker. "There's a wonderful woman chaplain here at Loma Linda that I wish you could meet. Her husband tragically died from a brain tumor about three years ago, and she seems really nice. Would you call her if I got her permission?"

"Is she an Adventist?" The question rose unbidden from the deep hurt inside. "After my trauma at the hands of the denomination, I don't want to get involved with another Adventist."

"No. I believe she is ordained in the Christian Church (Disciples of Christ)."

I brushed aside Claire's hint. People often make suggestions like these to the divorced and can't help playing matchmaker, so I refused to give it much thought. Claire telephoned again in a few days, and this time insisted I call. "I've told her about you, and she's anxious to hear from you."

I finally yielded and dialed the number, more out of curiosity than anything else. Karyn—Karyn Shadbolt, *Reverend* Karyn Shadbolt, a Christian Church (Disciples of Christ) chaplain—and I amazingly connected in that very first phone call. Over the next six months, we called each other regularly and often talked for hours. My phone bills reached obscene levels!

During the period of our long distance relationship, Karyn moved from Loma Linda, where she had been in Clinical Pastoral Education (CPE), to assume a full time position as Director of Pastoral Care at Long Beach Memorial, in Long Beach, California. Our relationship deepened, even though we had yet to meet personally. I seemed to have discovered in Karyn a true soul mate.

I flew to Los Angeles to meet Karyn. While the plane taxied toward the gate, the two photos she had sent flashed before me. One was a glamour black-and-white photo, taken five years earlier, revealing a stunningly beautiful, dark-haired woman. The other showed a woman with water dripping from her hair, taken on board a ship while she had been whale watching with other chaplain colleagues from Loma Linda. "In appearance," she had told me over the telephone, "I'm somewhat in between those two photos." What would she look like?

Coming out into the terminal I got my first glimpse of her, smiling nervously, her white dress beautifully accenting her tanned face and short, brunette hair. She was standing in the terminal, carefully watching the passengers emerging from the airplane and wondering whether she would recognize me. We instinctively moved toward each other, and then embraced. It felt good. It felt real good! She drove me to her home in Huntington Beach, where we enjoyed a wonderful weekend, including a trip to Catalina Island. This was where Zane Grey, the famous western novelist, had maintained a home and written most of his later novels. Getting acquainted with Karyn really exceeded all my fantasies. She swept me off my feet. She appeared to be everything I had ever wanted in a woman—beautiful, kind, compassionate, talented (she had been a professional operatic soprano when living in Hawaii), and, more importantly, deeply spiritual.

Barely five feet tall, she exuded a romantic energy that attracted everyone around her. Once she entered a hospital room, patients bonded with Karyn almost immediately. When a patient died, often the family would ask Karyn to conduct the funeral rather than their own pastor. And since she worked primarily in the intensive care wards, she officiated at scores of such funerals. Physicians, nurses, and other hospital staff also asked her to conduct their weddings. In the short time she had been at the hospital, she had literally become the "pastor" of Long Beach Memorial. And when she sang in worship, audiences marveled at the uplifting music that flowed effortlessly from her lips.

Karyn's husband, Bruce, a chemist, had died an agonizing death from a brain tumor four years earlier, while they lived in Kailua, Hawaii. He left Karyn with three children. Jim was married and living in Louisville, Kentucky. Deborah, or "Debbie," as we called her, was in Atlanta. Karyn's teenage son, Matthew, lived with Karyn in Huntington Beach.

Our relationship blossomed. Near the end of September we decided to get married and make our home in Huntington Beach. Living in a different part of the country would give me an opportunity to put the past behind me, I reasoned, including my life in Adventism. I hoped that Paula would accompany me to California and live with my sister until she could find a job and apartment, and that JoAnna would follow soon after her graduation from Kennesaw State. Thus, if all went as planned, my family would be reunited. As it turned out, Debbie and Paula became close friends, so that part of the plan appeared to work.

Because of the accelerated pace of our courtship, and the fact we lived on opposite sides of the country, I wanted to postpone our wedding until June. That would allow me to complete the full academic year at Richmont. Karyn and I also could get to know each other better, and could take more time to plan the transition. Moving to California was going to be a major change, so I wanted to go about it with some deliberation.

Karyn would hear none of this. "Why wait?" she pleaded. "We already know how well suited we are. What's the point of waiting?" Sensing my hesitation, she challenged, "Why don't you take the risk? Do something bold?" I gave in and we settled on January 2 as the date for the wedding. For some reason, however, I still didn't feel comfortable with this decision. It seemed to rush matters. I felt pressured. Although I didn't recognize it at the time, this uneasiness was a subtle omen of the future.

Yet Karyn seemed like an answer to my prayers. It felt so good to be with her and then, when we were apart, to talk by telephone. I looked forward to being with her in marriage. I prayed that God would grant me the humility to receive the obvious gift God had sent.

To resign my position at Richmont was more difficult than it seemed at first. I was reluctant to leave the safe haven I'd found there the past five years. It worried me, too, that I had no employment prospects awaiting me in California. Karyn kept reassuring me that she was financially well off enough to absorb my personal expenses for the time it might take to find a position in pastoral ministry or academia. "You'll have no problem finding just what you want," she confidently assured. Uncertainty plagued me but, taking Karyn's words at face value, I told myself that I had to "risk" something if I would ever succeed in restoring my home life. California represented a new life, a new marriage, starting over again in a new place. There would be a new denomination, so I could more decisively cut my ties to Adventism and become more deeply involved in the United Church of Christ.

All this was happening just too fast! I was just not emotionally over Laura. I wondered if I ever would be. Deep inside anger still smoldered, directed now primarily at her. At forty-nine, having to start over again! Develop a new relationship, a new home! I felt like someone had ripped off my arm, leaving me wounded and suffering. My love for Laura ran so deep that it just couldn't be expunged, at least, not easily. I tried repressing my feelings, trying by sheer willpower to purge them from my soul. *It's over,* I told myself time and again. *It's over! It's over! Get on with your life!* Sometimes the anger appeared as sadness, a sadness that lingered, a wound always aching. *What if Laura contacted me right now and wanted to come back? What would I do?* What-ifs choked my thinking, making it difficult for me to sleep at night. Deep inside, it seemed, I just couldn't let go.

I grappled with the notion of divine providence—reading the events happening to me as somehow pointing to God's will. "Lead me, O Lord, in your righteousness," I prayed, "make your way straight before me" (Ps 5:8). In its narratives, the Hebrew Bible characteristically represents divine providence as hidden behind visible events. The characters in the story don't recognize God's involvement until it suddenly jumps out at them. Joseph, sold into slavery by his brothers, rose to prominence as the vizier in Egypt, next in authority to the Pharaoh. Years later, when Joseph finally revealed his identity to his famished brothers, he made one of the classic biblical statements about divine providence. "God sent me before you to preserve for you a remnant on earth, and to keep alive for you many survivors. So it was not you who sent me here, but God" (Gen 45:7–8). Behind the brothers' earlier cruel betrayal, Joseph could now sense the strange working of God to turn those tragic circumstances into redemptive good.

Could the separation from Adventism, the divorce from Laura, and now the marriage to Karyn be God's effort to bring me to a new place where my life and ministry could become even fuller? Events now seemed to point to California, I reflected, a wholly different place than I would ever have imagined. If God was at work in my life in this way, however, it was hidden from me. It represented an unknown, requiring a new level of faith. Was God present even in the losses I had sustained, taking them in gentle hands, refashioning them for redemptive purposes?

Are all circumstances subject to God's transformation? I wondered. In a mysterious sense, the apparently random circumstances that occur may be transformed in the life of a person so that they become God's will. "Transformed" is the key. Circumstances, however apparently cruel they may seem, are divinely woven into the fabric of one's story. I realized that they eventually become integral parts of the redemptive pattern of our lives. God is at work, taking everything that happens to us, good or ill, and in some way refashioning it into a meaningful whole. The Great Alchemist is at work. This is one purpose of the Christian's life. "We know that all things work together for good for those who love God, who are called according to his purpose" (Rom 8:28). Some of the older Greek manuscripts of Romans simply read: "God makes all things work together for good."

Thus it was with mixed, troubled emotions—yet with a measure of hope—I brought my work at Richmont to an end. Arranging for JoAnna to move into her own apartment, I joined together with Mike, Deena, and Raymond in organizing home care for our aging mother, Laura, who was then suffering from heart disease and diabetes, and was living alone in Dalton. Loading my meager furniture, books, and clothes into a bright yellow Hertz rental truck, I left Mike's house that final morning to retrieve Paula's furniture from our house. Paula, thankfully, had decided to come to California with me.

Laura was at the house. "Was there ever a time during our separation when you thought reconciliation might be possible?" I asked, unable to resist still another plea. Getting this unexpected opportunity, I simply had to know her answer before I broke the final geographical ties.

"No," she emphasized. "After I moved out, there was no chance."

"All I ever wanted to do was love you," I responded. "All you need do now is to say the word. I'll unload this truck right here, cancel the wedding plans, and you and I can go on into the future together."

"No! It wouldn't work."

"Then all I can say is, may God help you in the path you've chosen!" My tone was icy and bitter. Angry and frustrated once again, I turned and climbed into the truck. The awful truth flashed into mind: I might never see Laura—my college sweetheart—again. My heart ached.

22

Enter the Disciples

In the Disciples tradition, individuals have the freedom to read, interpret, and apply the Scriptures for themselves. There are no creeds, statements of faith, or hierarchies that determine the way in which a person must read and understand the words they find in the Bible . . . The good news is that we are free to read, interpret, and live this word from God in a community of support rather than one of condemnation.

—Robert Cornwall

Paula and I traveled for four long days along Interstate 10 across the southern United States. Passing through Dallas, El Paso, Tucson, Phoenix, and across the Mojave Desert into southern California, we arrived at Huntington Beach on December 23. It was a jubilant arrival. It felt like I had come home. All my fears and reservations seemed to evaporate.

On January 2, with the sun setting over the Pacific Ocean, Karyn and I exchanged vows in a simple ceremony at my sister's home in Orange. In attendance were mother, Mike, Deena, and her husband, Roger, and a host of friends. JoAnna, Paula, and Debbie, Karyn's daughter, served as bridesmaids. We honeymooned in Georgia at my mountain cabin in Ellijay. From there we traveled to Cherokee, North Carolina, where we toured the native Cherokee sites. Karyn had some Cherokee ancestry, so this proved extremely interesting. At Pilgrimage United Church of Christ we "re-enacted" our marriage so that all my friends in Atlanta could attend, and the church gave us a reception.

For months afterward I experienced a peace I hadn't known for a while. The ten years of uncertainty, unfortunately, made it difficult for me completely to accept normalcy. How I still missed what I'd lost! The injuries of the past, as they often do, haunted the present. But I resolved to live in the present, to try to forget what was gone. Deep within, I knew, lay festering pockets of emotional and spiritual infection created and fostered by Adventism from which it no doubt would take the rest of my life to recover. Laura's sudden departure, too, tormented me. Thank God I now had an understanding and patient wife! I became even more determined to open the windows of my soul and let the Spirit of God cleanse and renew me.

I now began the job hunt in earnest. I sent short, one-page résumés to departments of religion at the universities and colleges in Los Angeles and Orange counties. At the same time, I circulated my clergy papers among the United Church of Christ congregations with pastoral openings. For a number of years, off and on, I had considered returning to parish ministry. Parish ministry had been my first career love. If no college or university teaching position became available, a return to parish life seemed like a viable option. Since Karyn was ordained in the Christian Church (Disciples of Christ), she suggested that since the United Church of Christ had a partnership arrangement in which the two denominations recognized each other's clergy, I should apply for ordained standing in the Disciples. "When you get it," she pointed out, "you'll be able to double the opportunities for a pastoral position."

When I had originally begun my search for a new denominational home, the Disciples, as they are usually called, had been on my short list of suitable denominations, along with the Lutheran, Presbyterian, Episcopalian, and United Church of Christ. I respected Disciples theology and polity, with its openness and commitment to the gospel, and felt as though, all other things being equal, I could be comfortable with the Disciples.

There were many things I admired about the Disciples. The denomination originated in the Midwestern United Sates in the early 1800s. Three individuals from Kentucky and western Pennsylvania, unbeknown to each other, had grown restless over the tight ecclesiastical control the Presbyterian judicatories of the time exercised over theology and local congregations.

In Kentucky, Presbyterian clergyman Barton Stone (1772–1844), clashed with the presbytery over the authenticity of the spontaneous conversions he had witnessed at the famous Cane Ridge revival in 1801. This celebrated event, called by many the "greatest outpouring of the Spirit since

Pentecost," drew an estimated ten to twenty-five thousand people.[1] The revival continued for over a week, marked by a frenetic outbreak of emotionalism that strained traditional Presbyterian credulity. For Stone, this remarkable outpouring of the Holy Spirit challenged the Calvinist doctrines of election and reprobation and brought him into conflict with the presbytery. He and five colleagues—Robert Marshall, John Dunlavy, Richard McNemar, and John Thompson—in protest withdrew from the presbytery and organized their own governing union they called the Springfield Presbytery. Later, they dissolved the Springfield Presbytery, and referred to themselves as merely "Christian." They felt that name was more consistent with New Testament practice.[2]

Stone believed that the divisive tensions and ever-multiplying religious denominations in American religious life could only be reconciled by a return to the simple faith in Christ found in the New Testament. He resonated with many others who felt that the only way forward for the church was through sloughing off centuries of accumulated tradition and recovering the original foundations of the church—in short, *restorationism*, an attempt to reconstitute or restore the apostolic church.

In Pennsylvania a few years later, Thomas Campbell (1763–1854) rebelled against the Scotch Seceder Presbyterian restriction that only members of that particular denomination, not even people from of other Presbyterian churches, could receive communion in a Seceder church. Sickened by such exclusivity, Campbell appealed for closer relations with all other Christians on the basis of the biblical text rather than the creeds. He rejected formal creeds as a foundation for unity. The presbytery brought him to ecclesiastical trial. Campbell immediately withdrew from the Seceder Presbyterians and organized what he called the "Christian Association of Washington [Pennsylvania]." He published his now famous "Declaration and Address" (1809), setting forth what would soon become the second historic emphasis of the Disciples—the unity of the church. Campbell insisted that the "church of Christ upon earth is essentially, intentionally, and constitutionally one."[3]

His son, Alexander (1788–1866), who was then studying at the University of Glasgow, also had become restive under the Scotch Seceder Presbyterians and dramatically walked out of a worship service in protest just as the Eucharist began. Coming subsequently to America, he joined his father's protesting movement. A study of the New Testament led Alexander Campbell to adopt baptism by immersion and the weekly celebration of the

1. Ahlstrom, *Religious History*, 433.
2. See McAllister and Tucker, *Journey in Faith*, 80–81.
3. Quoted in Cummins, *The Disciples*, 46.

Lord's Supper, which are still hallmarks of the Disciples. After an unsatisfactory, abortive attempt to unite with the Baptists, Campbell's movement became independent. They called themselves "Disciples."

In 1832 the followers of Stone and Campbell united. They referred to themselves as both *Christians* and *Disciples*, a compromise apparent today in the long, parenthetical designation of the denomination—*Christian Church (Disciples of Christ)*. By 1860 the fledgling denomination had 200,000 members.

After Barton Stone and Alexander Campbell died, the Christian Church (Disciples of Christ) went through a gradual moderation of its earlier idealistic theology. While it still maintains a strong commitment to the unity of Christianity, it has relinquished the futile quest to recover the teaching and polity of the New Testament churches. New Testament churches, it now recognizes, were never a single entity with a uniform doctrine or polity. For the Disciples, the local churches, the state organizations, called Regions, and the national offices, known as the General Church, all work cooperatively in covenant with each other. Disciples refer to these three aspects as "manifestations" of the church. The congregation is a "local manifestation"; groups of churches within a specific geographical region, a "regional manifestation"; and all the churches and other institutions within North America are known as the "general manifestation" of the church. Disciples often add a fourth designation, the "universal manifestation," which takes in all other denominations and churches in the world. These manifestations of the church exist in parallel to each other, bound by covenant, but none dominates the others. It is an ingenious, egalitarian way of being church.

This structure reflects the fact the denomination has accepted and encouraged the critical study of the biblical texts, and is willing to follow the new directions into which this study might lead, unlike the Adventism that I had experienced. By the 1950s the Christian Church (Disciples of Christ) was included among America's mainstream Protestant bodies.

With the Disciples I felt I would find a faith community committed to serious scholarship, true to the gospel, and focused on spirituality, but without ecclesiastical or theological rigidity. Within the context of their congregational polity, I felt I could find a spiritual home.

Karyn and I were driving from Long Beach, California, when I received a telephone call from Rev. Dr. Davida Crabtree, the Conference Minister of the Southern California Conference of the United Church of Christ. "Although we haven't formally met," her voice crackled over the cell phone,

"I've heard about you. I want to make you aware of a crisis that has arisen at our Corona del Mar, California, congregation, a few miles from where you live. The minister, who has been there for about seventeen years, has been accused of sexual indiscretion, so the Corona del Mar church has had to ask for his resignation. Because the particulars of his alleged indiscretions are confidential among only to a few key leaders, the congregation, among whom he was really popular, is in an uproar, as you can well imagine."

Crabtree requested I go to Corona del Mar as an intentional "supply" pastor for a three-to-six week period to see if I could help the congregation through the crisis. "Then, when the time comes," she emphasized, "you could become a candidate for the permanent senior minister."

"I'd like to help," I replied. "In fact, I'm anxious to help!" Crabtree's phone call seemed to come as an answer to prayer. I had been out of work, with no income, for exactly one month.

Through March and April, during the week I worked with the Corona del Mar Community Church (United Church of Christ), actively listening to members who wanted to process their anger and disillusionment, and then on Sundays, leading the worship. The Community Church is a picturesque New England style structure only a few blocks from a stunning view of the Pacific Ocean. Because of its scenic location, it had an extensive wedding ministry, with three to four weddings every Saturday, most of them conducted by the pastor. So officiating at these weddings became a routine event for me during these months. I had never officiated at weddings back-to-back for entire afternoons, so this was quite a new experience!

Dealing with the fallout on account of the allegedly offending pastor, however, proved much more difficult. Members, as expected, took sides, some against, some in favor. A few insisted the Southern California Conference had conspiratorially manufactured the charges. Others found in the alleged accusations a convenient reason to remove a minister they hadn't liked. Several more women in the congregation came forward with accusations of additional, previously unreported sexual indiscretions. Inasmuch as the United Church of Christ follows a congregational polity, the Southern California Conference couldn't simply force the pastor to resign, even though the Conference had to take the allegations seriously. Resignation had to be a congregational decision. However, the Conference could remove the minister's license. That made him technically ineligible for the position of senior minister at Corona del Mar. These were difficult days for the beautiful, stately Corona del Mar church.

Then John Townsend, chair of the pastoral search committee at First Christian Church (Disciples of Christ), located in Garden Grove, California, contacted me. While searching for a congregation we might attend,

Karyn and I had visited this church in January and found it to be a warm, friendly congregation. The Rev. Dr. Dennis Short, formerly chaplain at nearby Disciples-affiliated Chapman University in Orange, was serving as interim pastor. The church was situated on one of the busiest boulevards in Garden Grove, about three miles west of the famous Crystal Cathedral, where Robert Schuller then served as minister. The church had a membership of about 120 and a beautiful, new amphitheater-style sanctuary, seating 300, with a tall steeple crowned by a shiny aluminum cross. "The committee has seen your clergy profile and résumé and would like to have you come for an interview," Townsend said.

The search committee numbered eight people. We met around a conference table in the pastor's study as the committee questioned me about my life and philosophy of ministry. I only remember one query from that interview. Elwyn ("Butch") Laughorne, one of the elders, asked, "If you become our pastor, how do you intend to compete with the Crystal Cathedral?"

Later, I would discover that Butch, known for his humor, had asked this question somewhat in jest. Down the street from the Garden Grove church, the Crystal Cathedral took up an entire city block and employed hundreds of people. It was literally hundreds of times larger than First Christian Church. Butch and Helen, his wife, lived right in its shadow. I took his question in stride. "I'd try to give the Cathedral some competition!" Everyone chuckled. The interview went well, so they invited me back on Thursday night to preach a "sample" candidature sermon.

The sermon—on Matthew 4, the temptation of Jesus—apparently impressed them. The search committee recommended to the church board, and then to the congregation, that I be offered the senior pastoral position. On April 25 the congregation voted unanimously in my favor. Four months after arriving in California, I finally had a full-time pastoral position and a church! I was to begin May 3.

During the month remaining before May I made pastoral calls, counseled, and preached at Corona del Mar, I was surprised at how the academic world that had been my home for twenty years so quickly faded. Emerging from long-buried consciousness came my old love for pastoral life. Professionally and emotionally I enjoyed revisiting the parish, and longed for more. For years I had said I wanted someday to return to the parish. That day appeared to have arrived.

In the throes of the excitement, however, strange, conflicting emotions within me clashed. *Am I really doing this?* I mused at the church office in Corona del Mar. *Am I really working in a new denomination?* Accepting a pastoral position in another denomination had taken me finally and completely out of the Adventist orbit. The years of teaching in an Adventist

college and preaching only in Adventist churches seemed far distant, like
the teaching and preaching experiences belonged to someone else. *What
will Adventists think? Why do I care what Adventists think?* I felt angry all
over again that Adventism still had such a strong, addictive hold on me that
a perfectly normal act—accepting the call of a Christian church to be its
pastor—would cause me to feel guilty. Through my mind flashed the Adventist claim that it alone constituted the final, genuine manifestation of the
church in the world and that leaving Adventism for the pastorate of another
Christian denomination, from an Adventist perspective, constituted about
the worst possible form of apostasy.[4] All other churches were second-rate,
on lower rungs spiritually and theologically. For Adventist clergy to shift to
another denomination, as I had done, and to assume pastoral duties there
was exceedingly rare historically prior to the recent Adventist theological
upheaval. I knew that when word of what I'd done got out, I would be the
topic of conversation over dinner tables all across the Adventist world. Even
the thought of that notoriety momentarily unnerved me.

What chilled me most was that I recognized, on second thought, how
completely irrational were these thoughts. Today, I realize such unreason-
able ideas—and the feeling of guilt that goes with them—are symptoms of
post-traumatic stress syndrome (PTSD). I *knew* on one level there was no
real basis for the Adventist claim to be the final, true manifestation of the
church. I realized that, in accepting the Garden Grove pulpit, I was doing a
positive thing. But the old guilty feelings instilled from years of Adventism
raised their ugly head and tormented me with feelings that all but spoiled
the delight of what was happening right before me. Such is the power of an
addictive faith system, reaching long, painful tentacles across the years to
subvert present happiness.

---

4. God "has given a precious message to this church [the Seventh-day Adven-
tists] that is for His people in all churches," writes Richard O'Ffill. "To go back now
to being Methodist or Baptist or generically evangelical in our focus is not an option"
("Adventists the True Christians?" 45). One finds such supersessionist statements often
in Adventist literature.

23

The New Beginning Falters

> Security is mostly a superstition. It does not exist in nature . . .
> Life is either a daring adventure or nothing.
>
> —HELEN KELLER

Arriving at First Christian Church (Disciples of Christ) of Garden Grove in May, I was warmly welcomed by the congregation. Dennis Short, who had been the interim pastor for eighteen months, transferred that same day to the Corona del Mar Community Church, where I had been, as its new interim minister. He and I picked a day and merely exchanged offices. Thus Dennis and I became each other's predecessor *and* successor!

The Garden Grove congregation I met that first Sunday faced enormous challenges. Like many mainline urban churches, it had suffered a long, excruciating decline—from three hundred to a hundred twenty members over a decade. This sharp decline had left the congregation particularly vulnerable. The facilities consisted of three separate buildings. The older two, containing the original worship center, classrooms, a Montessori preschool, and offices, dated from the 1950s, when the church had been founded. They were in disrepair. The new worship center, a beautiful brownstone structure with a tall steeple, built in the 1980s, and featured seating for three hundred fifty. Its construction process unfortunately had alienated many congregants. Consequently, instead of filling its spacious new sanctuary after completion, the membership actually dwindled as dissatisfied members left. Now the fifty who met on Sundays felt depressingly overwhelmed by a sea of three hundred empty pews. Most of the remaining members were of retirement age or older. Nevertheless, they were brave, friendly, outgoing, down-to-earth people. They were under no illusions about the daunting future they faced in hoping to revitalize their church.

Typical of many congregations in urban settings, First Christian in Garden Grove, chartered in 1954, had seen the community change from predominantly an Anglo-American population nestled in the middle of vast orange groves to a multiethnic, cosmopolitan city of Korean, Vietnamese, Latino/a, Indian, and the older adult Anglo-American population. The city of Garden Grove exhibited signs of decline as well, with boarded up buildings, failing businesses, and the almost complete absence of new construction. Scarcity of land and the high costs of construction meant that new, developing ethnic congregations had to lease space in already existing churches. First Christian Church hosted four such congregations—a Korean Presbyterian and three Samoan churches, representing Congregational, Assemblies of God, and Independent denominations. This created a truly intriguing international mix of languages, cultures, and worship styles on a Sunday morning.

With a muddle of hope and fear, I realized I faced a daunting situation those first few months. Members spoke frequently of "closing our doors," or "trying to keep the doors open." I recalled the past when, as a young minister, a co-pastor and I had faced a similar challenge in the Appalachian Mountains in southern Kentucky. Here I was, starting my ministry again in another denomination, still a bit strange for me, in a new, second marriage, reliving in an entirely different setting an earlier chapter in my life!

On May 26 the Commission on the Ministry of the Pacific Southwest Region of the Christian Church (Disciples of Christ) granted me ordained standing as a Disciples minister. The previous evening, the Southern California Conference of the United Church of Christ had transferred my ministerial license from Georgia, so I was now officially clergy in *both* the United Church and the Christian Church (Disciples of Christ). When I returned to the church right after the Disciples Pacific Southwest Region Commission meeting, I went into to the empty sanctuary of the Garden Grove church, climbed into the pulpit, and looking out over the empty pews, imagining them filled with people, and recommitted my ministry in this place to God. I felt, for the moment, clean and whole again.

Some things about Disciples church life proved confusing, I soon discovered. The pastoral role isn't nearly as dominant or effective as it is in Adventism. Because they are congregational, Disciples churches operate much more democratically than their Adventist counterparts. Church affairs, like democracy itself, can seem unmanageable and messy. Disciples church operating boards often count half the congregation as members. In the Garden Grove congregation, in particular, it seemed as though things never got done after the decision to do them had been made. At the same time, the democratic approach invigorated congregational and personal freedom, and it was this, more than any other thing, that endeared me to the Disciples. The Adventist attempt to control the details of one's thinking, writing, teaching, and personal and family life, made me especially appreciative of the freedom so evident among the Disciples.

Enjoying this newfound sense of freedom made me want to share with the Garden Grove congregation something of my personal spiritual journey, so I preached a series of sermons on the theme, "Crisis of Faith." I described my struggle in Adventism, the crisis that had finally led to my leaving that denomination, and how I had now made my way to the Christian Church (Disciples of Christ).

The series received a mixed response. "You shouldn't talk about your struggle with Adventism!" reacted Myrna Kelly, the church office manager. "By doing so, you'll have to criticize another denomination. Disciples don't like to condemn others." Myrna was right. The Disciples are so tolerant of differences that they can rarely be coaxed into "criticizing" another faith community. Because my Adventist past had shaped me so definitively, however, I felt that Garden Grove should know my spiritual background. So I chose to recount it publicly. By so acknowledging it, I was determined not to let the past spoil the wonderful new life I had been graciously given.

The Garden Grove congregation proved to be an amazing faith community. The members surrounded Karyn and me with love, and acted like a surrogate, extended family. The congregation had no wealthy people. Most members came from ordinary, common backgrounds, just as had I, so I got along well with them. For the most part, they lived within a ten mile radius of the church. For pastoral visits this permitted me convenient access to their homes. I could interrupt my work in the office, slip out quickly for a visit in time of crisis, then return to resume whatever I was doing. Furthermore, their kindness really helped me along the road to recovery from the spiritual and marital trauma I had experienced. The entire congregation ministered to me in ways they have no way of knowing. Over time I developed a reverent respect for their gentle, Christian spirit.

Fuller Theological Seminary, located in Pasadena, contacted me later that year about teaching an extension class in the Old Testament prophets at Solano Beach, some sixty miles south of Huntington Beach. The class met on Monday evenings in a Presbyterian church educational center. I happily made the trek, excited that I could now, along with my pastoral work, teach once again. I had missed it. This began a custom—combining pastoral and teaching ministry—that would continue the rest of my professional life. It was nice to blend the practical duties of the parish with the formal academic study of Isaiah, Jeremiah, Ezekiel, and the Minor Prophets.

Despite these very positive developments, I still struggled with a sense of disconnectedness. Perhaps it was the physical distance from my daughters (Paula had by now moved back to Georgia.) I felt like an exile in a strange land. The two-thousand-mile distance from my daughters became, in a sense, metaphorical of the yawning chasm in my own life resulting from the divorce. Laura, it seemed, kept popping into mind. When this happened, triggering all over again the anger and disappointment, I kept wondering what I could have done—but failed to do—to save the marriage. Had I waited longer before remarrying, would it have made a difference? What if I had been content to remain single, allowing Laura time to think things through, would there have been reconciliation? I tormented myself.

The homesickness intensified during my mother's final illness. When I had left Atlanta, one major concern had been leaving my chronically-ill mother. Because she adamantly refused to go to an assisted living facility, Deena, Mike, Raymond, and I had to arrange for an in-home caretaker. She suffered from adult-onset diabetes, which aggravated an already existing heart condition. Several times heart congestion forced her into the hospital. Bypass surgery corrected the problem for a while, but eventually these chronic ailments caught up with her. Twice, when death seemed imminent, I made the two-thousand-mile journey back to Georgia. Both times, fortunately, she rallied.

Only days after her March birthday, however, she finally succumbed, dying peacefully while sitting in her comfortable recliner. Interestingly, despite having been a member for almost forty years, she had left explicit instructions that no *Adventist* minister was to conduct her funeral. Instead, Karyn and I officiated, although it proved emotionally overwhelming for me, and I was unable to finish. Mother also left instructions that her favorite ring, with a large ruby set in gold, be placed on her finger as she lay in state—a not-so-subtle defiance of the traditional Adventist prohibition against jewelry. Her Adventist friends must have stared in shocked disbelief at the ring sparkling under the soft funeral parlor lights. Probably they thought the funeral director had mistakenly placed the ring on her finger. I believe that mother's exclusion of Adventist clergy from her memorial service, and the ring, were posthumous acts of protest against a church that had been so damaging to the life of her children. Deena, Mike, and I had all been driven out, in one way or another, from the denomination. My mother was a powerful influence for good on my life, and I loved her dearly. At least I was left with the memory of our last telephone conversation the day before she died. "Jerry," she said, "I love you." It was as though she had premonition of what was about to happen.

Mother unfortunately didn't live to see JoAnna graduate from Kennesaw State University. JoAnna received her BSN on June 18, in a ceremony involving seven hundred degree candidates. She beamed as she crossed the dais to receive her diploma. During the ceremony I sat with Paula and JoAnna's friend, John, whom she had been dating. Laura and her relatives sat some distance behind us. After years of sacrificing to see JoAnna reach this milestone, we had come to this moment with a broken, fractured family. It really felt awkward. I thought of the weddings, births, and other important occasions that lay ahead, and winced.

So it was with a heavy heart I returned to California. I sighed for Laura, although I knew she would never be there with me again. My life was now centered in southern California, where I was now scheduled to teach an undergraduate comparative religions course in Judaism, Christianity, and Islam at Chapman University, a Disciples-affiliated university in Orange, California.

That fall course had scarcely begun when I started to notice subtle changes in Karyn's behavior. She seemed constantly depressed. She became more and more miserable and noticeably unhappy. Concurrent with these changes, our relationship started slowly, almost imperceptively, to deteriorate. This time I recognized the signs. I was acutely aware our relationship was faltering. We made the usual rounds of professional marriage counseling, but matters only seemed to worsen. We argued constantly, even about the smallest matters. Weeks would go by with only necessary, minimal communication . The angst of trying to hold the marriage together, while simultaneously attending to my pastoral duties, took its toll. I felt as though the entire burden of fixing things in the marriage was suddenly thrust upon my shoulders. Would I ever know marital peace again? I begin to wonder. I prayed earnestly on my drive to the church and again the twelve miles back, crying out to God once more to help me to know what to do. Karyn began to threaten divorce. Given my broken marital history, this sent chills down my spine. After one heated quarrel, "You and I are totally incompatible," she stormed. "We shouldn't have gotten married. I want out! *I want a divorce!*" I remembered her persistent urging originally that we get married sooner than I had wished because "we're so very suited for each other, and we know that." I was really confused by what appeared to me a sudden, precipitous about face. I couldn't figure out what had happened.

Several months went by before I reached the same conclusion. We were incompatible. I had made a serious mistake in marrying Karyn. I realized that now. I recognized that my initial attraction to Karyn, born out of loneliness and desperation, our whirlwind courtship stretching across the continent, the mistaken idea that God had brought our relationship into being, had all been part of my own faulty rationalization. I had been desperate, frantic even, anxious somehow to recover what I had lost. So I had attempted to take matters into my own hands, forcing premature closure and resolution by hastily getting into a new relationship. I hadn't been willing to surrender to God's own timing. I lacked the patience to trust that my life, under God, would finally reveal its own inner movements. So I forged heedlessly ahead with marriage to Karyn despite a deep, inner, almost unrecognized suspicion that our marriage was impulsive. Naively, I'd fallen prey to the blunder of many recent divorcees—marriage on the rebound. "Why don't you take the risk?" she had urged. "For once, gamble on something!" I had gambled, thinking I was somehow different than other divorced people. We could make it work. I had lost the bet. But since I didn't really believe in divorce, except under extreme situations, I was now in a quandary. I didn't know what to do.

As confusing as all this was, fortunately I didn't have to sort it all out. On April 25, four days after my fifty-third birthday, Karyn served divorce papers. They arrived at the church office by post in a plain business envelope. Initially, I was very upset. How would this affect my reputation in the Garden Grove congregation? How could I help troubled marriages in my congregation when I couldn't help my own? Once over the early, emotional shock, however, I felt a strange sense of relief. No matter how difficult the present moment might seem, in the long run, given our increasingly conflicted relationship, I was better off out of the marriage.

When I announced the impending divorce to the Garden Grove congregation, rather than sharp disapproval, which I feared might happen, the congregation offered its love and support. Never once did the church threaten my position as their pastor or even criticize the breakup. That was so different from the way it would have been treated in Adventism, where ministers who get divorced are quickly relieved of their pastoral positions. They are disgraced.

Relief, however, was coupled with a deep sense of embarrassment that, after thinking I had taken proper precautions, I could have made such a foolish, impetuous mistake. Having given up my academic career, quit my job in Atlanta, pulled up stakes and moved across the United States, leaving my daughters behind, I was now going through a second divorce! I was humiliated, distraught, and once more alone. Weeks slipped by before I had the courage to let Mike and Raymond know of my unfortunate circumstances. Deena, who lived in nearby Orange, found out almost immediately, and once again became a great source of emotional strength. Again, instinctively, I turned toward God. The closeness I had enjoyed with God since my first divorce had now faded. At the time, I was reading Friedrich Schleiermacher's classic, *The Christian Faith*, and thinking about the concept of the "feeling of absolute dependence," on which he based his theology.[1] God's mystical Reality began once more to feel like that to me, the absolute Bedrock upon which I could rest. I had no idea what might happen to me in the future, but once more there came over me an inexplicable sense of God's presence.

---

1. "The immediate feeling of absolute dependence is presupposed and actually contained in every religious and Christian self-consciousness as the only way in which . . . our own being and the infinite Being of God can be one in self-consciousness" (Schleiermacher, *Christian Faith*, 131).

24

Recovery and Redemption

I believe in Christianity as I believe that the Sun has risen,
not only because I see it, but because by it I see everything else.

—C. S. LEWIS

I moved into a spare bedroom at my sister Deena's modern, spacious home perched on one of the low lying hills northeast of Orange, and only nine miles from the Garden Grove Christian Church. It was the start of nine wonderful months living with Deena, her husband, Roger, and Deena's son, Darren, and later, Darren's wife, Mary. A breathtaking view of Orange County stretched out below the full-paneled glass French doors of my room. The room gave me a unique window on the world. At night I could tell when the Angels' major league baseball team was playing at Angels' Stadium, as well as catch a glimpse of the bright, flashing lights of Disneyland. In winter the Pond of the Mighty Ducks National Hockey League team lighted up the night, and the perpendicular streets stretching inward from the coast in long parallel lines crisscrossed with shorter, equally lined boulevards. They resembled colliding, lighted airport runways. Occasionally, on really clear days, I could glimpse the shimmering Pacific Ocean in the distance. Often, I opened the French doors at night and listened to the automobiles, trains, and ambulances—sounds of the city—beneath my window.

A few weeks later, I preached about how God seemingly doesn't speak to us as directly today as the Bible often represents God doing anciently. In this sermon, I admitted some of my own uncertainties about God's guidance in my marriage to Karyn. Just as worship started, Stan and Vanessa

Hickman entered. They had attended several months before, and had met Karyn. Stan had been in several of my classes at Southern Adventist University but, due to his own misgivings with Adventism, had left Southern—and the Adventist faith—ten years before. How will telling so candidly my marital struggle affect them? I pondered as I saw them take their seat. They had no inkling of what had just happened to me. Ignoring these reservations, I decided to talk openly about my marriage failure anyway. I avoided blaming Karyn by exploring only my own feelings. I told how, when Karyn and I had met, our relationship seemed so ideal that God simply *had* to be behind it. How well-matched we seemed to be! How overwhelming our love! God's grace in our relationship appeared to be so real. Now divorce? What did I miss? I asked. Where was God in all this? Had I missed a vital clue somewhere? Why would God lead me across the United States, requiring me to give up a good academic position and leave my daughters behind, into a marriage that, in the end, miserably faltered?

After the service, Stan, Vanessa, and I had lunch. We talked for over three hours. "When you started sharing so openly about your divorce with the congregation," Stan admitted, "I was impressed that, if this church would allow its minister to do that, I want to belong to it." Vanessa heartily agreed. "We want to become members."

I was thrilled! My honesty had deeply touched them. Stan and Vanessa gave me new appreciation for sharing openly in the pulpit one's personal struggles, something I'd been warned against in homiletics (preaching) class. I was again deeply moved about the strange ways in which God seems to work, the impenetrable mystery of divine providence. In the sermon I had reflected about why God allows certain mitigating circumstances to unfold, especially when one feels all along he or she has been following God's will. Exactly how divine providence works, I realize, has no ready answer, but I realized I needed to relax more in God's care and let God lead. Sitting there in the restaurant with Stan and Vanessa, I found myself relaxing more than I had in days. Tension started to drain away. For a fleeting moment, I let go of my obsession to control circumstances.

Stan and Vanessa weren't the only former Adventist acquaintances who suddenly reappeared. I reconnected with Ed Zackrison, my friend and colleague from Southern Adventist University. After being forced to resign from Southern on account of his alleged theological views, Ed had moved to southern California, where he taught first at an Adventist academy (high school), and then at La Sierra University, an Adventist university in Riverside. He and Joleen had also divorced—another sad sequel to the turmoil he had undergone at Southern. When Ed later married Dolcelyn, because his first marriage had not ended on "biblical" grounds,[1] he once more ran afoul of the Adventist leadership and was summarily dismissed from the La Sierra faculty. Such action surprised me because La Sierra had a reputation in the denomination for being more "liberal" than many Adventist universities. Many refugees from Southern had fled or migrated there to its friendlier environment.

Fresh from now his third vocational termination at the hands of Adventism and thoroughly disillusioned by this trauma, Ed turned up at Garden Grove. Later that week, we had lunch. There I met his wife, Dolcelyn, or "Dulce," as she liked to be called, a charming young woman, who was studying for her doctorate in psychology (PsyD) at the California Professional School of Psychology in Fresno. After hearing of my discovery of the Disciples, Ed asked about transferring his ordained ministerial standing to the Christian Church (Disciples of Christ). We must have talked for more than two hours. This was unbelievable! Who would have ever thought that Ed and I would reconnect under such circumstances?

A few weeks later, Ed and Dulce, along with Stan and Vanessa Hickman, joined the First Christian Church of Garden Grove. They increased the number of former Adventists already in the congregation. This was a moment of deep gratification. I had never thought of myself as a "bridge" for disenfranchised Adventists. I never envisioned myself helping former Adventists find out that there were real alternatives to the dogmatic church they had experienced. But that is exactly what began to happen at Garden Grove. Stan, Vanessa, Ed, and Dulce joined at least four other former Adventists in the congregation. Adventists started coming so frequently to the Garden Grove church that the nearby Adventist congregation broke with all denominational precedents and started granting letters of transfer to those who wanted to move their membership down the street a few blocks to First Christian Church. Because Adventists view all other Christian denominations as religiously corrupt, their polity doesn't allow granting such letters of transfer. The arrangement First Christian Church had with the large, thousand-member Adventist church a few blocks away was thus unique and unheard of.

1. Biblical grounds in Adventism means either adultery, a sexually immoral act contrary to the marriage covenant, or abandonment. These are considered "biblical" and therefore warrants for a legal divorce (see Matt 19:9; 1 Cor 7:15). No other grounds for divorce are recognized.

One Friday morning on my day off, in my room overlooking Orange and concentrating on paying my bills, I answered the telephone. I had not heard the voice on the other end for more than two years. It was Laura! She had come to Los Angeles for a workshop in pharmacology for psychologists. Unbeknown to me, Deena had invited Laura to dinner that evening. (Deena had remained in contact with her over the past five years.) Laura had phoned because she needed transportation from Los Angeles to Orange. "Is Roger there?" she asked, after a very nervous, but somewhat formal introduction. "I want to ask if he'll come and pick me up." My thoughts raced back to the last time Laura and I had spoken.

I had been in Georgia attending to mother's affairs following her death. I was at the townhouse apartment where JoAnna and Paula now lived, casually reading a magazine, when the doorbell rang. Since JoAnna and Paula were upstairs, without thinking, I went to the door. There stood Laura! Somewhat awkwardly, I acknowledged her, but without saying anything. We stood there for a few moments in an uncomfortable silence. Laura spoke. "Are the girls here?"

"Yes. I think they're in their rooms upstairs."

Laura walked up the stairs to Paula's room, noticeably anxious to get out of my uncomfortable presence. I went back to the sofa and picked up the magazine I'd been reading. Inside I felt resentment all over again, a smoldering, seething, yet now subdued anger. Although I definitely shared at least some of the responsibility for our divorce, still, in that moment I felt it was all her fault. *How could you shatter this family after twenty-six years of marriage? Why couldn't you at least try to work things out?* But I didn't say anything. This coincidental contact felt strangely morbid all over again. It was like reopening an old wound, tearing loose the sutures. I guess that's why they say divorce is worse than death. The spouse gone from your life has a tendency to reappear again and with them all the old feelings of loss and bitterness. Emotion suddenly drained out of me. Despair weighed me down.

Moments later, Laura came down the stairs, JoAnna and Paula in tow. She hugged each of them, then turned and silently walked out. Again, I didn't say anything. I felt lousy.

"No, Roger is out making calls for the building materials manufacturers he represents," I hesitantly responded to Laura's question, suddenly recalling at that earlier brief, unpleasant contact. "I'm here alone."

"Were you aware that Deena has invited me to dinner tonight?" she hesitatingly explained. "I need transportation to get there from my hotel, near LAX [the Los Angeles airport]. Deena told me to call Roger."

I let her finish, then took a deep breath, and said, "I happen to be free right now. I don't see why I can't come to the hotel and get you." Amazingly, in that moment all the anger and resentment I had felt three years earlier at JoAnna's and Paula's townhouse, and had self-righteously indulged since, seemed to drain away. I felt amazingly calm.

Had it been only a week before? Karyn and I had argued bitterly over the division of our joint property. My resentment toward Laura had resurfaced, as confusing as ever. *She's the cause of my present dilemma*, I thought accusingly, lashing out for someone to blame. Then something strange happened. Familiar lines from the Lord's Prayer penetrated my consciousness. "Forgive us our debts, as we have forgiven our debtors" (Matt 6:12). Had I forgiven Laura? If so, how could all this anger and bitterness still roil inside? Chastened and humbled, freely acknowledging my own failure in the marriage, and only days before her telephone call, I asked God to help me to forgive.

As I anxiously drove toward the hotel, located not far from LAX, almost an hour's drive from Orange, I reflected on my inner attempt at forgiveness the week earlier. Our initial meeting in the hotel lobby was surprisingly cordial, and we enjoyed a leisurely trip back to Orange. I detoured off the 22 highway so she could take a brief look at Garden Grove and the church where I worked. That evening we had dinner at Deena's. It didn't take long for me to notice that things seemed to have changed for Laura. The anger she had had at the time of our divorce had dissipated. Time, as the saying goes, heals all wounds. We seemed to reconnect as though we had never been separated. We were like two old friends picking up a conversation after years of mutual absence. It was like old times, except there was an unusual freshness, a newness that had not been there before.

When I returned to Georgia that summer for some vacation, I had several more "dates" with Laura. We literally rediscovered each other. The old spark had never really died! It was slowly, effortlessly coming back to life. One day, returning from lunch, I admitted, "All along I have loved you. I know that now. I know it more than ever. That hasn't changed in the five years we've been apart. Our breakup has been really difficult for me during my marriage to Karyn. I simply was never able to forget you. It was as though you were still there—or should still be there."

"Nor have I forgotten you," she said. "But I'm still not sure where this is going." She seemed to be groping her way along in this strange new/old relationship, unsure of her feelings.

As I was leaving for California, Laura asked if she could write. Originally, during our courtship in college, we had kept up a torrid correspondence in periods of separation. Thus began a stream of candid, honest, yet loving letters and telephone calls that started to rebuild our relationship, brick by brick.

Now I seriously began to think of returning to Georgia or the Southeast so I could be near JoAnna and Paula and, perhaps—if possible—reunite with Laura. I had come to California to begin a new marriage, to establish a new home. Now those dreams lay in utter ruin. I didn't really want to settle permanently in California, alone, far from all my relatives, except Deena. I wanted to move back to Georgia. But how? When? Where?

Quite unexpectedly, a few days later, a former student from Richmont Graduate University contacted me. Jenny Hamm explained that, after finishing the coursework for a doctorate in psychology, she realized she wasn't suited for a career in psychology, and so had decided to enter seminary. She was attending Columbia Theological Seminary, a Presbyterian school in Decatur, Georgia, and doing a pastoral internship in a local congregation of the Disciples. In the course of the conversation I told her about my recent divorce and desire to return to the Southeast.

"That's really coincidental," she responded, after I'd poured out my litany of marital woes. "First Christian Church (Disciples of Christ) of Marietta, Georgia, where I'm interning, is right now searching for a new senior minister. The Rev. Dr. Harold Doster, who has been here six years, is retiring." Jenny gave me the name of the pastoral search committee chair and urged, "Why don't you call him?"

It was the middle of the following week when I finally reached Larry Wright, the chair of the pastoral search committee. I explained my desire to return to the Atlanta area. "We've gone through about twenty-five applicants," he said, "and we've yet to find what we want. Hal Doster, who's from an academic background, has spoiled us, I'm afraid. It sounds like you have a similar background. How about sending us your résumé?"

Thrilled, I spent most of the next day putting together my search and call documents, the specialized résumé required by the Disciples denomination for applying for a pastoral position. My head spun from the exciting prospect. I kept reminding myself this might turn out to be just another dead end. It was, at best, only a possibility, perhaps even a remote one at that. Is God somehow involved? After my ill-fated marriage to Karyn, I admitted that I didn't know how to tell. Would God, as in the Old Testament case of Joseph, take hold of the negative events in my life, after the fact, and mysteriously weave them into a larger, redemptive plan? I wondered. Was God again moving in that way in my life? My life had been so tumultuous for fifteen long, difficult years. Things couldn't possibly turn around so dramatically!

25

God-Thing

I will repay you for the years

that the swarming locust has eaten,

the hopper, the destroyer, and the cutter,

my great army, which I sent against you.

—*THE PROPHET JOEL*

In October I once more returned to Atlanta to visit JoAnna, Paula, and now, Laura. I also wanted to touch base with the conference and regional offices of the United Church of Christ and the Christian Church (Disciples of Christ), respectively, to see about pastoral openings in the Atlanta and Chattanooga areas, or the smaller cities in between. The instant I arrived at the Hartsfield-Jackson, the world's busiest airport, a few miles south of Atlanta, I suddenly felt strangely nostalgic. Why did I feel so much at home here, even after a five-year absence? Why did I never want to leave once I set foot on the Georgia red clay? Was it the ever-changing climate? The green grass? All the pine trees? The rolling hills? The people? Was it something buried in my DNA, something that links people deep in their being with their native soil? I wondered whether my foray on the West Coast had taught me anything, made me stronger, better in some way. The humiliation of a second divorce was certainly chastening and embarrassing.

Laura invited me to go with Paula and her to the family home in Ninety-Six, South Carolina, for the weekend to celebrate her brother Oliver's birthday. Once again I found myself at the old Hayes farm house with the entire Hayes clan around, certainly surprised, but genuinely happy to see me. We ate until we were stuffed. We decorated the house with balloons and garish signs, and roared with laughter as Oliver opened some of his gag gifts. "It feels like you've come home," Laura whispered. Her sister, Ruth, fondly called me the "returning prodigal." It really did feel like I had come home.

Back in Atlanta, Laura and I indulged many long conversations. Each, seemingly, drew us closer. She loaned me her Toyota Camry to drive to Macon, about a hundred miles south of Atlanta, to confer with the Rev. Dr. David Alexander, the Christian Church (Disciples of Christ) Regional Minister for Georgia. Rain poured down in torrents, flooding streets and meadows—another reminder I was back in Georgia. Alexander seemed impressed with my background and indicated that he would assist in my seeking a pastoral position.

That evening I met the pastoral search committee of First Christian Church of Marietta. The T-shaped, light brown brick building, with a sanctuary and steeple cross on the northern side and a single story educational, administrative, and library wing on the southern side, sprawled alongside busy Fairground Street, running due north of the giant Lockheed-Martin aircraft assembly plant, in an older part of Marietta. Founded in 1949, the church had literally grown up on the acre site it now occupied. It started in a small chapel that had been physically moved—in pieces—from Kirkwood, Georgia, where it had once been an Episcopal church. Then came the building of the present sanctuary in the early 1960s; finally, the educational extension, added in the 1970s. Outside, like a welcoming beacon, stood the familiar church sign with the chalice logo of the Disciples: *First Christian Church (Disciples of Christ)*. While driving along Fairground Street several years before I had noticed the church. It was familiar. At the time I was casting about for a suitable alternative to Adventism, so I had made a mental note to visit it. Unfortunately, I never got around to attending.

For some inexplicable reason, I wasn't overly anxious when I met the committee. Larry Wright, Sam Bowers, Patricia Kern, Joanne Paller, and Rita Winfrey, who made up the search committee, quizzed me primarily about my pastoral philosophy. "With a membership of two hundred fifty, we're keenly interested both in the growth of the congregation and serving the downtown area," Wright emphasized. At the conclusion of the interview, they took me on a tour of the facility. The educational extension had been newly remodeled. The sanctuary boasted a typical 1960s décor, with natural blond pews, blue carpeting, and exposed ceiling beams. I was impressed with the functional, attractive facility. I really wanted to come here!

"You understand I'm divorced," I told the committee, realizing I honestly had to find out how they felt about my current marital status. That same afternoon, I'd contacted another search committee of a Disciples church in the area. When I told the chair of that search committee I was visiting the Atlanta area and would be available for an interview, he demurred, "In view of your divorce, our committee isn't seriously interested in talking with you." The rejection stung, frustrating me all over again. When Karyn initiated the divorce, I wondered whether I would encounter such prejudice against a divorced minister. Now, as I awaited an answer from the Marietta committee, I felt mortified at my painful, broken marital situation.

"That's not a problem with us," Wright said. "Some of us here on the committee are divorced. Your personal marital status is not an issue." Was I ever relieved! I respected the Marietta committee for being so understanding. It was the same tolerance I'd experienced at Garden Grove, the same tolerance I had come to realize was generally characteristic of the Disciples. My hopes leaped!

JoAnna, Paula, and I leisurely strolled through Hamilton Place Mall, near Chattanooga, a few days later, where we picked up some information to help JoAnna decide on a new car, and purchased a baby blanket, bibs, and a bumper guard for Paula's baby crib. She was expecting "our" first grandson around the first of November. How I loved referring to him as "our"! Could it really happen? Could we be a united family again?

Laura drove me to the airport the next day. She and I talked incessantly. On the way, we stopped by the Atlanta offices of the United Church of Christ to meet the Rev. Dr. Timothy Downs, the Conference Minister of the Southeast Conference, where I inquired about pastoral openings in that denomination in the Atlanta area.

I soon settled back into my California routine. The morning fog had not lifted as I returned from my run on a nearby high school track. I spotted Roger on the deck of his home. "Jerry," he called out as I came up the long drive, "you're to call Larry Wright in Marietta." This was it! I thought, negatively. Marietta is going to tell me that they aren't interested. I braced myself for the inevitable disappointment.

"Our church board," Wright began, "has decided to start negotiations with you to come as our new pastor." I couldn't believe it! It was simply too good to be true! "Larry, I would be delighted to enter negotiations with you. I'm grateful and honored to be considered." Wright, unaware of all the circumstantial, personal events that hung on my move to Atlanta, spoke of the negotiations as a "God-thing." What a wonderful expression for what appeared to be happening!

When making decisions, particularly big ones like this, I want to "feel" that a decision is good or not, quite apart from all the rational factors, which I also typically work out rather obsessively. I now had a strong sense that a move to Marietta was right. Not only right, but compellingly right! I *must* go. Something is there I need to experience. An unusual calmness came over me about the prospect of going, a peace I had rarely felt about any major decision. An added motive came soon in the birth to Paula of our first grandson—Spencer Allen—on October 30.

I received a card from Laura near the end of November. Enclosed were photographs of JoAnna, Paula, Laura, and me, along with a photo of little Spencer. Looking at them, tears came, no longer tears of bitterness, but tears of wonder, joy, and hope.

My farewell at Garden Grove dawned on Sunday, February 16. As I made my way to the church, I pondered how I could ever say goodbye to all these wonderful people, one of the finest congregations I had ever served. As the service unfolded, not sure that I could make it through without breaking down, I apologized for my restrained manner. Then I reflected about our life together, how the congregation had ministered to me when I needed healing after my years of struggle with Adventism. They had accepted me, a refugee from a harmful faith system, had loved and supported me, not only then, but during my divorce from Karyn. I reviewed all we had accomplished in the almost four years we had been together. As I neared the conclusion of my sermon, I couldn't hold it together any longer and broke down and wept. All over the congregation, people began to cry.

When the service ended, I never made it to the narthex, where I customarily greeted the congregation as it departed. People instead came out of the pews to intercept me, weeping, and then hugging. Someone observed later that it was like the funeral of someone greatly beloved. I felt like I was losing my dearest friends, my adopted family. I felt drained, torn by conflicting emotions raging within, ripping me apart. My tears mingled with theirs. The service and the reception following was wonderful, awesome, sad, and tragic, all rolled into one. That evening, I reread all the cards the Garden Grove congregation had sent me. I gazed on the beautiful framed picture of the church, with its bronze plaque giving my name and the dates of my tenure there, and wept inconsolably. I had no idea leave-taking could be *this* difficult.

A week later Laura arrived in California to help me drive the twenty-five foot rented Ryder truck, containing all my worldly goods, to Atlanta.

After four hard days of driving, most of through rain and damaged roads along Interstate 10, we arrived on February 25. I moved into my brother Mike's home for the second time, and on March 1 commenced my pastoral duties at Marietta First Christian Church.

As my redemptive time at Garden Grove had ended in worship, so it began at Marietta. Despite it being my first worship service there, everyone seemed relaxed and happy, alive with energy. I even managed to get through the liturgy, a bit different than Garden Grove's, with only a few minor bobbles. In the sermon I described my call to ministry, which had been the polar star through all the ups and downs of my life. I talked about my family background, taking a moment to introduce Laura and also Paula and JoAnna, who had come from Chattanooga, where they now lived, for my first service. Wilma Zalabak, a former student from Southern Adventist University, Jenny Hamm, and Skip and Stephanie Meboer, from Pilgrimage United Church of Christ, were also present. It was really a homecoming. After the service, there was a reception where I met many others. Everyone seemed warm and friendly, genuinely pleased that I had come to be their pastor. I knew then I would truly enjoy life as the pastor of the Marietta congregation. In spirit, they seemed very much like Garden Grove. Around them, one felt cherished, truly a part of an extended family.

Returning home later that day, I reflected on the strange, mysterious, and yet wonderful circumstances under which I had now come to live. Who would ever have believed this fairytale? God seemed to be doing in my life a work of grace that I would not have believed had I been told!

Living in two different regions of the Atlanta area, Laura and I often met in restaurants before or after work. One was the IHOP (International House of Pancakes) not far from the Marietta church. This restaurant held bitter memories because it had been the scene of one of our final, painful arguments prior to divorce. It was thus surprising one morning when Laura sat across from me at the IHOP, poking at her food, and confessed, "I threw away the best thing I ever had, and I know that now. I did it, and I'm to blame."

Some weeks later, we picked up the threads of that conversation. I gave her a birthday card and gift certificate. Our conversation drifted back to the events of the past when we had separated. "What's different now?" I asked.

"You've changed a lot," she smiled. "Yet you retain the values I'm now looking for—integrity and tolerance. I have changed, too. I guess you might say . . . I've grown up."

"What happened to us, in your opinion? Why did you want a divorce?"

"I'm not sure I yet know the 'whys and wherefores,'" she mused. "I'm still discovering the terrible damage done to me by the Adventist church and then by the community at Collegedale . . . it was really abuse . . . I'm still struggling not to try to absorb all the blame. You know we were taught that if there was anything wrong, it was always our own fault, not the church's."

"Oh, how well I know! I still struggle with that also."

She went on, struggling to put feelings into words. "Through the years, I wasn't permitted to disagree with you. The wife should 'submit' to her husband, and all that . . . As I felt the hurt generated by an abusive church, you were so closely attached to the abuser, I found myself distancing from you, too. Then those last three years of 'hell' at Southern really drove me away. You had one sustaining conviction: you knew you had done nothing wrong. But I had to support you with your anger—with no place to go with my own. My upbringing, together with the guilt-laden teachings of Adventism, reinforced that I was wrong even to be so angry."

I found myself empathizing with everything she was saying. I painfully recalled the excruciating agony of those three final years at Southern.

"Eventually, I had to get away from it all, unfortunately, including you. That became the bottom line. Remember that worship service we attended at the Marietta Adventist congregation no long after we moved to Atlanta? I hadn't wanted to go, but you insisted. I guess you were trying to hang onto what you could. I really resented being pressured to go. It was a terrible sermon, remember? Not a single biblical passage in it, just Ellen White quotes mostly condemning the Roman Catholics. Sitting there fuming, I got so angry I couldn't speak. I actually bit my finger nails until they bled!"

Her voice broke; tears streamed down her cheeks. "I'm still so angry at all that happened. I hate, I really *hate* the Adventist church and all it did to us. Were you still in it, I wouldn't even be sitting here talking to you!"

She paused, and took a sip of water. "I hadn't realized how raw that topic still is. I'm very busy with my psychological practice and with the girls, and now you. I don't want to waste any more time thinking about Adventism. People would be shocked, but as far as Adventism is concerned, the words of Rhett Butler in *Gone with the Wind* come to mind, 'Frankly, my dear, I don't give a damn!'"

Later, I mentally went over and over what Laura had said. She did seem to indicate a new level of understanding. Her words felt reassuring, giving me a warm glow.

At Marietta First, I again discovered the strong sense of community I'd experienced at Garden Grove and that seems to run through the whole Disciples denomination. It isn't perfect, I realized—no human experience is—but Disciples are one of the best religious communities I've ever known. When I first started in the ministry, I reminisced, at the Grove, Kentucky, Seventh-day Adventist church, a tiny congregation nestled in rural farmland south of Lexington, I had encountered a comparably strong sense of community. That was the exception in all my Adventist experience. Other than Grove, I never encountered what the New Testament calls *koinonia*, fellowship of the Spirit, anywhere in Adventism.

Why? Why is genuine community so seldom found in Adventism? Why has the denomination become so judgmental? Why has my life with the Disciples been so full of *koinonia*?

I had often thought about such questions. The real test of community, it seems to me, lies in embracing human diversity, accepting people for who they are, and loving them. Can a person who is different really find acceptance within a community? Adventism, with its tight political control and rigid theology and praxis, has no real way of creating an atmosphere of acceptance. In all my thirty-six years in Adventism, although there were notable exceptions, I *never* felt really accepted by its leaders or some of its people. Unless one conforms to the norms Adventism has set out, approval just isn't likely. With its philosophy of group-think and its judgmental tendencies, Adventism generates a toxic atmosphere inimical to spiritual development.

"What would you say," I hesitated, picking my words carefully. Laura and I were preparing lunch together in her townhouse in late summer. "What would you say if I asked you to marry me, eh . . . again?"

The awkward proposal, I could immediately tell, caught her by surprise. "Give me some more time," she replied. "I need more time to find out who I am."

I felt crushed. I was *so* sure by now she'd agree.

Later, she came to me, "I hope you didn't take my comment as a rejection."

"I felt embarrassed," I admitted, "like I was expecting too much, too fast."

"Don't. I didn't mean it that way. Let's talk about it later."

But I did take it as a rejection. Unsure of what it meant, I decided to back away from the whole issue and try to be as patient as I could. Then I would bring up the subject again. If she isn't willing at that time, I decided, I would just give up.

I enjoyed the falling leaves and the brilliant autumn colors—flaming maple reds, and poplar and hickory yellows crowning hills and valleys of my native land. The morning chill reminded me that winter wasn't far away. I realized how much I'd missed this eternal change of seasons, how much one's native soil courses through the bloodstream and embeds itself in a person's DNA.

In November I got to walk JoAnna down the aisle as she married Randy Noorbergen, son of Rene Noorbergen, the well-known freelance author. The Noorbergens—Rene and Judy—had been longtime friends of ours since Southern Adventist University days. JoAnna and Randy had practically grown up together. Randy had become a member of the Chattanooga Police Department and JoAnna a Registered Nurse at Erlanger Hospital, also in Chattanooga. Rene, to whom Randy had been especially close, had died several years earlier. From California I had written a letter of sympathy to his widow, Judy. Not only did I escort JoAnna down the aisle and "give her away," but then proceeded to the altar with Randy and JoAnna, pivoted to face the audience, and officiated at the wedding service itself.

What thoughts go through a father's mind at his daughter's wedding? Sadness? Joy? A mixture of feelings? Before I began the ceremony, I looked around. There present were Randy's mother, Judy, his sister, Wendy, and her husband, Robert, both of whom had been in my classes at Southern, and their four children. Other friends of Randy and JoAnna were scattered about. Paula and Spencer sat with Laura. I couldn't miss the significance of the occasion—once again we were all together, in the same room, celebrating as a family.

Six years' earlier, when the Adventist church had dealt my ministry its mortal wound, I had envisioned such a moment as this. Fearing I would never be able to officiate at my own daughters' weddings, I had sighed in anguish, but grimly determined, "You will not do this to me! I will not let the Adventist church destroy my ministry!" Now I was again especially gratified that I had made the decision to transfer to the United Church of Christ and the Christian Church (Disciples of Christ). This moment at JoAnna's wedding was reward enough.

"Dearly beloved," I began, "we have come here this day to celebrate . . . "

Redolent in its Advent decoration, the cross and altar of the chancel at First Christian Church seemed radiant amid scores of red and white poinsettias.

White Christmas paraments trimmed the pulpit, lectern, and communion table. The chancel glowed with a soft, golden light. The church had never seemed more beautiful.

Laura and I entered together, walking slowly down the aisle. Standing in our honor were Deena, Roger, Agnes Johnson, and Vanessa Hickman, members from Garden Grove who had come all the way from California. Opposite them, grinning from ear to ear, were Stephen, Oliver and Carol, Rosemary, Jon, Donald, and Ruth—Laura's family. Mike, my brother, energetically snapped photos. Billie, my sister-in-law, her daughter, Janice, and Evelyn Haley, a family friend from Dalton, had also joined the celebration. Flanking them on both sides of the aisle were members of the Marietta church and old friends whom Laura and I had known in years past.

At the altar, awaiting us, stood Ed Zackrison, clad in a long white cassock and a beautiful white pastoral stole. Now a Disciples minister and the transitional pastor at Garden Grove, he grinned as we approached. Could he and I, while on the faculty at Southern Adventist University, have ever imagined this setting, this occasion?

Two months before, Laura and I sat at her kitchen table, looking over the plans she was putting together for a vacation photography trip to Utah's Bryce Canyon. During our years apart, Laura had enthusiastically taken up landscape photography, and she used the photographs to paint water color and acrylic landscapes. She was really good at this and looking forward to the trip.

Gently laying aside a magnificent landscape photograph, she looked up at me, smiled, and said, "About your proposal, I thought you would like to know I'm now going to say yes. I've felt it for a long time, and now I'm sure. This time it's for keeps."

Time seemed to slow to a surreal crawl as we moved toward the chancel. I thought of Laura's words. I thought of God's "crazy, holy grace." At work all this time, in God's gentle, mysterious way, God had finally brought us full circle, and gave it all back again. "I will repay you"—I remembered the words of the ancient prophet Joel—"for the years that the swarming locust has eaten" (Joel 2:25).

Now all the swarming locusts were gone. Laura, the love of my life, stood beside me. Freed from the clutches of Adventism, we were together enveloped by a loving Christian community. As Ed pronounced us "husband and wife," I felt whole once more.

Epilogue

Whither Seventh-day Adventism?

In returning and rest you shall be saved;

In quietness and in trust shall be your strength.

—*The Prophet Isaiah*

A lmost two decades have now passed since Laura and I stood at that magical marriage altar. After ten successful years at First Christian Church (Disciples of Christ) in Marietta, I retired from active parish ministry to pursue research, writing, publishing, and part-time teaching of religion and biblical studies. Laura and I remain members of the Marietta congregation. Upon retirement, the congregation honored me with the title "Senior Minister, Emeritus," an honor I now humbly and gratefully share with only two other persons.

Life during those two decades, in contrast to the intense drama preceding them, has seemed somewhat placid, but in a good sense. It has been full, invigorating, and gratifying. In the first five years of my pastorate at Marietta, the church attendance and membership increased until all the off-street parking spaces were usually taken up on Sunday mornings. The congregation then undertook a renovation of the facilities to modernize its interior and enlarge the worship space. The subsequent five years, while they did not realize the hoped-for growth, did bring a healthy stability.

Life after Adventism, except for the period of our separation and divorce, has also brought peace and tranquility. Laura and I have never been happier. I wouldn't dare claim we have lived "happily ever after," but that's pretty close to what it has seemed. Laura continues her psychological practice, with offices now in Ringgold and Marietta, Georgia, and has joined me on the adjunct faculty at Richmont Graduate University. Our daughters, JoAnna and Paula, fellow travelers in this saga, now have families of their own. JoAnna is the Director of the Intermediate Care Unit and the North Wing at Erlanger Hospital in Chattanooga. Paula serves as receptionist and secretary in Laura's Ringgold practice. Our family has now been graced by the addition of three other grandsons, in addition to Spencer: Josh, Aidan, and Jasper.

Shortly after returning to the Atlanta area, I again accepted an invitation to teach at Richmont Graduate University. For several years since I've taught courses in Hermeneutics, Theodicy, and Comparative Religions. At about the same time, I also joined the adjunct faculty at Columbia Theological Seminary, a well-known Presbyterian seminary in Decatur, Georgia. There I've taught the book of Daniel, the Wisdom Literature, the Five Scrolls of the Megilloth, but mostly biblical Hebrew. Had I remained an Adventist, permanently branded among them as a heretic, I would never have been able to teach at the seminary or graduate level. Instead, with Richmont and Columbia, I have been privileged to do both.

That I have left Adventism doesn't mean I fail to appreciate the gifts it offered. Not all my Adventist experience was ill-fated. While an Adventist I acquired an enduring love of the Bible that sustains me to this day. The daily reading of the Bible is a practice I continue to cherish. From it I receive daily encouragement and hope. The Bible is also the focus of my scholarly work, and it is the focus of that work directly because of Adventism. Undeniably, the Bible remains the most important book in my life. Interest in the Bible translates into wider concern for theology, philosophy, and all things religious. I continue to read and study in all these fields. These are my professional passions.

The Adventist church also gave me some best practices for healthful living. Proper diet, exercise, rest, and temperance in all things go a long way toward promoting good health. It is this emphasis on healthful living, in my opinion, that is really Adventism's main contribution to the Christian world, not the Investigative Judgment or the church's apocalyptic speculations about the end of the world, as the denomination likes to think. I continue to practice many of these health customs.

One might describe my attitude today toward Adventism as similar to that of a person following a divorce. Although the conflict leading up to the separation, the divorce settlement, and the change in life afterward was excruciatingly painful, I don't wish the denomination any harm. I am perfectly willing to live and let live. But I have no desire to return to its community. Indeed, I wonder how I managed to remain "married" to Adventism for as long as I did. "Many of us have been harmed by religion," Scott Peck writes. "It is equally important to forgive your church for the sins it may have committed . . . Forgiving does not mean going back . . . without such forgiveness you cannot begin to separate the true teachings of that church from its hypocrisy. And you need the true teachings."[1] What would I have done differently had I known what I now know? Someone asked me that. So I replied: "If I could do all over again, I would probably attend the same Adventist college (after all, that's where I met Laura, and it was the nearest college to where I lived!). Upon graduation, however, I would have transferred to the seminary of another denomination and pursued a ministerial career there." We can't change the past, however. We can't go back and make different decisions. So looking back, I humbly accept the good things Adventism had to offer, try to recover from its abuses, and go on to build a life and ministerial career in the Christian Church (Disciples of Christ) and the United Church of Christ. In this endeavor God's grace has been given to me in spades.

It is therefore with mixed emotions that I look back on my experience in Adventism. Although my family and I are still in recovery from what someone aptly called "post-traumatic church syndrome," most of the resentment about the way we were unjustly treated has gradually faded. Sadly but characteristically, so far as I am aware, the Adventist church has never acknowledged its abusive, controlling practices, not to me nor to any others whom they have similarly treated. No Adventist leader has ever directly appealed to me to come back into the denomination. This silence speaks volumes. It suggests that the denomination has been relieved to have me—and many other similar "dissidents"—out of sight.

As a result, I have no regrets about leaving Adventism. Looking back on the struggle, I can now admit, the expulsion from Adventism was one of the best things that ever happened to me! Had I not been caught up in the doctrinal controversies, and specifically targeted for elimination because of them, I probably would never have reexamined the doctrines of Adventism as carefully as I have. I would still be within it, trying to live under its repressive polity, confusedly thinking in so doing I was somehow living out God's will.

What has happened to Seventh-day Adventism over these years?

My perspective on Adventism has now evolved into that of a genuine outsider. I am also by choice an outsider. I'm not privy to everyday life within Adventism, and only hear rumors about what that life is now like.

---

1. Peck, *Further Along*, 153.

When I severed the ties, I walked away and seldom looked back. Having gotten hold of a larger vision I could never go back to such an extremely narrow one. Today I keep up with Adventism, if at all, from a distance. My previous Adventist experience now seems more like a distant memory of another time, another place. It is like remembering an acquaintance of long ago, but who is no longer a part of my life.

In the interval Adventism has obviously changed, too. Many of the principal persons mentioned in this book have since died, retired, or otherwise left denominational employment. Not a few, as I, have left the denomination altogether. Modernism, postmodernism, secularism, political extremism, and the various social forces of cultural change have inevitably influenced Adventism. Some of the loudest, most dogmatic voices within the denomination have either died or lapsed into a tired, exhausted silence. There are no longer any witch hunts going on, as far as I am aware. As the result of the controversies recounted in this book, Adventism has now congealed into at least three perspectives. One is allied with mainstream evangelicalism, particularly around the Reformation gospel of justification by faith. Another has moved in a sectarian or even cultic direction, and continues to affirm the total reliability and authority of Ellen White. Still another finds more theologically compatible liberal, mainstream Protestantism.[2] All these perspectives now coexist—somewhat uneasily—within the same denomination. Diversity is often generational and geographical, with Adventists living near Adventist universities more liberal than those living in rural or urban areas. California Adventists are more liberal than those in Nebraska, Maryland, and the District of Columbia.[3] Adventists living in the Sunbelt are more conservative when it comes to church doctrine and practice than all others, as I certainly found out at Southern Adventist University.

Despite these socio-religious changes, however, Adventism still has not matured sufficiently to the point where thoughtful religious persons may expect to live peacefully within it. Dissent is not really tolerated. Clergy are still quite restricted on most matters and expected to see eye-to-eye with the generally conservative top leadership.

One thing has not changed, or at least changed only incrementally: the church's theology. Even a cursory glance at the second edition (2005) of *Seventh-day Adventists Believe*, cited often in this book, shows that the church still adheres to *all* its traditional doctrines. The church remains theologically—and politically—in the conservative camp. Biblical criticism, the

2. See Martin, *Cults*, 519.
3. See Rayburn, "Psychotherapy with Adventists," 217.

specific issue for which I was terminated at Southern Adventist University, while privately practiced today by many courageous Adventist scholars, remains under general suspicion.[4] In contrast, my current scholarly work routinely employs historical criticism and related methods. It is through historical criticism that I've been able better to understand *both* the human and the divine aspects of Scripture.

On the three issues that came under dispute in my story, the church holds essentially the same positions it did when the controversies first broke out. The widespread turmoil depicted in this memoir, sad to say, has had little or no effect on the church's formal teachings or praxis.

With regard to the *gospel*, the denomination does affirm, with Paul, that Christ has been made sin "who knew no sin, so that in him we might become the righteousness of God" (2 Cor 5:21). Through faith one receives salvation "through the divine power of the Word" as the "gift of God's grace." One is justified, adopted into God's family, born again, and delivered from the domination of sin. One then has "assurance of salvation now and in the judgment." Having experienced salvation, a person is expected to persevere in developing a character like Jesus. This is the process of transformation by the Spirit.[5] Even though these represent good evangelical statements, perfectionism still courses like a latent infection through Adventist life, always ready to break out, particularly in the more conservative, isolated communities of the church. This naturally leads to a great deal of existential guilt and shame.[6]

While the Reformation notion of objective justification is not specifically addressed in the church's current theological statement,[7] it seems to me there is enough room within the official statement for such an understanding. Had there been more tolerance on the part of church leaders in the 1980s for different views about the gospel there never needed to have been such vicious, damaging controversy.

The debate over the doctrine of the *Investigative Judgment* still finds the denomination clinging even more desperately to its traditional position,

4. See Biblical Research Institute, "Methods of Bible Study." See also Alberto Timm's recent claim that historical criticism sweeps away "the supernatural element of Scripture" and imposes on Scripture a "human principle in place of the Bible, thus distorting or even destroying the *sola Scriptura* principle" ("*Sola Scriptura*," 19).

5. General Conference, *Adventists Believe*, 133, 149–50. This refers to *sanctification*.

6. Rayburn, "Psychotherapy with Adventists," 219–20.

7. In the interpretation that follows Article 10 on the "Experience of Salvation," we find this statement: "Through justification by faith in Christ, His righteousness is imputed to us. We are right with God because of Christ our Substitute . . . we experience full and complete pardon. We are reconciled to God!" (General Conference, *Adventists Believe*, 137).

now offered in Article 24 as "Christ's Ministry in the Heavenly Sanctuary." In 1844, the culmination of the 2300 days (Dan 8:14), Christ entered the "second and last phase of His atoning ministry." This phase concerns an "investigative judgment" devoted to the disposition of sin. It will first determine among the deceased who are worthy to participate in the resurrection of life. Eventually the probe will pass to the living to determine who are "abiding in Christ, keeping the commandments of God and the faith of Jesus," and who are ready for the kingdom of God. When Christ completes this examination, human probation will close. This Investigative Judgment serves to vindicate God from all the unjust claims Satan has made against God, as well as vindicate God's people before the eyes of the watching universe. It answers the charges of Satan and gives "assurance to the unfallen creation that God will allow into His kingdom only those who truly have been converted."[8]

Interpretive notes to Article 24 also recall the denomination's many attempts since the 1980s to respond to the criticisms of the Investigative Judgment, from debate over how the Hebrew verb *nitsdaq* should be translated in Dan 8:14 ("restored" or "cleansed"?) to whether the 2300 "evenings and mornings" should be considered 2300 actual days (= years) or simply 1150 days. Rather than revise, the church has strenuously labored through its various theological study commissions to shore up this beleaguered doctrine.[9] In none of these apologetic studies do I, nor any other scholar I know who has taken the time to review them, find compelling reasons for retaining, without serious revision, the bizarre doctrine of the Investigative Judgment. Because Ellen White has endorsed the doctrine, unfortunately, the denomination remains stuck with the traditional interpretation. Given White's overweening exegetical authority, there is little chance of modification or reinterpretation. For outsiders, the doctrine still retains the impression of an elaborate, well-intentioned, but misguided attempt to cover up a failed prediction on the part of the nineteenth-century Millerite movement.

With *Ellen G. White* matters seem to have shifted slightly. The denomination now concedes that Ellen White frequently borrowed both the language and ideas of other, non-Adventist writers—without giving appropriate credit. When doing so, however, the church insists she didn't "mindlessly" adopt the thoughts or expressions of others, but modified them so that they would conform to her own thinking. Apparently, the reason for not giving proper credit is the fact she didn't want the reader to confuse "her own inspired message" with that of another (non-inspired) writer. The

8. Ibid., 347–69.
9. See Holbrook, *Doctrine of Sanctuary.*

opposite would seem to be the case. If clear credit were given for the other (non-inspired) authors, then the present-day reader of Ellen White would be able more easily to distinguish White's work from others. As it is, all blends together so that the reader cannot tell which is which. The reader is thus led to think all the content comes directly from Ellen White, which brings us right back to the original problem of distinction. Such a tautology doesn't solve the matter.

That Ellen White borrowed, sometimes extensively, was well-known to those contemporaries closest to her, as we have seen. Her editorial assistants, as well as many denominational leaders, were aware of this activity, although it wasn't widely known among the membership at the time. In her day, the practice of borrowing from other authors, without giving due credit, was commonplace. She merely followed the usual practice of her time and should not anachronistically be judged by our more definitive legal ideas of literary borrowing, Adventists claim. The denomination therefore rejects the charge that, based on current law about plagiarism, Ellen White illegally plagiarized.[10] Older defenses of Ellen White such as that of F. D. Nichol, who vigorously defended Ellen White, have been replaced by a "more open acknowledgement and discussion of Ellen White's use of borrowed sources."[11]

What Fortin does not mention are the implications the new "open acknowledgment" of White's sources has for the denomination's view of the inspiration of the Bible and its long-standing opposition to historical-critical biblical scholarship. If the denomination is now going to admit some of the methods of historical criticism into the study of Ellen White, whom it regards as inspired by the Holy Spirit in essentially the same manner as Scripture, it will also have to accept such critical methods for the study of the biblical text.

While he compliments Ellen White's originality and independence, the late Fred Veltman (d. 2006) admits that his source-critical research into fifteen chapters of White's *Desire of Ages* "was not able to ascertain the full extent of Ellen White's literary dependence." Many questions remain, but there can "no longer be any doubt that she used sources regardless of the subject content."[12] The impact of the appropriated theological content upon Ellen White is yet to be determined.

The denomination is also yet to face the effect all this has upon its excessive dependency upon the writings of Ellen White. Ellen White's

---

10. Denis Fortin, "Plagiarism," 1028–35.

11. Ibid., 1035. See Nichol, *White and Critics*.

12. Veltman, "*Desire of Ages* Sources," 770.

authority within the church seems largely undiminished—at least within the church membership—by the scandal over plagiarism. In Article 18 of the official Adventist beliefs, we read that her "writings are a continuing and authoritative source of truth which provide for the church comfort, guidance, instruction, and correction."[13] At the church's General Conference session at San Antonio, Texas, in July 2015, this statement was altered to read that Ellen White's writings "speak with prophetic authority." Delegates also voted to adopt a more lengthy statement called, "Statement of Confidence in the Writings of Ellen G. White." The relevant line reads:

> We reaffirm our conviction that her writings are divinely inspired, truly Christ-centered, and Bible-based. Rather than replacing the Bible, they uplift the normative character of Scripture and *correct inaccurate interpretations of it* derived from tradition, human reason, personal experience, and modern culture.[14]

Accordingly, Ellen White, it seems, is now given almost complete veto power over independent interpretation of Scripture. She "correct(s) inaccurate interpretations." Ellen White, in Alberto Timm's words, now functions as a divine prophetic filter, "able to remove false interpretations artificially imposed on the Bible."[15] In short, Ellen White decides by inspiration which interpretation is accurate or inaccurate! I shudder to think how this idea, taken seriously, will play out in Adventist religion classes in college and seminary. In the religion classes I taught at Southern, whenever Ellen White's view of a biblical passage seemed to go against an obvious reading of the biblical text, it posed serious problems. Now, it seems, future classes will have to adopt Ellen White's interpretation, even in instances when it runs (or appears to run) contrary to the reading of the biblical text. This is a serious problem because Ellen White's voluminous writings comment on about everything in the Bible, and therefore offer, presumably under inspiration, the *correct* interpretation of almost every text. How can this be, when her extensive borrowing from other writings shows that she also borrowed some of her interpretations, which were, in turn, based on "tradition, human reason, personal experience, and modern culture"? How can her writings be verified by the biblical text when it is Ellen White who decides whether the biblical interpretation that is used as evaluation of her is valid? The argument is circular. I'm reminded of the Mormon claim: "We believe the Bible to be the word of God as far as it is translated [i.e., interpreted]

13. General Conference, *Adventists Believe*, 247.

14. Quoted in Barker, "Adventists Revise Wording," 6–7. Emphasis added.

15. Trimm, "*Sola Scriptura*," 20.

correctly."[16] Where the Bible is not correctly interpreted, Joseph Smith's writings sufficiently caution the reader and supply the right interpretation. Adventists seem inevitably to be edging Ellen White into a similar canonical role. Contemporary Adventists are reminded of what one of Ellen White's cousins wrote about her in 1847:

> I cannot endorse Sister Ellen's visions as of Divine inspiration, as you and she think them to be; yet I do not suspect the least shade of dishonesty in either of you in this matter . . . *I think that what she had you regard as visions from the Lord are only religious reveries in which her imagination runs without control upon themes in which she is most deeply interested*. While so absorbed in these reveries she is lost to everything around her. Reveries are of two kinds: sinful and religious. In either case, the sentiments in the main are obtained from previous teaching or study. I do not by any means think that her visions are from the Devil.[17]

On two other issues, mentioned only tangentially here—the Sabbath and the special identity and vocation of Adventism—matters also remain much the same. Adventists continue to insist that the observance of the seventh-day Sabbath is a litmus test of loyalty to God that will eventually become universal in scope.

Perhaps it is best to allow Jan Paulsen, a recent General Conference President, summarize where Adventists are today with respect to the disputed doctrines:

> The historic sanctuary message, based on Scripture and supported by the writings of Ellen White, continues to be held to unequivocally. And the inspired authorities on which these and other doctrines are based, namely the Bible supported by the writings of Ellen White, continue to be the hermeneutical foundation on which we as a church place all matters of faith and conduct. Let no one think that there has been a change of position in regard to this.[18]

Adventists consider themselves specially chosen by God to proclaim a message of warning and hope for the world, symbolized in the three angels of Revelation 14. No one else is proclaiming their unique message, they assert. A corollary of this belief is that all other denominations and religions

16. Article 8 of the Articles of Faith of the Church of Jesus Christ of Latter-day Saints, cited in Richards, *Contributions of Smith*, ii.

17. Quoted by James White, *Word to Little Flock*, 29. Emphasis supplied.

18. *Adventist Review*, "Adventist President Says No to Changes," 2002, http://www.adventistreview.org/2002–1524/story3/html.

are consequently theologically deficient in some way and in critical need of the Adventist corrective message.[19] Despite this long-standing notion of superiority, however, relations between the Adventist and other Christian faiths have actually improved. Although they still set themselves apart, Adventists have nonetheless become friendlier toward other Christians. Their excellent clergy journal, the *Ministry*, available in both print and digital formats, is now sent to non-Adventist religious leaders around the world. Non-Adventist authors regularly appear in the author bylines. A motto boldly stands on the masthead of the *Ministry*: "Published by the Seventh-day Adventist Church. Read by clergy of all faiths." This effort, however, isn't entirely altruistic. The *Ministry* is sent to non-Adventist clergy with the hope of influencing them favorably—possibly even converting them—to Seventh-day Adventism.

Finally, I would say, whatever else it may be, Adventism is not what it boldly claims. It is not the remnant church. It is not the true church. It is not a movement chosen by God to bring to all religions long-lost and buried truths of Christian faith. In short, Adventism does not measure up to its exalted yet impossible claims. If Adventism wishes to have the respect of the thinking public in the modern world, it must alter—or better, abandon—its sectarian tendencies. It must humbly recognize that, in view of the biblical witness, it has no real, special, or privileged claim on God's favor. Rather, God is at work in all Christian denominations and movements—and even outside them. God is also at work in all nations, lands, and religious systems. If the denomination could humbly admit this ecumenical reality, Adventism might then take its place alongside other expressions of Christianity with the common goal of furthering God's work in the world. Contemporary Christianity recognizes the fertile, manifold witness of various denominations, and would welcome Adventism into that panoramic, pluralistic witness. Just as individuals may claim uniqueness without at the same time insisting they are the only "true" or "authentic" persons, so Adventism may affirm its uniqueness without thereby denying or depreciating the Christian (or religious) witness of others. This would obviously lead the church to a greater concentration on the central focus of Christian faith—Jesus the Christ—and less on its peculiar, idiosyncratic dogma. At least there would remain a healthy tension between the two, a dynamic that would guide the church toward a mature revisionism, a constant, ongoing reexamination of its doctrines in the light of the common Christian faith, *ecclesia reformata, semper reformando*, "a church reformed, yet always reforming."

19. See Griswold, "Three Angels' Messages," 20–22.

If—and when—such might happen, Adventism would move beyond its preoccupation with itself, its claims, its mission, and enter into a new era of ecumenical praise of its Lord. It might go from being a self-confessed "true" church to being "truly" church.

Bibliography

Adams, Roy. *The Sanctuary: Understanding the Heart of Adventist Theology.* Hagerstown, MD: Review and Herald, 1993.

Adventist Review. 2002. "Adventist President Says No to Changes." http://www.adventistreview.org/2002–1524/story3/html.

Ahlstrom, Sydney. *A Religious History of the American People.* New Haven: Yale University Press, 1972.

Alt, Albrecht. *Essays on Old Testament History & Religion.* Translated by R. A. Wilson. Garden City, NY: Doubleday, 1966.

Anderson, David E. "Adventists Seeking to Clear Name of Founder, Mrs. White." *Chattanooga News-Free Press,* September 26, 1981.

Anderson, H. George, et al., eds. *Justification by Faith: Lutherans and Catholics in Dialogue VII.* Minneapolis: Augsburg, 1985.

Andrews, John Nevins. *The Three Messages of Revelation xiv, 6–12, particularly the Third Angel's Message, and Two-horned Beast.* 5th ed. Nashville: Southern Publishing Association, 1970. First published 1892 by Review and Herald.

Armerding, Carl E. *The Old Testament and Criticism.* Grand Rapids: Eerdmans, 1983.

Bacchiochi, Samuele. *From Sabbath to Sunday: A Historical Investigation of the Rise of Sunday Observance in Early Christianity.* Rome: Pontifical Gregorian University Press, 1977.

Ball, Bryan W. "Saving Righteousness." *Ministry,* June 2010, 10–13.

Ballenger, Albion F. *Cast Out for the Cross of Christ.* Tropico, CA: N. p. [1909?].

Barker, Rick. "Adventists Revise Wording on the Prophet's Authority." *Proclamation,* Spring 2016, 6–7.

Barr, James. *Fundamentalism.* Philadelphia: Westminster, 1978.

Bear, David, et al. "Behavioral Alterations in Patients with Temporal Lobe Epilepsy." In *Psychiatric Aspects of Epilepsy,* edited by Dietrich Blumer, 197–227. New York: American Psychiatric, 1984.

Berger, Peter. *The Sacred Canopy: Elements of a Sociological Theory of Religion.* New York: Doubleday, 1967.

Berkouwer, G. C. *Faith and Sanctification.* Studies in Dogmatics. Translated by John Friend. Grand Rapids: Eerdmans, 1952.

———. *Faith and Justification*. Studies in Dogmatics. Translated by Lewis B. Smedes. Grand Rapids: Eerdmans, 1954.

Biblical Research Institute. *The Inspiration and Authority of the Ellen G. White Writings: A Statement of Present Understanding*. Report of the Biblical Research Institute of the Seventh-day Adventist Church, Washington, DC, 1982

———. *Methods of Bible Study*. Report of the General Conference of Seventh-day Adventists Committee Annual Council, Washington, DC, 1986.

Blanco, Jack J. *The Clear Word: An Expanded Paraphrase to Build Faith and Nurture Spiritual Growth*. Hagerstown, MD: Jack Blanco, 2000.

Bonhoeffer, Dietrich. *Ethics*. Edited by Eberhard Bethge. Library of Philosophy and Theology. New York: Macmillan, 1961.

Boyer, Paul. *When Time Shall be No More: Prophecy Belief in Modern American Culture*. Cambridge, MA: Harvard University Press, 1991.

Branson, W. H. "The Lord Our Righteousness." In *Our Firm Foundation*. 2 vols., 2:573–618. Washington, DC: Review and Herald, 1952.

Bright, John. *A History of Israel*. 3rd ed. Philadelphia: Westminster, 1981.

Brinsmead, Robert D. *Judged by the Gospel: A Review of Adventism*. Fallbrook, CA: Verdict, 1980.

———. "The Legend of Ellen G. White." *Evangelica* 2/5 (1981) 15.

———, ed. *Institute Syllabus 1971: The Fundamental Issues of the Reformation*. N.p.: Robert Brinsmead [1971].

Brown, Raymond E. *Biblical Exegesis & Church Doctrine*. New York: Paulist, 1985.

Brueggemann, Walter. *Theology of the Old Testament: Testimony, Dispute, Advocacy*. Minneapolis: Fortress, 1997.

Brunner, Emil. *The Christian Doctrine of the Church, Faith, and the Consummation*. Vol. 3 of *Dogmatics*. Translated by David Cairns and T. H. L. Parker. Philadelphia: Westminster, 1962.

Buchanan, John. *The Doctrine of Justification*. Grand Rapids: Eerdmans, 1977. First published 1867 by T & T Clark.

Butler, Jonathan. "Historian as Heretic." In *Prophetess of Health: A Study of Ellen G. White*. 3rd ed., 1–21. Grand Rapids: Eerdmans, 2008.

———. "The World of E. G. White and the End of the World." *Spectrum* 10 (August 1978) 2–13.

Butler, Jon, et al. *Religion in American Life: A Short History*. 2nd ed. New York: Oxford University Press, 2011.

Bultmann, Rudolph. "Is Exegesis without Presuppositions Possible?" In *Existence and Faith*, 289–97. Translated by S. M. Ogden. New York: World, 1960.

Burrows, Millar. *An Outline of Biblical Theology*. Philadelphia: Westminster, 1946.

Calvin, John. "The Author's Preface to the *Commentary on the Book of Psalms*." Translated by James Anderson. In *John Calvin: Selections from His Writings*, edited by John Dillenberger, 21–80. Missoula, MT: Scholars Press, 1975.

———. *Institutes of the Christian Religion*. Library of Christian Classics 20–21. 2 vols. Edited by J. T. McNeill. Translated by F. L. Battles. Philadelphia: Westminster, 1960.

Carson, D. A., ed. *From Sabbath to Lord's Day: A Biblical, Historical and Theological Investigation*. Grand Rapids: Zondervan, 1982.

Canright, Dudley. *Life of Mrs. E. G. White, Seventh-day Adventist Prophet: Her False Claims Refuted*. Salt Lake City: Grant Shurtliff-Sterling, 1998. First published 1919.

Chaij, Fernando. *Preparation for the Final Crisis*. Mountain View, CA: Pacific, 1966.

Chase, Lance. "Spaulding Manuscript." In *Scriptures of the Church: Selections from the Encyclopedia of Mormonism*, edited by D. H. Ludlow, 602–4. Salt Lake City: Deseret, 1992.

Clarke, M. G. *Sunshine and Shadows along the Pathway of Life*. San Francisco: Clarke, 1868.

Collin, P. H. *Dictionary of Law*, 2nd ed. Middlesex, CT: Peter Collin, 1992.

Collins, Adela Yarbro. "The Apocalypse (Revelation)." In *NJBC* 996–1016.

Collins, John J. *Apocalypse: The Morphology of a Genre*. Semeia 14. Missoula, MT: Scholars Press, 1979.

Conybeare, William John, and John S. Howson, *The Life and Epistles of Saint Paul*. 2 vols. London: Longman, Brown, Green, and Longmans, 1851–1852.

Corbett-Hemeyer, Julia. *Religion in America*. 7th ed. New York: Routledge, 2016.

Cornell, Merritt E. *Miraculous Powers: The Scripture Testimony of the Perpetuity of Spiritual Gifts. Illustrated by Narratives of Incidents, and Sentiments Carefully Compiled from the Eminently Pious and Learned of Various Denominations*. Battle Creek, MI: SDA Publishing Association, 1862.

Couperus, Molleurus. "Bible Conference of 1919." *Spectrum* 10/1 (1979) 27–57.

———. "Ellen G. White and Epilepsy." *Ministry*, August 1984, 24–25.

———. "The Significance of Ellen White's Head Injury." *Adventist Currents*, June 1985, 17–23.

Crenshaw, James. "Job, Book of." In *ABD* 3:858–68.

———. *Old Testament Wisdom: An Introduction*. 3rd ed. Louisville: Westminster John Knox, 2010.

Cummins, D. Duane. *The Disciples: A Struggle for Reformation*. St. Louis: Chalice, 2009.

Damsteegt, P. Gerard. *Foundations of the Seventh-day Adventist Message and Mission*. Grand Rapids: Eerdmans, 1977.

Daniells, Arthur G. *Christ Our Righteousness*. Washington, DC: Ministerial Association of Seventh-day Adventists, 1941.

Dart, John. "Plagiarism Found in Prophet Books." *Los Angeles Times*, October 23, 1980.

Davies, Horton. *The Challenge of the Sects*. Rev. ed. Philadelphia: Westminister, 1961.

Dockx, S. *Le Récit du Paradis: Gen. 2–3*. Paris: Duculot, 1981.

Douglass, Herbert. "God Does Not Play Word Games." *Ministry*, October 1974, 37.

———. *Perfection*. Nashville: Southern Publishing Association, 1975.

———. "Righteousness by Faith" In *EGWEnc* 1105–1108.

———. "The Unique Contribution of Adventist Eschatology." In *North American Bible Conference 1974*. Washington, DC: General Conference Biblical Research Committee, 1974.

———. "Why God is Urgent—And Yet Waits." Special Issue, *Review and Herald* 151, no. 20 (1974), 21–23.

Downing, F. Gerald. "Justification as Acquittal? A Critical Examination of Judicial Verdicts in Paul's Literary and Actual Contexts." *The Catholic Biblical Quarterly* 74/2 (2012) 298–317.

Edersheim, Alfred. *The Bible History: Old Testament*. 2 vols. Grand Rapids: Eerdmans, 1949. First published 1890.

————. *The Life and Times of Jesus the Messiah.* 5 vols. New York: E. R. Herrick, 1883.

Eissfeldt, Otto. *The Old Testament: An Introduction.* Translated by P. R. Ackroyd. New York: Harper & Row, 1965.

Eliade, Mircea. *The Sacred and the Profane.* Translated by W. R. Trask. New York: Harcourt, Brace & World, 1959.

Ellis, E. Earle. *The Making of the New Testament Documents.* Biblical Interpretation Series 39. Leiden: E. J. Brill, 1999.

Elwell, Walter A., ed. *Evangelical Dictionary of Theology.* Grand Rapids: Baker, 1984.

Erickson, Millard J. *Christian Theology.* 2nd ed. Grand Rapids: Baker, 1998.

Farley, Edward. *Ecclesial Man: A Social Phenomenology of Faith and Reality.* Philadelphia: Fortress, 1975.

Feiner, Johannes, and Lukas Vischer, eds. *The Common Catechism: A Book of Christian Faith.* New York: Seabury, 1975.

Festinger, Leon, et al. *When Prophecy Fails: A Social and Psychological Study of a Modern Group that Predicted the Destruction of the World.* New York: Harper & Row, 1956.

Fishbane, Michael. *Biblical Interpretation in Ancient Israel.* Oxford: Clarendon, 1985.

Fohrer, Georg. *Introduction to the Old Testament.* Translated by D. E. Green. Nashville: Abingdon, 1968.

Ford, Desmond. *Daniel 8:14, the Day of Atonement, and the Investigative Judgment.* Casselberry, FL: Euangelion, 1980.

————. "The Scope and Limits of the Pauline Expression 'Righteousness by Faith,'" In *Documents from the Palmdale Conference on Righteousness by Faith,* edited by Jack D. Walker, 1–13. Goodlettsville, TN: N. p. [1976].

Ford, Desmond, and Jillian Ford. *The Adventist Crisis of Spiritual Identity.* Newcastle, CA: Desmond Ford Publications, 1982.

Fortin, Dennis. "Plagiarism." In *EGWEnc* 1028–35.

Fretheim, Terrence. "Source Criticism, OT." In *IDBSup* 838–39.

Froom, Leroy E. *Movement of Destiny.* Washington, DC: Review and Herald, 1971.

————. *The Prophetic Faith of Our Fathers.* 4 vols. Washington, DC: Review and Herald, 1950–1954.

Gane, Erwin. 1980. "Is Justification the Act by which God Declares Righteous or Makes Righteous, or Both?" Faculty Working Paper, Pacific Union College, Angwin, CA.

General Conference of Seventh-day Adventists Biblical Research Committee. *North American Bible Conference 1974.* Washington, DC: General Conference of Seventh-day Adventists, 1974.

General Conference of Seventh-day Adventists. "Consensus Document: Christ in the Heavenly Sanctuary." *Ministry,* October 1980, 16–19.

————. "Parmenter-Ford Correspondence." *Ministry,* October 1980, 10–11.

————. *Seventh-day Adventists Believe: A Biblical Exposition of 27 Fundamental Doctrines.* Hagerstown, MD: Review and Herald, 1988.

————. *Seventh-day Adventists Believe: A Biblical Exposition of 27 Fundamental Doctrines.* 2nd ed. Hagerstown, MD: Review and Herald, 2005.

————. *Seventh-day Adventist Church Manual.* Rev. ed. Washington, DC: General Conference of Seventh-day Adventists, 1986.

————. "Statement on Desmond Ford Document." *Ministry,* October 1980, 20–22.

Gladson, Jerry A. "Battle over the Spirit of Prophecy, pt. 1." *Unlock Your Potential* 11/4 (1976) 6–7.

————. "Battle over the Spirit of Prophecy, pt. 2." *Unlock Your Potential* 12/1 (1977) 25–30.

————. "The Enigma of 'Azazel' in Leviticus 16." Master's thesis, Vanderbilt University, 1973.

————. "Recipe: Love." *Adventist Review*, November 12, 1987, 23.

————. "Retributive Paradoxes in Proverbs 10–29." PhD diss., Vanderbilt University, 1978.

————. *A Theologian's Journey from Seventh-day Adventism to Mainstream Christianity.* Glendale, AZ: Life Assurance Ministries, 2000.

————. *Who Said Life is Fair? Job and the Problem of Evil.* Washington: Review and Herald, 1985.

Goldingay, John. *Israel's Faith.* Vol. 2 of *Old Testament Theology.* Downers Grove, IL: IVP Academic, 2008.

González, Justo. *History of Christian Thought.* 3 vols. Nashville: Abingdon, 1970–1975.

Graybill, Ron. "Did Mrs. White 'Borrow' in Reporting a Vision?" *Adventist Review*, April 2, 1981, 7.

Grisar, Hartman. *Martin Luther: His Life and Work.* Edited by Arthur Preuss. Translated by Frank J. Eble. Westminster, MD: Newman, 1950.

Griswold, Scott. "The Three Angels' Messages and World Religions." *Ministry*, February 2016, 20–22.

Gritisch, Eric W. *Toxic Spirituality: Four Enduring Temptations of Christian Faith.* Minneapolis: Fortress, 2009.

The Guide to American Law. 12 vols. New York: West, 1984.

Gunneman, Louis. *The Shaping of the United Church of Christ: An Essay in the History of American Christianity.* New York: United Church, 1977.

Guthrie, Shirley C. *Christian Doctrine.* Rev. ed. Louisville: Westminster John Knox, 1994.

Hanna, John. *Life of Christ.* N. p.: American Tract Society, 1863.

Harink, Douglas. "Setting it Right." *Christian Century*, June 14, 2005, 20–25.

Harvey, A. E. *Jesus and the Constraints of History.* Philadelphia: Westminster, 1982.

Harrington, Daniel J. "The Gospel According to Mark." In *NJBC* 596–629.

Harrison, Roland K. *Introduction to the Old Testament.* Grand Rapids: Eerdmans, 1969.

————. *Old Testament Times.* Grand Rapids: Eerdmans, 1970.

Hassan, Steven. *Combatting Cult Mind Control.* Rochester, VT: Park Street, 1988.

Hasel, Gerhard. "General Principles of Biblical Interpretation." In *North American Bible Conference* 1974. Washington, DC: General Conference of Seventh-day Adventists, 1974.

————. "Daniel 8 and the Pre-Advent Judgment." Lecture at the First Seventh-day Adventist Church, Chattanooga, TN, May 9, 1981.

Hodder, Delbert. "Visions or Partial-Complex Seizures." *Evangelica*, November 1981, 30–37.

Holbrook, Frank B., ed. *Doctrine of the Sanctuary: A Historical Survey*, Daniel & Revelation Committee Series 5. Silver Spring, MD: Biblical Research Institute of Seventh-day Adventists, 1989.

Ingraham, J. H. *Prince of the House of David: Or Three Years in the Holy City.* New York: A. L Burt, 1857.

Indianapolis 1990: A Report and Analysis of the 55th General Conference Session of Seventh-day Adventists. N. p.: Universal Publishing Association, 1990.

Irwin, W. A. "Job." In *Peake's Commentary on the Bible*, edited by Matthew Black and H. H. Rowley, 391–408. London: Thomas Nelson, 1962.

Jemison, T. H. *Christian Beliefs: Fundamental Biblical Teachings for Seventh-day Adventist College Classes*. Mountain View, CA: Pacific, 1959.

———. *A Prophet Among You*. Mountain View, CA: Pacific, 1955.

Johns, Warren H. "Ellen White: Prophet or Plagiarist?" *Ministry*, June 1982, 5–19.

Johnsson, William. "An Evaluation of Geoffrey Paxton's *The Shaking of Adventism*." Faculty Working Paper, Andrews University, Berrien Springs, MI, 1978.

———. "Honest with God." *Adventist Review*, January 7, 1993, 7.

Jones, Alonzo T. *The National Sunday Law: Argument of Alonzo T. Jones before the United States Committee on Education and Labor, Dec. 13, 1888*. New York: American Sentinel, 1889.

Keck, Leander. *The Bible in the Pulpit: The Renewal of Biblical Preaching*. Nashville: Abingdon, 1978.

Kerr, H. T., and J. M. Mulder, eds. *Conversions*. Grand Rapids: Eerdmans, 1983.

Knight, George R., ed. *Questions on Doctrine*. Adventist Classic Library. Berrien Springs, MI: Andrews University Press, 2003.

Küng, Hans. *Justification: The Doctrine of Karl Barth and a Catholic Reflection*. 4th ed. Translated by Thomas Collins. New York: Thomas Nelson, 1964.

LaBrecque, Alexander. "The Scandal of the Gospel," *Evangelica* 1/1 (1980) 21.

Lacocque, André. *The Book of Daniel*. Translated by David Pellauer. Atlanta: John Knox, 1979.

Leith, John H., ed. *Creeds of the Churches*. Rev. ed. Garden City, NY: Doubleday, 1973.

Lindblom, Johannes. *Prophecy in Ancient Israel*. Philadelphia: Fortress, 1962.

Luther, Martin. *What Luther Says: An Anthology*. 3 vols. Edited by Ewald M. Plass. St. Louis: Concordia, 1959.

Macquarrie, John. *Principles of Christian Theology*. 2nd ed. New York: Charles Scribner's Sons, 1977.

MacGuire, Meade. *Lambs among Wolves*. Nashville: Southern Publishing Association, 1957.

Mann, Horace. *Life and Works*. 5 vols. Boston: Lee and Shepherd, 1891.

Martin, Walter. *The Truth about Seventh-day Adventism*. Grand Rapids: Zondervan, 1960.

———. *The Kingdom of the Cults*. Rev. ed. Edited by Hank Hanegraaff. Minneapolis: Bethany House, 1997.

Martínez, Florentino García, ed. *The Dead Sea Scrolls Translated: The Qumran Texts in English*, 2nd ed. Translated by W. G. E. Watson. Grand Rapids: Eerdmans, 1996.

McAllister, Lester G., and William E. Tucker, *Journey in Faith: A History of the Christian Church (Disciples of Christ)*. St. Louis: Bethany Press, 1975.

McAdams, Donald. "Ellen G. White and the Protestant Historians: The Evidence from an Unpublished Manuscript on John Huss." Unpublished Paper, 1977.

McBride, J. LeBron. *Spiritual Crisis: Surviving Trauma to the Soul*. New York: Haworth, 1998.

Minnery, Tom. "The Adventist Showdown: Will it Trigger a Rash of Defections?" *Christianity Today*, October 10, 1980, 76–77.

Miller, William. Letter to the Editor. *Western Midnight Cry*, December 21, 1844.

Mounce, Robert. *The Book of Revelation*. New International Commentary on the New Testament. Grand Rapids: Eerdmans, 1977.

Nestle, Erwin, and Kurt Aland, eds. *Novum Testamentum Graece*, 27th ed. Stuttgart: Deutsche Bibelgesellschaft, 1993.

Neufeld, Don F., et al., eds. *Seventh-day Adventist Encyclopedia*. Commentary Reference Series 10. Washington: Review and Herald, 1966.

Newsom, Carol A., with Brennan W. Breed. *Daniel: A Commentary*. Old Testament Library. Louisville: Westminster John Knox, 2014.

Nibley, Hugh W. *Since Cumorah: The Book of Mormon in the Modern World*. Salt Lake City: Deseret, 1967.

Nichol, Francis D. *Answers to Objections*. Washington, DC: Review and Herald, 1952.

———. *Ellen G. White and Her Critics*. Washington, DC: Review and Herald, 1951.

———. *The Midnight Cry*. Washington, DC: Review and Herald, 1944.

Numbers, Ronald. *Prophetess of Health: A Study of Ellen G. White*. New York: Harper & Row, 1976.

———. *Prophetess of Health: A Study of Ellen G. White*. 3rd ed. Grand Rapids: Eerdmans, 2008.

Oates, Wayne. *The Christian Pastor*. Rev. ed. Philadelphia: Westminster, 1964.

Oden, Thomas C. *The Justification Reader*. Classic Christian Readers. Grand Rapids: Eerdmans, 2002.

O'Ffill, Richard. "Are Adventists the True Christians?" *Adventist Review*, September 2000, 43–45.

Olsen, V. Norskov. "The Sabbath: Its Expanding Place in Christian Belief." *Loma Linda University Scope*, May/June 1972, 12.

Olson, Robert W. "Books, Preparation of Ellen G. White's." In *EGWEnc* 663–68.

———. "Was Ellen White Like the Bible Prophets?" Working Paper, Prophetic Guidance Workshop, Takoma Park, MD, 1976.

Ott, Helmut. *Perfect in Christ: The Mediation of Christ in the Writings of Ellen G. White*. Washington, DC: Review and Herald, 1987.

Pache, René. *The Inspiration and Authority of Scripture*. Translated by Helen I. Needham. Chicago: Moody, 1969.

Pals, Daniel L. *The Victorian "Lives" of Jesus*. San Antonio: Trinity University Press, 1982.

Payne, J. Barton. *Encyclopedia of Biblical Prophecy*. New York: Harper & Row, 1973.

Paxton, Geoffrey. *The Shaking of Adventism*. Wilmington, DE: Zenith, 1977.

Patterson, Gary. "Difficult Times and Enormous Loss: The Case of Jerry Gladson." *Adventists Today*, November/December 1995, 9.

Peck, Scott. *Further Along the Road Less Traveled: The Unending Journey Toward Spiritual Growth*. New York: Simon & Schuster, 1993.

Perkins, Pheme. "The Gospel of Mark." In *NIB* 8:507–733.

Peter, Carl J. "The Decree on Justification in the Council of Trent." In *Justification by Faith: Lutherans and Catholics in Dialogue VII*, edited by H. George Anderson et al., 218–229. Minneapolis: Augsburg, 1985.

Peterson, Donald I. *Visions or Seizures: Was Ellen White the Victim of Epilepsy?* Boise, ID: Pacific, 1988.

Peterson, William S. "A Textual and Historical Study of Ellen White's Account of the French Revolution." *Spectrum* 2 (1970) 57–69.

Priebe, Dennis. "Will the Real Gospel Please Stand Up?" *The Layworker,* January 1983, 18, 22–24.

Provonsha, Jack. "The Church as a Prophetic Minority." *Spectrum* 12/1 (1980) 18–23.

————. 1980. "Was Ellen G. White a Fraud?" Working Paper. Loma Linda University, Loma Linda, CA.

Questions on Doctrine. Washington, DC: Review and Herald, 1957.

Ramik, Vincent. MEMORANDUM OF LAW LITERARY PROPERTY RIGHTS 1790–1915 (Diller, Ramik, and Wight, Washington, DC, 1981).

Ratzlaff, Dale. *The Cultic Doctrine of Seventh-day Adventists.* Glendale, AZ: Life Assurance Ministries, 1996.

Rayburn, Carole A. "Psychotherapy with Seventh-Day Adventists." In *Handbook of Psychotherapy and Religious Diversity.* 2nd ed., edited by P. Scott Richards and Allen E. Bergin, 207–230. Washington, DC: American Psychological Association, 2014.

Rea, Walter. *The White Lie.* Turlock, CA: M & R Publications, 1982.

Rebok, Denton E. *Believe His Prophets.* Washington, DC: Review and Herald, 1956.

Rice, George E. "How to Write a Bible." *Ministry,* August 1986, 4–7.

Rice, Richard. *The Reign of God: An Introduction to Christian Theology from a Seventh-day Adventist Perspective.* Berrien Springs, MI: Andrews University Press, 1985.

Richards, Le Grand. *A Marvelous Work and a Wonder.* Salt Lake City: Deseret, 1950.

Richards, Stephen L. *Contributions of Joseph Smith.* Salt Lake City: Church of Jesus Christ of Latter-Day Saints, n.d.

Robertson, John. *The White Truth.* Mountain View, CA: Pacific, 1981.

Rordorf, Willy. *Sunday.* Translated by A. A. K. Graham. Philadelphia: Westminster, 1968.

Schaef, Anne Wilson, and Diane Fassel. *The Addictive Organization.* San Francisco: Harper & Row, 1988.

Schaeffer, Francis A. *The God Who is There.* Downers Grove, IL: InterVarsity, 1968.

Schleiermacher, Friedrich. *The Christian Faith.* 2nd ed. Edited by H. R. Mackintosh. Translated by J. S. Stewart. Edinburgh: T & T Clark, 1928. First published 1830.

Schroeder, Henry Joseph, ed. *Canons and Decrees of the Council of Trent.* St. Louis: Herder, 1941.

Schwartz, Richard W. *Light Bearers to the Remnant.* Mountain View, CA: Pacific, 1979.

Schweitzer, Albert. *The Quest for the Historical Jesus.* London: A. and C. Black, 1910.

Sanders, E. P. *Paul and Palestinian Judaism: A Comparison of Patterns of Religion.* Philadelphia: Fortress, 1977.

Smith-Christopher, Daniel L. "The Book of Daniel." In *NIB* 7:16–194.

Smith, Preston. "Perfection in Christ." *Review and Herald,* September 16, 1965, 9–10.

Smith, Uriah. "Our Righteousness." *Review and Herald,* June 11, 1889, 376–77.

————. *The Prophecies of Daniel and the Revelation.* Nashville: Southern Publishing Association, 1944.

Soggin, J. Alberto. *A History of Ancient Israel.* Translated by John Bowdon. Philadelphia: Westminster, 1984.

Soulen, Richard N., and R. Kendall Soulen. *Handbook of Biblical Criticism.* 3rd ed. Louisville: Westminster John Knox, 2001.

Sproul, R. C. *Faith Alone: The Evangelical Doctrine of Justification.* Grand Rapids: Baker, 1995.

Strand, Kenneth A., ed. *The Sabbath in Scripture and History.* Washington, DC: Review and Herald, 1982.

Taylor, Greg. *Discovering the New Covenant: Why I Am no Longer a Seventh-day Adventist.* Glendale, AZ: Life Assurance Ministries, 2004.

Thomsen, Russel J. *Seventh-Day Baptists—Their Legacy to Adventists*. Mountain View, CA: Pacific, 1971.

Thurston, Nancy Stiehler, and Winston Seebobin. "Psychotherapy for Evangelical and Fundamentalist Protestants." In *Handbook of Psychotherapy and Religious Diversity*, 2nd ed., edited by P. Scott Richards and Allen E. Bergin, 129–53. Washington, DC: American Psychological Association, 2014.

Tietjen, John. *Memoirs in Exile: Confessional Hope and Institutional Conflict*. Minneapolis: Fortress, 1990.

Tillich, Paul. *Systematic Theology*. 3 vols. Chicago: University of Chicago Press, 1951–1965.

Toulouse, Mark G. *Joined in Discipleship*. Rev. ed. St. Louis: Chalice, 1997.

Trimm, Alberto. "*Sola Scriptura*: The Reformers and Ellen G. White." *Ministry*, October 2016, 19–20.

Veltman, Fred. "The *Desire of Ages* Project." Working Paper, General Conference of Seventh-day Adventists, Washington, DC, 1989

———. "'The *Desire of Ages* Project': The Data," *Ministry*, October 1990, 4–7.

———. "'The *Desire of Ages* Project': The Conclusions." *Ministry*, December 1990, 11–15.

———. "The *Desire of Ages* Sources, Study of." In *EGWEnc* 766–70.

———. Report to PREXAD on the E. G. White Research Project. Washington, DC, 1981.

Walker, Jack D., ed. *Documents from the Palmdale Conference on Righteousness by Faith* [1976].

Waxman, S. A., and N. Geschwind. "Hypergraphia in Temporal Lobe Epilepsy." *Neurology* 30 (1980) 314–17.

Weatherhead, Leslie. *Daily Readings from the Works of Leslie D. Weatherhead*. Edited by Frank Cumbers. Nashville: Abingdon, 1968.

Wesley, John. "Sermon 45: The New Birth." 140 Sermons of John Wesley. http://godonthe.net/wesley/jws.45.html.

White, Arthur L. *Ellen G. White: Messenger to the Remnant.* Washington: Review and Herald, 1969.

———. *The Ellen G. White Writings*. Washington, DC: Review and Herald, 1973.

White, Ellen G. *Child Guidance*. Nashville: Southern Publishing Association, 1954.

———. *Christ's Object Lessons*. Washington, DC: Review and Herald, 1900.

———. *Counsels on Health*. Mountain View, CA: Pacific, 1951.

———. *Counsels to Writers and Editors*. Nashville: Southern Publishing Association, 1946.

———. *Early Writings*. Washington, DC: Review and Herald, 1945. First published 1882 by Pacific Press.

———. *Education*. Mountain View, CA: Pacific, 1903.

———. *Evangelism*. Mountain View, CA: Pacific, 1946.

———. *Fundamentals of Education*. Nashville: Southern Publishing Association, 1923.

———. *The Great Controversy between Christ and Satan*. Washington, DC: Review and Herald, 1911.

———. *Life Sketches of Ellen G. White*. Mountain View, CA: Pacific, 1915.

———. *Messages to Young People*. Nashville: Southern Publishing Association, 1930.

———. *The Ministry of Healing*. Mountain View, CA: Pacific, 1909.

———. *Prophets and Kings*. Mountain View, CA: Pacific, 1917.

————. *Selected Messages.* 3 vols. Washington, DC: Review and Herald, 1958–1980.

————. *A Sketch of the Christian Experience and Views of Ellen G. White.* Saratoga Springs, NY: James White, 1851.

————. *Sons and Daughters of God.* Washington, DC: Review and Herald, 1955.

————. *The Spirit of Prophecy.* 4 vols. Washington, DC: Review and Herald, 1870–1884.

————. *Steps to Christ.* Mountain View, CA: Pacific, 1956.

————. *Testimonies for the Church.* 9 vols. Washington, DC: Review and Herald, 1885–1909.

————. *Testimonies to Ministers and Gospel Workers.* Mountain View, CA: Pacific, 1923.

White, James. "Gifts of the Gospel Church." *Review and Herald,* June 1853, 13–14.

————. "The Judgment." *Review and Herald,* January 29, 1857, 100.

————. *A Word to the Little Flock.* N. p.: James White, 1847.

Wilson, Neal C. "This I Believe about Ellen G. White." *Adventist Review,* March 20, 1980, 8.

Wintermute, O. S. "Jubilees." In *The Old Testament Pseudepigrapha.* 2 vols., edited by James H. Charlesworth, 2:35–142. New York: Doubleday, 1985.

Wood, John W. 1980. "'We Must All Appear': The Investigative Judgment in the Writings of Ellen G. White." Working Paper, Seventh-day Adventist Glacier View Consultation, Glacier View, CO.

Wood, Kenneth. "Ellen White's Use of Sources." *Adventist Review,* September 17, 1981, 3.

————. "The Goal is Perfection." *Review and Herald,* November 30, 1967, 2–3.

————. "The Role of the Seventh-day Adventist Church in the Great Controversy in the End Time." In *North American Bible Conference 1974.* Washington, DC: General Conference Biblical Research Committee, 1974.

Wylie, J. A. *The History of Protestantism.* 4 vols. London: Cassell, Petter & Galpin [1874].

Yao, R. 1987. "Addiction and the Fundamentalist Experience." Paper presented at the 95th Annual Convention of the American Psychological Association, New York, NY.

Yost, Frank H. *The Early Christian Sabbath.* Mountain View, CA: Pacific, 1947.

Young, Edward J. *The Prophecy of Daniel.* Grand Rapids: Eerdmans, 1949.